The Gunslingers of '69

ALSO BY BRIAN HANNAN
AND FROM MCFARLAND

In Theaters Everywhere: A History of the Hollywood Wide Release, 1913–2017 (2019)

Coming Back to a Theater Near You: A History of Hollywood Reissues, 1914–2014 (2016)

The Making of The Magnificent Seven: *Behind the Scenes of the Pivotal Western* (2015)

The Gunslingers of '69

Western Movies' Greatest Year

Brian Hannan

McFarland & Company, Inc., Publishers
Jefferson, North Carolina

ISBN (print) 978-1-4766-7935-8
ISBN (ebook) 978-1-4766-3727-3

Library of Congress and British Library
cataloguing data are available

Library of Congress Control Number 2019040309

Front cover (left to right): Ben Johnson, Warren Oates, William Holden and Ernest Borgnine in *The Wild Bunch* (Warner Bros./Photofest)

Printed in the United States of America

McFarland & Company, Inc., Publishers
Box 611, Jefferson, North Carolina 28640
www.mcfarlandpub.com

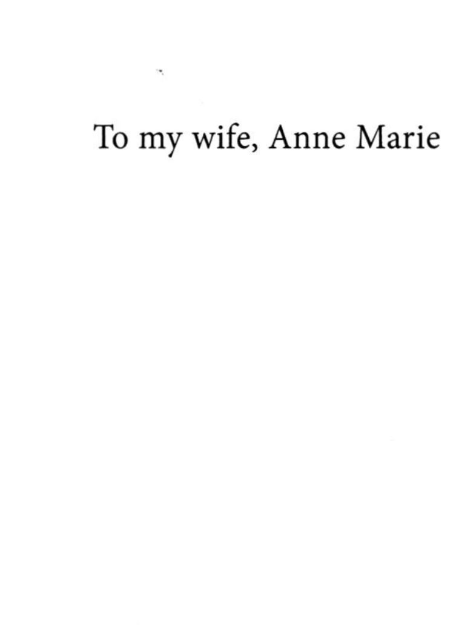

To my wife, Anne Marie

Table of Contents

Preface

This is an experiment. Prior to embarking on my first book *The Making of* The Magnificent Seven*: Behind the Scenes of the Pivotal Western* (McFarland, 2015), I watched a large number of westerns, but in no particular order, just viewing them as I felt the urge, following *Red River* (1948) with *Jubal* (1956) and then *The Cimarron Kid* (1951). I later wondered what my impression would have been of these various pictures if I had seen them in sequential order. If I had, in other words, experienced these pictures in the same way as an ordinary moviegoer; if I had not let historical perspective get in the way. I thought it would be an interesting experiment to gauge my reactions to watching films in this fashion, so that I would be, for example, seeing *Fort Apache* (1948) without any knowledge of what was coming later, say, *Winchester '73* (1950) or *The Searchers* (1956). In researching my *Magnificent Seven* book, there was no requirement, except in the case of that film's sequels, to look further forward than 1960. So, having decided I would like to write another book on westerns, I felt that it might be more useful to concentrate on one particular year than a decade. I selected 1969 because it was the year of some of my favorite westerns.

I was 15 in 1969, and going to the pictures cost more than my weekly pocket money, so I saw very few of these films upon their initial release. Some I caught later on television or VHS or DVD, but for many I have played over the past year it was the first time (*Support Your Local Sheriff, The Great Bank Robbery, Young Billy Young, The Stalking Moon, The Undefeated, Tell Them Willie Boy Is Here, et al.*). Some of the other films were lodged in my brain as a result of repeated viewings, but it felt to me that I had not seem them in context. I had viewed them almost as historical artifacts, my views sometimes colored by academic studies or biographies.

So I sat down to watch these pictures in exactly the same order as a moviegoer of the period would have done, starting with *The Stalking Moon* and ending with *Tell Them Willie Boy Is Here*. The experiment proved thrilling, for lack of a better word. I was faced with an astonishing variety of product, one moment engrossed in a moody drama, the next laughing out loud at a rip-roaring comedy, then a full-tilt adventure. I saw films high on panorama, intent on filling the screen with action, and then more intimate examples, pictures with big stars, and films with actors and actresses making debuts (or near enough). Because I had no choice in the matter, not having pre-selected my viewing in order to test an academic theory or to enjoy the entire portfolio of a specific star or director, I felt very much like the person who goes to the theater without any idea of what they are going to see. Consequently, I saw things in movies that I had never seen before and discovered a new way of looking at movies, not, as I said, from the academic perspective but from that of the ticket-buyer who enters the theater more in hope than expectation. I believe I felt the same excitement as a moviegoer of the period coming across a movie that told a story in a different way, or dealt with characters and issues in a novel fashion, or that used techniques that had never been seen before. I was, to that extent, a movie virgin, able to enjoy without the weight of analytical history on my shoulders.

Once I had watched an entire year's worth of good, bad and ugly westerns, I realized that this was a truly astonishing year for the genre, one which introduced so many new ideas while working within an almost hidebound format. When I started going back to the other years that I believed to be the best ever for westerns, I quickly realized that they might not, after all, be the pinnacles of achievement for the genre. I started to think that 1969 was the Year of the Western and so I came to write this book with that concept in mind.

Introduction

Nineteen sixty-nine was the year when westerns should have bitten the dust after *Easy Rider* and *Midnight Cowboy* revolutionized Hollywood. Instead, it was arguably the western's finest year. It was not just that 1969 produced four of the greatest westerns ever made (*The Wild Bunch*, *Butch Cassidy and the Sundance Kid*, *True Grit* and *Once Upon a Time in the West*[1]) and that, for once, critics and the public were in agreement, but that it set the pace for the genre and in some cases for the industry. The most obvious development was the increase in realistic violence. But it was also through the western that we saw the first "buddy movie," the first African American action star and the first credible western heroine since Barbara Stanwyck and Joan Crawford hung up their spurs. The tone for the year was both elegiac and gung-ho, reflective and political. While apparently rooted in decades-old genre convention, it began to deftly investigate deeper political issues relating in part to Vietnam and unrest but also to wider contemporary issues such as racism and the role of women. It set out the stall for the revisionist western. Westerns scored better at the box office and at the Oscars than ever before. It was the year that American directors hit back against the foreign invasion, reclaiming and reinventing and reinterpreting the genre. There was the rebirth of the comedy western. Western scores—influenced by pop and opera—took on a different complexion. And, as importantly, the great western movies of this year have stood the test of time.

Arguments have been made for other years as being the best for the western and it is worth considering the other candidates. Starting at the beginning brings us to *Stagecoach* (1939), considered by many the most influential western ever made. However, the John Ford western was at an advantage when it appeared because at that time it was not hard for a decent western picture to stand out since, prior to 1939, there was literally a handful—no more than ten—mainstream westerns (excluding singing cowboys and series movies) of any quality. The western did not take off in 1939 through the sole efforts of Ford, who had not stuck a toe into this particular genre since the silent era. There had been many—far too many, by some reckonings—westerns made during the 1930s, but the vast majority comprised inferior run-of-the-mill B-movies featuring stock characters. It is worth remembering, also, that Hollywood did not get much wrong in its estimation of public tastes. Audiences were fickle and already the 1930s had seen the speedy demise of gangster and horror pictures. A western with a likable leading actor and a few songs satisfied the general taste. More importantly, from the financial perspective, it was the kind of picture a Poverty Row studio such as Republic could turn out with ease, with little risk of a star, on whom after all such series depended, being poached by the majors. The flop of *The Big Trail* (1930) starring John Wayne put an end to Hollywood hopes of translating the traditional silent western into a more demanding talkie.

But it was not Ford who revived the genre. He was already three years behind the times when *Stagecoach* rolled out. Credit for kick-starting a moribund genre went to King Vidor and Cecil B. DeMille, when they released *The Texas Rangers* (1936) with Fred MacMurray and *The Plainsman* (1936) with Gary Cooper, respectively. Their box office success stimulated others of similar quality, but not in huge numbers: Richard Boleslawski's *Three Godfathers* (1936) with Chester Morris, Frank Lloyd's *Wells Fargo* (1937) starring Joel McCrea, and Michael Curtiz's *Gold Is Where You Find It* (1938) with George Brent and Olivia de Havilland. And it is true that 1939 was a year of particular excellence: In addition to *Stagecoach*, there came Tyrone Power as *Jesse James*, directed by Henry King, James Cagney as *The Oklahoma Kid*, helmed by Lloyd Bacon, Michael Curtiz's *Dodge City* with Errol Flynn and Olivia de Havilland, and DeMille's *Union Pacific* with Barbara Stanwyck and McCrea. But the main difference between 1939 and 1969 was that the earlier pictures were not contending with genre history, or having to find twists on traditional tales, nor being asked to tackle contemporary issues. The earlier westerns were made by top directors, who between them virtually invented the genre. And you could make pretty much the same assessment of 1948, the next outstanding year, because the Second World War had virtually stopped the new genre in its tracks, series characters and singing cowboys predominant, virtually the only ones worth mentioning being Raoul Walsh's *They Died with Their Boots On* (1941) with Flynn and de Havilland, three from William Wellman—*The Great Man's Lady* (1942) starring Barbara Stanwyck, The *Ox-Bow Incident* (1942) with Henry Fonda and *Buffalo Bill* (1944) with McCrea and Maureen O'Hara—and *Along Came Jones* (1945) with Gary Cooper. So when Ford came to make *Fort Apache* (1948), there was no precedent for cavalry westerns in the mainstream and when Howard Hawks produced *Red River* (1948), neither had any major westerns concentrated on the trail drive. By the time Anthony Mann brought out *Winchester '73* (1950), there were probably no more than, at tops, about 20 of what we would term top-quality westerns. And although you could make arguments for particular years—1948 (*Red River, Fort Apache*), 1950 (*Rio Grande, Broken Arrow, Winchester '73*), 1952 (*High Noon*), 1954 (*Apache, Vera Cruz*), 1956 (*The Searchers, Friendly Persuasion*), 1959 (*Rio Bravo*)—it was usually on the grounds that they threw up a classic or two.

But no individual year provided the combination of public appreciation by way of box office, critical and peer approval in the shape of Oscars, and, to that extent, retrospective appraisal from the likes of *Sight & Sound* or the American Film Institute, that was to be found in 1969. To back up my argument on these grounds, analysis of the Top Ten films at the box office prior to 1969 reveals that only seven westerns from the period 1946 to 1959[2] made the cut, and only four from 1960 to 1968; in other words, about one western every two years was an out-and-out hit. For 1969 alone, two films, *Butch Cassidy and the Sundance Kid* and *True Grit*, made the Top Ten. In term of Oscars, in only two years, 1963 and 1969, were westerns nominated in the major categories for more than one film—*How the West Was Won* and *Hud* in the former, and *Butch Cassidy and the Sundance Kid* and *True Grit* in the latter. Actual wins in any of the major categories were few and far between for westerns—only Warner Baxter as *In Old Arizona* (1928), Gary Cooper in *High Noon* and John Wayne in *True Grit* taking home the Best Actor Oscar, *Cimarron* (1931) winning Best Picture (although Kevin Costner's *Dances with Wolves* in 1990 and Clint Eastwood's *Unforgiven* in 1992 also won, but not in banner years for west-

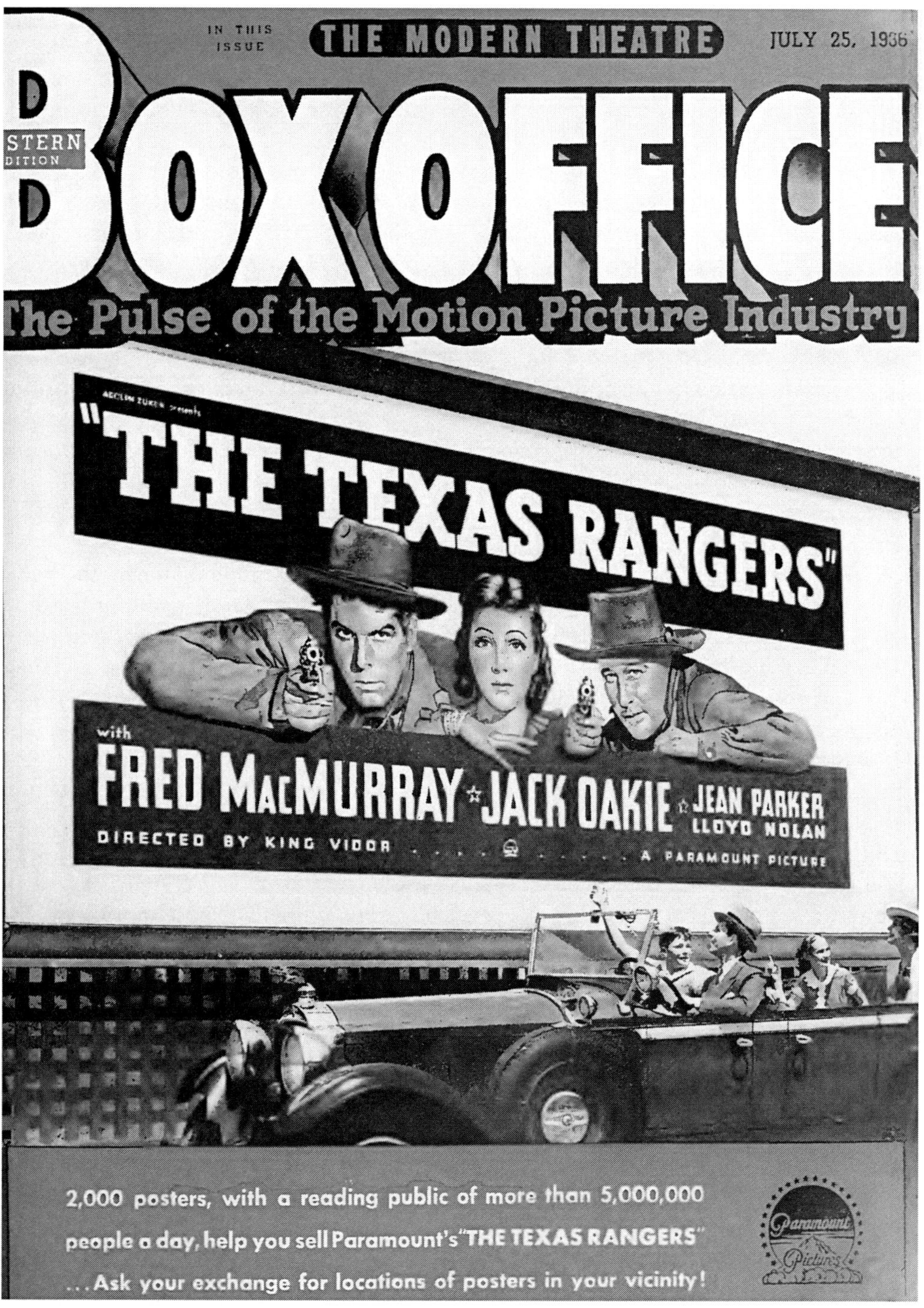

The most underrated actor of his generation, and among the most versatile, Fred MacMurray moved from westerns (*The Texas Rangers*, 1936, pictured) and film noir (*Double Indemnity*, 1944) to become Disney's go-to star for a string of comedies such as *The Absent Minded Professor* (1961), *Son of Flubber* (1963) and *The Happiest Millionaire* (1967). Trade press advertisement (*Box Office*, July 25, 1936).

erns). *How the West Was Won* and *Butch Cassidy and the Sundance Kid* also won Screenplay Awards. Admittedly, the Academy Award system managed to entirely overlook classics like *Red River* and *The Searchers*, so it is hardly a foolproof system of measurement. However, retrospective analysis favors 1969. The *Sight & Sound* once-in-a-decade worldwide Critics Poll (2012), in relation to westerns, featured two westerns from 1969, *Once Upon a Time in the West* (ranked third) and *The Wild Bunch* (fourth) in the top ten of that particular genre, more than for any other individual year.[3] In the Directors Poll that ran alongside it, three westerns from 1969 featured—*The Wild Bunch, Once Upon a Time in the West* and *Butch Cassidy and the Sundance Kid*—while in the other four years represented (1939, 1946, 1954, 1967) only one film from the genre was mentioned; and *The Wild Bunch* was voted equal first with *The Searchers*.[4]

The American Film Institute Western Top Ten had *The Wild Bunch* in sixth position and *Butch Cassidy and the Sundance Kid* one place lower, again more films for that year than any other.[5] The AMC Filmsite places *Butch Cassidy and the Sundance Kid* third and *The Wild Bunch* fourth.[6] From a more modern perspective, the movie magazine *Empire* rated only two westerns in its 2017 list of 100 Great Movies, *The Good, the Bad and the Ugly* and *Once Upon a Time in the West*.[7]

So what was it that made the last year of the 1960s so influential after the boom years of the 1950s, especially when at the start of the decade the demand for westerns had collapsed? Only two (*The Magnificent Seven* and *The Unforgiven*) appeared in the 1960 annual box office chart. After the financial failure of the big-budget spectaculars *The Alamo* (1960), *Cimarron* (1960) and *One-Eyed Jacks* (1961), the western had almost disappeared from sight, the success of *The Man Who Shot Liberty Valance* (1962) and *How the West Was Won* (1962) almost incidental. In 1964, for the first time in 15 years, there was not a single western in the annual box office top 25. The revival over the next couple of years had too many big-budget flops from some of its greatest exponents—John Ford's *Cheyenne Autumn* (1964), Sam Peckinpah's *Major Dundee* (1965) and John Sturges' *The Hallelujah Trail* (1965). The hits were led by *Shenandoah* (1965), the comedy western *Cat Ballou* (1965) and Richard Brooks' *The Professionals* (1966). John Wayne and James Stewart remained the biggest box office stars for westerns until from Europe the spaghetti western threatened the equilibrium. The traditional western took several realistic twists and turns but it was not until 1969 that the industry made an all-out assault on the genre, ironically at a time when Hollywood was in the middle of a financial meltdown.

By 1969, most of the majors had recently been taken over or were under threat of takeover and merger, Greek tycoon Aristotle Onassis rumored to be involved in the Kirk Kerkorian bid for MGM.[8] Those who had spent big like MGM, whose catastrophic losses would top $35 million by year's end,[9] now rued such extravagance and trimmed future budgets.[10] Even booming mini-major National General drastically reduced output.[11] Warner Brothers cancelled 23 pictures,[12] partly after incurring substantial costs from its merger with Kinney.[13] Twentieth Century–Fox rentals plummeted by one-third.[14] Although Disney remained optimistic with a $33 million slate, only two films out of the nine planned made it into theaters the following year.[15] European receipts were down across the board.[16] And most industry analysts feared the worst was yet to come.[17] Exhibitors battled in American courts to prevent the arrival of Pay-TV.[18] The industry also had to deal with hostile reaction from audiences and various representative bodies to the change in subject matter, away from the innocent comedies and roadshows to

Buddy Holly saw *The Searchers* and adopted its catchphrase "That'll be the day" for one of his most famous records. In advance of shooting *Lawrence of Arabia* (1962), David Lean studied the film to learn how to shoot landscape. Trade press advertisement (*Box Office*, May 12, 1956).

more disturbing contemporary fare and the increase in sex and violence.[19] Commentators were shocked to find nudity creeping into that most innocuous of genres, the "sexless cowboy" western. The protagonist for this—in what was seen as an unwelcome development—was *Hang 'Em High* (1968). Cutting closest to the immoral bone, sex reared its salacious head in 1969, in westerns such as *Sam Whiskey, Support Your Local Sheriff, 100 Rifles, Mackenna's Gold, The Wild Bunch, Tell Them Willie Boy Is Here* and *Butch Cassidy and the Sundance Kid*, although in more old-fashioned fare like *The Undefeated* bedroom scenes remained chaste.[20] The new ratings system introduced the previous year also brought fears of an onslaught of Adults Only pictures and further high-publicized clashes with the "moral majority."[21] When a raft of youth-oriented movies made on low or medium budgets—*Easy Rider* and Frank Perry's *Last Summer*[22] and a pack of biker pictures—raced through the summer[23] and the highly explicit *I Am Curious (Yellow)* threatened to shatter the foreign movie record held by the arthouse darling *La Dolce Vita*, studios tried to prevent the bloated Hollywood ship from capsizing by espousing the cause of youth.[24] Westerns were unlikely candidates to provide a universal panacea, especially given the perceived antipathy towards the genre from the younger generation. "Western Cycle Rides Again," ran one *Variety* headline.[25] That, in turn, led to "growing talk in film circles of westerns not as action programmers but as a source of first run feature fodder."[26] *International Motion Picture Exhibitor* predicted that the trio of *True Grit, The Wild Bunch* and *Once Upon a Time in the West* "would augur a resurgence of interest in one of Hollywood's most influential genres"[27] and that "the western is even more flexible and vital than it has been for at least the last 15 years."[28]

Thematic Impulse

It is quite clear from viewing nigh on 40-plus westerns released[29] in 1969 that certain themes and mini-themes emerged on a continuous basis as if some unconscious symmetry was at work. The main themes were: relentless pursuit (incorporating revenge), physical escape and psychological escape (dreaming), the changing position of women, and racism. Relentless pursuit is the central theme of *The Stalking Moon, Once Upon a Time in the West, The Wild Bunch, Young Billy Young, Butch Cassidy and the Sundance Kid* and *Tell Them Willie Boy Is Here*. While the pursued is usually an outlaw, he can also be a hero (*The Stalking Moon*) and, as with *The Wild Bunch, Butch Cassidy and the Sundance Kid* and, to some extent, *Tell Them Willie Boy Is Here*, the pursuit is seen from the villain's perspective, although, to a large degree, in this trio, the outlaws are given a sympathetic ride. Equally, in *The Wild Bunch, Mackenna's Gold, True Grit* and *Tell Them Willie Boy Is Here*, the character of the pursuer contains various shades of gray, sometimes downright dark, often quasi-outlaw in outlook, rather than the whiter-than-white traditional hero. In some films, pursuit is merely an element of the story rather than its overriding arch: Jim Brown in *100 Rifles* ends up in Mexico as a consequence of hunting an outlaw; in *The Undefeated*, Confederates are chased to prevent them escaping. Many of those running away believe they will find sanctuary in a foreign land or another region or in, in the case of Henry Fonda, in legitimate business. Some individuals simply escape into their own minds, dreaming of Paris (*Mackenna's Gold*), the Pacific (Morton in *Once Upon a Time in the West*), Bolivia (*Butch Cassidy and the Sundance Kid*), Australia (*Butch Cassidy and the Sundance Kid* and *Support Your Local Sheriff*), a quiet ranch (*The*

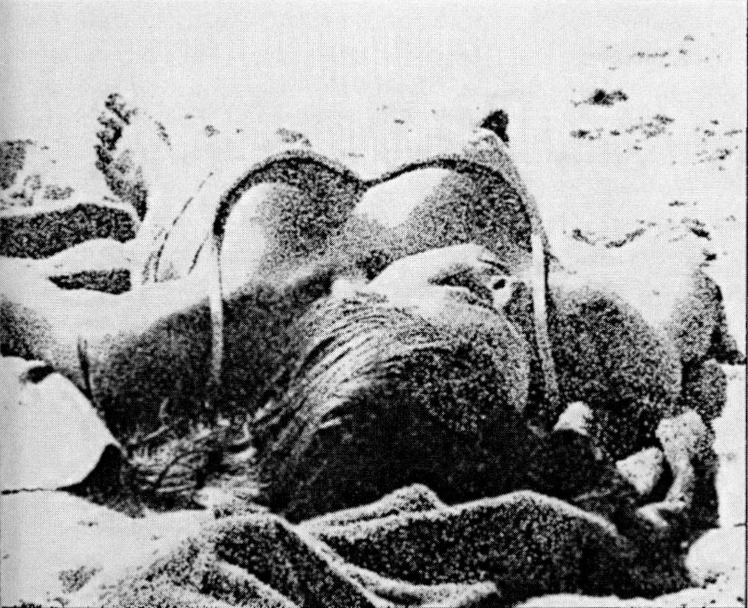

Sondra Locke turned down the *Last Summer* leading role. Trade press advertisement (*Box Office*, June 30, 1969).

Stalking Moon), something as indeterminate as the West itself (Jill McBain in *Once Upon a Time in the West*) or something as specific as a small library under a big elm (*The Undefeated*).

Representations of women ran the gamut from the dominant to the meek (and weak). Raquel Welch (*100 Rifles*), who had already made her western debut in *Bandolero!* (1968), emerges in 1969 as a latter-day Barbara Stanwyck or Joan Crawford and heads the list of 1969's tough-talking women and, except for illogical plotting, would have been the leader of the Mexican rebels. Jean Seberg in *Paint Your Wagon* turns traditional expectation on its head by taking two husbands while Katharine Ross in *Butch Cassidy and the Sundance Kid* has an implied *ménage a trois*, although her character changes substantially from the first half of the picture to the second, Initially, she is submissive but in Bolivia she not only takes charge, as only a teacher can, she joins the two men in their bank-robbing exploits. Claudia Cardinale's Jill McBain goes from submissive woman and semi-chattel to earth mother in *Once Upon a Time in the West.* In the sexuality department, Angie Dickinson in *Sam Whiskey* and Ina Balin in *Charro* are more than a match for their men and in *A Man Called Gannon* the female ranch owner beds two young cowhands. Two of the most original female characters, forthright, willful and often contrary, are Prudy in *Support Your Local Sheriff* and Mattie Ross in *True Grit*. But whereas Prudy is never in any real danger, Mattie is taken hostage and threatened with rape. Native Indian Hesh-ke in *Mackenna's Gold* is treated as chattel as is white woman Inga Bergerman, taken hostage. Native American Leloopa in *Heaven with a Gun* considers herself chattel, and Native American Lola in *Tell Them Willie Boy Is Here* is treated as chattel, and kills herself or is killed because she is a burden to her husband. Rape (*Heaven with a Gun*), or its threat (*True Grit, Mackenna's Gold, The Undefeated*), remains a constant, and often implied, theme.

There are also gender twists. In *Once Upon a Time in the West,* the woman inherits wealth through marriage; in *Support Your Local Sheriff,* it is the man. In *Heaven with a Gun,* a Mormon husband has two wives; in *Paint Your Wagon,* a woman has two husbands. And, in a more gut-wrenching twist, while white woman Sarah Carver in *The Stalking Moon* is vilified for not killing herself rather than be taken by a Native American, in *Tell Them Willie Boy Is Here* it is the Native American who kills his Native American wife (or she kills herself) rather than fall into the hands of the white man. Women are also betrayers (*The Wild Bunch*) and the idea of disrobing to distract the enemy or as a method of seduction is all too conveniently explored in *100 Rifles, Mackenna's Gold* and *The Great Bank Robbery.*

There is also a different attitude toward men. Although *Butch Cassidy and the Sundance Kid* is responsible for creating the new subgenre of the "buddy" movie, that was only a by-product of a revived interest in camaraderie whether it be the inner workings of a small group (*The Wild Bunch, The Undefeated, Journey to Shiloh*), two old friends (*Butch Cassidy and the Sundance Kid*), two newfound friends (*Paint Your Wagon*) or men thrown together by circumstance (*The Good Guys and the Bad Guys, A Man Called Gannon*).

African Americans are also shown in a new light with the first genuine action star in the shape of Jim Brown, the legendary footballer who had made his debut in *Rio Conchos* (1964).

But he is not just introduced in *100 Rifles* as a more muscular version of the western hero but is given a romantic entanglement with the heroine, breaking another taboo,

***Bandolero!* with Raquel Welch (pictured) was the second of three films featuring Dean Martin and George Kennedy. Part of the film was shot on the set built for *The Alamo* (1960) (Hannan Collection).**

that of on-screen miscegenation. Less controversially, because no promotional gain was made out of the fact, Marshal Patch in *Death of a Gunfighter* had an African American wife.

Attitudes toward Native Americans are explored in a positive manner in at least three instances. In *Heaven with a Gun,* the hero protects a defenseless Native American woman, in *Smith!* the hero defends a Native American in court, in *The Undefeated*, John Wayne's character has adopted a Native American boy. On the other hand, vicious racism against Native Americans is the driving force behind the action of *Tell Them Willie Boy Is Here*, by less-enlightened soldiers in *The Undefeated*, by citizens in *Smith!* and cowboys in *Heaven with a Gun*.

The railroad is a symbol of civilization (*Once Upon a Time in the West*), convenience (*True Grit*) and power (*The Wild Bunch*, *Butch Cassidy and the Sundance Kid*) and a method of imposing authority when employed as troop trains (*100 Rifles*, *Young Billy Young*). The coming of civilization impinges on the lawful and the lawless alike. *The Wild Bunch* and *Butch Cassidy and the Sundance Kid* face the end of an era, but so too does Marshal Patch in *Death of a Gunfighter*, turned out of his job for being too bloodthirsty. Even Rooster Cogburn in *True Grit* feels the breath of the defense lawyer on his neck.

The traditional is not ignored. There are one-to-one showdowns (*The Stalking Moon*, *Once Upon a Time in the West*, *A Time for Dying*, *Tell Them Willie Boy Is Here*, *Mackenna's*

Gold and *Day of Anger*) and there are battles (*100 Rifles*, *The Wild Bunch*, *The Undefeated*, *Guns of the Magnificent Seven*), and, of course, there is the glorious long shot to paint panoramas across the big screen.

Aims and Methodology

This book looks at the major westerns—including four I regard as masterpieces—that individually and in total make the argument that 1969 is the Greatest Year of the Western. It examines not just the changing of the West but the transformations attendant on the genre by the departure (death or retirement) of key directors and stars and discusses the longevity of various current stars (John Wayne, Richard Widmark, Glenn Ford, Robert Mitchum), the arrival of new stars (Clint Eastwood, Lee Marvin, Michael Sarrazin), as well as picking up on the innovations of the new breed of director, some of whom specialize in the format, and others coming to the genre for the very first time. One of the major influences on the 1969 western is that the majority of the old guard, led by John Ford, Howards Hawks and Anthony Mann, who had invented or reinvented the western, are gone. While newer talents such as Andrew V. McLaglen, Sergio Leone, Sam Peckinpah and Burt Kennedy have helped fill the vacuum, what is particularly striking about the year is how directors George Roy Hill (*Hawaii*), Robert Mulligan (*To Kill a Mockingbird*) and J. Lee Thompson (*The Guns of Navarone*), who had made their names in other genres, took up the challenge of reinventing this genre as if making a western had become a rite of passage in an era when they were no longer able to call upon such icons such as Gary Cooper, Randolph Scott and Alan Ladd.

Each film has been viewed in the order of its release in an attempt to replicate the response of the contemporary audience to the films. The introduction to each film explains how it came to be made, analyses the stars and directors behind the project, the context of the particular subgenre, and the problems faced in bringing visions to fruition. Each film is analyzed in terms of narrative, directorial style with considerable emphasis placed on how directors achieved their effects, and, in particular, utilized the camera, with the final section of each chapter devoted to critical response and box office (although overall box office is dealt with in more depth in the appendices). In my Conclusion, I point to the genuine depth of the western movie of 1969 and spotlight some of the hidden gems which so far have not attracted the cult following that appears to be necessary these days for reassessment.

As there is much confusion about the release dates of so many films (IMDb is not always accurate in this matter), I have taken another approach to this by examining the dates that films appeared in each city. This forms Appendix A. The dates mentioned here relate to the dates on which box office was reported in *Variety* magazine, which at that time was the only one of the trade magazines to consistently report these figures on a weekly basis. I have selected a sample of the 19 most prominent cities in order to show how quickly—or slowly—the release of each movie unfolded. It is also worth noting that not every movie opened in first run in each city, which means they went straight into a "showcase" release in that area, showcase being the name given to a local wide release long before national day-and-date wide release became the standard, or were not released at all in that city. Another element that this brings into relief is to show how congested release patterns were for westerns, sometimes with two or three major westerns opening

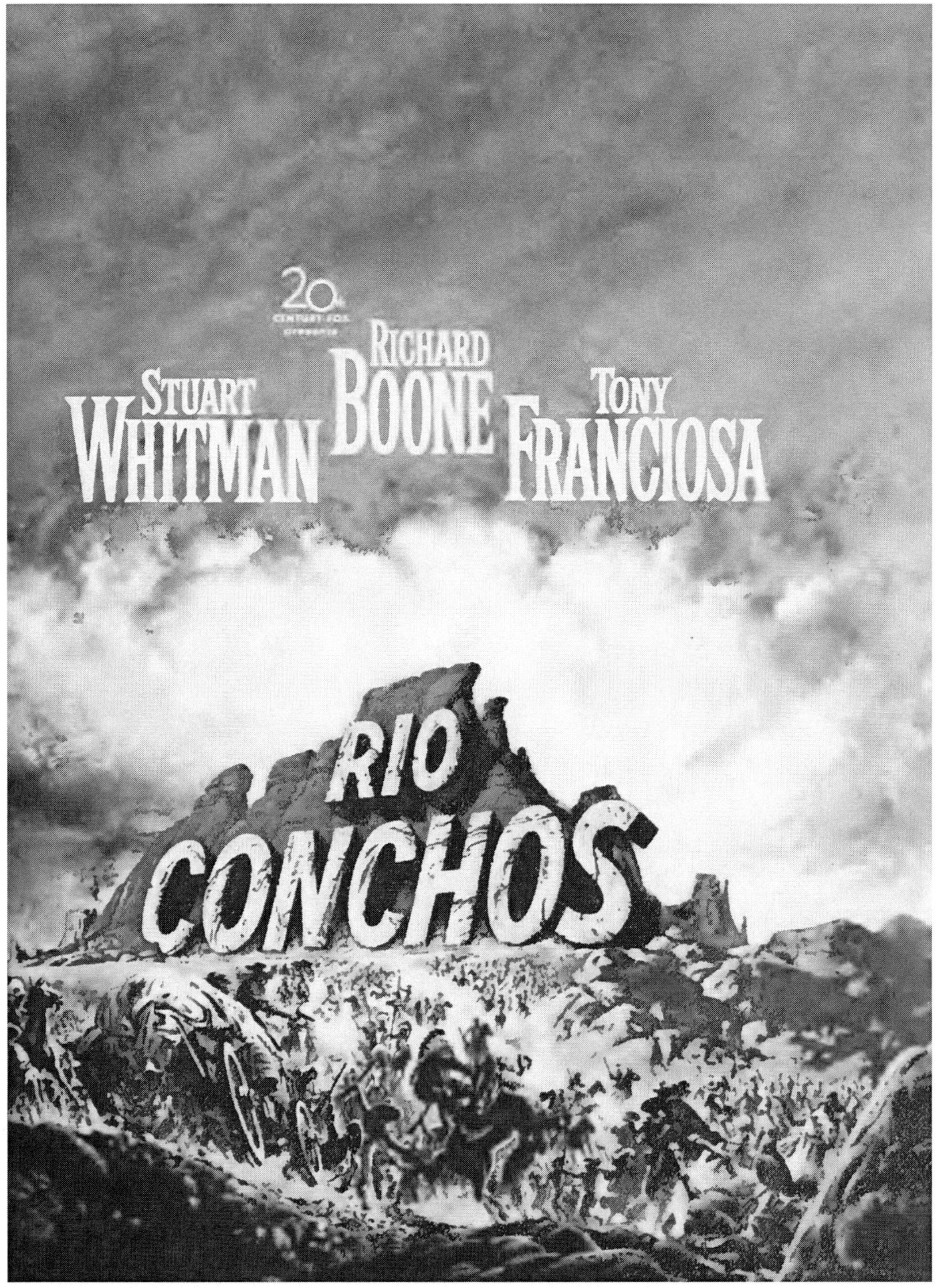

At the same time as *Rio Conchos*, Richard Boone was a television star with his own program, *The Richard Boone Show* (1963–64). *Rio Conchos*' world premiere was held in Cleveland, where Jim Brown was a football legend. Trade press advertisement (*Box Office*, September 21, 1964).

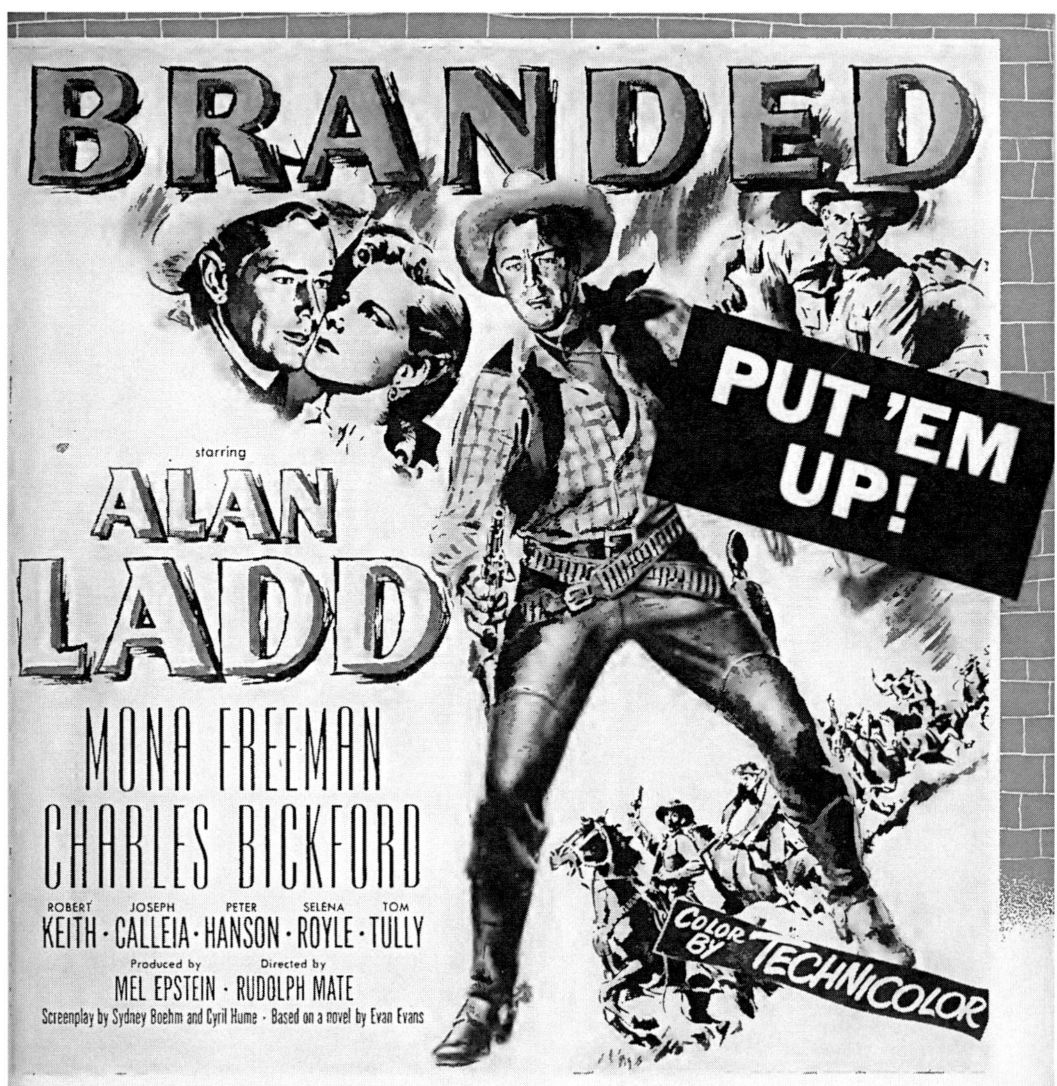

More posters—more promotion—more playing time! Make *plus* plans for the Ladd picture that's bigger than "Whispering Smith." Today, Paramount's great star is at the very peak of his boxoffice popularity as readers of one of America's largest circulation fan magazines vote for the third consecutive year:

ALAN LADD

The Most Popular Male Star—Modern Screen's Poll!

Branded director Rudolph Mate was nominated for five consecutive Oscars for Cinematography: *Foreign Correspondent* (1940), *That Hamilton Woman* (1941), *The Pride of the Yankees* (1942), *Sahara* (1943) and *Cover Girl* (1944). Trade press advertisement (*Box Office*, December 23, 1950).

in the same city at the same time or very close together, which may well have cannibalized returns.

Two further Appendices cover movie box office. Appendix B, relating to Appendix A, reveals the grosses[30] taken by each western of 1969 in the first week of its run in the selected cities. That enables the reader to evaluate how well each film did in relation to its competitors. Appendix C is a list of how well the westerns of the period 1960 to 1969 did at the box office. For a film to enter the annual chart, it has to have taken $1 million or more in rentals. For comparative purposes, in order to shed light on their impact in any particular year, this is done by showing their chart position for the year instead of the rentals[31] earned.

1

The Sound of Silence

The Stalking Moon

Starring Gregory Peck, Eva Marie Saint and Robert Forster; directed by Robert Mulligan; screenplay by Alvin Sargent, adaptation by Wendell Mayes, from the book by Theodore V. Olsen; National General Pictures; 109 minutes[1]

The Film That Should Never Have Been Made

By all that Hollywood held sacred, *The Stalking Moon* should never have gotten off the ground, at least not via National General Cinemas, the latest addition to the burgeoning mini-major roster. For National General, in keeping with the company name, had been set up to run theaters. And operating theaters and making movies ran counter to the Consent Decree of 1948 which had not only forced the major studios to jettison their chains of cinemas but also prevented them from functioning in that manner in the future. As a legal device, the Consent Decree had more than done its job; it had almost brought the entire industry to its knees since studios could no longer rely on the substantial profits generated from exhibition to bolster their moviemaking programs; the industry fell into a decade-long downward spiral. Although revenues recovered throughout the 1960s as a result of the promulgation of the roadshow, the Bond films and a variety of other audience-winning efforts, the underlying effect of the Consent Decree, that of reducing studio output, still had a radical impact on theater owners. Simply put, there were not enough movies to go around. A smaller number of movies corresponded to higher rentals, putting exhibitors under even more pressure to make a buck. To make the most of what *was* available, first-run owners, notwithstanding the standard lengthy contracts for roadshows specifying lengthy runs, took to running ordinary movies for longer than before, resulting in meager pickings for theaters further down the food chain. So when National General proposed upending the principles of the Consent Decree, there were few in the industry wishing to stand in their way.

National General owed its inception to the Consent Decree. It had been established in 1951 with the express purpose of taken over the running of the 550 theaters which Twentieth Century–Fox was being forced to relinquish. That number of cinemas was considered too high and a court order cut the number in half six years later.[2] By 1963, with earnings of $3.4 million, the organization ran 217 theaters as well as having real estate holdings and a sideline in renting equipment for mobile concerts,[3] by which time it had already instigated

Stalking Moon **co-star Robert Forster was nominated for an Oscar for Quentin Tarantino's *Jackie Brown* (1997). He played Native American Nakia Parker in the short-lived TV series *Nakia* (1974). Trade press advertisement (*Box Office*, January 8, 1968).**

court proceedings in order to annul or bypass the Consent Decree. It was not the first theater chain to aim to set aside the binding conditions of the Decree. Howco, owning 60 theaters, began low-budget production in 1954.[4] American Broadcasting-Paramount Theaters had made modest forays in this direction, primarily with program fillers of the sci-fi–horror variety, in the mid–1950s, and regional theater owner McLendon Films entered the production arena with *My Dog Buddy* (1960). But these were viewed as minor aberrations and not considered to breach the stout defenses of the Decree.

National General had bigger ambitions that could not be fulfilled without some alteration of the original Decree and in 1963 it went to court to seek a modification of the Decree ruling which, while safeguarding anti-trust measures, would nonetheless help arrest the rapid decline in production, which had seen output tumble from 408 features in 1942 to just 138 movies two decades later. As an "experiment," the government permitted NGC a three-year window.[5] NGC's new enterprise Carthay Center Productions announced its first movie nine months later: *What Are Little Girls Made Of*, a $2.5 million comedy produced by the Bud Yorkin-Norman Lear Tandem shingle. Carthay Center was also in talks with Stanley Donen (*Singin' in the Rain*, *Charade*).[6] A few months later, the infant outfit projected that it was on course to make four to six pictures a year with budgets in the $2 million to $4 million range, with *Divorce—American Style* now mooted as its first offering and a distribution deal with Columbia.[7] The hopes of expectant exhibitors were kept alive throughout the three-year period granted by the government. A three-picture deal was made with director Fielder Cook, who lined up prominent British playwright Harold Pinter to write *Flight and Pursuit*.[8]

Two years after receiving the governmental green light, none of these projects had come to fruition. To speed up production, Carthay sought to take advantage of the British government's Eady Levy (which subsidized film production in the U.K.) by making *The Berlin Memorandum* (later re-titled *The Quiller Memorandum*), based on the spy thriller by Adam Hall (aka Elleston Trevor), on a $2.5 million budget as the first volley in a six-film, 18-month production schedule.[9] By 1966, Tandem's *Divorce—American Style* starring Dick Van Dyke and Debbie Reynolds[10] had begun shooting. So had *The Quiller Memorandum* with George Segal and Alec Guinness as the marquee names, but without the involvement of Carthay.

However, by 1966, NGC was in a buoyant mood, underlining its ambitions by announcing a $10 million business-building loan.[11] More importantly, at the beginning of the year it had signed its first major star. Gregory Peck was to star in *The Stalking Moon*, with a $3.5 million budget and shooting to begin in spring 1967.[12] There was even talk at this stage that it "may be a hard ticket picture"[13]; it would give the new company prestige to enter the roadshow field. Although this was, technically, the eighth movie[14] on the NGC roster—and had previously been announced as such when movie rights to the Theodore V. Olsen western had been acquired pre-publication in December 1965[15]—it now, with Peck's involvement, shot up the production ladder.[16] Although screenwriter Wendell Mayes (*Anatomy of a Murder*, *Von Ryan's Express*) had been scheduled to act as producer,[17] Peck's production company Brentwood was also involved.[18] The picture acquired further cachet with the announcement that George Stevens (*Shane*) was to direct as well as produce.[19] There were now five co-producers: Stevens, Universal, Peck, NGP and Mayes.[20] In theory, at least, the arrival of heavyweights Peck and Stevens should have speeded up production. Instead, an endless series of delays and postponements ensued. The April 3, 1967, start date fell by the wayside when Stevens dropped out.[21] Although there was speculation that Steven's departure would lead to the movie being shelved,[22] Universal remained on board, at least for the time being, as distributor. Meanwhile, NGP took over production duties and reunited Peck with *To Kill a Mockingbird* director Robert Mulligan and producer Alan J. Pakula.[23] Before Stevens left, the start date had already been shifted to May 28[24] and when the dust on that had settled, it was set for an October 15 start.[25] But that proved over-optimistic and when it began rolling on January 5, 1968, the budget had increased to $4 million.[26]

NGP soon faced other difficulties. The battle to remain in the production business precipitated another round of legal and governmental negotiations.[27] The original three-year waiver that had expired in 1966[28] had been extended by a further three years and, although by this point the second largest movie chain in the country,[29] NGC had failed to fill the production gap that it was set up specifically to do. But its position was bolstered by CBS-TV launching its Cinema Center movie production arm and ABC-TV its Cinerama vehicle.[30] The company was so worried about *not* getting another government waiver that it considered a merger with Warner Brothers as a means of safeguarding production.[31] The Carthay name itself soon became defunct, the company reverting to National General Pictures (NGP) in order to identify, in the words of president Eugene V. Klein, "our picture-making activities as a major part of our company program."[32] In addition, it had fallen far short of its production schedule. Instead of releasing movies at the rate of one per month throughout 1968, only six films were ready for distribution—and none of them were actually made by NGC.[33] By year's end, the company's entire production fortune was riding on *The Stalking Moon*.

Catch a Falling Star

By the beginning of 1969, Gregory Peck looked a spent force. He had not made a film in three years, a dangerous length of exile in fickle Hollywood. The commercial and artistic peaks of the early 1960s—*The Guns of Navarone* (1961) and *How the West Was Won* (1962) both topping the annual box office charts in addition to winning the Oscar for Best Actor, at the fifth attempt, with *To Kill a Mockingbird* (1962)[34]—were ancient history. None of his other pictures came close to matching these in either commercial or artistic terms: *Captain Newman M.D.* (1963) ranked 21st for the year, and the Stanley Donen thriller *Arabesque* (1966) 16th. Most performed substantially below expectations. *Cape Fear* (1962), despite the involvement of *Navarone* director J. Lee Thompson and having incurred the Production Code's wrath,[35] finished 47th; in Peck's entire canon, only *Beloved Infidel* had done worse at the box office. The prestige offering *Behold a Pale Horse* (1964), directed by Fred Zinnemann and co-starring Anthony Quinn and Omar Sharif, proved an unexpected flop, 63rd for the year, while the thriller *Mirage* (1965), directed by veteran Edward Dmytryk, was 74th.[36] With his commercial status in question, the actor shuttered his production company Brentwood, although in an image-conscious industry, he came up with a more respectable reason: "We are far better holding ourselves available for acting jobs, and then producing only when the right elements happen to be there."[37]

From 1964 onwards, he was more commonly associated with films that did not get made. That year, Cinerama announced with considerable fanfare that he was going to star in the grand sci-fi project *The Martian Chronicles*, directed by Mulligan, adapted from the Ray Bradbury bestseller, with a $10 million budget.[38] Also failing to get off the ground was *The Night of the Short Knives*, planned as a co-production with veteran Walter Wanger.[39] At one point, Steve McQueen was mooted as a co-star until MGM's rival production *2001: A Space Odyssey* killed the idea stone dead.

In 1965, MGM signed him up, along with David Niven (another *Navarone* alumnus), James Stewart, James Coburn and George Segal, for *Ice Station Zebra*, based on an Alistair MacLean thriller, with a screenplay by Paddy Chayefsky[40]; when the movie finally appeared several years later, none of these actors were involved. In 1965, he also lost out

***Mirage* co-star Diane Baker was a Hitchcock protégé, having appeared in *Marnie* (1964). She had been nominated for a Golden Globe (Most Promising Newcomer) for *The Diary of Anne Frank* (1959) and for a Best Supporting Actress Oscar for *The Prize* (1963). Trade press advertisement (*Box Office*, March 22, 1965).**

on *They're a Weird Mob*[41] when the rights which he had held since 1959 elapsed. *Across the River and Into the Trees* with Virna Lisi, based on the Ernest Hemingway novel, did not get beyond the development stage.[42] It was hard to say what was worse, movies shelved before a foot of film was exposed, or pictures halted in mid-production, as was the case in 1966 when filming in Switzerland of *The Bells of Hell Go Ting A Ling A Ling* was suspended after five weeks due to unexpectedly harsh weather conditions. It was indicative of doubts about Peck's commercial standing that, once the weather cleared, the movie did not resume shooting, despite a budget outlay by this point of over $2 million.[43] In 1967, it was the turn of *After Navarone*,[44] *The Mudskipper*[45] and *Strangers on the Bridge* to stall on the starting grid.[46] Although the 1966 reissue of *Guns of Navarone* kept him in public view, during this period of enforced idleness Peck was more likely to be heard rather than seen, taking on narration duties for an ABC-TV documentary on Africa,[47] and a John F. Kennedy documentary,[48] although he enjoyed considerable publicity as president of the Academy of Motion Picture Arts and Sciences and as the inaugural chairman of the American Film Institute, taking up both roles in 1967. Although Peck was still a big marquee name when initially signed for *The Stalking Moon*, there remained a massive question mark, given nearly three years cinematic inactivity, over his ability to open a picture. In addition, the more obvious problem was whether a marketplace still existed for the Gregory Peck western given that, with the exception of *How the West Was Won* (1962), he had not been in the saddle since *The Bravados* and *The Big Country* in 1958, neither of which had turned a profit at the U.S. ticket wickets, and prior to those, *The Gunfighter* in 1950, another box office disappointment. He was hardly in the league of John Wayne or James Stewart, for whom the western was the default setting, both of whom had recently turned in strong commercial returns in the genre.

Oscars Abound

What the cast and crew had in common was Oscars. Director Mulligan had been Oscar-nominated for *To Kill a Mockingbird*. A graduate of live television, he was comfortable in a variety of fields, comedy in *The Rat Race* (1960), romance in *Come September* (1961) and dramas like *Love with the Proper Stranger* (1963) and *Inside Daisy Clover* (1965). Under his watch, Peck had won the Oscar for *To Kill a Mockingbird*, Natalie Wood had been Oscar-nominated for *Love with the Proper Stranger* and Ruth Gordon for *Inside Daisy Clover*. Producing partner Alan J. Pakula had also been nominated for *To Kill a Mockingbird*. *The Stalking Moon* was their seventh film together. Eve Marie Saint, who played Sarah Carver, the white woman on the run from her Apache husband, won an Oscar in her first movie role opposite Marlon Brando in Elia Kazan's *On the Waterfront* (1954). Over the following dozen years, she appeared in only 13 more pictures, but they were a diverse bunch including the female leads in Hitchcock's *North by Northwest* (1959), Otto Preminger's *Exodus* (1960), the comedy *The Russians Are Coming, The Russians Are Coming* (1966) and John Frankenheimer's epic *Grand Prix* (1966). Her apparent fragility concealed inner strength, although her deft comedic touch and passionate clinch with Cary Grant in *North by Northwest*, and her frantic reaction to the death of racing driver Yves Montand in *Grand Prix*, belied her reputation for onscreen coolness. In the Oscar stakes, cinematographer Charles Lang eclipsed them all with one win for *A Farewell to Arms* (1932) and 15 further nominations including *Some Like It Hot* (1959) and *One-Eyed Jacks* (1961). Although this represented a western debut for director, producer and leading actress, Lang had been the cinematographer for *The Man from Laramie* (1955), *Gunfight at the O.K. Corral* (1957), *The Magnificent Seven* (1960) and *How the West Was Won*. Sound editor Jack Solomon had been nominated in 1960 and editor Aaron Steel twice, in 1962 and 1965. Screenwriter Mayes had been nominated for Otto Preminger's courtroom drama *Anatomy of a Murder* (1959) and Horton Foote, who worked on *The Stalking*

Moon without receiving a credit, had won the Oscar for *To Kill a Mockingbird*. However, the final screenplay credit went to Alvin Sargent, in television since 1957. *Gambit* (1966) had marked his movie debut; *The Stalking Moon* his second picture. Actor Robert Forster made his debut in John Huston's *Reflections in a Golden Eye* (1967) and followed up with the role of Nick Tana in *The Stalking Moon*. Forster had a keen idea of his abilities, telling *Variety* that he only took roles that "would not compromise me or my wife or my agent. I don't know how an actor can agree to play a role that he doesn't feel he can do something special with." His principles led him to turning down a four-picture deal with Universal.[49] *The Stalking Moon* was the first and only picture for Noland Clay, who played Eva Marie Saint's son, as it was for Nathaniel Narcisco in the role of her husband Salvaje. This was composer Fred Karlin's third movie score after *Up the Down Staircase* (1967) and *Yours, Mine and Ours* (1968) and the music alternated between a lilting motif for the more idyllic sections and an urgent repetitive sound for the thrilling elements. Most of the picture was shot on location in Arizona (Wolf Hole, Wolf Hole Valley, Moccasin Mountains and the Paiute Wilderness Area), Nevada (Red Rock Canyon and Valley of Fire State Park) and Bavispe in Mexico (with interiors at the Samuel Goldwyn Studios).

Minimalist Script

The Theodore V. Olsen book[50] is quite different. In the novel, Sam Vatch (not Varner) has married Sarah without knowing that she has once been Salvaje's woman. Sarah Carver has two children not one, the other being an ill younger brother. In the book, she talks a lot. On the other hand, Sam Varner is looking for a home and, in any other kind of picture, her loquaciousness coupled with his need for domestic security would have brought them together emotionally. In the Olsen version, Salvaje, not Sarah, is the sole survivor of a massacre. But the film takes an entirely different approach.

In the movie version, instead of presenting the audience with a dialogue-heavy picture where emotional need is clearly stated, Mulligan is more interested in people who keep their feelings to themselves, who scarcely had a word to say, who lacked the dexterity to build up any lasting relationship. As much as the film is about the silences that can swamp individuals, it is also about characters watching each other for any sign of impending change, the kind that would normally be signaled by more vocal means. Such behavior is normally designated as brooding. Varney broods on what he should do, whether to help the woman or not, and just how far should he help, and when will helping her intrude on his privacy. Sarah Carver broods on the inevitability of her capture; and while that is temporarily postponed by the presence of Varney, it does not prevent her watching him for any sign that his attitude to her will change in a positive or, more likely, negative fashion. It is a revolutionary western indeed where the main characters do not exchange a kiss. Here, they hardly exchange a look. The one time they do come together could scarcely be termed a hug, more a gentle enfolding in his chest, minus his big manly arms around her.

"I Don't Mind Getting Out Alive"

The story of *The Stalking Moon* is simple enough: On the eve of retirement, Indian scout Sam Varner (Gregory Peck) helps the cavalry round up Indians to take to reservations.

One of these is American Sarah Carver (Eva Marie Saint) who, with her Apache son, is attempting to escape her vengeful Apache husband Salvaje. The extent of Salvaje's ruthlessness is seen within the first ten minutes: Varner agrees to take her to the nearest stagecoach post, and then to a train depot, and, finally, to his ranch in New Mexico where they enjoy a period of security. But wherever she goes, death follows, culminating in a shootout in the hills around the ranch.

But the treatment is far more complicated, often asking questions that cannot be answered, and placing the principals in situations that cannot be easily resolved. Sarah has not gone running in order to find a man to save her; she does not think she can be saved and accepts the inevitable. She feels guilty for "lacking the courage to die," of accepting Salvaje as her husband instead of dying along with the rest of her family when attacked a decade before by Indians. She is weak in other ways, hiding the identity of her husband from the Army and everyone else in case she is abandoned. She shows no great bond with her son, who, several times, attempts to escape.

Sam is very much an ordinary guy, just wanting to quit the Army and work his ranch. He is not the traditional extrovert western hero, nor the man who reluctantly takes up arms. He has no wish to get involved with Carver and each time he does agree to help, it is with a time-limited condition attached. These scenes lack any sense of meet-cuteness, no romantic interplay hastening him to a decision, little expectation that either party is angling to fall in love. It is practicality rather than intimacy that makes them share a blanket during a dust storm and he asks her to come to his ranch because he will get on with the work quicker if he has someone to cook. In fact, his honesty prevents that: He confronts her over the fact that she "put us out here knowing all the time that he'd come after us" and making her face the corpses of men who died because she hid the truth. He is honest with his emotions and he is determined ("I got a place to go and I'm going"). But he bears none of the normal western hero's traits, neither a hard drinker, loner or gunman. He is not gauche like James Stewart or malevolent like Clint Eastwood.

Even more unusual is the treatment of Salvaje. Despite the savagery of his actions, there is within him a sense of honor. He only chases his wife because she has stolen his son; there could be no greater affront to his dignity. The story is told from the point of view of the pursued, i.e., Sarah Carver. But, by turning that perspective on its head, *The Stalking Moon* more easily fits into the category of revenge western, characteristically a picture concerning chase and pursuit by someone who has been wronged. The director takes a bold step in the presentation of Salvaje. He is not seen at all in the first hour, then in just a few glimpses of a shape, his face only revealed at the climax. He is a ghost and a killing machine combined. Like a latter-day Terminator, he cannot be stopped, so skillful he evades capture, and relentless.

It is also, unusually for a western, a thriller. The tension mounts from the discovery, at the ten-minute mark, of Salvaje's first three victims, all fully armed soldiers, and the news, one minute later, that he single-handedly killed four troopers previously. At Hennessy, a stagecoach station, when Varner and Carver go out into a dust storm to search for her son who has run away, they return to find all dead. Everyone they left behind at Silverton, a train depot, is also killed. Initially, Carver appears impatient, not willing to wait five days for an Army escort, but once she reveals who the boy's father is, the reason becomes clear, and her desire for speedy travel creates more tension. In New Mexico, the death toll mounts once Salvaje arrives. Now the trap closes in on them. Even the ranch house cannot prevent Salvaje from sneaking in and kidnapping his wife, leaving her for

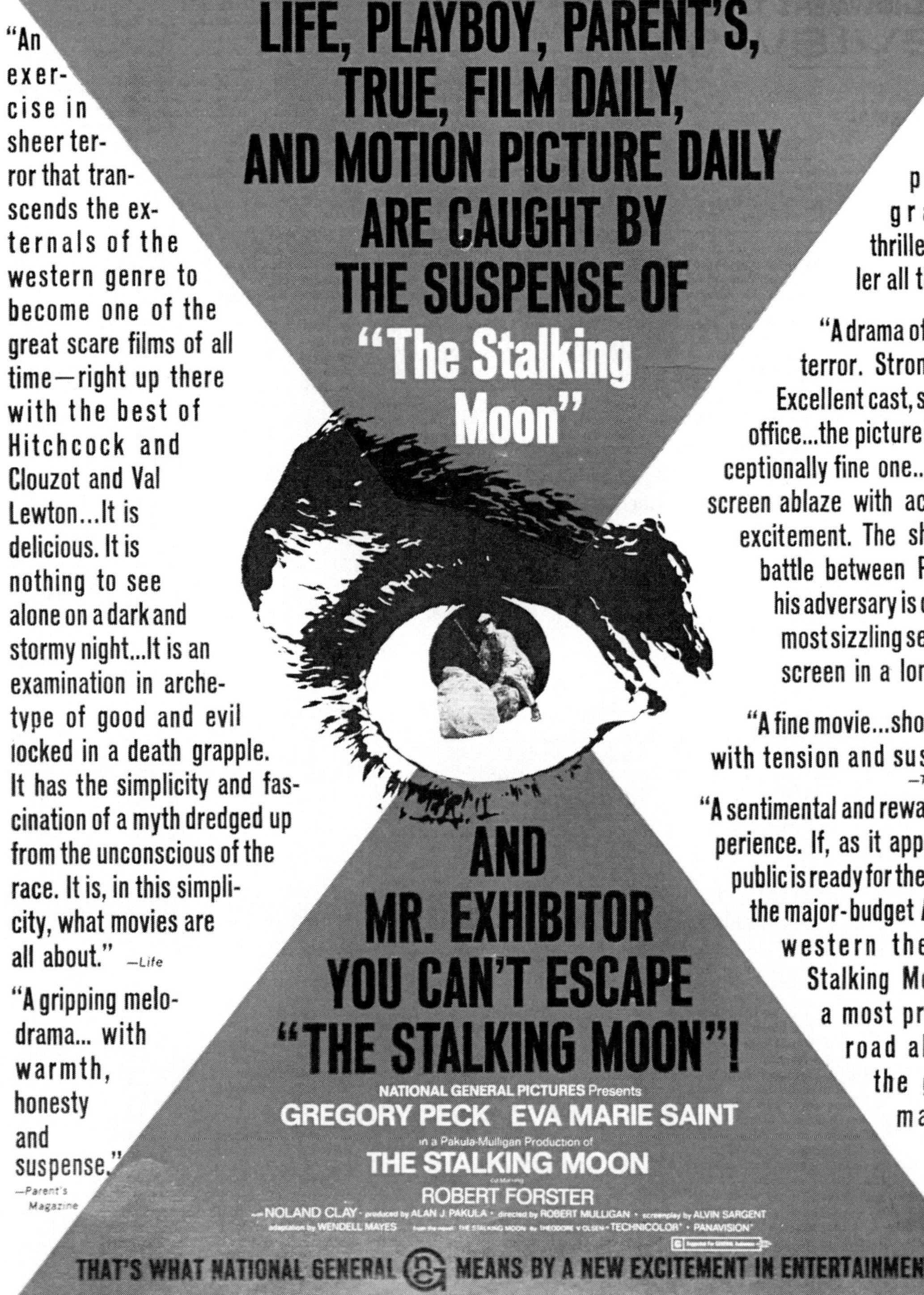

Universal ran a big Oscar campaign for *The Stalking Moon*, but it was not nominated in any category. Trade press advertisement (*Box Office*, December 23, 1968).

dead outside. When Varner and a fellow scout, the half-breed Nick Tana, attempt to turn the tables on Salvaje and track him down, it ends in Tana's death. Although most of the tension comes from the will- he-won't-he dynamic, there are number of Hitchcockian touches such as offscreen sound cues triggering alarm in characters.

In two instances, a door provides shock. In the first instance, as Sarah goes into the ranch house bedroom, we see a hand behind her pulling the door closed and then, as she turns, the sight of Salvaje leaping upon her. In the second example, towards the end of the film, Varner, trapped in the ranch house, sees light appearing around a closed door and then a shadow at the door.

At the end, Varner, pursuing Salvaje in the hills, walks into a kind of tripwire and a knife plunges into his thigh. The final battle between Varner and Salvaje twists and turns between one or the other having the advantage, sometimes literally interpreted as having the high ground, until, finally, both wounded, they scrap on the floor, Salvaje choking Varner on the wooden pole. Even when apparently fatally wounded, he still relentlessly crawls up the slope to attempt to strangle Varner.

Far from providing the expected relief, the ranch house merely provides a claustrophobic setting for the characters. Varner is trapped with an inarticulate pair. Instead of arrival at the ranch house precipitating emotional response and romantic interlude, as would be par for the course for other westerns, Varner finds himself stuck with a woman who refuses to talk and a boy who does not understand a word he says. The seven-minute scene where he sits down to eat and then has to virtually command mother and son to join him and encourage them to talk even if it is just to say "pass the peas," is one of the most awkward ever filmed. The movie is so darned awkward that you never laugh even at the few moments of comedy: the complicated issuing of train tickets, Varner keeping up a one-sided conversation at the table, Nick's attempts to teach the boy poker. Relationships are more likely to remain in limbo than move on to any romantic or sentimental plane.

The film has a tight structure, the first 40-odd minutes setting up the story and tracing Varner and Sarah's journey to the ranch house, the next 20 minutes at the ranch alternating between comfort and discomfort as emotional release battles with restraint, the final 40 minutes the physical battle between the mostly unseen enemy and the house occupants. Stylistically, it is exceptional. The first section is all open vistas, characters minute figures on vast landscapes. The middle section suggests harmony with nature, and the final battle alternates between being the hunter and the hunted. When we first see Varner, he is picked out along the edges of the screen as he leaps up or down or across rocky hillsides. That he appears and disappears at will could almost be the motif for the film. In action, Varner is immediately capable, striking down one Indian guarding horses before jumping on another and then firing his rifle to bring in the soldiers to round up the Indians.

There is almost a solemnity about the film. Virtually everyone is in long shot or medium shot for nearly the first half of the film. Peck is not given a big close-up right away. Instead he wanders on the periphery of the screen and the action. He enters scenes where something important is being discussed, such as Sarah's pleading to be allowed to leave the Army camp quickly. Most directors present Gregory Peck with aura intact, keeping him motionless on the screen to maintain his authority, but here he is always on the move, walking across open ground or confined spaces or darting across hillsides or through bushes, dashing on foot down slopes or racing on horseback. The script was viewed in many quarters as being underwritten, in particular Sarah's role, and that there were too many silences for comfort; but in the view of many, that is the strength of the picture. There is none of the easy dialogue, crackling lines, coarse confrontation, sentiment or raw emotion of other westerns. The movie hardly even skirts a cliché. This is in a class of its own in terms of the distance that characters maintain between each other. Varner has very little to say, Sarah's guilt restricts her vocabulary. In one regard, the thriller element gets in the way of a study of two remote characters.

Rather than anything in the Hitchcock canon, the film was most commonly compared to Tom Gries' *Will Penny* (1967), an unromantic western starring Charlton Heston[51] as a lifetime cowpoke who gets a job keeping trespassers off a cattle spread. As accidentally as in *The Stalking Moon*, into his life comes a mother (Joan Hackett) and son. The romance, initially awkward, soon develops into something emotionally deeper while at the same time Penny develops a deep bond with the son. Although the film reveals just how arduous the work of a cowhand is, and avoids most of the clichés about the western, and while the relationship with Hackett takes a while to flourish, the movie still has far more romance and emotion than displayed in *The Stalking Moon*, although, in the end, Penny leaves this behind and rides off.

If I have any reservations about *The Stalking Moon,* it is that is neither enough of a thriller nor enough of a character study. George Stevens might have sought emotional resolution and producer Alan J. Pakula, who later went on to direct *Klute* (1971) and *The Parallax View* (1974), might have proved more adept at marrying the thriller elements to personal anguish. Although *The Stalking Moon* may not have entered the pantheon of the greatest westerns, it is a very noble effort indeed. Its slow pace and lack of dialogue providing it with a very modern appeal.

Critical Reception

From the outset, NGC considered *The Stalking Moon* a major Oscar contender, rather a risky proposition for a western, and one whose temerity was likely to inflame the critics since only five in the last 20 years had been nominated: *How the West Was Won* (1962), *The Alamo* (1960), *Friendly Persuasion* (1956), *Shane* (1953) and *High Noon* (1952). Reviewers for the trades were divided: *International Motion Picture Exhibitor* called the movie "excellent" overall. *Variety* took the opposite view, complaining about the slow development and poor pacing, "clumsy plot structuring and dialog, limp Robert Mulligan direction" and "ineffective" stars, arriving at the conclusion that the movie was "109 numbing minutes."[52] *Motion Picture Daily* deemed it a "rewarding experience" and *Film Daily* called it "exceptionally fine." According to *Life,* it "transcends the externals of the western genre to become one of the great scare films of all time"; *Playboy* asserted it was "a tingle all the way"; and *Parents* Magazine termed it a "gripping melodrama."[53] "Western in character, universal in theme," was the summation in *The Showmen's Servisection.*[54] But Roger Ebert complained that the movie "doesn't work as a thriller … and doesn't hold together as a western, either." Vincent Canby in the *New York Times* complained that it was "pious" and "unimaginative."[55]

Strangely, nobody commented on the other link between Sarah Carver and her pursuer. In turning the heroine into the prey, in making the woman helpless, never knowing when the invisible hand would strike, Mulligan drew a clear parallel with the experience of the Indians, hunted down by the cavalry, harried off their lands, for no reason that could be understood.

The Stalking Moon has not exactly been subject to critical reappraisal in the years since its release, but French director Bertrand Tavernier in *50 Years of American Cinema* called it Mulligan's masterpiece. Writing in the March-April 2009 issue of *Film Comment*, Kent Jones cast more light on what the director was trying to achieve, thus putting the movie in more perspective, and aligning it closer than anyone thought at the time to the period in which the movie was made. Jones believed that the western aptly reflected the bewilderment of the times when, according to Mulligan, "We were in the process of a nightmare that I didn't understand. I mean, the riots were going on, the campuses were being burnt, the ghettos were being burnt, the marches that were going on, people were getting killed. It just didn't make any sense."

Mulligan took a pessimistic view of the outcome. "It just didn't work," he opined, "and a lot of that may have had to do with the basic silence of the movie." But what Mulligan actually meant is that the movie did not connect sufficiently with either audience nor critics. In fact, in my opinion, it is precisely because of the silences and the unwillingness of the director to tone down its emotional aspects and his refusal to play around with typical genre ploys that make *The Stalking Moon,* on second viewing today, such a rewarding experience. Reflecting on the movie's connection to Vietnam and the late 1960s riots, Kent Jones summed up his experience of the movie thus: "Robert Mulligan was the only filmmaker to wade into such painfully vexing and frightfully bourgeois territory and come out with a truly great film."

Box Office

The release date for *The Stalking Moon* had already been set for its general release in January 1969 but, figuring it had a critical winner on its hands, NGC, having put an Oscar win at the top of its promotional agenda, was faced with the problem of getting it out into a couple of theaters (one would have been enough, as long as it was in Los Angeles, according to the rules) in order to qualify for Academy Award consideration, and so it was deposited in a couple of first-run theaters (New York as well as Los Angeles, so that the New York market would not think it was being overlooked) just before Christmas 1968.[56]

The film ranked 47th in the annual chart with $2.6 million in rentals—"no better than fair, considering its cost," grumbled *Variety.* It ranked above *Once Upon a Time in the West*, but below other rivals in the genre.[57] It was reissued the following year as support for Universal's *Hellfighters* (1968) and NGC's *The Cheyenne Social Club* (1970). It received a warmer reception in Paris where, for the 1968–1969 season, it outgrossed *Mackenna's Gold* and *The Undefeated* as well as *Hang 'Em High* (1968) and *5 Card Stud* (1968), and did surprisingly well in Switzerland where its grosses were seen as indicative of a "box office upsurge."[58]

2

Controversy Runs Wild

100 Rifles

Stars: Jim Brown, Raquel Welch, Burt Reynolds; directed by Tom Gries; screenplay by Clair Huffaker and Tom Gries, from the novel by Robert MacLeod; Twentieth Century–Fox; 110 minutes

When Beefcake Met Cheesecake

100 Rifles was easily the most underrated film of the year. Even if the sum of all its parts did not add up to greatness, it had a lot more going for it than has generally been attributed. For a start, there was the attempt to build Jim Brown into a mainstream African American star. Secondly: the return of the bold female character that had largely disappeared since the heyday of Barbara Stanwyck, and Joan Crawford. Thirdly: the conjunction of these first two elements in a sex scene raised the issue of miscegenation that Hollywood had otherwise sought to avoid. Fourthly, and perhaps most hard-hitting of all: the issue of genocide, the mass slaughter of the Yaqui Indian population providing an uneasy parallel not just to the United States treatment of its own indigenous Native American population but also to its actions in Vietnam.

But there was a danger that, without both incisive direction and potent performances, the movie would spiral downwards into another simple case of "When Beefcake (Jim Brown) Met Cheesecake (Raquel Welch)."

Black Star Rising

For nearly a decade, Hollywood had pointed to Sidney Poitier as proof of its liberal credentials but while many of its leading figures espoused the Civil Rights movement, the industry itself could offer scant example of African Americans finding parity with whites. Poitier's elevation to the Hollywood A-list had been relatively recent. Despite picking up the Best Actor statuette for *Lilies of the Field* (1963)—following an earlier nomination for *The Defiant Ones* (1958)—Poitier struggled to gain acceptance as the star of big-budget films, more likely to be relegated to second billing, behind Richard Widmark in both the historical adventure *The Long Ships* (1964) and the Cold War thriller *The Bedford Incident* (1965) and James Garner in the western *Duel at Diablo* (1966), despite

Duel at Diablo (United Artists, 1996) director Ralph Nelson had previously worked with Sidney Poitier on *Lilies of the Field* (1963), for which Poitier won the Oscar. Nelson went on to make the controversial *Soldier Blue* (1970). Trade press advertisement (*Box Office*, April 25, 1966).

neither of these actors being considered substantial marquee attractions. Top billing in big pictures was denied Poitier even though his small films *Lilies of the Field* and *A Patch of Blue* (1965) performed exceptionally well at the box office. But the 1967 triple whammy of *To Sir with Love* (top billing, low budget), Norman Jewison's *In the Heat of the Night* (second billing to Rod Steiger, bigger budget) and Stanley Kramer's *Guess Who's Coming to Dinner* (second billing to Spencer Tracy, bigger budget) propelled him onto the A-list. Noticeably, each of these pictures dealt with racism, the third broaching the last taboo of Civil Rights, the marriage between an African American and a white woman, although a curtain was tastefully drawn over what the couple got up to in bed. Since nobody had expected Poitier to ascend the Hollywood ladder so fast, and in so doing become a trend, the industry had nobody lined up to ride in his wake and exploit what now appeared to be, at the very least, acceptance of African Africans as stars in their own right, or an audience ready to embrace a new kind of hero.

Never slow to recognize opportunity, Hollywood moved fast and by mid-summer the following year a number of African Americans had been slotted into major roles, if not necessarily the star part, in a number of forthcoming pictures. Most prominent were James Earl Jones, already a Broadway colossus, in *The Great White Hope* (1970), Sammy Davis, Jr., in *Salt and Pepper* (1968) and Jamaica-born Ester Anderson in *The Touchables* (1968), each of whom landed the star part in their respective pictures. Singer Diahann Carroll, fourth-billed in Otto Preminger's *Hurry Sundown* (1967), had been promoted to second billing in *The Split* (1968) and might have gone on to greater cinematic stardom had she not sidestepped into television for the series *Julia* (1968–1971), for which she won an Emmy. Raymond St. Jacques had been second-billed behind Dana Wynter in *If He Hollers, Let Him Go!* (1968), based on the Chester Himes bestseller, and took top billing in Jules Dassin's *Uptight* (1968) and was set for *Change of Minds* (1969) in which a white man's brain was transplanted into a black man's skull. But these were exceptions and mostly African Americans featured further down the cast list. Falling into this category was Bahamian-born Calvin Lockhart, Jr., third-billed in *Joanna* (1968). Despite leaping to fame after being second-billed in the controversial low-budget *Dutchman* in 1966, Al Freeman, Jr., was given scant regard when it came to the billing in *The Detective* (1968), the Francis Ford Coppola musical *Finian's Rainbow* (1968) and Sydney Pollack's World War II film *Castle Keep* (1969), although he received third billing in *The Lost Man* (1969) starring Poitier. Jazz legend Louis Armstrong's appearance in *Hello, Dolly!* (1969) was much trumpeted (pardon the pun!) but, in fact, he had a small role. Fleeting roles were accorded Jeff Burton in *Planet of the Apes* (1968) and Geoffrey Holder in *Krakatoa, East of Java* (1968). Although MPAA president Jack Valenti called for more African Americans in more African American films,[1] the number of highly touted big-budget African American–oriented pictures that offered stardom potential such as *The Confessions of Nat Turner*, based on the William Styron bestseller, *John Brown's Body* and *Dahomey* never made it out of the starting blocks.[2]

But there was one potential crossover star waiting in the wings: Jim Brown. While lacking Poitier's acting chops, he had the physique, looks and charisma. In that, he was closer to Woody Strode, whose impact in the John Ford western *Sergeant Rutledge* (1960) did not lead to stardom, instead to a succession of supporting roles where, occasionally, as with *The Professionals* (1966), he delivered a standout performance.[3] Brown was a Cleveland Browns football legend when he made his debut in the western *Rio Conchos* (1964), following up with supporting roles in MGM's *The Dirty Dozen* (1967), *Dark of*

Before *Dark of the Sun* (MGM, 1968), shown above, director Jack Cardiff was more celebrated as a cinematographer, winning the Oscar for *Black Narcissus* (1947) and nominated for *War and Peace* (1956) and *Fanny* (1961). He had been nominated as Best Director for *Sons and Lovers* (1960). Pressbook (Hannan collection).

the Sun (1968) and *Ice Station Zebra* (1968). But in terms of leading roles, his career was in danger of emulating that of Poitier: He hadn't managed to transition to the big-budget pictures. His first starring role was *Kenner* (1968), an independent production set in India. *The Split* (1968) was a heist picture at a football stadium while *Riot* (1969) was a prison hostage drama.[4] And there would have been a fourth picture that year had the proposed *The Gambling Sheriff* gone into production under the Dino De Laurentiis banner in summer 1968 as expected.[5] While all three pictures showed promise, they did not set the box office alight and, as much as they showcased his strengths, they also revealed that he was not best suited to the kind of drama at which Poitier excelled. Brown himself had no complaints:

> Hollywood has given me more opportunities than I ever got in any previous job including the Cleveland Browns. There is a vast group of whites who want no change but it's bound to come.... All you need is good luck and good timing. You can be dumb but if you're in the right spot, you've got it made. If you have a certain type of preparation in one field, that becomes your formula for success so transferring it isn't all that difficult. Maybe it's the momentum that carries you along. Let's face it. Cinema is a director's medium. It's a personality medium and Sidney's doing it well. In our capitalist society it's box office that counts and he's big there. As far as I'm concerned, Sidney's been good to me. But all I want to do is the James Brown thing.... It's still important for black and white audiences to face something that happens in real life.[6]

Brown's potential was recognized by *Variety,* which singled him out at the start of 1969 as one of its "new stars of the year" and judged him "the strongest contender to inherit some of Sidney Poitier's earning power."[7] Twentieth Century–Fox's *100 Rifles* offered the ideal solution. The previous year, Fox's *Bandolero!* had been the top-grossing western and Fox was willing to invest $3.92 million in the project,[8] more than the double the budget of any of his previous films.

Raquel Welch at the Gates

Raquel Welch was in a similar situation to Jim Brown regarding Hollywood acceptance. However, she was not in a minority as far as female stars were concerned. The 1960s had been dominated by the likes of drama queen (in more ways than one) Elizabeth Taylor (*Cleopatra*), comedy queen Doris Day (*That Touch of Mink*) and musical queen Julie Andrews (*The Sound of Music*), not to mention Audrey Hepburn (*Breakfast at Tiffany's*), Italian import Sophia Loren (*El Cid*), Jane Fonda (*Cat Ballou*), Natalie Wood (*Sex and the Single Girl*) and Shirley MacLaine (*Sweet Charity*). There was also an overabundance of new talent in Julie Christie (*Doctor Zhivago*), Vanessa Redgrave (*Blow Up*), Lynn Redgrave (*Georgy Girl*), Mia Farrow (*Rosemary's Baby*) and Faye Dunaway (*Bonnie and Clyde*). But those stars had more to offer than mere beauty, whereas Welch, having made her name primarily as a pin-up and as eye candy in movies like *One Million Years B.C.* (1966) and *Fantastic Voyage* (1966), had trouble shaking off the idea that she won more parts on the basis of her body than for the acting skills, appearing in a dry bikini in *Fathom* (1967) and a wet one in *Lady in Cement* (1968).

However, like Jim Brown, she was actively looking to fill a niche, and set out her stall as a player of dramatic intensity, and she found it in the most unlikely of places: the western. That she chose *100 Rifles* was interesting given her other choices. She was offered the Katharine Ross part in *Butch Cassidy and the Sundance Kid* when the lead roles had been offered to Steve McQueen and Warren Beatty and again when Paul Newman came into the frame. She was also up for the Faye Dunaway role for *The Crown Caper* (title later changed to *The Thomas Crown Affair*), again with McQueen, and a film with Terence Stamp (which was never made). But she clearly felt those roles were more decorative.

At one time, the female western star had been a staple. Claire Trevor was the star of *Stagecoach* (1939) and *Texas* (1941). Gene Tierney made her name with *The Return of Frank James* (1940) and *Belle Starr* (1941). Barbara Stanwyck carved out her own niche as a western icon after taking top billing in *Union Pacific* (1939), *California* (1947), *The Furies* (1950), *Cattle Queen of Montana* (1954), *The Maverick Queen* (1956) and *Forty Guns* (1957). While Maureen O'Hara took second billing in *Rio Grande* (1950), *McLintock!* (1963) and *The Rare Breed* (1966), she was the star of *Comanche Territory* (1950), *War*

Nine minutes of *One Million Years B.C.* footage was cut for the version released in the U.S., and 13 minutes from the Spanish version. The entire advertising campaign was based around Raquel Welch in a fur bikini. Trade press advertisement (*Box Office*, February 6, 1967).

In *Black Bart*, Yvonne De Carlo plays the real-life Lola Montez, once mistress of Ludwig I of Bavaria. But she never danced Salome or visited Arizona. The story was based on the real-life exploits of Charles Boles. Trade press advertisement (*Box Office*, March 6, 1948).

Arrow (1953) and *The Redhead from Wyoming* (1953). Yvonne De Carlo headlined for *Black Bart* (1948), *The Gal Who Took the West* (1949) and *Calamity Jane and Sam Bass* (1949). Shelley Winters did a feisty turn in *Winchester '73* (1950), *Untamed Frontier* (1952) and *The Scalphunters* (1968). Rhonda Fleming had the female lead in *The Redhead and the Cowboy* (1951), *The Last Outpost* (1951), *Pony Express* (1953) and *Gunfight at the O.K. Corral* (1957). *Johnny Guitar* (1954) achieved classic status largely on the performance of Joan Crawford. There had even been modern precedent: Inger Stevens had nearly cornered the recent market after *A Time for Killing* (1967), *Firecreek* (1968), *Hang 'Em High* (1968) and *5 Card Stud* (1968) while Angie Dickinson had followed *Rio Bravo* (1959) with more up-to-date turns in *The Last Challenge* (1967) and the soon-to-be-released *Sam*

Whiskey (1969) and *Young Billy Young* (1969). Claudia Cardinale went from a supporting role in *The Professionals* (1966) to top billing in the forthcoming *Once Upon a Time in the West*. However, precedent was two-sided, one example being when *Shalako* (1968) with Brigitte Bardot, still considered by many the sexiest woman in the world, and Sean Connery, the sexiest man, flopped at the American box office.

Raquel Welch set out to follow suit. In 1968's *Bandolero!*—originally titled *Mace* after the James Stewart character—she proved capable not only of holding her own against veterans James Stewart and Dean Martin but as adept on the pistol-packing side of things. Welch played a Mexican woman whose husband has been killed by Martin's gang. When Martin was rescued by brother Stewart, Welch was kidnapped and held hostage, while the gang was pursued by sheriff George Kennedy. To complicate matters, Welch fell for Martin. While Welch professed herself "no Anne Bancroft," she was pleased that she was not "running around half-naked all the time."[9] Twentieth Century–Fox released the film in a different manner to its normal big-budget films, following a sequential saturation technique, by which it bypassed first-run theaters in favor of a bigger number of houses in one area in a short space of time before moving on to the next. The studio believed Welch had not only acquitted herself well but brought an extra box office dimension to the picture—it earned $5.5 million in rentals.[10] So for the studio's next western, *100 Rifles*, she was offered the female lead.

Tyro Director vs. Veteran Screenwriter

Tom Gries had made his name as a director with his unflinching portrayal of the cowboy in *Will Penny* (1968). But that was not his debut. He was 32 when he wrote and directed the independent *Serpent Island* (1954), an adventure picture on an $18,000 budget. It was followed by Columbia's *Hell's Horizon* (1955) starring John Ireland before he turned to television. Although of the generation—John Frankenheimer, Sidney Lumet, etc.—that used live television in the 1950s as the springboard to movies, Gries operated in the more mundane section of television, the long-running series. Apart from the western *Mustang!* (1959), an independent picture released by United Artists, he spent his entire career in television, directing over 90 episodes (including seven of *Stoney Burke*, four of *Route 66*, *Combat!*, *Batman* and *The Court of Last Resort*, three of *Cain's Hundred* and *Checkmate*, two of *The Monroes*, *The Rounders* and *A Man Called Shenandoah* and single forays into *I Spy*, *Voyage to the Bottom of the Sea* and *The Man from U.N.C.L.E.*). In 1960, he wrote and directed the episode "Line Camp" for the Sam Peckinpah series *The Westerner* and several years later extended the idea into the feature *Will Penny*.

The script attracted Charlton Heston and Paramount provided the relatively low budget of $1.4 million. Primarily because of its honest depiction of cowboy life, the movie was well received by both critics and the public, ending the year 54th in the annual rankings ahead of *Villa Rides*, *Firecreek* and *Shalako*. But the rentals of $1.8 million covered little more than the negative cost and profits from the U.S. release would have been non-existent once marketing had been taken into account. Producer Marvin Schwartz had a four-picture deal with Twentieth Century–Fox after jointly producing *Blindfold* (1966) starring Rock Hudson and Claudia Cardinale for Universal, and, more importantly, again for Universal, joint producer through his Marvin Schwartz Productions and John Wayne's outfit Batjac of *The War Wagon* (1967) starring western heavyweights Wayne and Kirk Douglas.

The *War Wagon* screenplay had been written by Clair Huffaker, based on his own novel *Badman*. Huffaker had begun as a writer of western novels, then coupled fiction with writing for the small and big screen.[11] His work for all three media centered on the West. Between 1959 and 1960, he had written single episodes of *Riverboat, Rawhide, The Rifleman* and *Bonanza* and two episodes of *Colt .45* as well as 18 editions of *Lawman*. He would go on to contribute three episodes to *Outlaws* in 1961, the same number to *Destry* in 1964 and single episodes to *Twelve O'Clock High* (his sole non-western output) and *Daniel Boone* and a pair to *The Virginian*. But from 1960, he began to specialize in turning his own western novels into movies, beginning with *Seven Ways from Sundown* starring Audie Murphy, progressing quickly to the Elvis Presley vehicle *Flaming Star* (1960)[12] and Audie Murphy's *Posse from Hell* (1961). He received a joint credit along with James Edward Grant for adapting the Paul Wellman novel for Michael Curtiz's *The Comancheros* (1961) starring John Wayne, and another joint credit for *The Second Time Around* (1961) headlining Debbie Reynolds. With Joseph Landon, he adapted his own novel for *Rio Conchos*[13] (1964), and completely out of left field turned out *Tarzan and the Valley of Gold* (1967) based on the Edgar Rice Burroughs book. Next up were *The War Wagon* and an original screenplay about oil wildcatters, *Hellfighters* (1968), starring John Wayne and Katharine Ross and directed by Andrew V. McLaglen.

Marvin Schwartz brought him on board for *100 Rifles*. The basis of the film was Robert MacLeod's[14] *The Californio*, published in 1966, and the essence of the story concerned a "reckless stranger" who refused to turn the other cheek while innocent people were being killed. After Huffaker turned in his screenplay, Gries wrote two further drafts. It is safe to assume that the casting of Jim Brown came after the Huffaker script had been handed in. When Huffaker did not like the way his work had ended up on screen, he insisted on using the pseudonym Cecil Dan Hansen, as he had done on *The Second Time Around*. For *100 Rifles*, he was so upset at the end result that he demanded either his name be removed or the pseudonym installed, complaining that the finished product "bears absolutely no resemblance to my script."[15]

The movie was shot over a ten-week period in Spain beginning in July 1968.[16] Although that country had become a viable alternative for westerns looking to keep budgets low, in part in 1968 due to the devaluing of the peseta against the dollar,[17] the volume of films shot there had declined by nearly a third compared to the previous year.[18] Despite the popularity of the location, Almeria, the actual area of countryside where most spaghetti westerns were shot, was very small. This resulted in a limited variety of available landscapes compared with films shot in the U.S. such as *The Stalking Moon*. The actors had to contend with extreme heat, and Gries was laid low for three days after contracting typhus. Gries decided to get the sex scene out of the way on the first day of shooting, probably to insure that tension about the content was not allowed to linger until later in the shoot. However, it had the opposite effect. Neither Brown nor Welch had been given time to get to know one another nor to adjust to different styles of acting and to understand the perspectives of each other's characters. Welch was not happy with the scene and tensions between the two stars continued throughout the film, some press reports putting this down to squabbles over close-ups, others to unresolved sexual tension. Welch later complained that scenes edited out of the picture had reduced audience understanding of her motivations.[19] The MPAA also did some judicial trimming, axing Welch's shrieks during lovemaking.[20]

Twentieth Century–Fox had been affected by recent financial disasters such as *Doctor Dolittle* (1967) and *Star!* (1968); the former collecting $6.2 million in domestic rentals on a budget of $17 million, the latter $4.2 million in rentals after costing $14.5 million.[21] To counter mounting exhibitor panic about production being slashed, Fox had drawn up an ambitious program for 1969, promising one new movie every month. The program kicked off with a $7.7 million adaptation of the Lawrence Durrell classic *Justine* with Dirk Bogarde (January), followed by Michael Caine and Anthony Quinn in the $3.77 million film of the John Fowles bestseller *The Magus* (February) and the trendy $1.1 million *Joanna* from new director Mike Sarne (March). British star Maggie Smith in the $2.7 million *The Prime of Miss Jean Brodie* (April) came next with *100 Rifles* (May) and another Marvin Schwarz production, *Hard Contract* starring James Coburn, costing $4 million (June). Summer highlights were Omar Sharif in the $5.1 million biopic of *Che!* directed by Richard Fleischer (July) and Gregory Peck in the $4.9 million Cold War thriller *The Chairman* (August). Come fall it was the turn of Paul Newman and Robert Redford in the western *Butch Cassidy and the Sundance Kid* coming in at $6.8 million (September), Richard Burton and Rex Harrison as aging homosexuals in *The Staircase* costing $6.3 million (October) and Warren Beatty and Elizabeth Taylor in George Stevens' $10 million *The Only Game in Town* (November). The year ended with John Wayne and Rock Hudson in the $7.1 million Civil War western *The Undefeated* (December).[22] The studio needed several box office home runs because the following year it was already committed to three roadshows—*Tora! Tora ! Tora!, Hello, Dolly* and *Patton*—costing over $60 million. By spring it was clear that the first two movies in the schedule had been major flops, *Justine* bringing in only $2.2 million in rentals, *The Magus* $1 million. Income from *Joanna* and *The Prime of Miss Jean Brodie* barely exceeded costs.[23] By the time *100 Rifles* swung into action with two largely untried leads and a director making only his second major picture, the pressure was on.

"Whatever Is Customary"

The story of *The Californio* bears little resemblance to *100 Rifles.* Not only is the hero of the book, Steve McCall, white and not African African, he is a rawboned young man and not a lawman in his 30s. He is not a gunman either, being more proficient with the lasso. In fact, when forced into bloody action, he discovers that he abhors violence. The book could more aptly be described as a "rite of passage" novel where a young man, sent south "on legitimate business in the interests of the (U.S.) Federal Government,"[24] leaves home for the first time, becomes a man, loses his virginity and kills his first man. Nor is Yaqui Joe a bank robber in the book, and after they meet, they embark on further legitimate business. Maria, named Sarita in the film, is most like her feisty movie counterpart, and although in the MacLeod version she is married, that does not prevent her taking Steve's virginity. Of the villains, Verdugo (the name means "Hangman"), while not elevated to general, is still as ruthless, but the foreign adviser. Most of the film's action was invented by the screenwriters, including the concept of the 100 rifles, Sarita's sexy shower as a way of stopping the troop train, and the children being taken hostage (although in one episode in the book, children are shot).

***Opposite*: "Keep his shirt off and her [Raquel Welch's] shirt off and give me all the lines," Burt Reynolds reportedly advised the producers of *100 Rifles*, based on this novel. (Hannan Collection)**

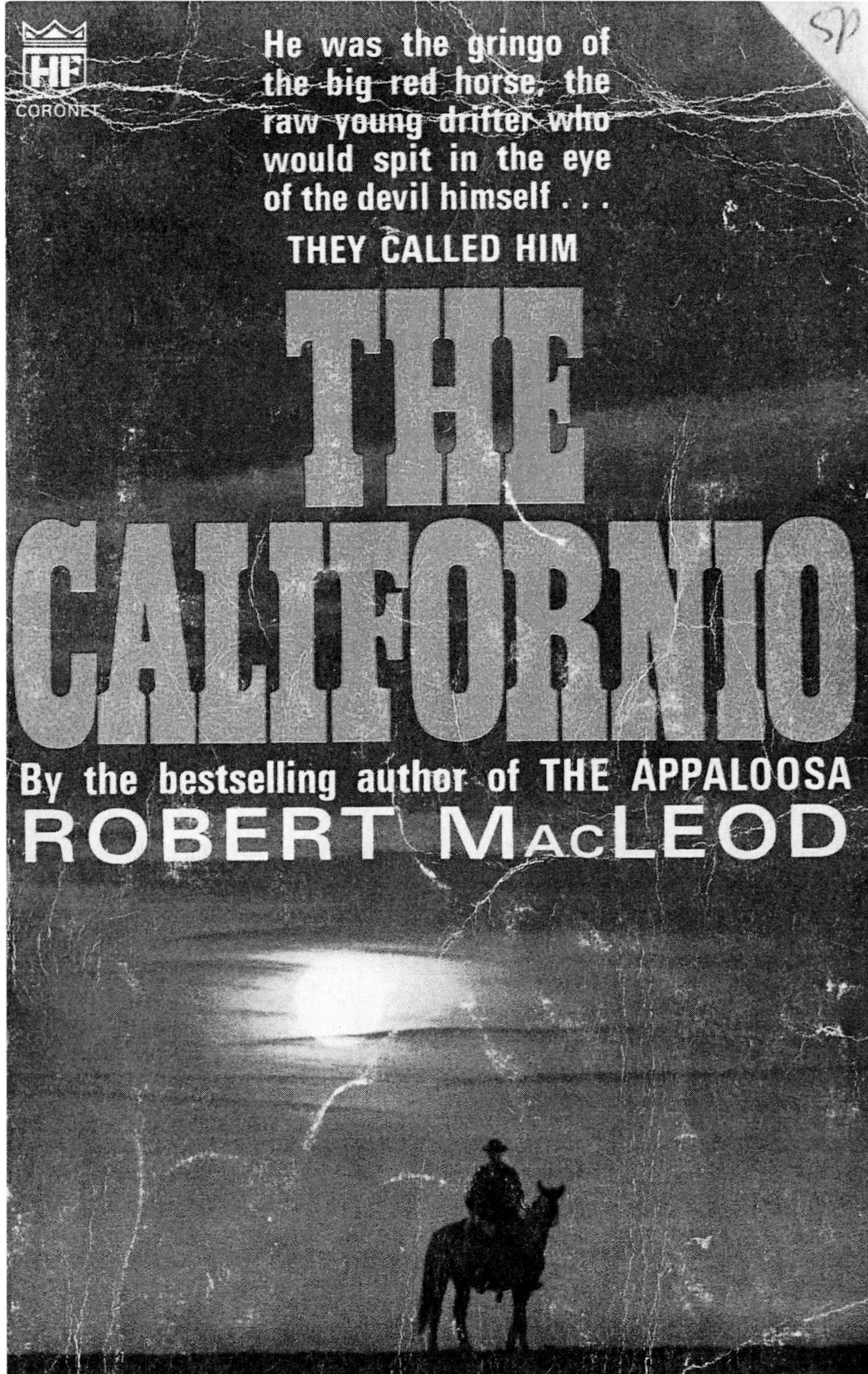
HF
CORONET
He was the gringo of the big red horse, the raw young drifter who would spit in the eye of the devil himself . . .
THEY CALLED HIM
THE CALIFORNIO
By the bestselling author of THE APPALOOSA
ROBERT MACLEOD

Trying to reshape the book to suit the new requirements of the characters makes the picture unnecessarily complicated. Arizona lawman Lyedecker (Brown) arrives in Sonora, Mexico, in 1912 on the trail of half-breed bank robber Yaqui Joe (Burt Reynolds). He finds the Mexican army callously executing Yaqui Indian rebels. To prevent further killing, Joe creates a diversion, which, while failing, permits the captured Sarita (Raquel Welch) to escape (this scene is drawn from the book). The $6000 that Joe stole from the bank has gone to buy the titular 100 rifles to help the rebel cause. Helped by Lyedecker, Joe escapes, picking up Sarita on the way. Both Lyedecker and the Mexicans are in pursuit, and the Mexicans soon recapture Joe and Lyedecker, who is now viewed as a rebel. Sarita again escapes. Lyedecker and Joe are returned to the garrison where the Mexicans have taken possession of the rifles. Just as the pair are put in front of a firing squad, Sarita, leading a group of rebels, frees them and steals the weapons. (Again, this is directly taken from the book.) In retaliation, the Mexicans attack a village, slaughtering the inhabitants and taking the children as hostages. At night, Lyedecker, Sarita, Joe and some rebels capture the garrison before the soldiers return, freeing the children. Lyedecker has been injured in the battle; after Sarita binds the wound, they make love. When they take the rifles to the rebel stronghold, they discover the rebel leader is dead. For no particular reason, the rebels elect Lyedecker their new "generale." The rebels decide to seize the Mexican troop train as a means of launching an attack on the main Mexican stronghold. Sarita creates a diversion by taking a shower under a water tower. The rebels storm the train. The empty train is sent cannoning into the town and in the ensuing battle Sarita is killed. (In the book, she survives[25] and Yaqui Joe is killed.) Yaqui Joe takes over leadership of the rebels while Lyedecker rides home.

While the capture-escape-chase-capture formula is overdone, the movie's biggest structural problem is Yaqui Joe, clearly turned into a drunk to avoid becoming a romantic encumbrance for Sarita, leaving the way clear for Lyedecker. His other contributions are to brawl with Lyedecker and try to get the American to give up his quest and stay and help the rebels. There are other unnecessary characters and touches. We know it is 1912 or some period more modern than the Wild West because there is a motor car involved as there would be in *The Wild Bunch*. The sole purpose of a German military adviser Von Klemme (Eric Braeden) is to act as a sounding board for Gen. Verdugo (Fernando Lamas), whose actions in any case speak louder than words. Railroad magnate Grimes (Dan O'Herlihy) is there to represent the equally callous big business. When Americans get drunk in westerns, that usually leads to fisticuffs, but when Indians knock back the liquor in *100 Rifles* they act like clichéd drunken Indians, tearing up the town, looting and destroying anything in sight.

These reservations apart, the film has a great deal to recommend it. On the whole, it is well directed, although without much of an eye for landscape. The film opens with Sarita, wearing a red headscarf,[26] offering a peasant a drink of water. A Mexican officer enters the scene, pulling the man away, putting him on a horse and hanging him. A hysterical Sarita launches herself at the dangling corpse, climbing up. We discover later that this is her father. "He dies for a rifle," says a soldier, "for nada," setting the movie's theme from the get-go. Sarita is lassoed and her screams are intercut by a train whistle that passes by other hanged men. As it pulls into a station, we cut to Yaqui Joe sitting up in bed with a naked woman and we see Sarita, easily recognized by the red headscarf, on a mule being escorted into the town. Then we cut to Lyedecker riding into town, but the fact that he is on an empty street, accompanied only by the sound of hoofbeats, does enough to introduce him.

Lyedecker finds an officer and hands him a wanted poster of Joe. A few minutes in and the characters are established: rebel Sarita, lawman Lyedecker and bank robber Joe. To give us all the other background we need, Gen. Verdugo tells Grimes that Yaqui Indians have been fighting Mexicans for 400 years and that the railroad track is on their land, hence why they keep on demolishing it. "What shall we do about it?" asks Verdugo. "Whatever is customary," replies Grimes. Verdugo proceeds to shoot three prisoners with one bullet. On a hotel balcony, Joe creates a diversion by wrestling with a half-naked girl. Four prisoners run but are shot while Sarita escapes. Joe is caught and we learn from Lyedecker that he stole $6000 12 days before but only has $50 left so the general surmises he has spent the rest on rifles. Joe says, "The general has been told to get rid of the Yaquis any way he can. He took the easy way. He's just killing everybody."

When Joe escapes by diving out the window, Lyedecker throws the guards out and helps him escape. As with *The Stalking Moon* and later *The Wild Bunch* and *Butch Cassidy and the Sundance Kid,* the escapees underrate the relentlessness of their pursuers. "I think we lost them," says Joe when they reach the apparent safety of an abandoned church. Sarita, no longer the passive woman of the opening scene, takes charge, turning on Joe, who has hidden the rifles, refusing to believe he will not personally profit from his action. Like Sarah Carver in *The Stalking Moon,* she is haunted by shame, in this case for not preventing her father's hanging, and possibly for being willing to sacrifice him in the name of freedom: "I helped him to die." There is a nod to *The Searchers* as Sarita leaves, silhouetted in the church doorway. When Lyedecker turns up, there is the sound of a punch offscreen and then Joe is on the ground. Lyedecker is intent on bringing Joe back to face justice. "I took a job nobody wanted," says Lyedecker. Returning Joe will guarantee him a job and a one-off payment of $200. But now Sarita has returned, minus the rifles. Possibly out of self-preservation, Joe asks Lyedecker to help the rebels. "Hell, no, it ain't my party," is the first of Lyedecker's stout rebuffs. Like Sam in *The Stalking Moon* it will take some time before he changes his mind.

When the soldiers appear, surrounding them, Sarita is taken away separately. But she has another weapon at her disposal: her body. She starts to undress in front of her captor, and, standing with her back to the camera, shows him her breasts. As he comes forward, she knees him in the groin (the method of choice for disabling an opponent that Butch Cassidy will later use). When she stabs him, the shock in her eyes suggests this is the first time she has killed a man. This may be what Welch was complaining about when she spoke of the cutting of scenes which explained her motivation. The narrative as it exists advocates that she is a feisty leader from the start, but this scene, and in particular her reaction, suggests otherwise, that it is the death of her father that has propelled her into action. But she proves to be capable of taking care of herself, and she, and not the two stronger men, is the one who escapes. In a homage to *The Defiant Ones,* Lyedecker and Joe are chained together. Back in the fortress, they see the stolen guns, the Indians guarding them, we are mercifully just told, skinned alive.

The genocide theme, pertinent both to American treatment of its own indigenous Native Americans and to the current war in Vietnam, is raised again. It is more trouble than it's worth for Gen. Verdugo to clear the Indians from their lands and ship them elsewhere, as the Americans had done when putting Indians onto reservations. (In *The Stalking Moon,* this is seen as being carried out as a peaceful exercise, none of the Indians rounded up at the start subject to fatal violence.) In other words, it is easier, as Joe previously explained, to kill them all. Verdugo has few compunctions. Later, he will slaughter villagers and carry off children as hostages. The other theme (common also to *The Wild Bunch* and *Butch Cassidy and the Sundance Kid*) explored at this point is the railroad. Its initial purpose, of facilitating the movement of people, has here been perverted. Here it is a tool of control. By loading up trains with troops and guns (including Gatling guns, also seminal to *The Wild Bunch*) and artillery, an army can be transported with ease across alien territory to keep the inhabitants in check. As exemplified by Grimes, railroads also represent the intrusion of big business into politics and ordinary lives, and the railroad man, while concerned that Lyedecker's possible execution could jeopardize U.S.-Mexican relationships and, by extension, possible halt the American railroad's expansion, is ultimately more apprehensive about the cost of damage to his trains than the cost in human lives of his partnership with the Mexicans.

Outside, where Lyedecker and Joe are still chained together, the firing squad goes into action, the first rebel falling in slow motion (a technique that would be used to greater effect later in the year in *The Wild Bunch*). Given that they are facing death and that, as far as the general is concerned, Lyedecker is aligned with the rebels, this seems an odd moment for Joe to try to dissuade Lyedecker from pursuing his ambition of becoming a lawman, especially as, Joe asserts, cops don't care about people. Soon Lyedecker and Joe are facing the firing squad. As the camera shows a soldier taking aim, he suddenly falls and behind him we see Sarita shooting. Ostensibly, she is rescuing the two men, but in reality she has returned for the rifles. Even so, this dramatic moment represents the transition of Sarita from loving daughter to leader. Again, they escape. Still chained together, Joe and Lyedecker start brawling on the edge of a cliff (some of the tension in the scene can be attributed to Jim Brown's genuine fear of heights) after Lyedecker has, for the third time, refused to get involved. At this point, Sarita takes charge, separating them by blowing their chains apart with a bullet. (Why she had not done this before is anybody's guess.)

Vietnam hovers over many of the westerns of 1969. The theme of being unable to escape a difficult situation, of relentless pursuit, of an implacable enemy, often with justice or morality or power on their side, who will never give up, are common to *The Stalking Moon, 100 Rifles, The Wild Bunch, Butch Cassidy and the Sundance Kid* and, in a twist on this, in *True Grit* where Rooster Cogburn is the one in fearless pursuit. Escaping this time, the rebels descend a steep ravine. But still Verdugo follows. Reaching the river, the rebels split up, Joe and the guns in one direction towards the rebel leader, Lyedecker and Sarita in another direction hoping to draw the enemy away. The splitting-up of the three main characters is a device to give Lyedecker and Sarita time together. When they reach a village, Lyedecker is greeted with awe by children (it's the first time they have seen a black man). He finds himself responding to them and gives a boy his knife. But this is not indicative of any change in intention. When he points out that Sarita could have killed him two or three times by now to prevent any risk of Joe being taken back, she responds, "I need you. If you stay, I won't worry about Joe. After, you can have him. I don't trust him but he's important for us now." (In exactly what way Joe is important is never properly explained, beyond the fact that he has brought the rifles. So far, he has done nothing but brawl.) But Lyedecker, unwilling to commit himself, replies, "No deal." With the Mexicans still in pursuit, they flee the village only to turn back when they hear shooting and see thick plumes of smoke rising into the air. Verdugo has slaughtered men and women and taken away the children. Lyedecker finds on the ground the knife he gave the child. This is his turning point, although no words are spoken, the decision

MR. EXHIBITOR, GET ON BOARD!

20TH HAS THE MOST EXPLOSIVE WESTERN IN YEARS
READY TO TRIGGER YOUR BOX OFFICE STARTING THIS EASTER!

20th Century-Fox presents

100 RIFLES

A MARVIN SCHWARTZ Production

Starring

JIM BROWN · RAQUEL WELCH
BURT REYNOLDS Co-starring FERNANDO LAMAS · DAN O'HERLIHY
HANS GUDEGAST

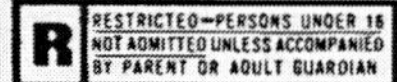

Produced by MARVIN SCHWARTZ · Directed by TOM GRIES · Screenplay by CLAIR HUFFAKER and TOM GRIES
Based on a Novel by ROBERT MAC LEOD · Music by JERRY GOLDSMITH · **COLOR** by De Luxe

DO YOU HAVE A PIECE OF THE **20th** ACTION?

100 Rifles stars Burt Reynolds and Raquel Welch re-teamed for *Fuzz* (1972), based on the Ed McBain series of crime procedurals. Trade press advertisement (*Box Office*, March 10, 1969).

shown in his eyes. Again, Sarita takes charge, deciding to free the children rather than follow the rifles. Under cover of night, the rebels storm the garrison and in the ensuing ambush of the soldiers free the children. As if he has donned the costume of a rebel, a wounded Lyedecker is seen brandishing a machete.

Further transformation takes place: Sarita, until now only seen in drab peasant clothes, the red headscarf serving only to conceal her looks, takes, as her share of the loot, a white camisole, still open, as it happens, at the back. This far, she has been unable to let down her guard, the job of keeping Joe in check and leading the rebel faction taking up all her time, action covering over grief at the death of her father. Because the bulk of journalists and movie executives were male, for them the sexual centerpiece of the film was Raquel Welch in various states of undress, forgetting that women, too, were apt to be partial to the sight of an unclothed muscular male. It is Jim Brown who is first seen shirtless. And it is Sarita who takes control of the scene, kissing him as a reward "for all the bad things I said to you." (A gender twist, for usually it is the man making reparation.) When he responds, she resists at first: "Not like this!" But Lyedecker turns tender and she is more responsive. The scene was shot without music. In retrospect, the awkwardness, especially given that it was the first scene shot, is apparent, but it still carries a molten energy. There is another tender scene involving Lyedecker and Sarita, ostensibly of the more traditional kind, the bold feisty leader apparently transformed into docile housewife, as Sarita cooks Lyedecker a steak. But there is another reading of this scene, more in keeping with her character. Throughout, Sarita is in charge. "You are my man," she says. "I will be your woman for as long as you want me." Not, you may notice, clinging to him, desperate for his love, but happy to enjoy the moment and let him go when the time comes (as Katharine Ross will in *Butch Cassidy and the Sundance Kid*, departing before the outlaws die).

In his first action as "leader," Lyedecker plans to attack the troop train. Sarita, the leader in all but name, points out that there is a water stop on the route, and she will force the train to halt by once again using her body as a weapon. As the train approaches the water tower, the soldiers see Sarita standing underneath dressed in only a man's shirt, taking a shower. The train shudders to a halt for this voyeuristic delight; the camera too, for the audience's sake, lingering on Sarita's curves. The Indians take the soldiers by surprise and seize the train. However, instead of commandeering it to drive into the Mexican-held town, Joe drives an empty train, jumping off at the last minute. The Mexicans are ready for attack, having been warned by Grimes, who escaped the train ambush. The Mexicans have Gatling guns (as they will in *The Wild Bunch*) and artillery and soldiers secured behind sandbags. The rebels stage a four-pronged attack if you count the initial assault of the train as it leaves the tracks and plows into the town's defenses. Sarita, wearing her red headscarf, is initially most prominent, climbing onto the roofs to tackle the Gatling gun. Joe is in charge of the cavalry while Lyedecker leads the ground troops. The battle is fierce: explosions, bullets and, in the end, machetes, to finish off Gen. Verdugo, whose horse has been shot from under him by Lyedecker. But when victory has been declared, a rebel appears carrying, in both arms, the dead Sarita, her head hanging down loose. Joe, the self-appointed leader, wears her scarf on his sleeve. And business is seen to take no sides, Grimes, reminding Joe that he will need trains to move men and supplies, gets him to command his rebels to begin fixing the wrecked train while Lyedecker rides off.

Although *100 Rifles* is ponderous and improbable in places, with too much emphasis on escape-and-rescue, it is nonetheless a highly effective western. It certainly does what it set out to do, establishing Brown as the first African American action star, providing Welch with a role she could get her teeth into, ensuring the combination is as sexy as all-get-out, while at the same time supplying enough shoot-outs and battle scenes to keep traditionalists happy. As important, director Gries is not afraid of using the film to make points, if sometimes a little heavy-handed, about Vietnam and genocide. All in all, a movie that deserves a good bit more respect.

Critical Reception

These ranged from sniffy to downright hostile. Perhaps like *The Stalking Moon*, advance publicity, although not this time pointing in the direction of the Oscars, had served to put critics off what sounded like an exploitative film. For the traditionalist, sex scenes were off-putting, and although naked breasts had started appearing in a handful of movies, there were precious few full-on sex scenes, never mind one that featured miscegenation. *Variety* judged it a "routine Spanish-made western with a questionable sex scene as a possible exploitation hook."[27] On the plus side, Welch's performance was "spirited" as was the Jerry Goldsmith score; Brown and Reynolds were just "okay." *The Showmen's Servisection* took a different view: "Fast pace, fine performances lift western several notches above the ordinary."[28] Roger Ebert in the *Chicago Sun-Times* called it "pretty dreary." Howard Thompson, the *New York Times*' second-string reviewer, said it was a "triumphantly empty exercise."[29]

Box Office

100 Rifles got off to a great start and Twentieth Century–Fox reported with delight that it had outgrossed *Bandolero!* by 40 percent in Washington (and by 500 percent in the ghetto areas), and by 300 percent in Philadelphia. In Baltimore it grossed $50,000 from a single theater compared to $80,000 from eight for *Bandolero!* and in Atlanta first-run it had been $61,000 for the new film compared to $38,000 for the previous one. However, while Brown and Welch fans were out in force in certain areas, that did not make up for less interest in regions where westerns were associated with bigger or more traditional names. Ultimately, *100 Rifles* fell short of expectations given the budget. U.S. rentals amounted $3.5 million, and it registered in 29th position on the annual chart—the sixth highest-grossing western of the year and ahead of *Mackenna's Gold*, *The Stalking Moon*, *Paint Your Wagon* and *Once Upon a Time in the West*.

3

The Cleverest Lawman in the West

Support Your Local Sheriff[1]

Starring James Garner, Joan Hackett, Jack Elam, Walter Brennan; directed by Burt Kennedy; screenplay by William Bowers; United Artists; 92 minutes

Different Jokes for Different Folks

The comedy western had been around for as long as the straight western. This subgenre tended to divide into four types. First were comedian-led properties where standard schtick was simply transferred into a western locale. Bob Hope was an arch-proponent of this, his films generally consisting of a hapless character, with the twin personality defects of cowardice and of believing himself attractive to women way outside his league, thrown into a sticky situation. He took this stock personality into *The Paleface* (1948), *Son of Paleface* (1952) and *Alias Jesse James* (1959). In the same vein could be counted Laurel and Hardy in *Way Out West* (1937), the Marx Brothers in *Go West* (1940), Abbott and Costello in *The Wistful Widow of Wagon Gap* (1947), Dean Martin and Jerry Lewis in *Pardners* (1956), Frank Sinatra and his Rat Pack in *Sergeants 3* (1962) and *4 for Texas* (1963), the British Carry On team in *Carry On Cowboy* (1965) and Don Knotts in *The Shakiest Gun in the West* (1968).[2]

The second kind of film was aligned to the first in that it was an extension of the fish-out-of-water concept centered around a mild-mannered man tossed into the rough-and-tumble of the Wild West, usually with a very sexy woman to contend with. Examples: James Stewart in *Destry Rides Again* (1939) coming under the spell of Marlene Dietrich and Kenneth More as the Englishman who unwittingly takes on the job of *The Sheriff of Fractured Jaw* (1958), in due course succumbing to the charms of Jayne Mansfield.[3] Thirdly came movies where a star normally associated with action or straight drama ventured into the broader field of comedy, examples of this being John Wayne in *McLintock!* (1963), Glenn Ford in *Advance to the Rear* (1964), Burt Lancaster in *The Hallelujah Trail* (1965) and Henry Fonda in *A Big Hand for the Little Lady* (1966).

The final category, and by far the most difficult to pull off, was the original comedy western. There were so few of these, that really the only outstanding example was *Cat Ballou* (1965) with Lee Marvin in a dual (and Oscar-winning) role as a lawman and drunken gunfighter.

And that was a shame because in the 1960s, U.S. audiences had turned to comedy in a big way. In the 1950s, around a quarter of the movies that filled the annual top 20 spots in the box office chart were comedies, but in the next decade this not only jumped to around 40 percent,[4] but virtually every year a comedy was ranked in the top five. *The Absent Minded Professor* finished second in 1961 with *The Parent Trap* third; the Doris Day-Rock Hudson pairing in *Lover Come Back* was third in 1963 and Cary Grant-Doris Day's *That Touch of Mink* fourth; *Irma La Douce* with Jack Lemmon and Shirley MacLaine came third in 1963; the Cinerama epic *It's a Mad Mad Mad Mad World* second in 1964; *What's New Pussycat* starring Peter O'Toole and Woody Allen fifth in 1965; Disney's *That Darn Cat* fourth in 1966, with *The Russians Are Coming, The Russians Are Coming* fifth; the James Bond spoof *Casino Royale* third in 1967; and *The Graduate* first in 1968 and Jack Lemmon and Walter Matthau as *The Odd Couple* fifth.[5]

An Unusual Combination

Most writers of comedy westerns specialized in writing comedy, primarily those who worked with established acts like Laurel and Hardy, Abbott and Costello and Martin and Lewis. In other situations, the movies were almost compiled gag by gag by a team of writers. Seven were employed on *The Paleface*, five on *Destry Rides Again* and three on *Son of Paleface*. It was unusual to find a writer of comedy westerns who had worked in other genres or had written straight westerns. The back catalog of W.R. Burnett, who received sole credit for *Sergeants 3* (based on the 1939 *Gunga Din*), included the crime drama *High Sierra* (1941), the war picture *Wake Island* (1942) for which he was nominated for an Oscar, the boxing drama *Iron Man* (1951) and the crime picture *The Racket* (1951); he also furnished the source material for *The Asphalt Jungle* (1950). John Gay, who penned the screenplay for *The Hallelujah Trail*, had previously been responsible for the submarine tale *Run Silent, Run Deep* (1958) and the drama *Separate Tables* (1958). Teddi Sherman, who wrote *4 for Texas* in conjunction with director Robert Aldrich, had shared the credit for the straight westerns *Four Faces West* (1948), *The Man from Bitter Ridge* (1955) and *Tennessee's Partner* (1955) as well as the war picture *Ten Seconds to Hell* (1959), and she turned in episodes for television western series including *The Rifleman, Cheyenne, Bat Masterson, The Rough Riders* and *The Virginian*.

William Bowers,[6] the writer of *Support Your Local Sheriff*, fell into this "unusual" category for he had written the classic western *The Gunfighter* (1950) directed by Henry King and starring Gregory Peck, as well as mainstream westerns like *Black Bart* (1948), *River Lady* (1948), *The Law and Jake Wade* (1958), *The Sheepman* (1958) and *Ride to Hangman's Tree* (1967). In addition, he had worked in virtually every other genre: musicals (*Sing Your Way Home* [1945] and *Something in the Wind* [1947]); comedy-mysteries (*The Notorious Lone Wolf* [1946] and *Mrs. O'Malley and Mr. Malone* [1950]); biopics (*Night and Day* [1946] and *The Best Things in Life Are Free* [1956]); crime dramas (*Convicted* [1950]) and thrillers (*Assignment Paris* [1952]). He had a septet of film noirs to his name: *The Web* (1947), *Larceny* (1948), *Cry Danger* (1951), *The Mob* (1951), *Split Second* (1953), *Tight Spot* (1955) and *5 Against the House* (1955). On the comedy front he could boast *My Favorite Spy* (1942) for radio personality Kay Kyser, *The Countess of Monte Cristo* (1948) for ice-skating star Sonja Henje, *She Couldn't Say No* (1952) starring Robert Mitchum and Jean Simmons, *My Man Godfrey* (1957) twinning June Allyson and David Niven, *Imitation General* (1958) with Glenn Ford, *The Last Time I Saw Archie* (1961) with

Robert Mitchum, and *Way... Way Out* (1966) with Jerry Lewis. Interspersed with his work in all the other genres were a handful of comedy westerns: *The Wistful Widow of Wagon Gap, The Gal Who Took the West, Alias Jesse James* and *Advance to the Rear.*

All movies, regardless of genre, are always, at some point, written with a star in mind or rewritten to a star's specifications. Comedies are even more specifically tailored to the best attributes of a particular comedian or, of a straight actor, to what they are capable of achieving from humor on screen. For obvious reasons, dialogue is far more important in comedy than any other type of picture, while sight gags, invariably a product of the writer's imagination, can as easily lose their impact in the hands of an incompetent director. To prevent what he believed was a perfect script from being mangled on its way to the screen, Bowers intended, for the first time in his life, to act as producer and director.[7] He took the script to James Garner, who liked it so much he put the idea to United Artists,[8] to whom he owed a film. But UA did not want to risk working with a first-time director and vetoed the idea, turning instead to Burt Kennedy, himself a scriptwriter, who had directed six westerns in the past five years, including the comedy western *Mail Order Bride* (1964). In theory at least, Kennedy could be trusted not to muck up the script. With a budget limited to just $1.75 million, there would be little room for stylistic diversion. As far as Bowers was concerned the role of the director was, effectively, to stay out of the way and let the words speak for themselves.

Solid But Not Spectacular

Although he was probably not aware of it, James Garner was coming to the end of his career as a Hollywood star. After *Support Your Local Sheriff* he would only retain marquee power for another five years. And there was a good reason for this. Despite his 14 years in the movie business, only a few of his pictures, *The Thrill of It All* (1963), *Move Over, Darling* (1963), *The Great Escape* (1963) and *Grand Prix* (1966), had been out-and-out successes, finding a slot in the annual top 20.[9] But the first two were Doris Day vehicles; Steve McQueen was the acknowledged star of the war picture; and for the motor racing spectacular, the actors took second place to the Cinerama production and John Frankenheimer's thrilling direction. The ratio of roles to hits was dismally low. However, Garner's movie career had followed an unusual trajectory, beginning as designated star of two war pictures, *Darby's Rangers* (1958) and *Up Periscope* (1959), and the romantic drama *Cash McCall* (1960)—all relatively low-budget movies. But no sooner had star status been conferred than it was lost and there followed a four-year hiatus in terms of top billing. He was billed third behind Audrey Hepburn and Shirley MacLaine in *The Children's Hour* (1961), and he was second-billed to Kim Novak in *Boys' Night Out* (1962), to Steve McQueen in *The Great* Escape, to Doris Day in *The Thrill of It All* (1963), to Lee Remick in *The Wheeler Dealers* (1963), and to Day again in the romantic comedy *Move Over, Darling* (1963). He regained marquee prominence in *The Americanization of Emily* (1964). But then, with the exception of *Grand Prix*, he did not exactly set the box office alight in *36 Hours* (1964), *The Art of Love* (1965), *Mister Buddwing* (1966), *A Man Could Get Killed* (1966), *How Sweet It Is* (1968) and *The Pink Jungle* (1968). Leading man in a dozen films and virtually all had sunk in commercial terms. If ranked at all in the top 100 movies of any given year, they were generally to be found at the lower end of the spectrum. In fact, five of those movies had brought in combined rentals of only $6.5 million—a woeful average of $1.3 million.[10] Only *The Art of Love* had produced "passable" returns of $3.5 million in rentals, still not enough to qualify as a verifiable hit. MGM blamed "public apathy to Garner" for *Grand Prix* not doing better at the box office and was so annoyed with the actor that initially he was turned down for their production of the adaptation of Raymond Chandler's *The Little Sister* (later renamed *Marlowe*).[11]

At the outset of his career, Garner had been "pegged as a 1960s cool successor to Clark Gable after audience enthusiasm for his appearance in *The Great Escape*." But he had thrown away that opportunity by taking on "indifferent comic assignments and misjudged roles."[12] There was a strong suspicion that the public was getting fed up with his "customary bewildered portrayals"[13] and there were complaints that his "reactive facial expressions were not enough" to convey internal conflict.[14]

That he remained a star at all under the circumstances was largely due to the fact that the bigger stars commanded such enormous salaries (Paul Newman, Steve McQueen, John Wayne, etc., were paid in the region of $750,000 to $1 million) that they priced themselves out of the smaller picture, leaving the way clear for the less popular stars like Garner (by comparison, he earned $150,000 for *The Great Escape*[15] and not much more for other films); more importantly, that his production company Cherokee was involved in the making of all his movies from *The Art of Love* (1965) onwards.[16] Operating a production company was not an unusual occupation for a movie star. Mary Pickford, Charlie Chaplin and Douglas Fairbanks had established United Artists in 1919 to take control of their careers and get a bigger share of the profits. In 1948, Burt Lancaster formed Hecht-Lancaster, which was responsible for the swashbuckler *The Crimson Pirate* (1952), the westerns *Apache* (1954) and *Vera Cruz* (1954), etc., while its successor Hecht-Hill-Lancaster produced *Trapeze* (1956), The *Sweet Smell of Success* (1957) and *The Unforgiven* (1960).[17] Kirk Douglas' production company Bryna was the driving force behind the western *The Indian Fighter* (1955), the anti-war *Paths of Glory* (1957) and the epic *Spartacus*[18] (1960). John Wayne's production entities Wayne-Fellows and Batjac put together *Big Jim McLain* (1952), *Hondo* (1953), *The High and the Mighty* (1954), *The Alamo* (1960), *McLintock!* (1963), *The War Wagon* (1967) and *The Green Berets* (1968). Paul Newman ran a company in conjunction with director Martin Ritt.

Owning a production company was not just a career option or a vanity operation, it was often seen as a financial necessity, an essential, and legal, method of reducing tax bills. Mostly, such companies remained relatively dormant, caught up in just making movies for the star who owned the company.[19] However, stars were rarely exposed to the normal financial risks this would incur since studios picked up the tab for their overheads in return for a "first look" agreement. Nevertheless, there was an upside for the studios since this way of doing business meant the actors often foregoing their usual fee or deferring it until the movie reached break-even point in terms of revenues,[20] thus lowering negative costs, in return for a bigger share of the profits. However, the whole point of running a production company in the proper sense was to take advantage of the ability to pick the best scripts to enhance the owner's standing. And, in that regard, Garner had failed miserably. He had demonstrated his skills in the mainstream genres: thriller (*36 Hours*), drama (*The Americanization of Emily* and *Mister Buddwing*) and adventure (*The Pink Jungle*). But extending his range, and therefore attracting better parts, proved beyond the capability of Cherokee since he was clearly more at home with comedy as witnessed by *The Art of Love, A Man Could Get Killed* and *How Sweet It Is* (1968). Even his more straightforward movies involved some element of humor.

Evan Hunter, the author of this novel, also wrote the novels on which the movies *Blackboard Jungle* (1955), *Strangers When We Meet* (1960), *The Young Savages* (1961) and *Last Summer* (1969) were based. Trade press advertisement (*Box Office*, September 12, 1966).

Part of the problem was the television series *Maverick* (1957–1962) which in large part was responsible for his screen persona, that of a character less interested in action than in finding a way around trouble or walking away from it, while at the same time holding substantial appeal for the ladies who seemed not to notice these traits. He had been forced into three seasons of the series, limiting his availability for outside projects at a time when demand for his talents as a potential rising movie star was at its peak. When he pulled out of the series, Warner Brothers retaliated by showing reruns for the next two years and holding his career back in a long-running contract dispute. He was also involved in expensive litigation with Warners which cost him $106,000, virtually his entire income from the television series. Although he won, and his seven-year pact with the studio was annulled, he was given a paltry $1750 (the equivalent of one week's salary) in costs rather than the punitive $341,000 he was seeking.[21] (It was somewhat ironic that, having jettisoned an exceptionally promising television career in favor of movies, he therefore missed out on the financial bonanzas many television stars began to enjoy in the mid–1960s: James Arness in *Gunsmoke* and Fess Parker in *Daniel Boone* enjoying annual salaries of $1 million.[22]) Where Steve McQueen had managed to capitalize on his early television fame as the star of *Wanted: Dead or Alive*, Garner was left in limbo, and facing the prospect of meeting the same fate as the stars of *Cheyenne* (Clint Walker) and *77 Sunset Strip* (Edd Byrnes) who had seen Hollywood pass them by. However, *Maverick* had dealt him a rather likable screen persona and without too much effort he was able to turn in decent, likable performances in the movies he was offered, or, through Cherokee, helped set up. Even so, he was handicapped by his old-fashioned square-jawed good looks, lacking the sense of edge and danger that Paul Newman, Steve McQueen and Lee Marvin brought to their roles. He was rarely considered, if at all, for the type of roles those stars had made their own. His westerns were tame compared to *Nevada Smith* (1965), *Hombre* and *The Professionals* (1966); his comedies lightweight compared to *Irma La Douce* and *The Graduate,* and his dramas were rarely dramatic enough. Although he had entered the production business[23] to get away from the "comedy groove" into which Universal and MGM had directed him in the early 1960s,[24] his lack of talent for drama meant that he was unable to break out of this typecasting.

So why, after years of underperforming movies and a career that appeared in terminal decline, was James Garner able to bounce back with the biggest hit of his career? Well, the fact was, the role of Jason in *Support Your Local Sheriff* fitted him like a glove. In one sense, this was hardly surprising since his company Cherokee had developed the project and could tailor it to his requirements. But there was something else in his screen persona that had often been overlooked. He was not a demonstrative actor, not one for over-the-top performance, his style quiet rather than aggressive, with the stillness that is the essence of movie acting. Not showing a great deal of genuine emotion onscreen would hardly be a drawback in a picture that called for none. His measured delivery, seasoned by years in comedy, provided him the timing essential for comedy. More importantly, his screen persona was of a man confident to the point of arrogance. So what if the picture was written to highlight his most appealing traits while making fun of his deficiencies? What if there was a picture that could take advantage of his "quiet effectiveness," his "flair for comedy," his "outstanding" aptitude for romantic comedy and his ability to appear as a "sarcastic sophisticate"?[25] What if, for once, he was the king of cool, in total command, rather than the victim of grand self-delusion? If the script was good enough, he could pretty much sleepwalk his way through it, letting the script do most of the talking.

Welcome to Mud Town

The plot was ridiculously simple. Gold is discovered in the tiny hamlet of Calendar, which grows virtually overnight into a raucous, lawless Wild West town dominated by the Danby family. Passing through "on the way to Australia," Jason (James Garner) takes on the unwanted job of sheriff. After jailing Joe Danby (Bruce Dern) for murder, he has to deal with the gunslingers sent to rescue Joe. In between times, he romances the scattergun Prudy (Joan Hackett), the mayor's daughter, prone not just to mishap but taking offense. The picture reaches a finale when, with his deputy (Jack Elam) and Prudy, the townspeople having voted to have nothing to do with the shootout, he faces off against Pa Denby (Walter Brennan) and a dozen cowboys.

But the plot was the least important element of a picture that came "close to annihilating every cliché in the genre."[26] Hilarity ensues from the get-go. What begins as a standard western funeral turns into anything but. After showing a close-up of a coffin and the music playing the equally standard "Shall We Gather by the River," the camera pulls back to reveal the accordionist playing the tune (a sight gag reprised by Mel Brooks for *Blazing Saddles* a few years later). Mayor Olly Perkins (Harry Morgan) can barely remember the name of the deceased ("Millard or whatever his name was") and his main concern is that "whatever deadly disease struck him down is not particularly contagious." The ceremony is rudely interrupted when Prudy spots gold in the newly dug grave (an idea repeated in *Paint Your Wagon*). In seconds, she is in the grave, staking a claim, laying about the others with a shovel.

Prudy is the first of the clichés turned upside down. The west has had its fair share of rowdy madams of the Shelley Winters variety, straight shooters of the Barbara Stanwyck sort, winsome maidens in the Grace Kelly mold, tomboys out of the Doris Day school, sex goddesses disguised as Marilyn Monroe or Jane Russell, and a fair sprinkling of hysterical females for whom the whole Wild West is just, well, too wild. But while Prudy Perkins combines feistiness with bashfulness, she is crazier than a sunburned rattlesnake and engages in fisticuffs in her first two appearances in the movie, going in the space of a few seconds from upstanding citizen to wildcat. So it is no surprise, really, that she kicks off the whole story by not just spotting the gold but reacting to it in a full-on distinctly unfeminine manner. By the time she pops up again, the town is "Klondike Central," out of control, rowdies shooting it up, the main street a swamp. The town worthies, who have already filled their pockets, get pretty sore at the Danbys filling their pockets at everyone's expense, demanding a 20 percent "tax" on every wagon that passes through their spread, as they must, in order to reach Galena where the gold is shipped east.

In the midst of this chaos, Jason rides into town dressed in black, another twist since that color usually denotes the bad guy (a nod, this time, in the direction of Yul Brynner's outfit in *The Magnificent Seven*). Gunfire erupts from the balcony of Madame Orr's House (another sight gag). This version of James Garner is quite different to previous models. The self-deprecation remains, but this time he is confident and self-contained and his aversion to violence appears not the result of cowardice but of a logical mindset. Where in previous movies he was thrust into the action as helpless as a fish out of water, here he is deliberately on the periphery, an observer, cool, adding up consequence, one step (if not several) ahead of everyone else. While cleverly avoiding direct confrontation, a character trait reminiscent of Maverick, in the saloon, Jason challenges Joe Danby over a gunfight which Danby claims he won fairly but Jason calmly explains he drew first while pretending not to ("an old Arizona trick"). When Jason goes outside to eat, he discovers food and accommodation are so expensive that he is likely "to go broke by 2:30 p.m." And when a fistfight begins, Jason calmly, not to say deftly, takes his plate and removes himself from trouble. When one of the rowdies aims a fist at him, Jason merely shakes his head, like a schoolmaster warning an errant child, and the man moves away. It is not long before he comes across Prudy, who has taken extreme umbrage at being knocked down trying to cross the muddy street, and is setting about the man with a length of wood and is soon drenched in mud. A tomboy is tame by comparison. Seeing an advertisement for a sheriff, Jason applies for the job. The town council is dumbfounded to find a candidate, since there have been three sheriffs in the past two months; one quit and two were shot. The job pays $150 per month plus lodgings at the mayor's house and food cooked by his daughter, whom we know, but Jason does not, is as likely to start a fight as finish it, setting up audience expectation of future mirth at the expense of the woman's culinary skills.

Shades of Sam in *The Stalking Moon* and Lyedecker in *100 Rifles*, Jason is not so keen on commitment, pointing out he is heading for Australia (the first big dreamer of the 1969 vintage). Realizing his demeanor does not carry the edge of a convincing law enforcer, Jason saunters across the room, throws a steel disc into the air and shoots a hole in it. This being a film of twist and double-twist, the mayor remains dubious. "Do it again," he demands. Duly obliging, Jason is hired. The sheriff's badge is noticeably busted up. Jason observes that it "saved the life of its wearer." But scriptwriter Bowers is ready with the verbal equivalent of a double-take. "Would have done," replies Perkins, "if not for the other bullets flying in from everywhere." And that really is the beauty of the movie. Yes, we have a sure-footed Garner, a charming treat, and a story filled to bursting with inanity, and the slapstick of Miss Prudy, but the script is so chockfull of zingers that there is pretty much a laugh a minute and when you hit such a solid comedy seam, really, everyone else just has to stand back. On the way to arrest Joe for murder, Jason has to first stop the mass brawl. Which is a tricky proposition in this genre because mass brawls are meant to never end, not until every punch has been thrown, every table and chair broken, windows smashed, horses and god-knows-what dragged in. Cue one of the many imaginative solutions dreamed up by the resourceful Mr. Bowers. Jason does not even raise his voice, he simply turns on the fire hose and drenches the brawlers into submission. One brawler, Jake (Elam), has the temerity to draw on the newly appointed sheriff only to see his weapon blown clean out of his holster, a demonstration of speedy gunplay that would be emulated a few months later by the Sundance Kid. The cool Jason then instructs Jake to go to the saloon and tell Joe that he is about to be arrested. "What you gonna do after he kills me?" asks Jake. With perfect timing, Jason replies he will "arrest him for both murders."

Jason is so laid-back about detaining Joe and clearly so confident of his own powers that the next thing he does is delay the arrest, a quite untoward development in a genre where confrontation is the name of the game, the only acceptable reason for stretching out the time between a call for action and its realization being to build up audience tension. But this runs counter to *High Noon* and every other western where shootouts are the highlights of the picture. (Just how long, in genuine dramatic terms, the tension prior to a shootout can be elongated will shortly be demonstrated in *Once Upon a Time in the West.*) In terms of lengthening the tension prior to the anticipated shootout, Jason first

Around the time *Support Your Local Sheriff* was made, politicians got behind the campaign "Support Your Local Police." Trade press advertisement (*Box Office*, March 24, 1969).

checks out the jail and in so doing spoofs Howard Hawks' *Rio Bravo* (1959). From a comedy perspective, this is the best jail ever. It lacks one essential ingredient: bars. Unperturbed, Jason draws a chalk line in front of the space allocated the cell and dribbles red paint on the floor, leaving not just the audience but the town council to wonder why. The payoff is some way distant since Jason is still is in no hurry, his priority now to collect his bedroll and take it over to the mayor's house where Prudy is trying to wash that mud out of her hair. As she hasn't had time to change her clothes, she is appalled to see her father leading the new sheriff towards the front door. Rushing around trying to hide from the visitor, Prudy, naturally enough, being Prudy, ends up in a tree. There is something so endearingly bizarre about Prudy that nothing she does would surprise you. This is a meet-cute to behold. Intent on turning every western cliché on its head, Bowers takes time out to play about with the word "departed," normally used to describe the death of a loved one. "Wife dead?" asks Jason, setting up the punch line, "No, just departed."

Now, with all the jail stuff and house stuff and Prudy stuff out of the way, it is time to get down to the confrontation. Although Jake has balked at the prospect of passing on Jason's instruction, the new sheriff tries to recruit him as deputy. But commitment being what it is in the western of this era, Jake is reluctant, and will remain so for some time. The saloon has a party atmosphere, everyone in town gathering to see Joe kill the new sheriff. Bad guys always get to mouth off in westerns, but Jason has had enough of it and probably speaks for the entire audience when he says, "It's bad enough having to kill a man without having to listen to a whole lot of stupid talk first." Stupidity is another recurrent theme. Moviegoers have become so accustomed to not just villains but heroes acting so dumb that audiences no longer question crass stupidity. Well, now somebody has. But just as Jason readies to make his move a man at the top of the stairs gets the drop on him. In the process of pretending to drop his holster (another trick from Arizona?), Jason shoots the man. He hears other shots from behind. Jake has killed another bad guy. In the jail, Jake again turns down the job, outraging Danby that the new sheriff is attempting to recruit "the town character," a fine example of misplaced arrogance given the entire Danby family (father and three sons) would struggle to find a single brain cell they could call their own. Jake retorts that he "was the town character, now the deputy sheriff," taking on the job for the most bizarre of reasons, because he has been insulted. Naturally, Joe mocks the jail-without-bars, especially when Jason explains, as if to a child slow to learning, that the chalk line will act as the door. Danby queries the red marks on the floor. "That's the poor feller that crossed the line earlier today." Joe is not so dumb as Jason thinks and soon works out that a chalk line is not, in fact, a door and escapes, only to be instantly caught and reprimanded, returning meekly to his cell when informed that the gun he has stolen is without bullets only to later discover that it is not. Meanwhile, Jake asks the question that has been on the audience's lips. How come a gunslinger like Jason has slid under the bush telegram? "Why have you not got a reputation?" asks the deputy. "Good way to get yourself killed," comes the logical reply.

Some western heroes in this particular calendar year know exactly where they are headed. Their faith is touching, if naïve. Sam in *The Stalking Moon* looks forward to retiring to his little spread in Mexico. It's pretty much a dream as he has not seen it in 15 years and left the running of the ranch to an old man. He is lucky that there is any halfway decent ranch at all, for other western heroes appear to pluck a dream out of the air on no greater authority than having read a book about it in the Chicago Library, as Jason now confesses to Jake. (Another unlikely haven, Bolivia, pops out of Butch Cassidy's mind.)

With the level of verbal wit on offer, the audience would not have been expecting some decent slapstick (the mud brawl hardly counting), But now there is a beauty: Prudy in the kitchen wearing one of her best dresses. You expect the fun will rely on Prudy's much-vaunted cooking. Instead, it is crazier. Prudy is baking and in the process of checking on her guests happens to pat her face, forgetting her hands are covered in flour and shortly she is wearing a white beard of flour. Neither is her best dress, sticking out in all directions, suitable for the kitchen and, as she swirls around, it catches fire, and she ends up serving up the food oblivious to the smoke and flames shooting up her rear. When Jason douses the flames, Prudy takes immediate offense.

In a nod to *My Darling Clementine*, Jason's natural inclination is to sit in his office with his feet up on the desk and that is how Pa Danby (Walter Brennan) encounters him when he arrives, pistol at the ready, to rescue his son Joe. Brennan is an ideal choice for the role of the head of the villainous clan not just because he played the same part in *My Darling Clementine* but because, otherwise, his role in westerns is the ornery old guy who gives the hero his comeuppance. Any audience familiar with Howard Hawks' *Red River* (1948) or *Rio Bravo* will anticipate what happens next. Except that screenwriter Bowers has anticipated that anticipation and instead allows Pa Danby to be disarmed by Jason, who simply blocks the pistol barrel with his finger, thus, according to Jason, incapacitating the weapon, a measure of the old man's idiocy that he accepts the explanation. When he leaves, Danby muses, "He strikes me as being a lonely man." In typical western parlance, Jake replies, "He's a mean no-good lowdown bushwhacker." "See," retorts Jason, "no wonder he's lonely." Such psychological insights lead the audience to believe that he will unerringly bowl over Prudy. Although she sits with him in the swing in the porch and looks all set to be bowled over, his confidence gets the better of him and turns into conceit, and romance is put on hold. Which is just as well we have to wait for that element to sort itself out because Jason has pretty much sorted out everything else. To prevent rowdies racing into town on horseback, he runs along the street a rope that he tugs to sent racing horsemen flying.

In the film, James Garner does stick his finger in someone's gun. His co-star Joan Hackett made her Broadway debut in *Much Ado About Nothing* in 1959 and collected an Obie for her performance in *Call Me By My Rightful Name* in 1961. Trade press advertisement (*Box Office*, March 24, 1969).

Pa Danby has hired a motley collection of gunslingers to free his son. Killing seems a waste to Jason and after outdrawing the first bad guy, he chases the next one out of town by throwing stones at him. The time-honored trick of freeing a prisoner by having horses pull away the ropes tied round the cell bars is turned in its head, the bars now having been installed more solidly than usual to prevent such an occurrence. Joe laments, "Pa got a heart as big as the whole outdoors but he don't got one brain in his poor old head." Pa Danby resorts to his final option, strength in numbers, summoning the entire extended Danby clan and hired hands, around a dozen or so riders. When Prudy warns of impending attack, Bowers again springs a surprise. "Might just leave town," says Jason. Surprise number two is Prudy's reaction. "One of the most mature things I've ever heard a man do. Almost any other man would have to stick around to prove they are a man." Any other man, of course, abides by the rules of western convention, no matter how ludicrous.

In the end, Jason does decides to stick around, but the town council, in the best *High Noon* tradition, decides to leave him to it. In a more visual nod in the direction of *High Noon*, Jason is seen as the lone man in an empty street, while the audience watches the bad guys thundering towards the town. There is still time for a few more gags during the final shootout—Jason, Jake and Prudy vs. the rest—Jason reproving Prudy's marksmanship in lacking the ability to wound, and Jason calling a truce so he can cross the street. As instanced in *100 Rifles*, when an enemy appears implacable, the only way to win is to be extra-implacable, and as with the Tom Gries western, one of the best ways to resolve a situation is by taking a hostage: Jason tying Joe Danby to a cannon and threatening to blow him to Kingdom Come ensures the bag guys drop their weapons. Sadly, the only time the exploder of clichés falls into the cliché trap itself is at the very end when it turns out the cannon is not old and useless and it destroys Madame Orr's House. Romance will, of course, out, however William Bowers counters that cliché by having Jason marry Prudy for her wealth.

Director Burt Kennedy did the necessary and kept out of the way. Most scenes are shot without resort to stylistic device, the town council filmed in groupings or two, three or four people, the actors clearly chosen so that their different heights added clarity to such compositions. Kennedy makes the most of low angles to emphasize Jason's laziness when he lounges with his feet up. Occasional offscreen action is indicated by sound effects, but generally he just keeps the camera pointing in the right direction and allows his cast to make the most of Bowers' script. The only time he permits intrusive flourish are the impressive shots of the gang of bad guys approaching, initially in the distance as tiny figures cresting a hill and this particular composition shot through the branches of a tree; and one other terrific shot of the riders in one line. Everyone else is at the top of their form, Elam and Brennan in particular not tipping the wink at the audience. Joan Hackett, in a complete reversal of her character in *Will Penny* (1968), proves a natural comedienne, even though, in reality, she has never undertaken such a role before, her acclaimed parts on the stage much more serious roles, and her performance in *Will Penny* the opposite of Prudy, subtle rather than loud and ostentatious. For James Garner, this proves the best role of his career, one that manages to corral all his appealing characteristics, allowing his natural clipped delivery full vent, making no emotional demands that his eyes are not capable of expressing, and carrying the audience along with his own particular charm.

Critical Reception

Comedies play best when there is an audience. Laughter is infectious and when there is enough of it, then it is like an epidemic nobody can escape. However, in press screenings comprising a handful of critics, the opposite can as easily hold sway: If nobody laughs, then the movie is endured in puzzled or hostile silence. Critical response was generally good, *Variety*, not usually a big fan of Burt Kennedy, commenting that he was the "best choice to direct" and that the film was "delightful."[27] *Box Office* called it "sheer entertainment from start to finish."[28] Judith Crist in *New York* magazine gave it a "near rave" review. The *New York Daily News* ("a wonderfully tipsy western in the same corral as such spoofs as *Cat Ballou*") and *Cue* magazine also gave favorable reviews[29] while for *The Washington Post* it contained "consistently funny lines."[30] The far more influential Vincent Canby at the *New York Times* called the inventive western "unimaginative."[31] In Britain, it was generally well received, *Sight & Sound* considering it "no mean achievement to maintain a comic tone with the Western form."[32] The British Film Institute's *Monthly Film Bulletin* called it "refreshing," and the *New Statesman* "a fairly refreshing if protracted joke." Richard Roud in *The Guardian* carped that it was "the kind of film you will like only if you like to go to the movies."[33]

Box Office

Since there was no attempt by the major studios to carefully conserve their best pictures so that they would not go head to head with rivals, *Support Your Local Sheriff* turned up in theaters at the same time as *100 Rifles*, which had a bigger budget and therefore a bigger advertising budget, and the low-budget *Smith!* Nor was it possible to achieve an uniform release date in the late 1960s—the openings of *Support Your Local Sheriff* in the key cities were four weeks apart. Space in first run theaters was at a premium in part because of a logjam created by long-running roadshows (*Funny Girl*, *The Lion in Winter*) and extended runs of hits (*The Thomas Crown Affair*). The false impression has been given in some quarters that the movie struggled to find an audience and only survived through the efforts of theater managers to hold onto it until the public turned up in sufficient numbers. In the first place, this is just wrong and in the second place could not be more wrong because movie exhibition was a hard-headed business and nobody in their right mind would keep on a picture that was not performing when it could be showing a film that was. However, it is true to say that box office response varied: "wham" in Philadelphia, "strong" in Kansas City, "lusty" in Providence, but "only fair" in Boston and "thin" in Los Angeles where it was unexpectedly trounced by *Smith!*[34] However, the picture showed "legs" and would either enjoy a lengthy run in the same theater, especially in the less prestigious houses in the smaller cities and towns, or make return visits in the immediate future. Given its budget, and Garner's declining appeal at the box office, the film did far better than expected and proved a highly profitable venture for Cherokee Productions and distributor United Artists. With rentals of $5 million,[35] it was the third-best-performing western of 1969 at the U.S. box office, finishing in the 20th spot in the annual rankings ahead of *The Wild Bunch*, *The Stalking Moon* and *100 Rifles*.

4

Kill the Messenger

Heaven with a Gun and *Smith!*

Heaven with a Gun

Starring Glenn Ford, Carolyn Jones, David Carradine, Barbara Hershey; directed by Lee H. Katzin; screenplay by Richard Carr; MGM; 101 minutes

The Star Next Door

Of the actors still in full employment, Glenn Ford had more westerns (21) to his credit than any other, including John Wayne if you discount the volume of B-pictures to which the Duke was consigned in the 1930s following the flop of *The Big Trail* (1930). Ford's western debut *Texas* (1941) had been intended as a star-making vehicle for himself and William Holden, but it did the former the more good and when the pair were reteamed in *The Man from Colorado* (1948) it was the unassuming Ford whose career had taken off, thanks in part to the electrifying film noir *Gild*a (1946). Although James Stewart was considered the screen "every man," Ford was in a similar vein, that of "the star next door." Ford was most at home, according to film historian Patrick McGilligan, with "warm, decent, idealistic fellows with backbones of steel"[1] and most likely to appear in a "series of pure-hearted inarticulate do-gooder roles."[2] Unlike Stewart, he was not tall and languid, but small and compact, and although his clipped delivery served him well, it was his face that delivered the goods, his eyes in particular able to express every emotion under the sun. And he was also a coiled spring, a fuse which you lit at your peril.

However, what set him apart from John Wayne and James Stewart was that for most of his career he did not appear in big-budget pictures; the exceptions were *The Teahouse of the August Moon* (1956), *Cimarron* (1960), *The Four Horsemen of the Apocalypse* (1962) and *Is Paris Burning?* (1965), in which he played a supporting role. He was versatile and, according to Sidney Poitier, "there was more variety in his body of work than in comparable actors."[3] Ford was equally at home with romance (*It Started with a Kiss*, 1959), film noir (*The Big Heat*, 1953), drama (*Blackboard Jungle*, 1955), comedy (*The Teahouse of the August Moon*), war (*Torpedo Run*, 1958), and, unusually, could hold his own against kids (*The Courtship of Eddie's Father*, 1963). His domain was the medium-budget movie and in that respect he was a no-risk option. Very often his presence pulled routine movies

***Blackboard Jungle* was not shown at the Venice Film Festival for fear it cast the U.S. education system in a poor light. The book by Evan Hunter was based on his own experiences. Trade press advertisement (*Box Office*, April 23, 1955).**

out of the rut or turned them into huge hits, and occasionally his popularity went through the roof, such as in 1958, when he was named Star of the Year. Never in the $500,000 to $1 million bracket, he compensated by working hard, and in the 1950s his name regularly emblazoned three movies a year, five in 1953 and 1955, four in 1956 and 1958[4]; in the 1960s that declined to two per annum, three in 1964.

It was probably this aspect of his character that extended his career in the 1960s, when the hits died up. For, even when the production hothouse of the 1940s had been trimmed by the Consent Decree and television in the 1950s, and ongoing financial turmoil in the 1960s, producers still needed to churn out movies, otherwise they would not get paid. Ford still had some kind of following out there and could be hired for a relatively small sum by the standards of the day. However, he had seriously begun to lag behind his contemporaries. Robert Mitchum, one year younger, starred in bigger pictures, William Holden, two years younger, would star in *The Wild Bunch* with a budget three or four times larger than any recent Ford effort, while John Wayne and James Stewart, nine and eight years older, respectively, were at the top of their game, box office prowess undiminished in the wake of the previous year's *The Green Berets* and *Bandolero!* Ford was only 53 at the time of the release of *Heaven with a Gun*, still relatively young for one who had been a major star, but these days the success of old films was no guarantee of ongoing appeal.

Analysis of the performance of his most recent films made grim reading. Of his last eight pictures, none had earned over $1 million in rentals,[5] and his previous film *Day of the Evil Gun* (1968) had originally been made with television in mind. In fact, he was only available to make *Heaven with a Gun* and *Smith!* because another proposal to film a Zane Grey adaptation had fallen through.[6]

An idea of how low Ford's career had fallen was that, although appearing under the MGM aegis (although this was far from the industry giant of old, struggling with $40 million losses[7]), *Heaven with a Gun* was an independent production from the King Brothers,[8] B-movie specialists, and this would be the last of the 27 films—the company was now diversifying into the diamond-selling business[9]—they had made since 1941's crime thriller *Paper Bullets*, which cost $19,800. In more recent times, especially due to *Trumbo* (2015),[10] they are better known for employing blacklisted writers in the 1950s.[11] However, they were one of the regular B-movie suppliers in the 1940s and 1950s, output dramatically curtailed in the 1960s when that market collapsed. Primarily they made thrillers (*Dillinger*, 1945) and westerns (*Bad Men from Tombstone*, 1949), drifting into sci-fi with *Rodan* (1956) and *Gorgo* (1961) and fantasy with *Captain Sinbad* (1963). Some indication of the level of their budgets can be shown by the fact that Glenn Ford was the biggest star the brothers had ever employed with the exception of Robert Taylor (*Return of the Gunfighter*, 1967), at one time a far bigger attraction than Ford but by then a much smaller one.

Director Lee H. Katzin was making his movie debut after four years in television (*Branded*, *Mission: Impossible*). Writer Richard Carr had been in television since 1952, most recently working on *The Virginian*, *Gunsmoke* and *The High Chaparral*, but his movies had been restricted to the drama *Too Late Blues* (1961) starring Bobby Darin and Don Siegel's war film *Hell Is for Heroes* (1962) starring Steve McQueen. In the wake of Clint Eastwood's *Dollars* trilogy, *The Magnificent Stranger* (1967) was compiled from two 1959 episodes of the TV series *Rawhide*,[12] on which Eastwood had worked. Apart from Ford, *Heaven with a Gun* had no other proven marquee attractions, relying on names more famous from television to add cachet. Female lead Carolyn Jones (who plays saloon owner Madge MacLeod) was better known as Morticia in television's *The Addams Family* (1964–1966), her movie career dormant since starring in *A Ticklish Affair* (1963).[13] David Carradine (the wayward Cole Beck) had essayed the title character in the television series *Shane* (1966). *Heaven with a Gun* was the sophomore picture after the Doris Day comedy *With Six You Get Eggroll* (1968) for upcoming actress Barbara Hershey (Leloopa, a Hopi

Indian). For character actor John Anderson (Asa Beck, father of Cole), this was the first of three 1969 westerns, the others being *The Great Bank Robbery* and *Young Billy Young*, and he had been as prolific the year before in Henry Hathaway's *5 Card Stud* and *Day of the Evil Gun*, which, coincidentally, starred Glenn Ford. There were cameo roles for J.D. Cannon (the gunslinger Mace), Noah Beery, Jr. (Asa Beck's right hand man Garvey) and William Bryant (rancher Bart Patterson).

Kill the Messenger

This tightly written picture about a range war comes somewhat undone towards the end when it has "message" written all over it. Up until then it has worked very well. The story has twists without unnecessary complications, and spins a merry tune with disinformation. While some of the characters are straight from Central Casting, it is a brave attempt to widen the scope of what a low-budget picture could achieve in the genre.

The pre-credit sequence is succinct. The film opens with a shepherd guarding his flock. As he turns up to the hills behind, shots are fired. We cut to a barn being set on fire and sheep being scattered. An Indian is chased by two horsemen, one later revealed as Cole Beck, lassoed and dragged along the river bed and out onto dry land where he is hanged. We are not shown the hanging, just a man pulling on a rope on which clearly a heavy weight is attached and then the corpse's dangling feet.

We cut to Jim Killian (Glenn Ford) riding up and the Hopi girl Leloopa (Barbara Hershey) hiding in the bushes. The girl watches as the horseman digs a grave for the Indian. The two horsemen return and accost the gravedigger. Cole Beck orders, "String him up again." With his usual quiet steel, the man replies, "I don't think I will." Beck shoots into the ground but the man throws a shovelful of dirt in Beck's face, whacks Beck's accomplice with the shovel and gets the draw on both. When the grave-digger rides off, the girl emerges from her hiding place and lies on the grave. Five minutes in and we know a range war is taking place, that the stranger (Ford) is not to be tangled with, that the girl is probably fatherless, and that Cole Beck is ruthless.

In the town, Killian buys a livery stables for $400, promising payment the next day. Entering the saloon of the hotel-cum-bordello, he sits down with Cole Beck at a poker table. We cut to a crowd watching as the stakes increase and to an overhead shot of Madge (Carolyn Jones) in the hotel balcony. When Killian wins, Cole Beck accuses him of cheating. "There was a time you'd be dead in a few seconds if you'd said that," says Killian. Madge, the hotel owner, intervenes, despite Cole Beck suspecting that Killian is a "gunslinger hired by the sheepmen." Madge is disappointed to find he has not come on account of her, to rekindle their former romance. Here comes twist number one. His winnings come to $590, enough to cover the cost of the stable, and the first of several instances where the audience is misled by its own assumptions. A man offers $400 for a livery stable, you assume he has the cash, right? Not that he has to finance the purchase by gambling. Eleven minutes in and we know Jim Killian is far from what he seems, more than just a righter-of-wrongs, but a clever operator.

Cole Beck arrives at his father's ranch where horses are being broken in. As with *The Stalking Moon*, the "cowboy" elements are taken seriously. Normally, in this kind of picture, fathers are tough on errant sons, but Asa Beck (John Anderson) is indifferent to the death of the Indian. His men have captured a trespassing sheepman, Scotty Andrews

(Ed Bakey), and set about shearing him. "Send him back without a hair on his body," orders Asa Beck. Killian arrives when the man is bloody and scalped. "Turn him loose," says Killian. "I'm only going to say it once." Asa offers Killian double what the sheepmen are offering. Again, there is an edge of realism: Asa Beck would "rather pay" than lose two or three men in a shootout. Killian says he will give his answer the next day in town at noon. Twist number two: as Killian leaves, Scotty tries to hire him. So he's not a hired gun after all—or not yet. He gives Scotty the same answer: tomorrow at noon. High noon?

Back at his house, the Hopi girl, a half-breed we learn, cooks baby rattlesnake. Her father is dead, mother dead long ago; "Now I belong to you." Never has it been so brazenly put: Woman as chattel, a continuing undercurrent of the female in the western, is posited in realistic fashion. Killian is discomfited, not in the John Wayne-Gregory Peck old-cowpoke bashfulness in front of the opposite sex, but for proper reasons. He is an older man, she is young and vulnerable and he will not take advantage. But the scene ends with some stereotypical light comedy as he makes her take a bath.

Twist number three: Killian has turned the livery stables into a church and he intends to be a preacher. I know the title gave it away, but I assumed the title had something to do with how comfortable a man was with his weapon. As we later discover, there is a secondary meaning, relating to that very point. Although religion has been an integral part of many westerns, especially when it comes to funerals, the gunslinging preacher does not figure much in the canon. Mormon[14] and Quaker influence was seen in *Bad Bascomb* (1946), *Angel and the Badman* (1947), *Friendly Persuasion* (1956) and *Jubal* (1956), the latter also starring Ford, but there have only been a handful of preachers, most prominently Joel McCrea in *Stars in My Crown* (1950), Van Heflin in *Count Three and Pray*

Heaven with a Gun **screenwriter Dalton Trumbo had his name removed from the credits. Trade press advertisement—advertising supplement (Hannan Collection).**

(1955) and Robert Mitchum in *5 Card Stud* (1968). (Also, in a minor role, a preacher is one of the Good Men of Hadleyburg in *Mackenna's Gold.*) One of Beck's men challenges the idea of preacher-gunman: "No man can be both." Killian then proves his point by wounding two men who draw on him.

The various plots develop. On being taken to the store for new clothes, Leloopa fears she is going to be sold. Madge, worried that Killian has fallen for the girl, dresses her like a whore. When cattle-ranching husbands refuse to attend church in the presence of hated sheepmen, their wives intervene. Scotty is unable to come to terms with the prospect and kills one of Beck's men with shears. Twist four: Killian is a practical preacher, producing scientific argument that prove that cattle and sheep can share the same pastures and overcoming traditional suspicion that cows and sheep cannot drink the same water. "Why can't you fellows get along the way the animals do?" he asks. But his momentum is suddenly halted by the arrival of Mace (J.D. Cannon) and in twist number five we learn that Killian is a convicted murderer.

Despite this, some cattlemen and sheepmen agree to attempt to work in harmony, but Asa Beck remains opposed and his men set fire to Scotty's barn and house. The scalped man, now willing to give in, takes his wife to Santa Fe for safety. In a touching scene, two of Madge's whores tell Killian that Beck is planning to block access to the lake to sheepmen. The girls, almost in disguise attending church in normal attire rather than bordello outfits, say they will understand if Killian does not want them to attend church now he knows their profession. "If the Lord closed his house against sinners," replies Killian, "I don't think I'd be able to get by the front door." But the fragile position of women in the west is underlined when Cole Beck rapes Leloopa. Killian beats him up with fury, and walks down the street, past all those who might judge, with his arm around Leloopa. Aware how inappropriate it is to share a house with such a young girl, Killian arranges for a rancher to take her in.

A sequence rounds out the characters of the bad guys by touching on the realities of herding cattle. Asa Beck talks about the worth of what he does. "Night. Good moon out. Herd of cattle of your own. Gives a man a feeling that he has done something with his life important." Scotty returns and kills Cole Beck with shears before being shot by Mace. Furious, Asa sends messengers to call the other cattle ranchers to his side and dispatches four men, including Mace, to shoot Killian. While three men burn down the barn, Mace confronts Killian in the saloon. "You ever draw from a sitting position?" asks Mace, full of confidence. "I have. Takes a certain knack." Killian shoots him just the same. He kills two of the gang. Leloopa is felled by a horse's hoof and, when she recovers, she asks if she has to leave. When she is reprieved, the look on Madge's shows she has lost all chance of winning him back. The townspeople have put out the fire but the church is a blackened shell. Madge points to the waiting citizens: "To me, they've always been suckers. They pay too much to drink and then they pay to climb the stairs, but I never promised them Heaven up there." She tells him he has to choose between the gun and God. Killian walks into the church and in front of a blackened cross drops his rifle and unbuckles his belt.

Now, unfortunately, the movie falls apart. The message takes over. Pacifism can win. Killian rounds up a huge convoy of townspeople, mostly women, and sets out for the lake where he knows Beck's men are waiting to ambush the sheepmen. They abandon their wagons to clamber over the hills to reach the lake by sunrise and intervene. Beck fires a warning shot at Killian. The camera tracks Beck's rifle as it takes aim. But Beck is forced to back down by his foreman. Cue the theme song "A Lonely Place." Leloopa stands beside Killian while Madge, with consolation or perhaps incipient romance in mind, takes Beck's arm.

It's hard to say what is so awful about such a happy ending. Nobody is needlessly shot. Cattlemen and sheepmen can work together. Women have helped save the day. Yet it still seems contrived. Up that point, it had been well-knitted together, and if anyone is better suited to show the internal conflict facing a killer preacher, it is Glenn Ford. But the ending is so ridiculous, it verges on the sublime. Although the film sports many a cliché—gunman seeking redemption, etc.—and features lynching, rape and shearing, I found the first two-thirds impressive. Not quite a hidden gem, but not rubbish either, and certainly with more succinct storytelling than many other prestigious westerns that year.

Critical Response

Howard Thompson of the *New York Times* called it "plodding."

Box Office

Heaven with a Gun, one of the biggest flops of Glenn Ford's career, failed to find a place in the Annual Rentals Chart, which meant it earned less than $1 million.

Smith!

Starring Glenn Ford, Nancy Olson, Dean Jagger; directed by Michael O'Herlihy; screenplay by Louis Pelletier, adapted from *Breaking Smith's Quarter Horse* by Paul St. Pierre; Walt Disney; 112 minutes

Too Much Talent, Not Enough Story

You were pretty much down on your luck if you accepted the male lead in a Disney picture in the late 1960s. There was precedent, of course, largely in the shape of Fred MacMurray who had headlined *The Shaggy Dog* (1959), *The Absent Minded Professor* (1961), *Bon Voyage* (1962), *Son of Flubber* (1963), *Follow Me, Boys* (1966) and *The Happiest Millionaire* (1967), all comedies except the last, all hits except the last. Disney's other go-to star, Dean Jones (*That Darn Cat!*, 1965, *The Love Bug,* 1968), had a considerably less auspicious career than either MacMurray or Glenn Ford. And Disney was also down on its luck, reeling from losses incurred by *The Happiest Millionaire*, production cut to the bone with only three pictures scheduled for 1969.[15] However, Ford had another reason for taking on the role. He had Canadian Blackfoot Indian in his blood and held an honorary position with the Federal Bureau of Indian Affairs.[16]

Ford's co-stars were of the veteran variety. Nancy Olson (playing Norah, his wife) had made her debut in 1949 in *Canadian Pacific.* Earning an Oscar nomination for *Sunset*

Hollywood producers always looked on the bright side. The *Smith!* pressbook contained "slugs" that could be attached to posters saying "held over! 3rd action week!" It is unlikely that ever occurred. Pressbook (Hannan Collection).

Blvd. (1950) had given her enough leverage to star three times opposite William Holden (*Union Station*, 1950, *Submarine Command*, 1951, and *Force of Arms* 1951) and John Wayne in *Big Jim McLain* (1952). But her movie career went into cold storage following *Battle Cry* (1955) and afterwards she only worked for Disney in *Pollyanna* (1960), *The Absent Minded Professor* and *Son of Flubber* with another lengthy hiatus—she believed, oddly, that making fewer films would extend her stardom—until *Smith!*[17] Dean Jagger (Judge James C. Brown) went even further back, his first picture being *Woman from Hell* (1929). He had also been in Oscar's sights, winning Best Supporting Actor for *Twelve O'Clock High* (1949) and picking up meaty roles in *The Robe* (1953) and *Elmer Gantry* (1960). In the previous year he had appeared in two westerns, James Stewart's *Firecreek* and Ford's *Day of the Evil Gun*. Keenan Wynn (Vince Haber) would be seen in another pair of westerns in 1969, *Once Upon a Time in the West* and *Mackenna's Gold.* Colombian Frank Ramirez (Gabriel Jimmyboy) had been in three episodes of television series before *Smith!* However, the supporting cast featured three unusual actors: Warren Oates (as Walter Charlie), Chief Dan George (Ol' Antoine) and Jay Silverheels (McDonald Lashaway). Oates' rugged features seemed made for westerns. After coming to attention in the television series *Stoney Burke* (1962–1963), he had appeared in *Ride the High Country* (1962), *Major Dundee* (1965), *The Rounders* (1965), *The Shooting* (1966), *Return of the Seven* (1966) and *Welcome to Hard Times* (1967). "I started out playing the third guy on a horse and worked my way up to number one bad guy," he said.[18] Chief Dan George, son of a tribal chief and born on a reservation in north Vancouver, played, unusually, the same character Ol' Antoine in two episodes of the television series *Cariboo Country* (1960), one of *Festival* (1966)[19] and *Smith!*[20] Silverheels was more famous as Tonto in the television

Comic books and comic strips had been a part of the Hollywood promotional machine for many years when *Smith!* went down that route. Pressbook (Hannan Collection).

series *The Lone Ranger* and two movies, *The Lone Ranger* (1956) and *The Lone Ranger and the Lost City of Gold* (1958). Typecast ever since, he had only found work in television before *Smith!* Director Michael O'Herlihy, brother of actor Dan O'Herlihy, was making his movie debut while writer Louis Pelletier was a Disney regular responsible for *Those Calloways* (1965), *Follow Me, Boys* and *The Horse in the Gray Flannel Suit* (1968). Canadian author Paul St. Pierre campaigned for 20 years for recognition of the current problems facing Indians and was a representative in the Canadian Parliament. While his book *Breaking Smith's Quarter Horse* was based in British Columbia, the movie action was shifted to the Washington region and Idaho. The movie was filmed after *Heaven with a Gun*, but reached theaters earlier.

Smith! has more pertinent things to say about the position of the Indian than most of the revisionist westerns beginning to appear but not much else. In one part it is a traditional Disney family picture, with the Smiths happily married, and features important roles for two boys. Smith, raised by Ol' Antoine, is more sympathetic to their plight. The film begins with Smith returning home to his ranch where the Indian Jimmyboy has taken refuge after being accused of murder. Jimmyboy soon flees to a nearby cave where he is tracked down by the Smiths' ten-year old son and his friend, who keep his whereabouts a secret. Indian-hating sheriff Vince (Keenan Wynn) attempts to tracks him down. The son confides in his father, and Smith goes to the cave. Jimmyboy is gone: Ol' Antoine persuaded the fugitive to turn himself in, and been arrested himself. Smith initially only attends the trial because the Indians he is relying upon to help him bring in the harvest are there. He spends his savings going to the trial. Smith manages to free Ol' Antoine. When he discovers that the interpreter Walter Charlie is on the side of the sheriff, he dismisses the interpreter and takes the job himself. The highpoint of the trial, with Smith placed in the central dramatic role as the interpreter, does not focus on the actual allegations against Jimmyboy so much as a speech by Chief Dan George, who does not speak good English either, about the historic injustice Indians have suffered. Jimmyboy is freed and the Indians help him bring in the hay while Ol' Antoine begins breaking in the son's Appaloosa.

The film is not dramatic in the manner of Ford's previous westerns, nor is he central to many elements of the action and it is not his impassioned speech that saves the day but his interpretation of words actually spoken by Chief Joseph of the Nez Perce, who had defied a 3000-strong U.S. army in 1877 by leading his people on a 1000-mile march to the safety of the Canadian border. (He failed in the end and had to surrender.) Among the words spoken at the trial were the famous words, "From where the sun now stands,[21] we will fight no more forever."

Critical Response

Variety called it a "pleasant modern western" but nobody else had anything good to say about it, many critics being offended by its patronizing tone.

Box Office

It did reasonably well for a picture of its budget, bringing in $1.3 million in rentals. This may be partly due to the fact that it was sent out on a double bill with a reissue of the Disney favorite *The Incredible Journey* (1963).

5

Western as Opera

Once Upon a Time in the West

Starring Claudia Cardinale, Henry Fonda, Jason Robards, Charles Bronson; directed by Sergio Leone; screenplay by Ario Argento, Bernardo Bertolucci and Sergio Leone; Paramount; 165 minutes (cut for U.S. release to 144 minutes)[1]

Three Guys Meet ... in the Projection Booth

Just before Christmas 1966 in Rome, Sergio Leone, Bernardo Bertolucci and Dario Argento met in the projection booth of a screening of *The Good, the Bad and the Ugly*. At the time, Argento was a film critic and enthusiastic supporter of the first two *Dollars* films, but several years away from making his own directorial debut in *The Bird with the Crystal Plumage* (1970).[2] Bertolucci was the director of the critically acclaimed *The Grim Reaper* (1962) and *Before the Revolution* (1964). Soon afterwards, the trio began collaborating on the screenplay of *Once Upon a Time in the West.* This was despite Leone, on completion of *The Good, the Bad and the Ugly*, declaring, "I do not want to make any more Western films. I have finished with that kind of film, that kind of story."[3] He rejected an invitation from United Artists to direct Clint Eastwood in *Hang 'Em High*.[4] The collaboration lasted two to six months (opinions vary) until a story took shape about how the beginnings of the railroad, triggering a sea-change in the West, would displace the sometimes lawless pioneers,[5] a mythic tale about the ending of a myth, "a formidable fable of the twilight and resurgence of the American West."[6] The writers drew upon Nicholas Ray's *Johnny Guitar* (1954) for its baroque nature, John Ford's *The Searchers* (1956) for the massacre at the McBain ranch, *The Magnificent Seven* (1960) for the impassive Charles Bronson, George Stevens' *Shane* (1953) for the funeral, and John Ford's *The Man Who Shot Liberty Valance* (1962) to explore political pressure plus "all those films about the building of the railroad."[7] Leone employed five stereotypes (the lone avenger, the killer who wants to be a businessman, the idealistic outlaw, the whore, and the businessman with ambitions of becoming a gunfighter) as a framework to create a homage to the mythical west and "a cinematic fresco on the birth of America." Despite the time the three men spent together, they ended up with only 80 pages of script, and Leone then turned to Sergio Donati, uncredited contributor to *The Good, the Bad and the Ugly*, who wrote the script in 25 days, inventing the fly sequence and the idea of Morton, the railroad magnate, having no legs, that the railroad could bridge the Atlantic and Pacific oceans,

Paramount Pictures
Presents This Summer's
Great Boxoffice
Excitement
From Sergio Leone,
The Man Who Gave
The Old West A New Look
And Big Boxoffice.

A
SERGIO LEONE
FILM

CLAUDIA CARDINALE

HENRY FONDA JASON ROBARD

CHARLES BRONSON

IN

ONCE UPON A TIME IN THE WEST

WITH
GABRIELE FERZETTI · WOODY STRODE · GUEST STARS (IN ALPHABETICAL ORDER) JACK ELAM · LIONEL STANDER · PAOLO STOPPA · FRANK WOLFF · KEENAN WYNN · SE

PRODUCED BY FULVIO MORSELLA · EXECUTIVE PRODUCER BINO CICOGNA · MUSIC BY ENNIO MORRICONE · A RAFRAN-SAN MARCO PRODUCTION · TECHNISCOPE® · TECHNICOLOR® · A PARAMOUNT PICTURE

M Suggested for MATURE audiences (parental discretion advised).

Once Upon a Time in the West director Sergio Leone leased the area where the town of Flagstone was set for ten years, aiming to rent it out to other productions. Trade press advertisement (*Box Office*, June 2, 1969).

and much more of the detail.[8] Leone was not the first foreigner to take aim at the traditional American western: Fred Zinnemann (*High Noon*, 1952) and Fritz Lang (*The Return of Frank James*, 1940, *Western Union*, 1941, and *Rancho Notorious*, 1952) had both been born in Austria, while William Wyler (*Friendly Persuasion*, 1956, and *The Big Country*, 1958) had originated from Germany.[9] For Italians, this was more than a chance to rewrite history. According to Hank Werba, "Leone believes he will restore the plainsman in a more accurate perspective and thereby provide a more fundamental insight to the potent development of American civilization.... The big point ... is that his characters are truly representative of a period marked by violence and lawlessness and in which the survivors passed along the steel and spirit that placed America at the head of the world."[10]

Once Upon a Time in the West would be Italy's biggest movie since Dino De Laurentiis let John Huston loose on *The Bible* (1966).[11] With a $5 million budget,[12] "it would mark the biggest breakthrough to date in the American market [and] confirm that America can count on Italy to produce motion pictures for world audiences."[13] Euro-International, which committed $2.5 million to the western, had bankrolled 18 pictures costing $32 million with the U.S. a prime target, having set up a marketing unit there.[14] After considerable investment, Hollywood was beginning to question its financial exposure in Europe. As well as *Once Upon a Time in the West*, Paramount was funding or part-funding Lewis Gilbert's adaptation of the Harold Robbins bestseller *The Adventurers*, the Julie Andrews-Rock Hudson musical *Darling Lili*, Lindsay Anderson's *If...*, *Two Gentlemen Sharing* with Judy Geeson and Ester Anderson, Peter Medak's *Negatives*, *The Assassination Bureau*, the satirical World War I musical *Oh What a Lovely War*, Tony Curtis and an international cast in the comedy *Monte Carlo and All That Jazz* (*Those Daring Young Men in their Jaunty Jalopies*) and Sergei Bondarchuk's *Waterloo*.[15] With a budget 12 times larger than *A Fistful of Dollars*, *Once Upon a Time in the West* presented an opportunity to crack America—the *Dollars* films not the huge successes imagined[16]—and for this, Leone required stars with marquee appeal.

Atop his list was Henry Fonda. Leone wanted an "ignoble assassin ... and to act the part of such a bad man I needed someone who had always represented 'the good.' I needed Henry Fonda."[17] However much this was a great idea from the perspective of Leone, who imagined the shock an audience would experience at seeing the killer with those iconic baby blue eyes, it was also a miscalculation since Fonda had long-ago lost his box office cachet, no longer receiving automatic top billing after the dismal box office of *A Big Hand for a Little Lady* (1966) and *Welcome to Hard Times* (1967). His next film *Stranger on the Run* (1967) was made for television and after that he was reduced to second billing for *Firecreek* (1968) and *Madigan* (1968).[18] Nor did he bring to the project the iconic status Leone imagined, not being a frequenter of Oscar's high table, just two nominations 17 years apart, for *The Grapes of Wrath* (1940) and *Twelve Angry Men* (1957). The other problem was: Fonda did not want the job. He rejected the proposal until Eli Wallach's intervention,[19] whereupon he watched parts of the trilogy before signing up.[20]

Actor and director differed considerably in their interpretation of how the part should be played. In 1973, Fonda told an AFI seminar audience that he perceived the character as a traditional villain and had grown a mustache after the fashion of Gregory Peck in *The Gunfighter* (1950) and been fitted with dark contact lenses to hide his baby blues. When Fonda arrived on set, he was told to shave off the mustache and get rid of the contact lenses. "Where are the big blues?" Leone reportedly wailed. But it was only when he came to shoot the McBain scene that the actor realized the point of the blue

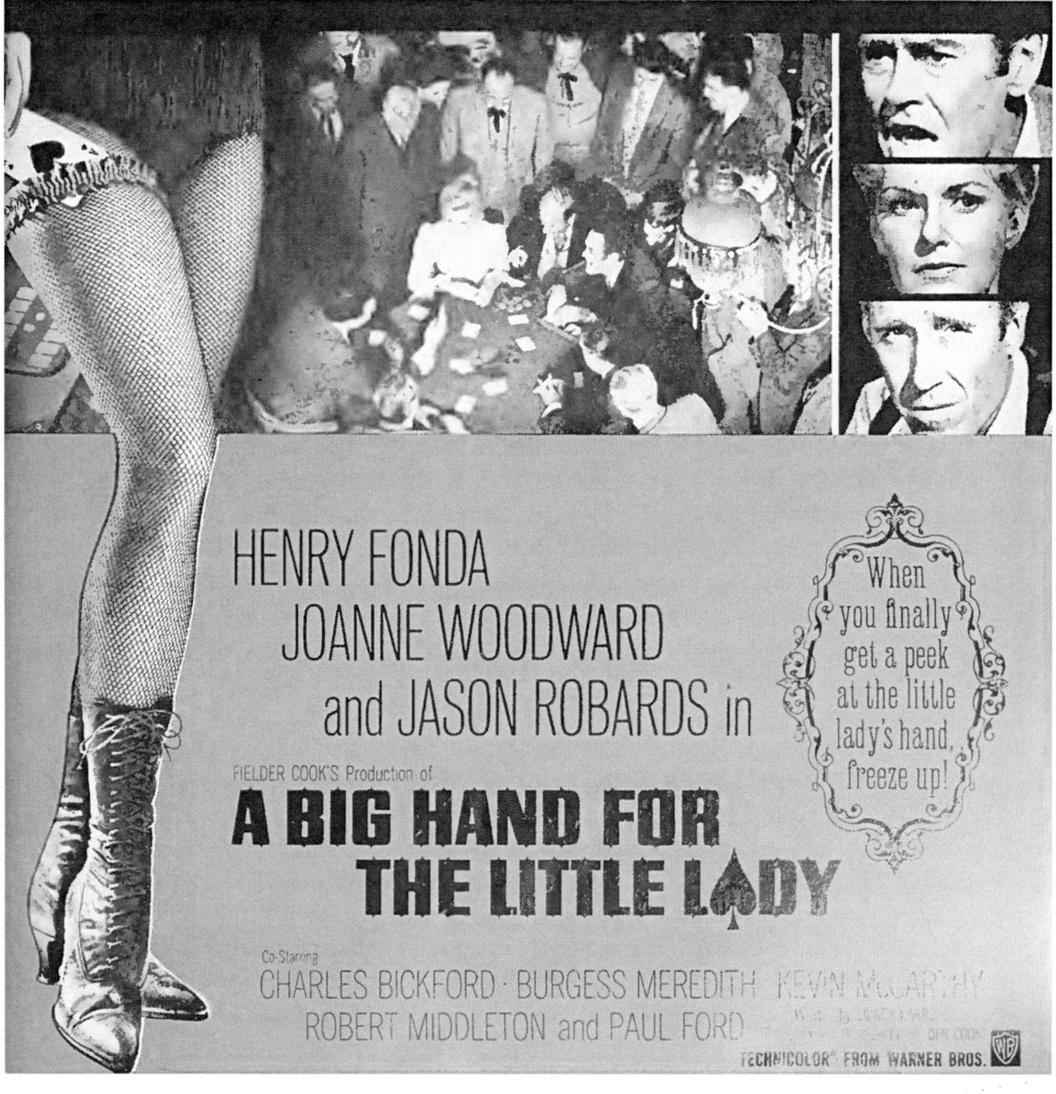

***A Big Hand for a Little Lady* was the second movie for director Fielder Cook. He made his directing debut a decade before with *Patterns* (1956). Trade press advertisement (*Box Office*, May 16, 1966).**

eyes. "That leaves a nine-year-old boy standing in the middle of the worst massacre you can imagine," recalled Fonda. He understood the audience reaction as the five gunmen approached the terrified boy and the camera cut to the leader of the gang: "Jesus Christ, it's Henry Fonda."[21]

But such realization of director intent did not smooth over other issues. They had different ways of working. The actor's obsession about finding the proper hat seemed over-meticulous to the director, although that revealed Leone's lack of experience with actors of the highest caliber who often fussed intensively over their costume or finding the correct pair of spectacles or the right kind of walk. Despite his reputation, Fonda saw himself as someone who took orders, and wanted to carry out those instructions exactly.

Leone did not understand why he was being pestered with "banal questions" such as which hand Fonda should use to hold a glass. Fonda, for his part, could not come to grips with acting to the sound of a tape of the score being played in the background, or to the long hours. Leone recollected:

> Henry seemed uneasy, uprooted in his unaccustomed role, as if he were embarrassed at finding himself in this different kind of part and it seemed to me that he was reacting with a performance which was monotonous and underdeveloped. Then finally I saw the rushes and it was my turn to say, "Now, I understand!" He had created such a mosaic of subtleties in his expression; he had designed a character so real and human that he ran the risk of having his personality overwhelm the other actors around him.[22]

At this point, Clint Eastwood, the most obvious choice for the monosyllabic Harmonica, was not an established Hollywood star and, indeed, still struggling to be offered leading roles. Although actor and director had fallen out on *The Good, the Bad and the Ugly*, Eastwood met with Leone. But after watching his erstwhile mentor act out the first 15 minutes of the picture, he turned down the role,[23] instead choosing *Hang 'Em High* (1968). That proved a wise decision since it pushed Eastwood up the Hollywood pyramid far faster than if he taken the Leone picture.[24]

Other names that came into the frame for Harmonica included James Coburn,[25] Terence Stamp, Rock Hudson and Warren Beatty,[26] Paramount was dead set against hiring Bronson,[27] who would be pushing 50 by the time the movie appeared and had never stepped up to movie stardom; he was regarded as a steady supporting actor in movies despite leading man roles on television. He had made his movie debut (as Charles Buchinsky) in 1952 in *My Six Convicts* and he had occasionally delivered an eye-catching performance: *The Magnificent Seven* (1960), *The Great Escape* (1963), and in a non-action role in *The Sandpiper* (1965). But he generally went straight back into television, and even after *The Dirty Dozen* (1967) his next gigs were in television's *The Virginian* and *Dundee and the Culhane*. The situation wasn't improved by the flops *The Guns for San Sebastian* (1968) and *Villa Rides* (1968) in which he received third-billing and fourth-billing, respectively. Disillusion with Hollywood sent him scurrying to France for *Adieu L'Ami* (1968),[28] a move that would, astonishingly, alter his fortunes. Harmonica came from the same cinematic mold as the Man with No Name. For Leone, Bronson had a "face made of marble ... a sort [of] granite block, impenetrable but marked by life ... always an impassive look on his face ... expresses sadness with his harmonica."[29] Bronson, realizing the significance of his role, and that he was not center stage in the way of Clint Eastwood, spent a great deal of time discussing with Leone how he should move, rather than, as with Eastwood, essentially stand still.[30] He remained granite-faced offscreen too. Claudia Cardinale recalled, "It was difficult to get a smile out of him," although he was not exactly immobile, continuously bouncing a rubber ball.[31]

Jason Robards was an unusual choice for Cheyenne. He was primarily a stage actor; that's where Leone first came across him and noted his "unsettling force of character."[32] In romantic films, he was the "leading man" rather than the star, second billed to Lana Turner in *By Love Possessed* (1961), to Jennifer Jones in *Tender Is the Night* (1962) and to Jane Fonda in *Any Wednesday* (1965). He was as likely to be a featured support, third billed in *A Big Hand for a Little Lady*, behind Fonda and Joanne Woodward, in *Divorce American Style* (1967) behind Dick Van Dyke and Debbie Reynolds, and in *Isadora* (1968), behind Vanessa Redgrave and James Fox. When he garnered a rare starring role, he was usually outgunned by a co-star, the acting plaudits for *A Thousand Clowns* (1965) going

Sergio Leone turned down an invitation to direct *Villa Rides* because he objected to Yul Brynner playing the lead. It was the first movie to feature Charles Bronson and his wife Jill Ireland. Trade press advertisement (*Box Office*, June 3, 1968).

to Martin Balsam who won the Best Supporting Actor Oscar. Britt Ekland as a stripper hogged the limelight in *The Night They Raided Minsky's* (1968). Kudos for his stage work was not replicated on screen: no Oscar nominations. Second-billed to James Garner in John Sturges' *Hour of the Gun* (1967), he had impressed as Doc Holliday[33] and believed Cheyenne was "tailor-made for him.... Jason Robards was as close to him as anyone could be." But screenwriter Sergio Donati disagreed[34]: "He's one of those actors who, in the industry phrase, doesn't translate to the big screen. He hasn't got any eyes, I think that's his problem."[35] It was not the only problem. Robards was an alcoholic, drunk during his interview with Leone. He was given a second chance at the instigation of his agent

Robert Ryan headed up *Hour of the Gun*'s Clanton Gang. Screenwriter Edward Anhalt had a small role in the picture. Trade press advertisement (*Box Office*, September 11, 1967).

and after agreeing to a penalty clause if he turned up drunk on set.[36] Leone saw Cheyenne as a kind of corollary to the Eli Wallach character in *The Good, the Bad and the Ugly*, "a mixture of drollery and sadness." However, as befitted his stage origins, Robards had an extraordinary voice, as evidenced in the post-synchronization. "[He was] one of the greatest dubbers I ever saw," said executive producer Fulvio Morsella, "he could really use his voice."[37]

Claudia Cardinale: "After Spaghetti, Italy's Happiest Invention"[38]

Perhaps by default, Leone already had his star—Claudia Cardinale—although she was not the only contender. An Oscar winner for *Two Women* (1960), Sophia Loren was in the running at the prompting of husband Carlo Ponti when he was potentially a funder. Leone commented: "I somehow couldn't see her as a tart from New Orleans"[39] despite the fact that she had been nominated for an Oscar for *Marriage, Italian Style* (1964).[40] Loren had starred opposite the cream of the Hollywood A-list—John Wayne (*Legend of the Lost*, 1957), Cary Grant (*The Pride and the Passion*, 1957, and *Houseboat*, 1958), William Holden (*The Key*, 1958), Clark Gable (*It Started in Naples*, 1960), Charlton Heston (*El Cid*, 1961) and Marlon Brando (*A Countess from Hong Kong*, 1967). She received top billing in *The Millionairess* (1960), *The Fall of the Roman Empire* (1964), *Lady L* (1965), *Operation Crossbow* (1965) and *Judith* (1966), several of which were big hits.[41] She was 34 in 1967 but with Fonda 62, Bronson 46 and Robards 45,[42] Leone might have feared a deadly case of middle-age spread. Cardinale, while not in the Loren class in terms of acting skill or box office appeal, was, along with Gina Lollobrigida, the next best thing, and currently pulling down $500,000 per picture.[43] While this paled alongside the director's reputed $750,000-plus percentage,[44] she was by far the best-paid actor on the movie. Tunisian-born, she was a 20-year-old beauty contest winner when she film-debuted in a minor role in *Goha* (1958)[45] with Omar Sharif. After signing a seven-year contract with Italian producer and future husband Franco Cristaldi, she moved quickly into the first rank of Italian female stars with roles in several artistic successes: Luchino Visconti's *Rocco and His Brothers* (1960) and *The Leopard* (1963) and Fellini's *8 1/2* (1963). Hollywood snapped her up for *The Pink Panther* (1963) and Samuel Bronston's *Circus World* (1964) and from 1966 onwards she worked almost exclusively in America: the female lead in the thriller *Blindfold* (1966) opposite Rock Hudson, the war film *Lost Command* (1966) opposite Anthony Quinn, the western *The Professionals* (1966) opposite Burt Lancaster, the comedy *Don't Make Waves* (1967) opposite Tony Curtis, the adventure *The Hell with Heroes* (1968) opposite Rod Taylor and the crime film *A Fine Pair* (1968) opposite Rock Hudson. While her box office was more spotty in the U.S. than Loren, she scored huge hits with *The Pink Panther* and *The Professionals*, the latter in particular almost a template for the kind of feisty heroine essayed by Raquel Welch in *100 Rifles*. But with solid gold marquee appeal in Italy, she was "a star who would satisfy the Italian investors."[46] In addition, she had reached a professional peak, winning the Best Actress David—the Italian equivalent of the Oscar—for her performance in *Mafia* (1968).[47]

Visconti described her as a "splendid cat … waiting to be petted … [but] who will become a tiger" while Fellini, conversely, had cast her as a earth mother figure.[48] Putting a woman center stage was a radical departure for Leone, not a fan of females in westerns.

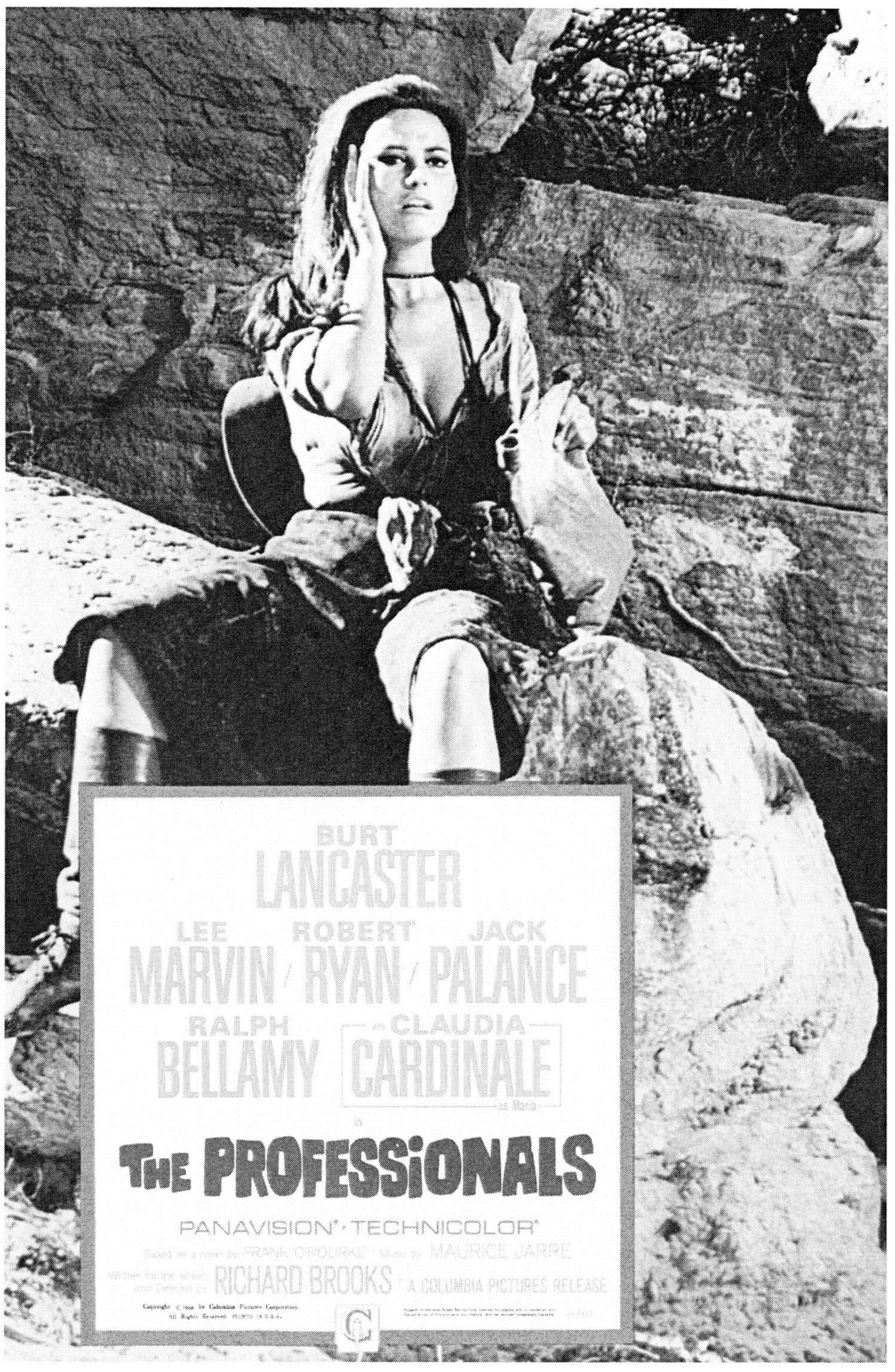

Frank O'Rourke, who wrote the novel *A Mule for the Marquesa* on which the movie *The Professionals* was based, also wrote the source material for *The Bravados* (1958) and *The Great Bank Robbery* (1969) (Hannan Collection).

He opined, "If you cut the woman's role out ... the film became much better"[49]; in his previous films, women were featured in stereotypical minor roles. It is interesting to contemplate how her role—and her billing—might have changed had Clint Eastwood consented to take part. Eastwood exuded a sex appeal that none of her co-stars could match, and that might have encouraged Leone to take advantage of sexual synergy of the kind that Jim Brown and Raquel Welch displayed in *100 Rifles*. On the other side of the coin, the fact that she was the unquestioned star, with top billing in both Europe and America (sometimes billing changed according to country, but not in this case), meant that her physical presence was central to a picture where, in reality, she was a pawn on a larger chessboard rather than, initially at least, the controller of her own destiny. In the end, she virtually ran the gamut of all the roles allocated to women in a western—the reformed whore, the submissive woman, the chattel, the object of lust, the spitfire—before finally emerging as the earth mother, bringing succor to the railroad laborers, but rich and the pioneer of a new town on the verge of a new era of civilization. In return, Leone used her charismatic features in trademark close-ups. Where Fonda found Morricone's music being played in the background off-putting, Cardinale welcomed Leone's distinctive approach to direction. She was already familiar with the music when he interviewed her for the part. She recalled:

> While he was speaking, we were listening together to the music of the film. And, while I listened, I understood every moment of the film, shot by shot, before seeing any of it on film.... Every time I had to act a scene, he would put on my music, the music for my character. And this really helped me to concentrate, to remove myself from the real world.[50]

She also benefited from shooting scenes in Monument Valley[51] which she felt exerted a "certain kind of emotion" and where the ghost of John Ford hovered; the crew was housed in the same accommodations as Ford.[52]

Just as with *100 Rifles*, the director began shooting with a love scene, Fonda and Cardinale. The principals suffered the same agonies of embarrassment as Brown and Welch, going into such an intimate scene not long after being introduced, the occasion not helped by the studio calling a press conference before the cameras rolled to announce "the first true love scene of Henry Fonda's entire career." Cardinale, against complete nudity, arguing her way out of such a scene in *The Professionals*, kept her scruples intact, and although naked there was not much on show. Of course, Leone, too, was filming the first love scene of his career and "betrayed his tension by always playing with something in his hands."[53]

Ennio Morricone: The Fifth Star

Music was so instrumental to Leone's films that it had made a star out of Ennio Morricone, the theme tune for *The Good, the Bad and the Ugly* even topping the singles charts in Britain. Written in advance, the music for *Once Upon a Time in the West* accompanied the director and stars on every location. The *Dollars* films had relied on unusual instruments and sound effects—the maranzano, choruses, whipcracks and pistol shots. By comparison, this score was almost sedate and in certain instances, such as Jill McBain's arrival in Flagstone, regulated "the speed of the crane ... in time with the musical crescendo." The main theme "summoned the wide open spaces" but the effect of the harmonica was "sinister." The sound of waves punctuated the theme for railroad boss Morton, even Leone's trademark whistling softer, while the final shoot-out built up into a stunning musical climax. Cheyenne's theme was rewritten at the recording studio after Leone had described the character in terms of "the Tramp" from Disney's *Lady and the Tramp* (1955). Also eliminated was music intended to be used for the opening sequence at the Cattle Corner Station, replaced by exaggerated natural sounds: the buzzing of the fly (attracted to the marmalade coating Jack Elam's beard), the creaking door, an irritating windmill, footsteps, the station agent's fearful voice, a caged bird, a cock, a slamming door, splashing water. "The best music I've ever composed," said Morricone, whose idea it had been to dispense with an orchestra.[54] Western films with significant theme tunes did not usually bind so closely to the action, *The Magnificent Seven*, for example, most copiously reproduced when the gunmen were riding across the landscape, the famous "Do Not Forsake Me, O My Darling" nowhere in evidence during the climactic scene in *High Noon*. Conversely, Leone filled the screen with music and sound effects, from the soaring operatic to the stop-start of Cheyenne's motif and the mournful harmonica. Morricone's contribution was deemed so significant that he was accorded billing on the advertising material.

From Monument Valley to Almeria

Shooting took place between April and July 1968, about the same time it took to film *The Good, the Bad and the Ugly*. There were four main settings: the Sweetwater ranch, the town of Flagstone, the railroad and the desert. First to be shot, in Cinecitta in Rome, the 500th production to be filmed there,[55] were the interiors, then the crew moved to Almeria and Granada in Spain for exteriors before heading to Monument Valley, chosen as much for commercial as artistic reason.[56] In Spain, Leone selected as locations Sierra de Baza and Sierra de Los Flibres because the coloring of the landscape was similar to the red earth found in Utah and Arizona.[57] The railway line near Estacion de Calahorra in Spain doubled for the Cattle Corner station sequence, which had a four-day schedule and was the last scene to be filmed in Spain.[58] Art director Carlo Simi built the two-story ranch house out of logs, outhouses and a stone well, speckled around with rosemary and sage bushes and olive and almond trees, that comprised Sweetwater close to the village of Tabernas, 30 kilometers from Almeria. The set of Flagstone—costing $250,000, more than the entire budget for *A Fistful of Dollars* (1967)—was a few hundred yards away, near the existing railway line, with the Sierra de Baza mountains forming a backdrop (Leone had leased a thousand acres of land there). The town was only half-built, as it would have been at the time while awaiting the completion of the railroad, but it was fitted out with station, hotel-saloon (at the heart of the town), barber shop, theater, offices, houses, etc. El Paso, Texas, was the inspiration for the set. Interiors were built for the saloon, stables, barber shop and station. The inn where Cheyenne meets Harmonica was deliberately dimly lit because bars in traditional westerns eschewed authenticity when it came to lighting. A shallow canyon on the way to Sweetwater had been set aside for the railroad. One of the locomotives was rebranded to resemble the 1875 "Genoa" type. The Morton train was designed in elegant fashion but the workers' train was basic. In Monument Valley, Leone used as background West Mitton Butte, East Mitton Butte and Merrick Butte on the Arizona side. The brick arch where Harmonica's elder brother was hanged was built 15 miles north of the valley on the other side. As much effort went into creating a rich seam of period detail: fading photographs, rosary beads, ancient documents in Sweetwater; sacks of feed, crates and barrels being unloaded from the train at Flagstone along with cattle, a soldier, a well-dressed little girl, black porters, carpetbaggers and a prospector.[59] The Flagstone set cost $500,000.[60] Leone's insistence on the long coats known as "dusters," originally derided by American critics, was based on his obsession with detail, this particular attire more practical than the tight pants favored in the traditional American western.[61] Leone strived for a specific look:

> I wanted to make the audience feel, in three hours, how these people lived and died—as if they had spent ten days with them: for example, with the three *pistoleri* at the beginning of the film, who are waiting for the train and who are tired of the whole business. I tried to observe the character of these three men, by showing the ways in which they live out their boredom ... so we had the fly, and the knuckles and the dripping water. They are bored because they are inactive.[62]

The Epic That Never Was

The full version of *Once Upon a Time in the West* is an epic in the way that *The Good, the Bad and the Ugly*, of comparative length, is not. Western epics had a poor record at the box office, the list of flops including *The Alamo* (1960), *Cheyenne Autumn* (1964) and *The Hallelujah Trail* (1965), with only *How the West Was Won* (1962) with an all-star cast and the benefit of the Cinerama widescreen escaping the curse.[63] The most important constituent of an epic is length and it is what the director does with such length that decides whether it is successful or not. Filling the time with countless characters and subplots is not the way. The best epics use the time to involve the viewer in the dynamics of the world they are entering. Films as different as *Lawrence of Arabia* (1962) and *Grand Prix* (1966) immerse you in their unusual locales, David Lean by taking the audience first on Lawrence's journey through the desert to meet Prince Faisal, then sustaining interest by further focusing on its desolation, beauty and inherent danger at the same time as establishing intimacy via Lawrence's scenes with Sherif Ali (Omar Sharif), his battles with authority and his battles with himself over the violence he unleashes. In similar fashion to Leone, *Grand Prix*'s John Frankenheimer used natural sound, the revving and roar of engines, at the start and concentrated on the danger and thrill of the races, driver rivalry the core of the drama; while there are numerous characters, their many deaths along the way emphasize the perilous nature of the sport. Frankenheimer's film is set in a small locale, or a series of them, in the cramped arena of a racing circuit and the garages, hotel rooms and houses the characters occupy. So while the audience receives a whirlwind tour of the world, the action and the resulting personal dramas are played out on similar stages every time. Lean used Lawrence's journey to engross the viewer; we see what he sees when he sees it. Leone, on the other hand, was dealing with familiar, rather than novel, locales. So although he used crane shots and long shots to establish panoramas (the vast stretches surrounding Cattle Corner, the isolated ranch house, Flagstone, Monument Valley), he only did so after he had created intimacy. We know the characters before we see the land. We watch the gunmen being annoyed by having to wait for the train prior to discovering where they actually are; we see Brett McBain shooting game and the young boy desperate to grow up imitating his father with a weapon fashioned from his fingers in advance of seeing the ranch; and we see the expectation and wonder on Jill McBain's face as she arrives at Flagstone before the majestic crane shot revealing where she is; and it is through her trip on the buggy out to Sweetwater that we see that world in its larger form, the forbidden emptiness of Monument Valley, a vast expanse dominated by monolithic structures that seem impossible to tame. Slow exposure, giving the viewer time to absorb detail and character nuance, is essential to the epic. *Once Upon a Time in the West* is deliberately, almost achingly, slow, as Leone evokes a world that the audience has never before seen in its entirety, comparing the broken-down, tired old Cattle Corner station with the new, youthful vigor exhibited at the Flagstone railroad, the thrifty regime at the ranch (where every slice of bread is counted) with the opulence of Morton's railroad carriage. An audience needs time to take this all in. There is a subtlety at work.

The movie begins, literally, in the old west, a cattle-loading bay that is already out of favor, in a railroad station long past its best, with a decrepit old man in charge. As the picture shifts from locale to locale, we see a new west unfold, an infant town taking shape, a different future being planned; we pass the workers pushing the railroad ever forward; and we see power transfer from a businessman as ruthless as any gunman to a woman from New Orleans who represents a more humane approach to the developing world. We begin with the kind of lawless ambush prevalent in the older days, the final shootout at the Sweetwater ranch almost a sideshow to progress, as the railroad sweeps ever onwards.

And there is mystery. Generally, the western is the most direct of all the genres, characters establishing from the outset who they are and what they want by action or dialogue. But Harmonica, Jill McBain and Cheyenne are all, on initial appearance, mysterious. Leone takes the conventions of the western and turns them upside down, not just in the reversals and plot twists that confound audience expectation, but in the slow recounting of the tale, where character motivation and action constantly change, and where everything is inevitably consumed by progress as the onset of civilization puts paid to a time when justice was meted out by the bullet.

Another director would have made shorter work of the opening sequences. For all we learn about character and story in the opening 20 minutes, it could have been heavily cut, beginning with the train pulling into Cattle Corner, the gunmen emerging from the station and the shootout; with Brett McBain struggling with his collar, brief exchanges with his children, and the shootout; with Jill McBain (excising entirely her arrival at Flagstone and the ride through Monument Valley) arriving at her husband's funeral; in other words, a speedier, action-filled opening. One attempted murder to establish Harmonica's speed with the gun; the ranch massacre showing Frank's ruthlessness; Jill arriving only in time to see her dreams evaporate; and still we would have the mystery of the who and the why. But that would be like asking Lean to cut back Omar Sharif emerging out of the horizon in *Lawrence of Arabia* or for Hitchcock to trim the endless scenes of James Stewart following Kim Novak in *Vertigo* (1958). There is something hypnotic in these two scenes and it is the same quality that Leone seeks from his western. Time is the enemy of all auteurs. The director wants us to stop thinking about time, to submerge ourselves in his version of the world, to fall under his mesmeric spell. And that is what the opening sequence sets out to do. This world is both cliché and original. We are over-familiar with desert backdrops, railway stations, gunmen hanging around, trains puffing in the distance. But Leone conspires to create a world contrary to our expectations. He invites us to linger in exquisitely observed boredom. He refuses to build tension in the normal fashion. There is no jagged score, the gunmen do not fiddle with their weapons;

there is not even a sense of impending showdown because we are not shown the opponent until the train has departed. But tension nonetheless builds, and in unique fashion. Leone has taken a shortcut to expectation by handing the roles of the three gunmen, Stony (Woody Strode), Snaky (Jack Elam) and Knuckles (Al Mulock[64]), to actors with iconic faces: Strode the good-guy muscular bowman from *The Professionals*, Elam's crusty face familiar from a dozen television series plus *The Rare Breed* (1966), *The Way West* (1967) and *Firecreek* (1968); and the Canadian Mulock who played the one-armed bounty hunter in *The Good, the Bad and the Ugly*. Yet only Snaky proves mean-spirited, treating the station master with lack of respect, pulling apart the telegraph wires, until the audience warms to him as he is tormented by a buzzing fly disturbing his rest.

Instead of music, there is a whole distorted symphony of sounds each as distinct as a single note played on a piano. In the first shots we hear a creaking door, chalk scraping down a blackboard, and the infernal rusty windmill before the camera pans up to Stony. The toothless, beaky station master (Antonio Palombi[65]) looks round to see Snaky silhouetted at one door and the camera tracks left to show Stony at another.[66] We see a squaw in the background as three men enter. There is a caged bird. Stony blows away the tickets the terrified station master hands him and a cock crows in the background as the old man is shoved into a cupboard. A door slams and the first title slides in from the side. Stony puts his hat on and we see the squaw running off into the desert and the exterior, with the words Cattle Corner painted on a water tower, and the wide stretch of timber revealing a working station whose only purpose is the loading of cattle on and off trains. As Stony strides across the wooden planks, the windmill noise almost drowns out his footsteps and he walks past Snaky sitting in a rocking chair. A crane shot of Stony walking reveals cattle pens in the background and grassland and isolation. The man stops, we realize, at a vantage point. Knuckles is at the water trough at the other end of the planking. The two men have taken up positions. Then Snaky hears the ticker tape of the telegraph. Annoyed, he leans over and tears out the wires and then, satisfied, leans back and tips down his hat. Stony is fanning himself in the heat with his hat but puts the hat on when his bald scalp is hit by dripping water. He could move, but does not, because he has chosen his position and because he is impassive, as impervious to disturbance as his colleague is irritated by it. Knuckles sees a whining dog and starts to crack his knuckles. The fly lands on Snaky's beard and he pantomimes trying to blow it off. We cut to Knuckles cracking his fingers and back to the fly as Snaky rocks in his chair and blows through the side of his mouth. We have a close-up of Stony, ignoring the sound of water dripping on his hat. We hear the windmill and the fly. Snaky captures the fly in the barrel of his gun, a low-key example of the speed of his reactions. The buzzing becomes high-pitched. Snaky puts the pistol containing the fly to his ear and rocks away, happy.

The sound of a train is heard. We see the train from underneath and hear screaming brakes. Stony drinks the water that has gathered in his hat. We hear the fly and the train. Knuckles sees the train approaching. Stony loads his rifle. Snaky gets to his feet and they all move in the direction of the railroad and we can see that they are spread out, positioned to cover the train's arrival. Carriage doors open, trunks are thrown out. The men move together. The train pulls out. Without showing any puzzlement or confusion, the men turn away from the train.

We hear the sound of a harmonica. The men turn in a four-shot, Shaky and Knuckles in dusters on the left, Harmonica in the middle and Stony wearing jeans and shirt on the right. There is a close-up of Harmonica accompanied by the instrument's haunting refrain. Letting go of the instrument, Harmonica asks, "Frank?" Snaky says, "Frank sent us." "You bring a horse for me?"

Snaky grins, "Looks like we shy one horse." Harmonica responds, "You brought two too many." Another four-shot, this time with Harmonica on the right in deep background and the others spaced out. Snaky reaches for his gun but Harmonica shoots first and guns them all down while taking a bullet from Stony. We cut to the windmill and its ragged sound. We cut to a close-up of Harmonica's eyes. He gets up to the sound of the windmill. This whole sequence lasts seven minutes and we learn very little except that gunmen get as bored doing their jobs as anyone else and that Leone has pulled out the first of many reverses, for in *High Noon* it is the villain who is met at the station. The opening has a hypnotic quality. Nothing happens until death. Harmonica has been double-crossed by Frank, but who Frank is and why this meeting has been arranged and why Harmonica needs to die is another reverse, because normally at the start of westerns we are left in no doubt about character and motivation. This is not, then, a western, it's a mystery. Although there are a limited number of locations (ranch, train, hotel, town), we never return to Cattle Corner Station.

We cut to a rifle poking out of the grass. We hear shots. Birds fly up. We get a close-up of red-haired Brett McBain (Frank Wolff[67]). There is no establishing shot of the terrain. Where are we? A young boy, running after the birds, pretends to shoot.[68] The boy comes running up the slope with dead birds in both his hands and races past the camera, which then shows in the background the ranch nestled at the foot of the mountains with a table laid out in front. As she prepares the spread, Brett's freckle-faced daughter Maureen hums "Danny Boy" (the only music so far, and that is off tune, the rest of the sequence relying again on sound effects and sound's dangerous opposite in this wilderness—silence). We get a close-up of McBain as he responds to sudden silence. His older son Patrick gets into trouble for not being ready to go to the train station and meet his mother. The boy snaps, "My mother died six years ago." The sound of the slap he receives for this response is like a whip crack. McBain tells his daughter that the woman will be "wearing a black dress and the same straw hat she was wearing when we met." McBain, who has just whacked his son, now looks dreamy and romantic. Maureen fetches fresh water from the well, the older boy leads out the buggy. There is silence again and the wind ominously blows up dust. The boy is on the buggy. Birds fly up and Maureen, smiling, watches them. There is the sound of a shot. McBain's eyes go to the sky, thinking someone is hunting the birds. In long shot, he sees Maureen stumble and fall. He runs towards her. Two shots hit him and Patrick. The younger boy comes running out of the house. His face in close-up is accompanied by momentous chords of music. In long shot, we see three men in dusters emerging from the bushes. They wait for another man who strides forward past them to the front. (Convention dictates they let the boy go, that they turn away, job done; the audience knows this.) Instead, the five men converge on the boy. There is a two-shot, in the tradition of two men facing each other in a duel, of the boy and the leader of the gang. The camera pans around to show Frank's face (first audience gasp—it's Henry Fonda!). He is chewing tobacco. Close-up of Frank, close-up of the boy, a terrified innocent freckled face straight out of Disney casting, a shot of the five men. One says, "What we gonna do with this one, Frank?" Frank replies, "Now that you've called me by name," as if seeking an excuse when, as we learn later, execution is unavoidable in case the boy stands to inherit. Frank draws his gun and points. Close-up of the boy, close-up of Frank. Those baby blues. A bell rings. The gun fires.

Cut to: screaming brakes as a train in a distant haze hauls into Flagstone. Cattle are unloaded and we see a beautiful woman, Jill McBain (Claudia Cardinale), in the aforementioned straw hat, delighted and expectant leaning out of a railway carriage. "Flagstone City" (not just "Flagstone" and not "Flagstone Town" for this place has ambitions) is painted on a water tower, as though the purpose of this tower and that of Cattle Corner is to establish locality when, in reality, the towers are the most vital part of any enterprising community, for without water the trains cannot run and the cattle, removed from pasture, will die. This station is considerably more animated than dead-end Cattle Corner, and all sorts of people harboring myriad dreams emerge from the train, businessmen and families and gold prospectors. Then we cut to Jill looking at a clock showing 7:55 and she is puzzled and sad. Her theme swells up and in the most glorious shot of the whole picture the camera pans up from the station building (painted, new, solid and not inhabited by decrepit old men) in a crane shot that for the best part of a minute pulls up to show us the busy half-built town.

Then Jill is on a buggy staring at buildings as they pass, an attorney-at-law, clothing, a co-operative, but in all the openness there is still mystery. Sam the buggy driver (Paolo Stoppa[69]) dashes the last of Jill's hopes when he calls her destination, Sweetwater, "a stinking piece of desert" and Brett McBain "a loony." But not everyone welcomes progress, as shown when Sam lashes his buggy to force the railroad workers to step aside (he risks unemployment if trains replace buggies as the preferred mode of transport). Leone lavishes more music on the Monument Valley scene, as the buggy rolls through it in long shot, and without question the most obvious nod to the influence of John Ford. However, this is not the old west of John Ford, with John Wayne leading a cavalry expedition against marauding Indians. This is a landscape that has, to some extent, been tamed, for the buggy does not trundle through an entire wilderness, instead it follows a well-worn track.

We know what lies ahead for Jill, there is no tension left to extract, so Leone can afford to pull off to the side to introduce the movie's final character. Sam stops at what is very much a working man's saloon. It's not the usual drinking parlor of a town with honky-tonk music and whores, but an all-in-one blacksmiths, stables, accommodation, bar, bathing house (bath "only three people used it this morning"). When McBain enters, it is only in part with wariness and for the first time we see the beginnings of something heroic beneath the flashy clothes and the beautiful face. She is not a feisty Cat Ballou or Sarita from *100 Rifles*, quick with fist and gun, but she is not the timid pampered female her attire might suggest, and she is not afraid of entering such establishments. We learn she's from New Orleans (another twist, actually, for strangers in westerns rarely say where they come from). From outside we hear horses neighing and pistol shots. Jill stares at the door. Conventionally, when shots are heard outside, it is a dying man who enters, usually facing the bar. In this case, Cheyenne (Jason Robards) stumbles in backwards. Close-up of Cheyenne. We hear his strange clippetty-cloppitty stop-start theme as if his identity is not as fully established as that of Harmonica or Jill. When he drinks at the bar, we see he is handcuffed. In truth, this is an awkward sequence, a rambling means of introducing Jill to Harmonica and Cheyenne, the attempts to mislead the audience by creating create tension between Harmonica and Cheyenne misplaced, while the method of releasing himself from the handcuffs is laborious (could he not have shot through the chains himself?). Its primary purpose is to over-extend mystery: Were Cheyenne's men responsible for the ambush on Harmonica?

To get the right kind of faces in the background, *Once Upon a Time in the West* director Sergio Leone paid $14 a day to locals with the requisite British, American and Scandinavian looks. Pressbook (Hannan Collection).

Jill arrives at Sweetwater in time for the funeral, the bodies laid on the same tables we previously saw bearing the food for her reception. She tarries over the corpse of McBain but she strokes the cheek of the dead Timmy, the younger boy, in a wholly female gesture that immediately makes the audience warm to her. We discover that Jill and Brett are already married. What merely appears poignant acquires greater plot significance, since inheritance is the key to the story. Cheyenne's involvement in the massacre is hinted at by the discovery of a piece of cloth from the dusters. Jill is urged to leave, but she retorts, "This is my home." This appears another poignant moment, but Jill has reasons beyond sentiment for staying. She upends the ranch house looking for, we assume, money. She finds her wedding bouquet. In the ranch house, as throughout, Leone accords his star plenty of close-ups and often the only opportunity we have of measuring her state of mind is through these close-ups. Cardinale does an excellent job at various times of portraying her torment, fear, anger and toughness.

Harmonica accosts a man at the laundry, almost strangling him as he pulls his necktie through a wringer. The man had been charged with setting up the meeting between Harmonica and Frank that ended in, we now realize, betrayal and ambush. Barely minutes after Cheyenne's potential involvement in the McBain massacre has been introduced, it is resolved, Harmonica determining that one of Frank's ploys is "faking evidence."

Back at the ranch, Jill finds toys—of the town, a station sign, a train. Then we hear, offscreen, the harmonica. She blows out the lamp, but does not cower and, not intimidated, reaches for a rifle in the manner of someone familiar with the weapon and without hesitation begins blasting out the window. She appears to have kept watch all night, for in the next shot it is morning and she returns the rifle to the wall, tidies herself and without a word picks up her bag and gets ready to leave. Cheyenne, not Harmonica, enters. He has been on the run. He asks her to make coffee. But domesticity, it transpires, is not her strong suit, or perhaps she is accustomed to less basic circumstances, and it is Cheyenne who has to light the fire. Now that she is in the same room as her family's killer, she toys with killing him. Even in supposed civilization, she, like any of the men, is prone to savagery and revenge. Cheyenne appears to be toying with her: "So this here's where I'm supposed to do the killing." McBain misinterprets, expecting further violation, as if this is a condition to which a woman of these times must become accustomed (but also a clue as to her profession), and she says that even if men take her, "I'll still be what I was before," that is, someone with a real identity, with an inner resolve that cannot be broken. Along with Mattie in *True Grit* and Sarita in *100 Rifles*, Jill is one of the toughest female characters in the 1969 western, but she is also the most rounded character, not driven solely by revenge, but given opportunity to express warmth and love as well as submission and determination and, above all, unflinching self-appraisal.

Curious reversals are at play in the scene in the carriage of railroad magnate Morton (Gabriele Ferzetti[70]). It is the crippled businessman who shows remorse at killing all the McBains, the killer who acts the entrepreneur ("It happens in business") and the magnate who harbors a sentimental dream of seeing the Pacific. Frank appropriates his boss' chair, cigar and whiskey, but Morton reminds him, in a premonition of the future, that money can control gunplay. Back at the ranch, Jill explains that she was ready to exchange her life in New Orleans to become a housewife, have kids. Cheyenne is not taken in, believing there is still "money left around somewhere," and he introduces a different concept of Jill, contrary to the one which has already impinged on audience imagination, that of earth mother. But she is not convinced she has any future here and is taking her bags to the buggy in the outhouse when she hears the harmonica again. This time it is Harmonica. "This isn't the time to leave," he informs her, and then proceeds to strip her (with an intimation of rape) of the finer parts of her clothing, ripping off the lace, until her cleavage is revealed. Harmonica orders her to fetch water from the well. The last time that instruction was issued, the audience is aware, was prior to the massacre. It is also the fourth visual or verbal reference to water.

We cut to a pair of riflemen on the slopes above the ranch and they ride down and are shot by Harmonica. We cut to Cheyenne watching, with the suggestion that he has also appointed himself guardian, expecting such an attack. Leone's previous heroes never held such high principles; whatever they did was for money. Now we have two men conspiring to keep her alive. But it is not so clear-cut as all that. Both hold grudges against Frank and it is entirely possible that she is being kept alive as future bait.

Harmonica tells the laundryman he knows everything and wants to negotiate with Frank, then follows the underling to Morton's train. Frank spots Harmonica's shadow on the roof, and Harmonica is captured. We see hazy flashbacks of a younger Frank. Frank kicks the laundryman out of the train and shoots him. As he falls to the ground, we cut to Cheyenne perched underneath. Harmonica begins reciting his litany of the people Frank killed. Interrupted by Morton, Frank goes after Jill. Cheyenne demonstrates his skills by shooting the guards, one through a boot. Jill is beginning to piece the mystery together, seeing the piles of lumber and nails close to the ranch, and the sign for a station, but inside the ranch Frank is waiting, holding the toy sign. Morton goes to Frank's hideout to make a deal but Frank kicks away his supports to make him crawl. Cheyenne and Harmonica at the lumberyard are also making connections. This material is for building McBain's town, the ranch having the only water for miles around, but McBain will lose the rights to the land if the station is not built by the time the railroad line arrives. Cheyenne sets his men to work.

The love scene, if it can be called that, is one of the most unusual ever filmed. In the background is Jill's theme as ironic counterpoint to the action. Jill is submissive to Frank. Does she fear being shot like the rest of the family? Is she simply acting like a whore and pretending to be attracted to a client? Is she submissive to the more powerful male? Or is she attracted to the rich man, the way she was to Brett McBain, who can take her away from New Orleans? We never find out because Leone gives all the dialogue to Frank, who takes pleasure in pointing out that she is in the "hands of the man who killed her husband." He asks, "Is there anything in the world you wouldn't do to save your skin?" But she has lost that kind of pride long ago. Where she comes from, pride like that can get in the way of ambition, in the way of staying alive. He taunts her with his knowledge that she was a high-class whore. Throughout, she does not react, playing the role of a whore who submits to a man's desire, whatever that might be. "I could marry you and the land would be mine," he teases, but there is also another solution, "quicker, simpler," leaving the audience imagining, with the way his hands crawl over her body, that he intends strangulation. But the price for a wannabe businessman is the need to follow, or be seen to follow, the rules and so an auction is held at the hotel. Meanwhile, to keep the subplot ticking along, Morton hires Frank's men to kill Frank. No outlaw is more ruthless than a businessman. It is not quite a fair auction, Frank's gang silencing anyone foolish enough to bid. But Harmonica has the money and though not in ready cash and—in similar fashion to *Heaven with a Gun*—has an audacious plan, paying for it by the $5000 reward for Cheyenne, bringing the outlaw in at gunpoint.

At the hotel, Jill tells Harmonica, "You don't look like the defender of poor, defenseless widows." When Frank arrives, Jill goes upstairs for a bath (water again). It should be a classic confrontation. Instead it is both a reversal and a logical development. Frank, too, is effecting a transformation in this new world of progress and civilization and, now "a real businessman" rather than a killer, offers to buy the land for one dollar over the $5000 price paid. Harmonica declines but, sensing an ambush outside, goes upstairs, kicking open the door of Jill's room, where she is in the bath, and from the vantage point of the window helps his adversary avoid being killed by his own men. Jill is outraged: "You saved his life." Harmonica offers a different perspective: "I didn't let them kill him and that's not the same thing." Frank returns to the train where he finds the other men dead and Morton outside in a ditch, still dreaming of reaching the Pacific (not just water, but the sounds of waves) before he dies.

Harmonica and Frank revert. They ignore progress, civilization. They are two ruthless, relentless killers. Outside the ranch, they come together for a showdown. When Frank says, "Nothing matters now, not land, not money, not women," he is speaking for them both. Harmonica may be a justified killer but that is the thin line civilization will not cross. In contrast to this, Cheyenne is making sure that civilization is helped along its way, sending Jill down with water for the laborers finishing the railroad approaching the completed Sweetwater railroad station. "And if one of them should pat your behind, just make believe it's nothing." He is making one obvious point here: If men are going to be men, women will just have to accept it. But he is also making a subtle point, that Jill is a fine woman, not a whore any more, and normally a woman like her would not tolerate such behavior, but she would be doing the men a kindness, like a queen consorting with her subjects, by disregarding such offensive groping. Jill, of course, has put up with worse, but he is doing her a courtesy all the same.

For the climactic scene, you have the impression Leone wanted to create the greatest-ever screen showdown. That, of course, is unmistakable, but he is equally conscious that most of the previous shootouts, including many in the legendary category, take a huge chunk of artistic license in a bid to keep things clear and simple and not muddied by the semantics of gunplay. So here he has Frank first of all getting comfortable, removing a cumbersome jacket that would inhibit arm movement. Nor does Frank advance towards his opponent in a straight line in the way gunslingers do in every western main street, but circles him, to gain advantage, to find, as the three *pistoleri* at Cattle Corner, the best position.

Other directors don't use music quite the way Leone does. Where Frank moves, Harmonica remains still, and the camera tracks Frank but pans round Harmonica's face as he watches Frank circle. Frank halts in center screen. Now Harmonica closes the gap. There is silence except the wind. A close-up of Frank is followed by one of Harmonica. Then we discover Harmonica's explanation, the reasons for this pursuit, in flashback, not by monologue. Harmonica, as a child, keeping his hanged brother aloft on his shoulders, tears streaking down his cheek, knowing that if he moves his brother dies, Frank approaching the boy, sticking the harmonica in his mouth, the boy stumbling. As the boy falls in flashback, in the present day Frank and Harmonica shoot. Cut to Jill. Frank tries to holster his gun but twists and drops it and falls. Still mystery. "Who are you?" croaks Frank. By way of explanation, Harmonica rams the instrument in his enemy's mouth. Whether Frank has time to register this before he dies is a moot point, but, anyway, is death not usually meted out in the old west by a stranger?

There is a curious ambiguity at the finale. In merely surviving, Jill is rich. She has left New Orleans in search of a new life and now she has it. But still she looks back, beyond the invitation of independence, free to make her own choices without the need to submit to a man or his desires. Instead, she makes a play for Cheyenne: "You're sort of a handsome man." Cheyenne has acquired sudden wisdom: "But I'm not the right man and neither is he" (meaning Harmonica). Jill is setting the table with the red-checked tablecloth that Maureen used at the beginning. She tells Harmonica, "I hope you'll come back some day." Harmonica replies, "Some day." As Harmonica departs, Cheyenne slaps her butt and mutters, in his wisdom, "Make believe it's nothing."

But there are no tears as Jill watches both leave. Out of her vision, Cheyenne comes off his horse. (He has been wounded while escaping the guards taking him on a train to prison.) He dies with Harmonica watching over him. The train arrives. The camera catches the station sign. Laborers leap off the moving train. Jill's theme swells up as she emerges from the house carrying flagons of water and the camera pulls back in one final shot to establish the new era and the earth mother in its midst and then the camera tracks across to see Harmonica trotting away, leading the corpse of Cheyenne tied to his horse.

The slowness of the movie permits reflection. In the edited version, the longest

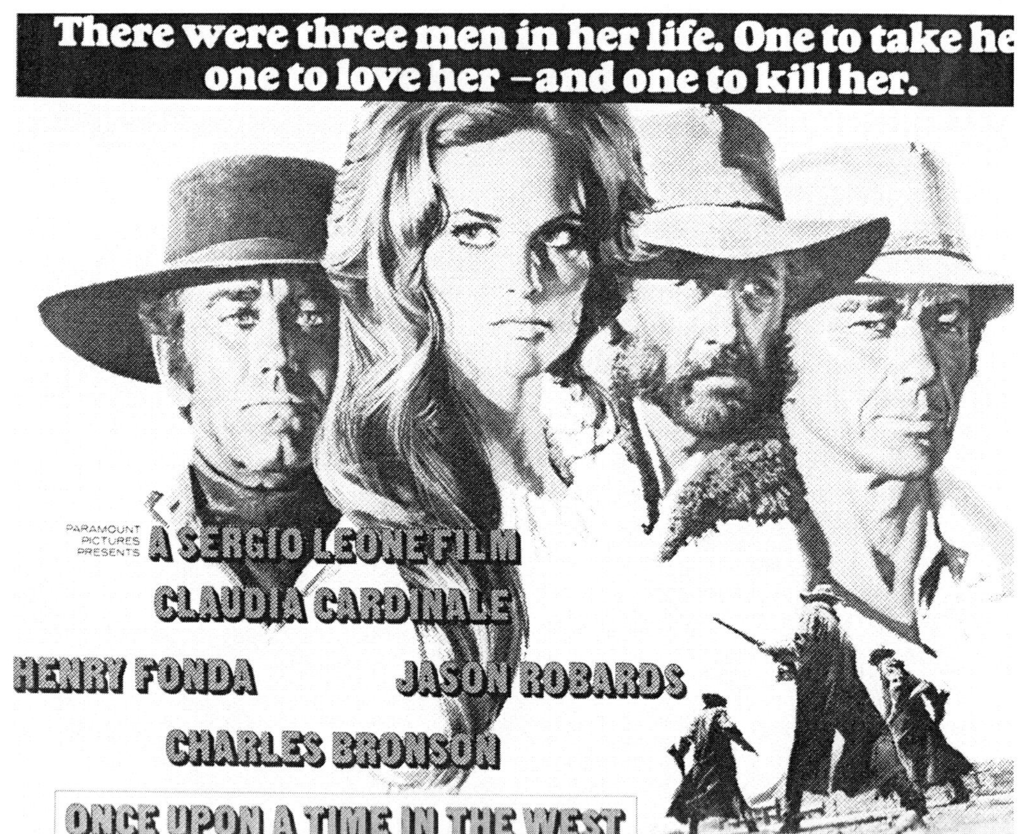

Claudia Cardinale enjoyed an unusual contract with her management team Vides Productions in Italy: She was paid a monthly salary whether she worked or not. This allowed her to reject inferior material (Hannan Collection).

sequence eliminated is the trading post sequence where three "good guys" meet, but in the extended version that does appear as a longer scene, and since length is a major constituent of the epic, its inclusion puts the viewer into a more relaxed, contemplative mode. Admittedly, *Once Upon a Time in the West* does have, for such a straightforward story, a convoluted subplot, of double-crossing and betrayal, and, were it not for Cheyenne's philosophizing you could almost believe his only role was as a *deus ex machina*, to provide a reason for rescuing Harmonica on the train, and to act as the guarantor in the deal to buy the land. So it is, for good reason, a mixture of lawlessness and lawfulness, of barbarity and civilization, as one era of the west gives way to another. Frank orders an ambush and a massacre but still follows the rule of law to acquire land he might have done obtained more easily by eliminating Jill. The civilized businessman Morton turns to the unlawful when he needs to get rid of Frank. Harmonica helps the villain escape death only for the pleasure of killing him himself. Jill drifts between the good and the easy, between carrying out Brett's wishes and submitting to Frank, between taking on the responsibility of Sweetwater station and living under the protective wing of Harmonica or Cheyenne.

Yet only Jill seems capable of change. Though she is prevented from escaping, she sees how easy it is to become wrapped up in a dream, of moving from New Orleans to

Sweetwater in search of a proper home and family life, and finally she comes to accept her fate as earth mother, even if some of the men might still treat her as a saloon girl in their patting of her butt. You can almost sense her sense of pride in ownership, in becoming part of a new kind of world, of identity, when she strides out with a smile on her face to bring solace to the workers. Of course, it is a fable, the railroad did not bring peace and prosperity to the west, and trains were robbed as much as banks, and the Wells Fargo stagecoaches, which had assisted many to move west, went out of business, and the railroad workers who died by the hundreds to build the new iron highways were not compensated by grateful magnates; instead the magnates grew wealthy beyond imagination, and more corrupt as they created a new class that came to dominate the American labor market for the next century.

Outside of such oversimplification, Leone's picture reflects the changing nature of the Wild West and investigates the means by which it is tamed. Those who cannot accept civilization have to move away or they are steamrolled. The western movie stereotypes on which Leone grew up are brought to vivid life and move through the film with a self-awareness that is lacking in most westerns. Strangely, the driving force of the story is often mystery: Jill does not know the true aspirations of her husband nor why he should die; Frank does not know who hunts him; Cheyenne does not know why he should be set up; even Morton is mystified when his protégé turns against him. Of course, the deeper nuances of the film are not as immediately as visceral as the camerawork and the music, the violence is not dwelt upon as in *The Wild Bunch*, nor relationships romanticized as in *Butch Cassidy and the Sundance Kid*. The Indian threat, which underpins *The Stalking Moon* and *Tell Them Willie Boy Is Here*, is non-existent. The whore, the outlaw, the killer, the gunman and the businessman are given an extraordinary cinematic framework. Some scenes are shot with stunning directorial bravura: Cattle Corner, the crane shots at Flagstone, Monument Valley, the emergence of Frank from the bush, the baby blue eyes of innocent Timmy staring into the baby blue eyes of the killer, the funeral, the love scene in which one of the participants does not know whether she will be alive at the end of it, Frank surviving in Flagstone with the aid of Harmonica, and the final shootout. But there are many other scenes that demonstrate character with simplicity, Snaky's fly, Harmonica as brutal in his treatment of the laundryman as Frank, the cripple Morton pulling down his lattice grid as if that will provide all the assistance he will need, and Jill, alone in the ranch house, tormented by her thoughts, her golden dream dashed.

Leone thought he was making "a labyrinth," a movie where the parts were so closely interconnected that to remove one piece was to destroy the whole picture. Even with Paramount's interference over the running time, the film's themes remain intact, but over the years greater significance has attached to the visuals and the music, in the same way that *Vertigo* has grown in critical and public esteem because the film exerts a hypnotic quality that no amount of words can replicate.

Critical Reception

Leone's *Dollars* trilogy had not gone down well with the critics in America or Britain, though the new style was welcomed in Europe, particularly in Italy and West Germany, where this type of western flourished, and in France where the critics appreciated the director's artistry. It was a critical and box office success in France where it opened around

Christmas 1968, but Paramount grew nervous about its reception in the U.S. According to accepted lore, this was following a negative reaction to a preview screening, but in fact the decision had been made long before the movie was unspooled anywhere in the U.S. In February 1969, it was reported that Paramount would release the film in a 150-minute version in the U.S.,[71] in reality a 144-minute version, with 24 minutes cut from the 168-minute feature shown in Italy, removing the meeting of Cheyenne and Harmonica (and Jill) at the inn, a two-minute scene between Morton and Frank (which, in reality, does not make much sense), a shorter scene of Frank returning to Morton's carriage and the death of Cheyenne. There was precedent for editing Leone films: *A Fistful of Dollars* had lost five minutes between Italian debut and American launch, *For a Few Dollars More* two minutes, and *The Good, the Bad and the Ugly* 19 minutes followed by further cuts when it went into general release.[72]

The editing of *Once Upon a Time in the West* did not have the desired effect. *Variety* was on the whole positive ("an extraordinarily regular beautiful flow of images") but doubted whether the film "could capture and sustain a wider audience" partly because of its length and partly because it was a "straight" western rather than the "camp" style of the director's previous work.[73] Roger Ebert in the *Chicago Sun-Times* also had mixed views, calling it "good fun" but complaining, in response to the running time, about the director's "inability to call it quits."[74] But *Time* gave it the bullet, insisting it was "tedium in tumbleweed … intent operatic, effect soporific."[75]

Box Office

Euro-International was on a roll after its unexpected commercial success as the Italian distributor of the German-made sex-education movie *Helga* (1967)[76] and artistic success as the producer of John Cassavetes' *Faces* (1968), winner of four awards at the Venice Film Festival, and the resurgence of the western in that country.[77] It was in a strong financial position to give *Once Upon a Time in the West* a sizable launch in Italy where it faced tough opposition from *2001: A Space Odyssey*, *Where Eagles Dare*, *Lady in Cement* and Disney's *The Jungle Book*.[78] It soon became clear that grosses would fall far short of the anticipated $8 million record gross, and, in fact, it would turn out to be Leone's worst performer at the box office—only $3.8 million compared to $4.3 million for *The Good, the Bad and the Ugly*, $4.6 million for *A Fistful of Dollars* and $5 million for *For a Few Dollars More*.[79] Paramount strove to give the film a decent send-off; after all, they had nearly $2.5 million, plus marketing, invested in the project. It opened in New York on Memorial Day, two weeks ahead of the rest of the country, in two theaters, the State 2, only available because of the under-performing roadshow *Chitty, Chitty, Bang, Bang*,[80] and the Orpheum, which often worked in tandem, as did many other of the city's first-run operations.[81] "Paramount presents this summer's big box office excitement, from Sergio Leone, the man who gave the old west a new look and big box office," ran the advertising campaign to trade magazines while the consumer advertising centered on violence and Claudia Cardinale: "There were three men in her life … one to take her, one to love her—and one to kill her." Even rival studios were convinced that Leone would strike gold again, United Artists piggybacking on the new release by reissuing a double bill of *A Fistful of Dollars* and *For a Few Dollars More* in April and May to surprisingly good box office.

However, in retrospect, that might only have served to remind audiences of the type of picture that Leone had eschewed here. Contrary to essays by academics and book authors, the film was not an instant flop, opening strongly in New York, the best western of the year so far at the box office, outgunning *The Stalking Moon*, *100 Rifles* and *Mackenna's Gold.* It did better in its first stanza in the Big Apple than *The Wild Bunch* a few weeks later. But it was on first run for a limited period only, Paramount having already booked it into one of the five New York showcase (multiple release) operations for July 16.[82] Once the picture moved into wider release, audiences responded with less enthusiasm, and in its New York showcase circuit release, out of seven movies in play that week, it finished fifth in terms of gross.[83] It ended the year in 47th spot in the annual chart, a poor return on its substantial budget. However, its overseas performance, especially in France and Italy, went some way towards break-even. It ran for a year in Paris[84] and became one of the year's top earners in France and Germany. In terms of admissions (14.8 million), it registered the seventh-highest figures of all time in France[85] and was the third-highest (13 million) in Germany. There was no opportunity for audiences or critics to immediately revise their opinions since the movie was sold almost immediately after initial release to ABC-TV to air in the 1970–1971 season.[86]

Re-Evaluation

Over the next 50 years, the merits of *Once Upon a Time in the West* were regularly discussed and re-evaluation began. In an act of atonement in 2008, *Time* placed it in its Top 100 Films of All Time, and the film magazine *Empire* named it the top western of all time in a 2008 poll, as did the British newspaper *The Guardian*. The last once-in-a-decade *Sight & Sound* Poll in 2012 (where only four westerns featured in the overall Top 100) placed it third in the list of top westerns behind only *The Searchers* and *Rio Bravo*.

6

The Roadshow That Never Was

Mackenna's Gold

Starring Gregory Peck, Omar Sharif, Telly Savalas, Julie Newmar, Camilla Sparv; directed by J. Lee Thompson; screenplay by Carl Foreman; Columbia; 128 minutes

A Roadshow to Rival Funny Girl *and* Oliver!

Originally intended as a three-hour movie[1] for roadshow release, Columbia's *Mackenna's Gold* was to be shot in early 1966 by writer-producer Carl Foreman (*High Noon*, 1952; *The Guns of Navarone*, 1961; *Born Free*, 1966), who would also be in the director's chair.[2] Until recently, Columbia had doubted whether the extra cost involved in opening a movie as a roadshow was worth it. David Lean's *The Bridge on the River Kwai* (1957)[3] fulfilled all the criteria for a movie destined for roadshow: prestigious project, William Holden and Alec Guinness providing marquee appeal, a three-time Oscar nominee in director David Lean,[4] intriguing story, and with length also a major consideration to ensure the need for an intermission clocked in at 161 minutes. The roadshow had been in use since the silent era but then only sporadically until the advent of the widescreen and Cinerama in the 1950s.[5] However, Columbia was only beginning to find its feet as a genuine "major"—until the early 1950s, it had ranked as one of the "Little Three" rather than the "Big Five"[6] studios. They had two concerns about employing roadshow for the release of *Bridge on the River Kwai,* its biggest-ever financial gamble. Firstly, roadshow slowed down the speed at which receipts came in and, secondly, required an extra injection of expenditure for marketing. So the company had severely curtailed roadshow availability.[7] Even after MGM's *Ben-Hur* (1959) demonstrated the enormous potential for a roadshow, Columbia got cold feet about releasing *The Guns of Navarone* in this fashion.[8] Columbia eventually succumbed to pressure and sent *Lawrence of Arabia* (1962) down that route on a wider scale but still felt that hard-ticketing, as it was known, had been an unnecessary expense and that the film would have done better without it. The success of Fred Zinnemann's *A Man for All Seasons* (1966), whose star Paul Scofield[9] was largely unknown to movie audiences, had changed Columbia's perspective.[10] The length of its roadshow run had been a marketing coup all on its own, opening up the film to a much wider audience than could have been anticipated for a movie that was essentially a historical drama about a moral dilemma. It resulted in staggering box office, the film rated fourth in the annual rankings for 1967.[11]

Nonetheless, roadshows fell foul of a problem that was on the increase as the 1960s drew to a close. The issue was that there were both too few and too many roadshows. Too few of the kind that remained in theaters for six months or more and made massive profits for exhibitor and studio alike, and too many flops or movies that would never have qualified for roadshow exhibition except for the fact that there were too few roadshows. In the early 1960s, exhibitors, primarily at first-run houses, had upgraded their theaters and installed expensive specialist projection equipment at considerable expense to meet public demand for the likes of *Lawrence of Arabia, Spartacus* (1960), *West Side Story* (1961), *Cleopatra* (1963) and *It's a Mad Mad Mad Mad World* (1963). By the time *The Sound of Music* (1965) and *Doctor Zhivago* (1965) appeared, the future of the roadshow seemed settled. Hollywood had created the "event" movie, one that was shown on a wider screen than normal, projected in 70mm or Cinerama, that audiences had to book in advance to see and only at specific times, limited often to only ten showings a week, and at separate times, breaking one of the industry's golden rules: that people could drop in on a movie at any point in the day, even halfway through the picture. The fuss to get to see a roadshow was in keeping with the hoopla attendant on going to the legitimate theater. Given the advance planning involved, it made sense to extend the evening to include a visit to a restaurant or cocktails, and as with watching a show on stage there were supplementary purchases, a lavishly illustrated program as a souvenir of the experience, and soft drinks, popcorn and ice cream at a scheduled intermission. If a roadshow was in high demand, it might take months before you could see it. All these factors, especially the waiting and anticipation, made a roadshow an event. Even when the public taste dramatically changed with the proliferation of spy films and risqué comedies and dramas, and when the release structure altered so that more people could see more movies more quickly, there was still room for the roadshow as pictures as varied as *Oliver!*, *The Lion in Winter* and *2001: A Space Odyssey* testified in 1968.

Not all roadshows were hits. But as the flops cost huge amounts, the disparity between budget and income was larger than for a normal film. Of course, there had been flops from the very beginning: for example, *Can Can* in 1960 and *King of Kings* the following year. But when the flops began to outweigh the hits and the industry endured a year (1967) of turkeys like *Doctor Dolittle*, *Half a Sixpence* and *The Happiest Millionaire*, incurring losses which threatened to sink studios, then questions began to be asked about the merit of the roadshow as a release vehicle.

Coupled with the problem of roadshows that fell short of expectation was the question of roadshows being in short supply. To get around that problem, and in some instances simply to use the prestige of a roadshow as a marketing device to help launch a movie, pictures that had not initially been made with roadshow in mind were simply blown up from 35mm to 70mm,[12] for example, the World War I aerial drama *The Blue Max* (1966), the historical *Mayerling* (1968), the adaptation of Jacqueline Susann bestseller *Valley of the Dolls* (1968) and the western *Shalako* (1968). In the wake of flops and movies not fit for roadshow purpose, companies began to examine more closely the type of film that was worth the extra expense of a roadshow launch, weighing that against the probability that it could see a far quicker return on costs (though not necessarily a larger profit in the long run) by going down the normal release route. Furthermore, studio honchos had to consider whether the public would be willing to fork out high ticket prices for a film that might not have achieved its full script potential, especially if the critics subsequently gave the picture the thumbs-down.

One of the factors against roadshowing *Mackenna's Gold* was that westerns were not considered a natural medium for the process. Although *How the West Was Won* (1962) had been a rip-roaring success, it had other things going for it. For a start, it was the first dramatic film to be shot in Cinerama, secondly it boasted a genuine all-star cast including Gregory Peck, John Wayne, James Stewart and Debbie Reynolds, and thirdly, it was helmed by the likes of John Ford and Henry Hathaway. On the other hand, John Ford's *Cheyenne Autumn* (1964) and John Sturges *The Hallelujah* Trail (1965) were surprising roadshow flops. Audiences could have been put off by the lack of marquee names, Richard Widmark toplining the former and Burt Lancaster (notwithstanding his box office record in the genre) the latter, and length, the first coming in at 154 minutes and the second 165 minutes. Or it could have been the subject matter: *Cheyenne Autumn*, a downbeat tale about Native Americans, *The Hallelujah Trail* a comedy about the battle over a cargo of whiskey. Their failure was the main argument against not taking a roadshow risk with westerns. It would take some hell of a persuading to make them change their minds.

Mackenna's Gold **was shown in 70mm at the Odeon Leicester Square, London. It received rave reviews from the British newspapers** ***Sunday Telegraph*** **("smashing adventure"),** ***Sunday Times*** **("miraculous effects") and the** ***London Evening News*** **("stupendous climax ... not a dull moment"). Trade press advertisement (*****Kinematograph Weekly*****, April 19, 1969, 22).**

Carl Foreman was just the man to do it. In a bid to achieve the prestigious roadshow launch he craved, Foreman persuaded Columbia to increase *Mackenna's Gold*'s budget to $5 million and agree to film the movie in Cinerama. (Over 25 percent of the budget was allocated to Cinerama to license the name and use the equipment–$1.35 million in total negative costs.[13]) In January 1967, Columbia launched the marketing campaign with full-page advertisements in the trade papers promoting the fact that the movie would be filmed on location in the U.S. in Cinerama and that it would bring together the "creators of *The Guns of Navarone*," meaning, at this point, Foreman and director J. Lee Thompson. The advertisement also highlighted author Will Henry, on whose novel the film was based (as the "author of *San Juan Hill* and *From Where the Sun Now Stands*"), and plugged the book as "a novel of Apache gold and Apache revenge based on the search for the fabulous Lost Adams Diggings."

By the following year, Foreman's star was in the ascendant after the Parisian revival of *High Noon*.[14] At the same time, any reservations Columbia had about roadshows had vanished, in keeping with the entire industry, now that a total of 26 movies entering production in 1968 were set for roadshow release[15] including ten that would use the Cinerama process.[16] Columbia was concentrating on three major pictures for roadshow release in 1968–69: *Funny Girl*, *Oliver!* and *Mackenna's Gold*.[17]

By this time, Columbia had reshaped its marketing effort to provide the specialist support re-quired for promoting roadshows. In early 1967, it had poached sales guru Leo Greenfield from Buena Vista with the aim of setting up an effective unit to market hard-ticket product—"first assignment—*Mackenna's Gold*, *Oliver!* and *Funny Girl*"[18]—to the record number of Cinerama theaters[19] and those desperate to accommodate roadshow. By the end of 1968, both Cinerama and Columbia had reported record revenues and profits, the former turning a $290,000 loss into a $679,000 profit,[20] the latter on an unprecedented streak of success with a gross profit of $9.3 million profit on a gross income of $239 million.[21] Columbia soon added another roadshow prospect to its slate, Sydney Pollack's World War II drama *Castle Keep* starring Burt Lancaster, and was so confident about the two non-musicals that it expected the western and the war picture to run consecutively from late spring 1969 well into the following year at Loews Hollywood in Los Angeles.[22] The studio, by targeting advance booking group sales, believed it had hit a marketing mother lode, those for *Funny Girl* topping $550,000 compared to the normal $80,000.[23] By the beginning of December 1968, Columbia began planning what it expected to be the triumphant launch of *Mackenna's Gold*. The world premiere was to be held in Phoenix, Arizona, on February 15, 1969, with the roadshow launch set for the DeMille theater in New York five days later.

Within the next month, however, the world premiere was called off. Work began on editing down the near-three-hour running time, and plans for a roadshow release were quietly dropped. What caused Columbia to get cold feet? It could have been a simple reaction to the indifferent public and critical response to *The Stalking Moon*. If audiences had not taken to star Gregory Peck in one western, what made anybody think they would do it for another? Or it could have been something to do with two other Cinerama movies, *Custer of the West* (1967) starring Robert Shaw and Mary Ure and *Krakatoa—East of Java* (1968) starring Maximilian Schell, and the flop of Universal's roadshow *Isadora* (1968). The first was a western with British actors in the leading roles, the second a disaster movie with a German star; the third again toplined a British star, Vanessa Redgrave. Although *Mackenna's Gold* boasted a better marquee line-up, it was relying on Cinerama special effects to lift it out of the western rut. *Krakatoa—East of Java* had spent the bulk of its budget on special effects, far more than had gone on *Mackenna's Gold* which climaxed with an earthquake. *Custer of the West* had been a major misfire at the box office and when news leaked out that Cinerama was going to limit roadshows of *Krakatoa*, confining it in the main to normal release and in most areas not in 70mm, it made Columbia question its own strategy. If *Mackenna's Gold* was to be marketed as a drama in a western setting rather than a shoot-out in the tradition of *100 Rifles*, then Columbia looked with trepidation at *Isadora*, boasting an 177-minute running time; its roadshow run in Los Angeles was swiftly truncated, and the movie butchered in a bid to find an audience.[24] In addition, Columbia recalled the saga of *Casino Royale* (1967), as big a financial risk as *Mackenna's Gold*, and how it had refused to give in to producer Charles K. Feldman when he demanded a roadshow release. The studio, convinced it was not suitable, found

Custer of the West originally took shape as _The Day Custer Fell_, to be directed by Fred Zinnemann. The stars were low-paid by Hollywood standards: Robert Shaw receiving $350,000, his wife Mary Ure $50,000. Trade press advertisement (_Box Office_, April 29, 1968).

its decision justified when the spy spoof raced to $10.2 million in rentals and placed third in the annual box office chart.[25] By now the cost of *Mackenna's Gold* was hovering around the $7 million mark, not counting marketing, and just to break even, the western needed to pull in at least twice that amount, and even *How the West Was Won* had not managed that. Columbia, comparing advance bookings against that of its other roadshow biggies *Oliver!* and *Funny Girl*, had found that the group market which had responded so enthusiastically to the musicals had shown scant interest in a big-budget western, despite the Cinerama effects, and possibly because of the lengthy running time.

The studio decided on a different tack. The world premiere shifted to Munich, West Germany, in March,[26] with most of the rest of the European capitals holding gala premieres before the picture made its U.S. debut in Phoenix on May 10. But the picture unveiled in Phoenix was a ghost of the original. The running time technically came in at 128 minutes, but, in effect, was under two hours long, the introductory narration lasting eight minutes and the end credits accounting for further time. What was oddest of all about the whole business of the release was—setting aside all the genuine reservations about the movie's fitness for roadshow—the 18-month gap between completion and world premiere. Filming had begun on May 16, 1967, and wrapped on September 29. Of course, there were special effects to be added, but it was unlikely these would take a year, or anything like.[27] In other words, Columbia had shelved one of its biggest budgeted movies for nearly 15 months and the reasons could not all have been to do with an argument over roadshow.

The Curse of the Hyphenate

Hollywood employed a wide array of hyphenates: writer-directors, producer-directors, actor-directors, writer-producers and writer-producer-directors.[28] The purpose of carrying out more than one task on a movie was to exert greater control on the end product and/or to realize a bigger share of the profits. Sometimes directors were producers in name only, but were given this credit as a way of reducing their tax bill[29] or to earn a percentage of the profits. For actors, the producer credit performed a similar role but was often nothing more than a sop to vanity. Among the most significant writer-producer-directors were Billy Wilder[30] and Charlie Chaplin and top producer-directors included Otto Preminger, David Lean, Alfred Hitchcock and John Ford. Actors tended not to become hyphenates as often because the process was so time-consuming and could substantially detract from their earnings as a star. Laurence Olivier was actor-producer-director on *Henry V* (1944),[31] Frank Sinatra actor-producer on *Sergeants 3* (1962) and *Robin and the 7 Hoods* (1964) and actor-producer-director on *None But the Brave* (1965),[32] Gregory Peck was actor-producer on *Pork Chop Hill* (1959) and another five films.[33] John Wayne carried out the same three roles in *The Alamo* (1960) and, under the Wayne-Fellows and Batjac umbrellas, in another 24 movies was either producer-only or actor-producer. There was an upside to studios conceding such control, especially to actors since they were particularly useful when it came to marketing and were, either because they had their own money tied up in a movie or relied on its box office for deferred salary and a share of the profits, more willing to tour the U.S. and/or the world to help promote the picture. In the normal course of things, actors commanded media attention in a way that few directors could (Hitchcock the most obvious exception) and if making their directorial debut, for example, attracted even more newspaper and television coverage. However, the downside of one person having so much control was that often that resulted in *too* much control, a neophyte director not always able to turn a script into an appealing commodity,[34] and experienced hyphenate unwilling to subjugate his vision to the general good.

Carl Foreman had been a writer-producer for most of his working life, either as a partner in the Stanley Kramer company (*Champion*, 1949, and *High Noon*, 1952) or as an independent (*The Key*, 1958, and *The Guns of Navarone*, 1961). And he was also now a marketing dream due to his personal history, forced to flee Hollywood for Britain in 1952 during the anti–Communist hysteria. Although initially struggling to regain the status he had lost, he found that Britain and other European countries did not attach any stigma to him. The fact that the movies he made as an independent producer always carried an "inherent message" made him a marketing godsend. In addition, he soon realized that making films in Europe could add immeasurably to the marketing mix. For *The Guns of Navarone* marketing, his presence alone was often enough to galvanize the media in major European cities.

But he had always viewed becoming a producer as a way to protect his screenplays and as a stepping stone to becoming director. After the departure of Alexander Mackendrick

Directed by Stanley Kramer and written by Carl Foreman, *Champion* was reissued in 1955 with another collaboration between the two men, *Home of the Brave*. Carl Foreman's first script was *Spooks Run Wild*, a B-picture for the long-running East Side Kids series. Trade press advertisement (*Box Office*, April 18, 1949, 3).

(*The Man in the White Suit*, 1951) from the *Navarone* director's chair, Foreman had agitated unsuccessfully to be his replacement,[35] finally gaining the opportunity to operate as a triple-hyphenate on the three-hour World War II epic *The Victors* (1963). Since then, although he had not been the actual producer, he had, through the production company High Road, acted as executive producer on films such as *Born Free*, one of his biggest successes, costing just $1 million but grossing $8 million worldwide.[36] And he had a full slate of upcoming projects: *High Dam*, a sequel to *The Guns of Navarone*,[37] *Fifteen Flags* set in World War I, *Mistress Masham's Repose* to be directed by Joshua Logan, and a long-cherished ambition to make a Winston Churchill biopic. His relationship with Hollywood was sometimes uneasy, but it had not prevented Columbia from bankrolling his operation from 1957. But since acquiring his new position as a top producer, he had not made a movie in America. So, amongst other reasons for taking on *Mackenna's Gold* was the opportunity to work in his homeland for the first time since 1952.

To make the movie, he had to come to an accommodation with the person who owned the rights to the *Mackenna's Gold*[38] novel—Dmitri Tiomkin, who was entering into a class of his own as a hyphenate, that of composer-producer. Tiomkin and Foreman had first worked together in Frank Capra's Army Signal Corps unit in 1941 and the composer had scored *High Noon* and *Navarone* and had received record fees for his scores (*Navarone*, *Solomon and Sheba*, 1960, and *How the West Was Won* all set new highs) as well as pressing studios for a bigger share from sales of original soundtracks and music publishing rights.[39] After suffering a debilitating eye illness, the composer had determined to expand his horizons and move into production, principally a biopic of Tchaikovsky.[40] His initial foray into production came in 1964 when he purchased the rights to *Mackenna's Gold* from novelist Will Henry, one of the most prolific and highly regarded writers of westerns. Will Henry was a pseudonym, one of two that Henry Wilson Allen used for writing westerns, the other being Clay Fisher. He also wrote screenplays for cartoon shorts under the pen names Heck Allen and Henry Allen. Westerns made from his novels were *Santa Fe Passage* (1955) starring John Payne, *The Tall Men* (1955) starring Clark Gable and Jane Russell, *Pillars of the Sky* (1956) starring Jeff Chandler, and *Yellowstone Kelly* (1959) starring Clint Walker. At the same time as *Mackenna's Gold* was sold, his 1960 book *Journey to Shiloh* was being set up under the title *Fields of Honor* to be directed by veteran Mervyn LeRoy.[41] When this fell through, it was made into a film under the original title in 1969 with newcomer James Caan. *Who Rides with Wyatt* was released as *Young Billy Young* starring Robert Mitchum in the fall of 1969.[42] Tiomkin agreed to sell the rights to Foreman in April 1965 in return not just for a fee and an agreement to compose the music[43] but also the vital producer's credit necessary to launch him on a new career.[44]

As mentioned above, Foreman's original deal with Columbia was that he would direct as well as write and co-produce.[45] When the Churchill film was postponed, *Mackenna's Gold* moved to the top of Foreman's agenda. Although the original shooting start date of spring 1967 was pushed back, the project kept gathering momentum until it would become one of the studio's three biggest pictures. Initially, Foreman was keen on filming in Spain where production would not only be cheaper but the film would take advantage of generous government subsidies.[46] But while Foreman won the battle, at least initially, to turn the project into a big-budget Cinerama picture that would be released as a roadshow, he lost the war to become its director.

There was ample reason for Columbia to harbor doubts. *The Victors*, a pet project, had not been a success commercially or critically. And while *The Victors* and *Mackenna's*

Opera singer Maria Callas was at one time going to play *The Guns of Navarone*'s female lead. Cary Grant had asked for first refusal rights on the role that eventually went to Gregory Peck (Hannan Collection).

Gold both boasted large casts, those hired for the western were substantially more experienced than the war film and might require a more skilled director. In addition, Columbia did not want to offer the producer any reason to divert his energies away from the complex logistics of a location shoot where much of the time the crew would be 50 miles from the nearest town and where, despite the desert environment, they could be subject to storms and flash floods. J. Lee Thompson came on board as director. Although Thompson's career had stumbled of late with poor business for *Return from the Ashes* (1965), Eye *of the Devil* (1966) and *Before Winter Comes* (1968), he had considerable experience of handling big stars. Gregory Peck, Anthony Quinn and David Niven had headlined in *The Guns of Navarone*, Peck and Robert Mitchum in *Cape Fear* (1962), Yul Brynner and Tony Curtis is *Taras Bulba* (1962), Brynner again in *Kings of the Sun* (1963), Shirley MacLaine, Paul Newman and Mitchum in *What a Way to Go* (1964), MacLaine in *John Goldfarb, Please Come Home* (1965), Niven and Deborah Kerr in *Eye of the Devil* and Niven in *Before Winter Comes*. (Thompson was also at this point lined up to direct Charlton Heston in *Planet of the Apes* [1968].) Moreover, as he had proved with *The Guns of Navarone* and others, he was at ease with a film complicated by plot, action, an extensive parade of characters and the problem of fitting multiple actors into the same scene.

However, Thompson was interpreting Foreman's vision and, as had occurred on their previous film together, their relationship did not run smoothly. This was partly due to disagreements over the heavy-handed tone of the film and how it was ultimately cut. But there were other times when the producer felt the director was lackadaisical about doing his job. Foreman recalled, "I was not very happy with the work of J. Lee Thompson on that film and entirely apart from that we still got into trouble in terms of scheduling and so forth and our relationship was always a problem."[47]

Logistics were always going to be a problem on a picture of this scale, shot almost exclusively on some of the most inhospitable places on Earth. The buzzard section was filmed in Monument Valley on the Arizona-Utah border, and other scenic wildernesses included the Glen Canyon of Utah, Spider Rock in Canon de Schelly in Arizona, Kanab Valley, Sink Valley, the Panguitch Fish Hatchery in Utah, and Medford, Oregon. A writer-producer was the worst kind of hyphenate as far as a director was concerned in that, as suggested previously, the producer might be more apt to protect his original vision and dialogue than adapt the screenplay, which is only ever intended as a blueprint, to other ideas as the movie went into production. The opening of the picture is pure Foreman, on a par with *Guns of Navarone*'s introductory section, and the extensive use of narration ran counter to a director who felt the camera should tell the story.

But it is worth examining Foreman's contribution as the screenwriter. Will Henry's 1964 source novel was, by today's standards, a slim volume. The principal idea of Mackenna being given a map by a dying Indian comes from the book, as does the capture of the white woman (named Francie in the novel), and a surprisingly erotic description of Hesh-Ke's attempted seduction of Mackenna in the pool, the Apache mysticism and, equally surprisingly, the earthquake denouement. Some white men do join the party, but they are of rougher stock, the "Good Men" of Hadleyburg entirely Foreman's invention. Foreman turned Mackenna into a lawman rather than just a prospector, made the map more tangible (in the book, it was drawn in the sand), gave Mackenna a past with Hesh-Ke and with the outlaw Colorado (named Pelon in the book), and, just as *Once Upon a Time in the West* director Sergio Leone did with Henry Fonda, realized that a handsome, attractive villain was far more interesting than the "jug-eared, ugly man" described in

Henry's book. Foreman made Tibbs a sergeant and added 20 years to the raw-boned youngster of the book.

But in the original, Hesh-Ke was accidentally killed just after the pool incident, and it was another outlaw, Hachita, who killed Colorado so that the climactic fight on the ledge was between the axe-wielding Hachita and the unarmed Mackenna rather than between Mackenna and Colorado, but Henry had the white woman taken hostage kill the Indian. The various shoot-outs and chases are primarily a Foreman invention. He gives Mackenna more depth, and the vices of gambling and alcohol. Most important, it was Foreman who added the visual grandeur. There is no Shaking Rock in the source material, and no waiting for sunrise or for a shadow to point the way to the entrance to the canyon.

Starry, Starry Cast

Gregory Peck was not the first choice for the title role in *Mackenna's Gold*. He only got the part after Steve McQueen and then Clint Eastwood turned it down[48] and even then Peck wavered, only agreeing to the project after pressure from Foreman, and in recognition of their work together on *The Guns of Navarone*.[49] Omar Sharif, who had leapt to fame in *Lawrence of Arabia* and cemented his reputation as a matinee idol in *Doctor Zhivago* (1965), had been the insurance in case audiences did not warm to Barbra Streisand in *Funny Girl* and as, the outlaw Colorado, was about to do the same in *Mackenna's Gold*, although this time his character, in ruthless pursuit of gold, eschewed any element of romance. In retrospect, the Columbia sales team may have quickly realized the folly of trying to sell such a distinctively unromantic Sharif, despite the prospect of the star lolling naked beside a pool, to the women who made up the core of group advance bookings, and, although it is unfair to say that Sharif was miscast for a role which he carried off with a certain vigor, it is certainly true that for a movie intent on roadshow release, denying Sharif a romantic interlude had a negative impact on audience interest. However, Sharif's marquee appeal had taken a tumble in the previous few months. MGM's *Mayerling* and Twentieth Century–Fox's *Che!* had flattered to deceive at the box office.

Over the past few years, Telly Savalas had discovered the harsh reality of Hollywood. An Oscar nomination for Best Supporting Actor in *The Birdman of Alcatraz* (1962) had done less for his career than the odious Maggott in *The Dirty Dozen* (1967), after which he was promptly promoted to third billing on *Sol Madrid* (1968), *The Scalphunters* (1968) and *The Assassination Bureau* (1968). Although he retained that billing on *Mackenna's Gold*, he did not appear until halfway through, suggesting that his role as Sgt. Tibbs had been a casualty of the editing needed to reduce the running length. The two female leading roles, rivals for Mackenna's affection, were taken by Sweden's Camilla Sparv as hostage Inga Bergerman and Julie Newmar as Hesh-Ke. Sparv had been James Coburn's leading lady in *Dead Heat on a Merry-Go-Round* (1966), Stephen Boyd's in *Assignment K* (1968) and Rod Taylor's in *Nobody Runs Forever* (1968). Newmar[50] was a decade older and despite 15 years in pictures was best known for playing Catwoman on the *Batman* TV series (1966–1967). Foreman had given her the leading female role opposite Zero Mostel in *Monsieur Lecoq* (1967) but the movie was unfinished, although Newmar still attracted attention after stills from the picture appeared in *Playboy* magazine. The two characters were polar opposites, Bergerman, terrified and repressed, Hesh-Ke feisty and jealous.

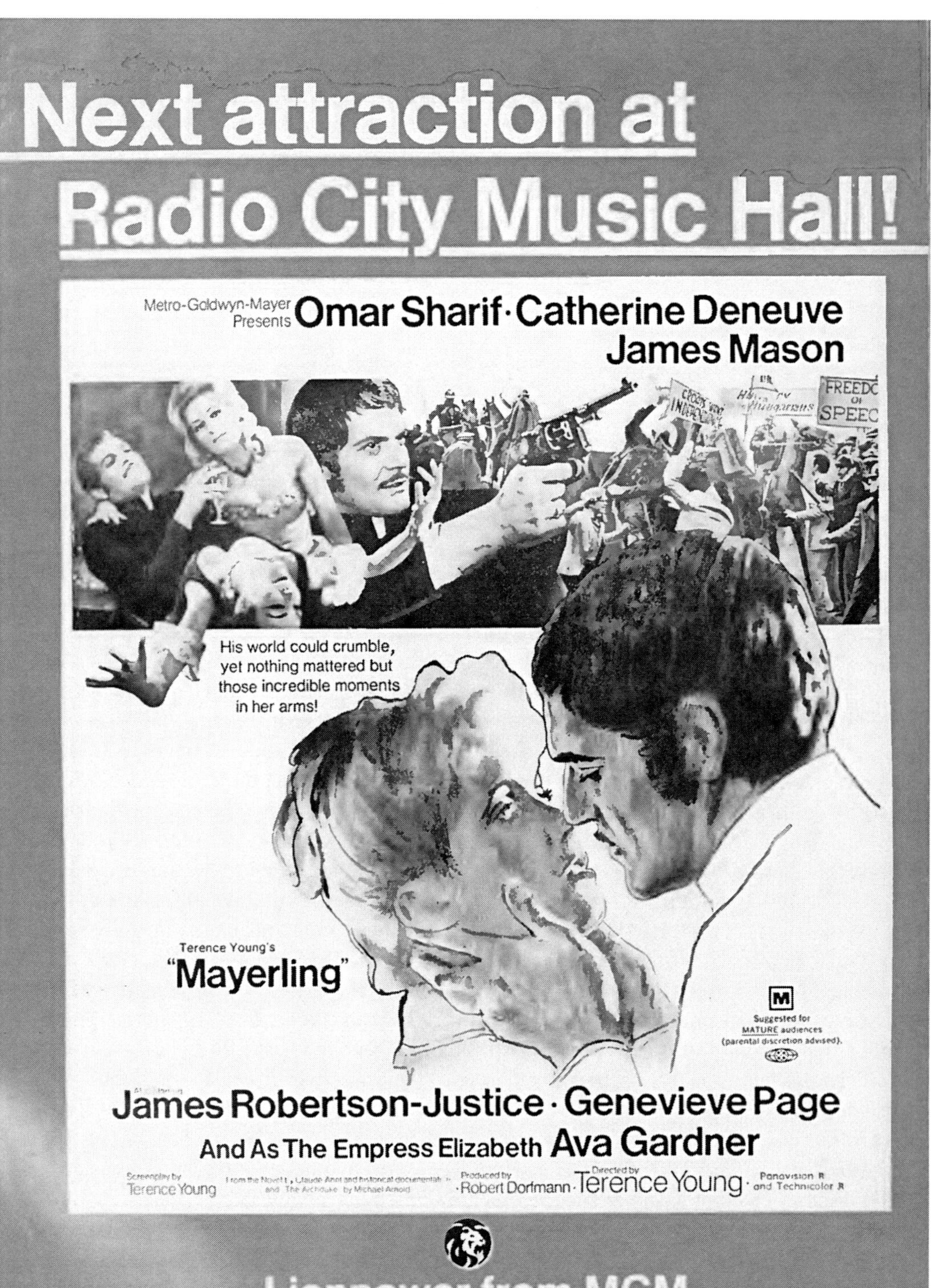

Mayerling had originally been intended as a vehicle for Audrey Hepburn. France's 1936 version had Charles Boyer in the lead. Pressbook (Hannan Collection).

Rounding out the supporting roles within the outlaw gang were Chicago-born Robert Philips as Monkey, Pepe Callahan as Laguna, New Yorker Shelley Morrison (later a regular on the *Will & Grace* television series) as the Pima squaw, Rudy Diaz (of Apache descent) as Besh, Madeleine Taylor Holmes as the old woman, plus Italian Eduardo Ciannelli as Prairie Dog. The all-star cast had been a Hollywood marketing ploy from *Grand Hotel* (1932) to *Around the World in 80 Days* (1956) but in the 1960s it was utilized on a far wider basis, often as a way of making supporting roles more attractive to audiences, as evidenced by *The Longest Day* (1962), *Judgment at Nuremberg* (1961), *How the West Was Won*, *It's a Mad Mad Mad Mad World* and *Casino Royale*. Now *Mackenna's Gold* aimed to set a new standard for the quality of actors in supporting roles, including Edward G. Robinson, Lee J. Cobb, Burgess Meredith, Anthony Quayle, Eli Wallach, Raymond Massey, Keenan Wynn and Ted Cassidy.

The George Lucas Connection

In some respects, the involvement of George Lucas (*Star Wars*) in *Mackenna's Gold* has overshadowed that of director J. Lee Thompson. Committed to bringing through a new generation of talent, Foreman had established an internship for the picture. Lucas was one of four winners. The internship funded the winners to shoot a short film on the location. Foreman immediately became a fan because of the quality of Lucas' effort. Foreman explained:

> He did the shortest one of the lot and the most technically accomplished. It ran only one minute and 47 seconds and it had no title—he gave it a date—and then we agreed we'd call it *A Desert Poem* because he went out on the desert and did a lot of stop-action photography. George really knew his camera and he played with his camera and it was around and about the film—he was doing the desert more than anything else but in the desert was the film company with its parasols and all that shimmering in the distance and he played around with little things where the sun was shining and the film company was working. And then it began to rain, and it rained like hell, and then the sun came out again. It was awfully good. He did a lot of trick stuff with his camera and that's what the boys resented, that he could just go out by himself and do that.[51]

"The boys" resented him for more than his technical accomplishment but Foreman's admiration for the neophyte director increased after seeing a display of professionalism that put the other professionals to shame.

> We were … in a very difficult location … near the place where we had painted in this great seam of gold.… We got to the big scene, the scene where [the actors discovered the gold], and they all started running towards it.… But [the location] was in a kind of ravine and there was a problem about the light—you could only shoot it … at that time of year when the sun was more or less directly overhead or had just begun to go down or had just passed the meridian.… [But when Foreman arrived on location] the entire company was just sitting there. Lucas therefore pointed out in an indirect manner that the scene had not been rehearsed because J. Lee Thompson was waiting for the sun to rehearse it during the precious moments when the sun was there instead of being ready for when the sun was there.[52]

Simplicity Complicated

The story of *Mackenna's Gold* was simple and as old as the hills, as old at least as John Huston's *The Treasure of the Sierra Madre* (1948): A group of men hunting for gold are driven mad by gold fever. But what should have been a straightforward plot was complicated by an avalanche of characters and the necessity for not just introducing them but keeping them in focus. Big movies often had slow openings; CinemaScope pictures in the 1950s used the first minutes to establish an exotic locale and the extravagant roadshow of the 1960s usually began with a lengthy segment that was an extension of the overture. But for a movie that had, in terms of its budget, a lean running time of just over two hours, it seemed almost perverse to waste the first six minutes on scenery, narration and the theme song "Old Turkey Buzzard," sung by Jose Feliciano.[53] The stunning effects—a close-up of the sun cutting to a close-up of a buzzard's eye, the bird's eye view of the peaks of ancient canyons, the widescreen and Cinerama drawing in the viewer—would have been prerequisites of the earlier Cinerama travelogues whose intention had been to show Americans a country they have never properly seen unless they had the opportunity to fly over such canyons. It was a very slow start, ideal perhaps for a movie intended as a near-three-hour epic but not for the shortened version. It was almost as if producer Foreman, having spent all that money on the glorious cinematography, was loathe to lose it to speed up the story. Then came two minutes of narration by Victor Jory while the camera repeated what had just been shown. That Foreman was keen on narration had been shown in *The Guns of Navarone*, which began with an extensive animated sequence explaining the history of heroes in ancient Greece that had nothing to do with the actual movie. For *Mackenna's Gold*, the first section of the narration is equally redundant, a retelling of the "Appointment in Samarra" tale made famous by Somerset Maugham.[54] Then we get two minutes of the theme song. Finally, Jory's narration becomes more pointed, explaining the Apache legend of a fabulous hidden seam of gold, the Indians gaining strength by resisting its temptations, and that an explorer called Adams had found it (but could never find it again) and that in 1874 it had become known as Mackenna's Gold.

It is not until the seventh minute that a human being appears, an Indian on horseback, way down on the valley floor. This section, the real opening of the film, is a perfect example of visual and verbal exposition. The Indian hears hoof beats. Mackenna (Gregory Peck) makes his entrance, also on horseback, badge gleaming (so we know he is a lawman). The Indian shoots Mackenna's horse and shatters the bottle of whiskey (so we know he is partial to a drink) in his pocket. After an exchange of gunfire, Mackenna shoots the Indian. "You are Mackenna the marshal," says the Indian. Mackenna reckons Colorado (villain of the piece thus introduced) paid the Indian to shoot him. But the Indian says he fired at Mackenna because the lawman is looking for gold. "I quit gold hunting a long time ago," replies Mackenna. He finds no gold in the Indian's belongings but does locate a map of the Canyon del Oro, location of the Adams gold. "You will wish you never saw this map," the Indian says before he dies, thus presenting the western's central thesis. True to his word, Mackenna burns the map.

We cut to a ranch commandeered by an outlaw gang, a mixture of white men and Indians, headed by Colorado (Omar Sharif). Their anxious reaction to the approach of U.S. Cavalry suggests they are not law-abiding individuals, a fact proven when they take Judge Bergerman's wife Inga (Camilla Sparv) hostage, the husband killed trying to protect her. Mackenna is interrupted digging a grave for the Indian by the outlaws. "Remember I told you I would come for you," says Colorado, twisting around the motif of the relentless lawman from *The Stalking Moon* and *100 Rifles*. Colorado attacks Mackenna after finding the remains of the burned map and, insisting the marshal can remember its details, takes him hostage. The story takes an odd turn when the Indians among the outlaws refuse to bury the dead Indian under rocks and are adamant that they should take the corpse with them, indicating an undercurrent of mystical force. And now the set-up is virtually complete, Colorado and Mackenna deadly enemies forced to work together, two hostages in Mackenna and Bergerman, the mystery of the map and already a sense of gold fever. The setting-up of the story has been well done, both in terms of the screenplay and the direction.

Cinerama lends itself to certain types of scenes, height being one, and the process comes into play as the group attempts to cross a rope bridge high in the canyons. Mackenna, imitating *100 Rifles*, is stretched over a horse, bound and helpless. When one man's foot goes through a plank of wood on the bridge, the camera swirls out of control, another signature Cinerama effect. Then, for no reason, we are subjected to further narration, explaining (as if the audience could not work this out for itself) that Colorado's hideout is in a box canyon where the group has headed and is now eating. Bergerman is thrown to the ground, also bound and helpless, but ignored. We now discover that the dead Indian was Old Prairie Dog. When Hesh-Ke (Julie Newmar) appears from the back of the cave, it is immediately clear from Mackenna's reaction that he knows her. Colorado, who often acts as an additional narrator, explains, "She remembers you." Mackenna replies, in unenthusiastic tones, "I remember her, too." And that is the last piece of the emotional jigsaw, that, as much as Mackenna and Colorado have an inescapable past, so, too, do Mackenna and Hesh-Ke.

Colorado introduces another theme, that Indians are beginning to "behave like white men" towards the gold. Mackenna tries to discourage gold fever, asserting that there is "not enough gold to fill your back tooth." Colorado takes another tack, trying to bribe Mackenna into complying, offering him "the girl" (Bergerman), "all the women you want" and, finally, "Scarface" (aka Hesh-Ke). When this elicits no response, Colorado again punches Mackenna while Hesh-Ke menaces him with a knife, although this disguises her true feelings. "She still likes you," says Colorado; "Too bad I already gave her to Monkey."

Mackenna and Bergerman are imprisoned for the night in an improvised cell underground, an obvious device to let them get to know each other, and so that, for narrative purposes, Mackenna can develop an attraction towards her. The Camilla Sparv role is underwritten, partly because the screenwriter believes the audience needs no reminding about her predicament: that she is likely to be raped. As early as the silent era, in films like *The Invaders* (1912) and *The Battle at Elderbush Gulch* (1913), it is expected that rape will be the fate of a white woman captured by an Indian.[55] Bergerman is terrified, reacting to being a captive of the Indians the way any white woman would. Mackenna owes his job to her father and had tried to mend his ways as a drinker and a gambler, although clearly, as we have seen, he has struggled to give up whiskey. So although he appears honest in his dealings with Colorado, there is still a part of him that is dishonest. A knife-wielding Monkey enters the cave, clearly intent on ravaging the woman. Armed with only his belt, Mackenna fends him off until the fight is halted by Colorado.

The men from Hadleyburg arrive, led by Ben Baker (Eli Wallach). Instead of being a posse hunting down the renegade, they have come to join the party to hunt for the gold. One of Colorado's men, Laguna, has betrayed knowledge of the gold and their hideout and he is promptly dispatched by the outlaw. Their purpose in story terms is clear, to show that it is not just outlaws and a wayward marshal who fall prey to the temptation of gold, but upright, decent citizens. But their presence is cumbersome, intrusive. There is enough going on—the uneasy truce between Mackenna and Colorado disguising deep enmity, the promise of romance between Colorado and one woman or the other, the disquiet of the Apaches, and the mystery of the map—without them disturbing what is a finely balanced and taut storyline. They are such obvious stereotypes; five out of the seven lack names, identified only by profession or nationality. Suddenly, nearly one-third of the way into the picture, a large number of people have to be introduced and, to some extent, given storylines.

When critics refer to impressive composition in a movie, they tend to be talking about a scene framed in an interesting fashion. John Wayne going through the door at the beginning and end of *The Searchers* is a classic example. But in reality, composition is what a director does to arrange the characters in a scene so that they are presented in an interesting fashion. In this case, with so many new arrivals, Thompson has them seated in different depths in the cave, while Colorado walks among them introducing them. The outlaw mocks the Older Englishman (Anthony Quayle), the Storekeeper (Burgess Meredith) and the Preacher (Raymond Massey). Because of the composition, as Colorado moves across the floor, the audience expects more of the same when the outlaw reaches the little old man standing out from the rest courtesy of his dark glasses. But this is Adams, the original finder of the gold, who was blindfolded by Apaches when they took him to the gold, and the only survivor when the Indians massacred the rest of the group. He is certainly the most impressive character among the honorable men of Hadleyburg because, although clearly blinded by the incident, he still cannot resist the lure of the gold, and inflames others with this hunger, for he came back with "a little nugget worth $190." Another of the Indians, Sanchez (Keenan Wynn), mocks the Younger Englishman with the long blond hair (Robert Porter), unable to make up his mind whether this is a boy or a girl—gender confusion a surprising feature of earlier westerns[56] while white men were often stripped by Indians[57]—and kissing him to find out. The young man reacts, swiftly punching Sanchez in the stomach. Mackenna prevents Sanchez using his knife and tries to dissuade the Editor (Lee J. Cobb) from pursuing the gold.

Colorado sows suspicion and distrust, telling the visitors that Mackenna killed Prairie Dog and burned the map. The scene abruptly changes tone, and now Mackenna appears on trial. "You were a drifter, a man from nowhere," says the Editor. For no apparent reason, Hesh-Ke interrupts, bringing in Bergerman. Colorado offers a glib explanation for her presence: that they stopped at the ranch to buy food, but the owner started to shoot, and out of the goodness of his heart, the outlaw has made Bergerman a partner in the scheme so she will get a "full share." He need not have bothered, nobody wants to know about the outlaws' misdeeds, not even when Mackenna claims "the best man in your town has been murdered." The cavalry (another relentless force), who are in the habit in this picture of interrupting the outlaws, are again sighted, forcing outlaws and good citizens to escape. Out of nowhere, the narrator explains to the audience the outlaws' clever plan to hoodwink the cavalry, getting the Pima squaw so drunk she could not talk, sending her into the enemy to make out she had been attacked by Indians, thus providing the misdirection required for the gold hunters to escape. "That was the plan," says the narrator in arch tones, "and with a little bit of luck it could just work." (Was there ever a more annoying narrator?) Mackenna has other ideas, breaking away from the group with Bergerman, but he is easily caught. The narrator drones on: "So now they are together—the good citizens and the outlaws, Mackenna and the girl," destination the waterhole, "a kind of neutral territory."

However, the cavalry men catch up. The good people of Hadleyburg try to evade capture by pointing out they are the good people of Hadleyburg and not to be confused with the outlaws, but their protests are drowned out by gunfire, and in a significant twist on the theme of massacre (*100 Rifles, The Wild Bunch*) it is the white people who are mercilessly mowed down. Before Adams dies, his dark glasses fall off, revealing the empty sockets: He was punished by the Apaches in the worst way possible, never able to see gold again. Hearing the gunfire, Mackenna again tries to escape with Bergerman. This time when caught, he is dragged by rope behind a horse across the rough ground in another piece of Cinerama expertise, the camera point-of-view as scenery hurtles by, while Hesh-Ke, demonstrating her dominance and making clear her intentions regarding Mackenna, lashes Bergerman with her belt.

The demise of many of the Hadleyburgers allows the story to get back on its feet. In the first of a series of visualizations, we see Mackenna imagining details of the map. This is pretty redundant as well and gets to be as annoying as the intrusive narrator. The rules of moviemaking regarding the guide are simple enough: let the camera follow him. Exposed in the canyon to the baking sun, Bergerman slips off her horse. When Mackenna goes to her aid, Colorado, drawing his pistol, says, "Leave her," but the marshal stands over the fallen woman, pointing out there is plenty of water "less than two hours from here." Which is the kind of dialogue we want from a guide, full of narrative purpose and employed in moments of crisis, not someone offscreen filling in details of the plot. Arriving at a pool with a waterfall, Colorado dives in naked, as does Hesh-Ke. "Excuse me," pipes up Bergerman in one of the most asinine lines ever written, "but is there something between you and that Indian girl?" Mackenna explains that their relationship ended when he was responsible for her brother being hanged. This is a good example of the curse of the hyphenate: The director has shown us by the way Mackenna continually glances at Hesh-Ke that he is both wary and attracted to her. Why the relationship finished is immaterial; what is more interesting to the viewer is why the marshal became enmeshed with the Indian woman at all. Although this is a kind of miscegenation and probably as frowned upon as that of *100 Rifles*, it is passed over without comment. In this, one of the most sexist movies of the year, where women are treated as chattels and where captive women will not be rescued by upstanding citizens if it gets in the way of gold, there is something appealing about the fact that Mackenna and Hesh-Ke once enjoyed a more equal relationship. And it is a shame about the dialogue because the subsequent action, and one of the best scenes in the movie (and written by the same guy, I should point out, as was responsible for the terrible line), tells us everything we need to know about Hesh-Ke's state of mind.

Mackenna and Bergerman are tempted to get into the water. The woman keeping on her clothes seems natural but for Mackenna to do so is downright odd when the opposite would have added to the subsequent developments. The water is pretty murky for an undisturbed pool in the middle of a desert and is dark enough to conceal the full extent of Hesh-Ke's nudity. (In what seems a gender-equality titillation trade-off, the "voyeuristic admiration of the male body,"[58] Colorado at this point is lolling naked on the rocks.)

Despite complaints about the "blatant sexuality"[59] of *The Outlaw* (1943) and *Duel in the Sun* (1946), and in the 1950s "trend in the treatment of women ... [of placing] an emphasis on their bodies,"[60] this was largely limited to relatively demure scenes like bathing in a pool where the most you might expect to see is a woman's naked shoulders breaking through the surface or a woman in a bathtub covered by bubbles. However, voyeuristic scenes involving women were often mirrored by those featuring men: In *The Hallelujah Trail,* after soldiers spy on the temperance women bathing, Burt Lancaster in his bath is accosted by Lee Remick, while it is Eli Wallach who is given the bath scene in *The Good, the Bad and the Ugly.*[61] Spaghetti westerns had contained fleeting nudity—*For a Few Dollars More* (1965), for example—but the stringent U.S. Production Code restricted excess until that form of self-censorship was lifted in 1968 and replaced with the new ratings system. Ted Post's *Hang 'Em High* (1968) broke that taboo.[62] However, especially on the giant screen, and with a greater depth thanks to Cinerama, the nudity in the *Mackenna's Gold* pool scene is audacious—and effective—as the audience is shown pretty much all of Hesh-Ke's naked body. The Indian woman swims underwater and sinuously wraps her body around Mackenna. At first, he appears to respond and they come to the surface in a lip-locked embrace, but then he pushes her away. Hesh-Ke swims off and still underwater seizes hold of the fully clothed Bergerman and pulls her down and begins choking her until Mackenna comes to the rescue. It is a stunning, wordless scene, Hesh-ke's emotions tipping over into jealousy and fury. Hesh-ke's anger is not over and at night, armed with a knife, she advances on Bergerman. This time it is Colorado who intervenes.

If the audience is still wondering what happened to the Hadleyburgers who escaped the cavalry onslaught, now they have the chance to find out, and this time the slaughter is carried out by a band of Apaches. In this largely redundant scene, the Storekeeper tries to bribe his way out of impending death, and blonde locks cannot save the Younger Englishman. The purpose of the scene and the next is to remind the audience that the outlaws have not escaped, being chased by not one but two relentless pursuers, the Apaches, who do not want them to reach Canyon del Oro, and the cavalry intent on taking Colorado prisoner. The reappearance of the soldiers is the cue for the narrator who informs us that leading this small patrol is Sgt. Tibbs (Telly Savalas). "'Foxy Tibbs,' his men called him" is sending his men back to the main troop to "show the lieutenant the trail," but in so doing reduces his own ranks until it is "five against five." The odds appear in Colorado's favor and he intends doubling back and picking off the soldiers. Mackenna suggests an alternative: send Bergerman back to the soldiers to slow them down. But Bergerman, realizing she has become too great a burden on Mackenna, takes matters into her own hands and races off to the pursuing soldiers. We see Tibbs cocking his rifle, Mackenna and Colorado watching anxiously, but instead of shooting the woman, Tibbs turns on his own men and shoots them. Up pops the narrator: "Now there were only four [outlaws] left.... It made things better for Mackenna. Only thing was Hesh-Ke had ideas. She wanted Mackenna back. And now the girl was gone, she figured there was nothing to stop her" (as if the audience had not worked this out for themselves).

Foreman was pretty scathing about Thompson's performance as a director, despite the exceptional pool scene, and the way he has shown Mackenna's character from his reactions and facial expressions allowed action to dictate story, and would have created a picture with more pace had the writer-producer not insisted on giving so much screen time to the men from Hadleyburg, the narration and the scenery. I mentioned before how important proper composition is to a movie and in this regard the next scene shows Thompson is at his peak. It begins with a three-shot as the outlaw watches Hesh-Ke unroll her bedspread, the audience after the narration in no question about what will happen next. Still in the three-shot, Colorado hears someone coming. Cut to Sgt. Tibbs and Bergerman arriving. She blurts out, "He's a murderer." Tibbs is as glib with the explanations as Colorado: He says that the other soldiers will think his soldiers were killed by the outlaws. He also brings his dead men's horses, which will come in useful for loading up gold. Now Thompson moves into a six-shot: Mackenna and Bergerman kneeling on the left hand side with Hesh-Ke and Monkey standing behind them with Tibbs just off-center moving forward in the shot and Colorado to the right. As Mackenna stands up and faces Tibbs, the camera shifts to a three-shot with Monkey in the background, Mackenna in the middle and Tibbs with his back to the camera in the center. Then we switch to a three-shot with Mackenna and Tibbs on either side of the screen and Colorado lighting a cigar in the middle, but further back. We cut to Colorado then back to three-shot as Tibbs says, "No hard feelings, Miss Bergerman." Three close-ups follow in quick succession: Bergerman, Colorado and Mackenna, but Mackenna is pulling back to throw a punch. We cut to a two-shot as the punch lands on Tibbs, a close-up of Monkey stepping forward, a six-shot as Mackenna punches again and Tibbs going for his gun but being stopped by Colorado, who says, "Bergerman? Daughter of Judge Bergerman?" This is an excellent example of how fluid camerawork explores the arrival of a new person into the schematic, how the camera, once the positions of the principals have been established by the six-shot, can, with a series of slight moves, draw us closer into action.

The scene ends with the sound of approaching horses and another of Mackenna's map visualizations and in long shot the relentless cavalry. Cue the narrator: "To get away from the cavalry, they headed for the ferry on the Yellow River. They figured they could cross over on the raft there and then double back on the trail later but what they didn't know was the Apaches had taken over the whole of the Yellow River territory."[63] Yet again, all of this is irrelevant. The camera shows what they do and we scarcely need to know the politics of the Yellow River situation. But now the movie springs into real action and for the first time Cinerama shows its truth worth, its dizzying effect when used to real purpose only hinted at before. Previous movies shot in Cinerama always had a scene that involved speed, the rollercoaster ride in *This Is Cinerama* or a runaway train (*How the West Was Won*) and the effect is achieved by the audience being pitched into the camera point-of-view, the wide rounded screen creating the sense of the viewers being placed in danger. Firstly, as the Apaches tear through the trees, the camera is placed low for the Cinerama point of view. Just as the action is speeding up, in wades the narrator: "And there was another thing they didn't know. Some other Apaches had already burned down the ferry but they had been in a hurry so the raft was still afloat. They still had a chance." This is a completely pointless intervention. If there is still a raft there, who cares about the semantics? But Cinerama rides to the rescue with POV shots of descending a steep slope and shaky camera, the scene continuing for a few minutes. The outlaws reach the river, push off in the raft, and get caught up in a shoot-out, one of the most powerful shots being a horse with an arrow through both sides of its neck. But they are also caught in a strong current, another Cinerama trope (*How the West Was Won*), and tension mounts as the camera switches to the POV of the racing water and the oncoming rapids and the sound, magnified in six-track stereo, of the thundering waterfall that lies ahead. The outlaws mount their horses and jump into the river and reach the shore in safety, the only casualties the extra horses, while the Cinerama effect continues as the raft is smashed in the rapids.

Now comes the time to tie up a loose end. As they sleep, a horse approaches. Colorado awakes, sniffing. The horse carrying the corpse of Prairie Dog appears. Colorado shoots at it to scare it off but Monkey shoots back. There is another visualization, with which the audience will be more familiar, for a picture of a tall rock pillar is the main image in all the advertising. The narrator says, "Now they were there. They had made it. The place Mackenna knew as Shaking Rock." This is redundant since Mackenna also says, "We're here." For reasons not explained to the audience, they must wait here until sunrise.

Now that they have arrived, Mackenna realizes that, despite Colorado's promise, it is unlikely he will leave the canyon alive. He tells Bergerman not to go into the canyon tomorrow. This could easily be done with a scene involving the two hostages, but Thompson maintains the emotional pressure by having Hesh-Ke watching. Another verbally underplayed element of the picture now comes into play as Mackenna asks Colorado for his gun (and the girl). Although there have been fisticuffs aplenty, and although tradition dictates that a shootout between hero and villain must come at the end, Mackenna's helplessness when stripped of his weapon has been one of the repeated plot points: In a western, a man without a gun is always at the mercy of someone else. Although many westerns contain sections where the hero is beaten up (the spaghetti western raised the stakes on this particular game), rarely has a hero been so vulnerable for so long.

This little section also humanizes the otherwise ruthless Colorado. Just as in *Support Your Local Sheriff*, Colorado has an unlikely dream, of getting to Paris, and has hoarded advertisements picturing its delights. And there are three final twists: Bergerman is afflicted with gold fever, and wants to see the gold before departing; the first kiss of Mackenna and Bergerman is witnessed by Hesh-Ke; and Monkey kneels before the pillar as if praying. This trio of neatly observed moments will play out at the denouement.

The sunrise is worth waiting for. It is a glorious scene. After a close-up of the rising sun and the pillar, and the screen changing color, the shadow of the pillar creeps across the canyon floor and points to a crack in the canyon wall. The crack is a tunnel entrance and on the other side, the sun is shining on a seam of bright gold. We have another section of pure Cinerama lasting two minutes as the camera races down the twisting track leading to the gold, alternating audience POV with shots of the riders. (Disappointingly, there also some matte shots.[64]) As they ride down, Hesh-Ke tries to push Bergerman over the edge, but it is the Indian who falls to her death. When they reach the gold, there is eerie music like a heartbeat, as if the canyon is alive. Bergerman gives in to temptation and wallows in a pool of golden mud. Then we are treated to a series of stills showing their wild enjoyment (this particular novel effect was overshadowed by its use in *Butch Cassidy and the Sundance Kid*). Mackenna has spotted an escape route above the gold seam and begins to climb toward it with Bergerman. Sgt. Tibbs gets a tomahawk in his chest. Colorado draws his pistol to shoot Monkey, but Monkey has removed the bullets. "Spirits tell me what to do," he says. "This is Apache gold. They tell me kill everyone today." As Monkey bends over Tibbs to retrieve his tomahawk, Colorado throws a knife in his back and, for no apparent reason except to have the compulsory battle between enemies and because he is relentless, Colorado, tomahawk in hand, pursues the escapees up the rock even though the easier exit route lies in the opposite direction. When they reach a ledge, the battle begins, but not the traditional shootout because neither has a gun. Colorado, courtesy of the tomahawk, has the edge. Thompson eschews traditional music (compare this, for example, to the operatic climax of *Once Upon a Time in the West*) and the only sound is that of the wind. Bergerman at last comes out of her torpor of helplessness and pulls off her belt to throw to Mackenna as a weapon, but her aim is off and it sails over the edge. The close-quarters fight in the confined space is

Had everything gone according to plan, *Mackenna's Gold* would have been the fifth U.S. roadshow in Omar Sharif's career following *Lawrence of Arabia* (1962), *The Fall of the Roman Empire* (1964), *Doctor Zhivago* (1965) and *Funny Girl* (1968). Pressbook (Hannan Collection).

enthralling, but just as Mackenna gains the upper hand, bullets ring out. The Apaches are galloping out of the tunnel and down the winding track. The volume of noise disturbs the canyon and suddenly the rocks begin to shake, some tumble down, the sand ripples and the ground heaves up. The Indians escape the way they have come. As Colorado, Mackenna and Bergerman reach the canyon floor and mount horses, the earthquake grows in intensity. The special effects are awesome for the time (but timid and amateurish by today's standards) and the escape against the background of the worsening quake is very effective, the entire three-minute sequence containing no music, just sound effects. The tunnel collapses behind them but they are still not safe out in the open as the Shaking Rock collapses.

There is a happy ending, of sorts. All escape, but Mackenna, this time the relentless one, tells Colorado before he rides off, "You know I'm coming after you." And there is one final twist. Bergerman, to show she is free of gold fever, tosses away gold dust. Mackenna smiles in approval as the camera pans down to his saddle bag, which is bursting with gold nuggets.

Who knows how much better—or worse—*Mackenna's Gold* would have been if released at its original length. But working from the truncated version, there is certainly an argument that it would have been a lot better with another 20 minutes or so lopped out, the good men from Hadleyburg eliminated, Sgt. Tibbs' betrayal of his soldiers sufficient to make the point about the effect gold has on decent men, although that "message" needs little further emphasis. There is more than enough conflict—Mackenna vs. Colorado, Hech-Ke vs. Bergerman—to keep the tension level high, never mind the hidden agenda of Monkey and his belligerence towards Mackenna, never mind Bergerman's hatred of Colorado and her fears about her fate. Cavalry and Apaches provide enough chase and escape, Mackenna enough fights, the two hostages enough other drama. The scenery would have greater impact if limited and, of course, the narrator should be taken out and shot. This is nothing more—or nothing worse—than a decent western wrapped up in the bloated shadow of a roadshow. And it is a shame that the word "roadshow" ever entered any discussions about developing Will Henry's novel into a movie.

Critical Reception

Variety came out in favor of *Mackenna's Gold*: "splendid western, stars plus special effects and grandeur should insure box office success."[65] *The Hollywood Reporter* predicted, "Audiences should queue up," and *Film Daily* proclaimed it "a Fine, exciting western adventure."[66] But Vincent Canby in The *New York Times* called it a "truly stunning absurdity," The *New York Daily News*, while generally positive, nonetheless complained that it was "pretentious." *New York* magazine and the *Washington Post* were among the naysayers.[67] Perhaps Peck's own opinion was the most damning: "*Mackenna's Gold* was a terrible western, just wretched."[68]

Box Office

Star fatigue did not occur in the days of the studio system, when releases were carefully spaced out to give the public breathing room between each release. Actor independence meant timing of releases was removed from studio control. Gregory Peck's movies in 1969 came from three different companies, Universal (*The Stalking Moon*), Twentieth Century–Fox (*The Chairman*) and Columbia (*Mackenna's Gold*), and Omar Sharif was in the same position with MGM for *Mayerling*, Fox for *Che!* and *Mackenna's Gold* from Columbia. As you might expect, releases were not coordinated, studios did not sit down around a table and discuss how to avoid each other's movies clashing. So in the first six months of 1969, audiences were treated to three pictures apiece from the stars. Worse, both had movies in direct competition, Fox bringing out *The Chairman* and *Che!* at the same time as *Mackenna's Gold*. Worse again, both actors were recovering from the poor showing of films released in the U.S. earlier in the year, Peck from *The Stalking Moon* and Sharif from *Mayerling*, although the latter was a big hit overseas.[69] So by the time *Mackenna's Gold* finally reached theaters, audiences may have been suffering from star fatigue or even lack of interest given the response to the earlier movies. Whatever the reason, *Mackenna's Gold* did not race out of the gate. Its final rentals tally of $3.1 million—42nd spot in the annual chart,[70] ahead of *The Stalking Moon* and *Once Upon a Time in the West*, but well below the much less expensive *Support Your Local Sheriff* and *100 Rifles*—put it in the category of flop, if not, given the budget, disaster. However, it was a huge hit in India, setting a record in Madras for the best showing for a foreign picture.[71]

7

Retread of a Retread

Guns of the Magnificent Seven

Starring George Kennedy, James Whitmore, Monte Markham, Bernie Casey, Joe Don Baker; directed by Paul Wendkos; United Artists; 105 minutes.

Misguided Misfire

There would have been no sequel to *The Magnificent Seven* (1960) except for the success United Artists had enjoyed with reiterations of the James Bond, Pink Panther and Beatles films. The company had come to believe that repetition could guarantee success. However, a second western in this particular series was a greater risk than a new spy picture, comedy or pop musical for the simple reason that the original *Magnificent Seven* had flopped, just $2.3 million in rentals, finishing a disappointing 38th in the annual chart. UA had panicked before release, demanding 20 minutes of cuts, and when this request was refused, throwing the picture out in wide release (known at the time as "saturation") at a time when that method of distribution was reserved for low-budget movies, or ones expecting poor word-of-mouth.[1]

Though domestic box office did not stack up compared to its cost, the western did generate word of mouth, returning time and again to neighborhood theaters in the U.S., and doing substantially better business abroad.[2] *The Magnificent Seven* might have been considered a prime target for reissue except for the fact that it been sold almost immediately to television, holding the unwelcome record for the fastest-ever transfer to the small screen of a big-budget picture. It made its small-screen premiere on February 3, 1963.[3] So desperate was UA to develop ancillary income that it had toyed with the idea of creating a 90-minute television series with Sam Peckinpah acting as executive producer.[4] The movie remained in the public's memory thanks to Elmer Bernstein's theme tune being adopted for the Marlboro TV commercials and the release of *The Great Escape* (1963) which featured several of the western's alumni.[5] A sequel, to be called *The Return of the Magnificent Seven*, was first mooted in 1964 with Yul Brynner reprising his role as Chris[6] but a lawsuit by Anthony Quinn, who had at one time been offered a part in the original,[7] and the prospect of an Elmer Bernstein-John Sturges musical version of the western[8] put that idea in cold storage.

When the concept was revived in 1965, it went through two sets of writers and directors, Burt Kennedy replacing Walter Grauman, months of delays, and a switch of location from Mexico to Spain before filming finally began on February.[9] However, where the budgets for James Bond spy films had increased with every new adventure, the budget for *Return of the Seven*, as it was now known, went in the opposite direction, down to just $1.78 million.[10] One of the byproducts of the low budget was that the producers simply plundered the previous score, with little additional extra music, and Bernstein received a second Oscar nomination for effectively the same compositions as *The Magnificent Seven*.

The ongoing popularity of the original was in part due to the wealth of up-and-coming acting talent involved, Steve McQueen now a major movie star, James Coburn on the verge of a breakthrough into the major leagues after *Our Man Flint* (1966), Charles Bronson also on the threshold and Robert Vaughn hot on television in *The Man from U.N.C.L.E* and producers Mirisch, hoping to repeat the trick, brought in to support Yul Brynner television favorites Robert Fuller (*Laramie*, 1959–1963, and *Wagon Train*, 1959–1965), Warren Oates (*Stoney Burke*, 1962–1963), Julian Mateos (*Primera Fila*, 1964–1965) and newcomer Jordan Christopher in his sophomore role after *The Fat Spy* (1966).[11] But this was not so much a sequel as a remake, the story revolving around saving a village from psychotic Mexican rancher Lorca (Emilio Fernandez[12]). The *New York Times*' Vincent Canby condemned it as "philosophical twaddle" and *Variety* complained it was a "plodding, cliché-ridden script." The public appeared to be in agreement and *Return of the Seven* wound up with a dispiriting $1.6 million in domestic rentals, taking 70th position in the annual rankings.[13]

Like its predecessor, *Return of the Seven* did much better business abroad, gunning down $3.4 million, enough to persuade United Artists it was worth a third go-round. However, by this time UA was in financial trouble and would soon record an industry pre-tax loss of $85 million.[14] Mirisch was also in trouble: "In an unpredictable market, we sought further safety in presold material."[15] So the budget for *Guns of the Magnificent Seven*—originally it was to be called *The Magnificent Seven Ride Again*[16]—decreased yet again, now down to $1.36 million, and the ingredients appeared inferior. Director Paul Wendkos[17] (*Gidget*, 1959, and *Gidget Goes to Rome*, 1963) had only made two movies in the past five years, the low-budget programmers *Johnny Tiger* (1966) and *Attack on the Iron Coast* (1968). Finding someone willing to follow in Brynner's shoes proved problematic.

"It wasn't easy to cast the part," said Walter Mirisch.[18] He gambled on George Kennedy, who had won critical acclaim and an Oscar[19] for his role in *Cool Hand Luke* (1967). But this marked the first time he had received top billing; strong supporting roles (*The Dirty Dozen*, 1967, *Bandolero!*, 1968, *The Boston Strangler*, 1968) were previously seen as his forte. The rest of the cast were largely movie unknowns. Drawn from television were Monte Markham (*The Second Hundred Years*, 1967–1968), who played Keno, and Wende Wagner (*The Green Hornet*, 1966–1967), who had the female lead, Tina. While James Whitmore (Levi) had some acting heft, Reni Santoni (Max) was a novice and Bernie Casey (Cassie) and Joe Don Baker (Slater) were making their movie debuts. At least writer Herman Hoffman,[20] who had scripted Wendkos' last movie, came up with a change of plot.

Before going to the impregnable El Cavadad de Rata Jail, Mexican revolutionary Quintero (Fernando Rey[21]) hands over $600 to his followers to buy guns and continue the campaign. Max decides to use the money to free their leader and crosses the border to recruit legendary gunslinger Chris Adams (Kennedy). As with the other pictures in

One of the many action scenes from *Guns of the Magnificent Seven* (1969). Apart from Yul Brynner, Fernando Rey was the only actor to appear twice in a "Magnificent Seven" movie (Hannan Collection).

the series, each of the "seven" is introduced with a cameo demonstrating their personality and skills. Max sees Chris trying to save horse thief Keno from an unjust trial, which he eventually achieves with his trigger finger. Chris agrees to help Max and sets out to hire five others at $100 apiece. First to sign on is Keno, an expert in hand-to-hand combat. Next is dynamiter Cassie, a former slave. Slater is a one-armed gunslinger, P.J. (Scott Thomas) a chronically ill wrangler and Levi the knife-thrower. However, there are obvious connections to the original. Once they witness the brutal treatment of the peasants, the mercenaries become less mercenary. Instead of adopting a whole village as in the original, they adopt a boy whose father is on a chain gang with Levi acting as his father figure. There is a love interest, P.J. falling for peasant girl Tina. As before, there is conflict with the people the mercenaries are trying to help. When the rebels discover what the $600 has been used for, they refuse to assist. Chris and his men, after casing the prison from outside and realizing their small contingent is not enough for the job, have to train a prison gang (three wagon loads) they have freed, one of whom is the boy's father, and another, in an extremely unlikely twist, is Zapata. In preparation for the assault on the jail, Chris and his men steal uniforms and liberate sulphur wagons, using this method of transport as an excuse to enter the fort, since conceivably they could be arriving from a nearby sulphur mine. The attack is well-planned, Levi disabling the watchtower guard,

Cassie scaling the walls and taking control of the watchtower's Gatling gun (as ferocious a weapon as in *The Wild Bunch*), and the doors ripped open by explosives. However, the combined forces of the mercenaries and the trained peasants are not enough to win the day until the rebels suffer a change of heart and race to the rescue. Four of the "seven" are killed and, in the mandatory act of generosity, the three remaining leave the $600 behind.

In truth, it is far from awful. There is a core twist in that the Seven act as attackers rather than defenders, assaulting a stronghold as in *The Professionals* (1966), rather than waiting to be attacked as in the 1960 original. This allowed the director time for more detailed planning rather than simply improving the line of defense. The script has some nice touches, each character provided with an interesting back story, and the action is well-handled. Also, the film should have benefited from the trend towards "group" action pictures, as epitomized by *The Dirty Dozen* (1967), *The Devil's Brigade* (1968) and *Where Eagles Dare* (1969), which "in an age of specialization ... seem to have unlimited appeal."[22] However, all three pictures, especially the first two where training was an essential element, put considerably more imagination and drama into the assaults and the areas under attack (a heavily fortified palatial mansion, a strategic Italian hilltop and an Alpine castle). More importantly, the trio boasted bona fide stars (Lee Marvin, William Holden, Richard Burton and Clint Eastwood); *Guns of the Magnificent Seven* came up short in that department. George Kennedy, while dangerous-looking in a rough-and-tumble fashion, lacked the menacing stare and icy demeanor of Yul Brynner. In the absence of a charismatic star, there is only so often you can go to the well before it runs dry.

The producers made one other miscalculation. According to *International Motion Picture Exhibitor*, "Contrary to many recent westerns, the Magnificent Seven are not violence-prone anti-heroes. Clean-shaven and attractively moral, they should have extra appeal to those offended by the excessive violence of other westerns." In reality, the dumbing-down of the original Magnificent Seven, whose morals were questionable even if they occasionally undertook upstanding actions, and who lived by their skills with the tools of violence, was more likely to work against the picture, in an era when the new generation of western heroes had grubby beards and few morals. Mirisch–UA also had doubts about the finished product: Filming began in Spain in April 1968,[23] and then the movie was shelved for nearly nine months. While it opened in the summer, the traditional period for opening westerns, this year it faced an uncommonly high standard of opposition in *Once Upon a Time in the West*, *Mackenna's Gold*, *The Wild Bunch* and *True Grit*.

Critical Response

Variety optimistically said the movie was "able to rise above routine storyline via rugged treatment."[24] *International Motion Picture Exhibitor*: "well-acted, action-packed western."[25] Mainstream critics were harsh, Howard Thompson in the *New York Times* leading the attack with "all the magnificence of a dead burro."[26]

Box Office

There was even less public interest in the second sequel than to the first retread. Rentals of just $1.5 million were recorded in the U.S. though again it did better abroad with $2.5 million.[27] Despite the lackluster domestic box office, or perhaps to make up for it, UA–Mirisch embarked on another gamble. *Return of the Seven* returned to screens just three years after its debut in August 1966, in some respects in direct competition with the latter stages of the general release of *Guns of the Magnificent Seven*, and also in competition with a UA reissue double bill of *The Good, the Bad and the Ugly* and *Hang 'Em High*, almost as if the purpose of the second sequel was to act as a trailer for the first sequel, and, also, as it happened, offering an unwelcome comparison to the deficiencies of the new film compared to the older one.

8

Tough Rider

True Grit

Starring John Wayne, Glen Campbell, Kim Darby; directed by Henry Hathaway; screenplay by Marguerite Roberts; Paramount; 139 minutes

The King Expands His Kingdom

It is not generally known, or admitted, that the reason John Wayne became a top star in the early 1950s was not due to westerns but from films in other genres—war films like *Sands of Iwo Jima* (1949),[1] which garnered him his first Oscar nomination, and *Flying Leathernecks* (1951), the romantic comedy *The Quiet Man* (1952) and the adventure films *The High and the Mighty* (1954) and *The Conqueror* (1956). All of these were among the Top 20 Films of their year at the box office whereas *Rio Grande* (1950) and *Hondo* (1953) were not.[2] The success of *Stagecoach* (1939) had not catapulted Wayne onto the Hollywood A-list, nor did his marquee value increase much during the war when many top male actors were called up. For much of the decade he received second billing, often to women: to Claire Trevor in *Dark Command* (1940), to Marlene Dietrich in *Seven Sinners* (1940), to Joan Blondell in *Lady for a Night* (1942), to Joan Crawford in *Reunion in France* (1942), to Ray Milland in *Reap the Wild Wind* (1942), to Jean Arthur in *A Lady Takes a Chance* (1943), to Robert Montgomery in *They Were Expendable*, and to Claudette Colbert in *Without Reservations* (1946). He received third billing behind Dietrich and Randolph Scott in *The Spoilers* (1942). But the box office performances of *The Searchers* (1956) and *Rio Bravo* (1959) restored his faith in the genre and in the 1960s he made more westerns—11 in total—than anything else.

There was more to it than that, of course. He was, James Stewart and to some extent Bette Davis apart, just about the only survivor of the Golden Age of Hollywood, and his range was limited. Wayne wasn't cut out for the musicals, comedies, historical adventures, contemporary dramas[3] and spy pictures that dominated that decade. So, in some senses, the western was his default. And it had served him well. With the exception of *The Comancheros* (1961), all these westerns had been big hits.

After his initial battle with lung cancer, he enjoyed an extended period of success in Henry Hathaway's *The Sons of Katie Elder* (1965), Howard Hawks' *El Dorado* (1967) and Burt Kennedy's *The War Wagon* (1967). He diversified with the Vietnam war picture *The Green Berets* (1968), which he directed, and which was a hit, and the same-year

The Comancheros was the last film of legendary Hollywood director Michael Curtiz, who had helmed *Casablanca* (1942), *Mildred Pierce* (1945) and *White Christmas* (1954). Trade press advertisement (*Box Office*, October 2, 1961).

adventure *Hellfighters* which fell short of his high box office standards. So when any big western picture was mooted, it was either Wayne or James Stewart whom producers first approached.

Charles Portis was a journalist with one modern novel, *Norwood,*[4] published in 1966, to his name when he wrote *True Grit*, published in 1968. Unusually for a western, it lasted 22 weeks on the *New York Times* bestseller list. The main attraction for a reader was the equally unusual first-person narrator, Mattie Ross, an old lady telling the tale of how as a 14-year-old in Arkansas she sought bloody revenge for the death of her father. The narrative voice was highly individual with colorful phrases, punchy dialogue, and a taut storyline.

Producer Hal Wallis snapped it up. Wallis had been making his own pictures for over two decades, having originally overseen films as varied as *Captain Blood* (1935) and *Casablanca* (1942). As an independent, he was responsible for launching the careers of the comedy duo Dean Martin and Jerry Lewis (*My Friend Irma,* 1949) and Charlton Heston (*Dark City,* 1950) and instrumental in the work of Burt Lancaster (*I Walk Alone,* 1947) and Elvis Presley (*Loving You,* 1957). He was at home in all genres from the historical drama *Becket*[5] (1964) to the comedy *Barefoot in the Park* (1967). And he also had a western pedigree, having set up John Sturges' *Gunfight at the O.K. Corral* (1957), *The Sons of Katie Elder* (1965) and *5 Card Stud* (1968).

There was barely a year between the *True Grit* publication and the movie's world premiere. From the start, Wallis had John Wayne in mind for Rooster Cogburn, with Robert Mitchum as back-up. Mia Farrow turned down the role of Mattie Ross when she found out the director was to be Henry Hathaway, Wayne wanted Michele Carey (*El Dorado*), who was unavailable, or his daughter Aissa, whom Hathaway ruled out, Sally Field from the television series *The Flying Nun* was also considered, but the part finally went to 21-year-old Kim Darby.[6] She had been in the movies since 1963 (an uncredited role in *Bye Bye Birdie*) and had mostly been confined to guest roles in television series such as *The Fugitive, Star Trek, Gunsmoke* and *Bonanza.* Elvis Presley was touted for the role of Le Boeuf but his manager Col. Parker insisted his client receive top billing. So the role went to another popular singer, Glen Campbell, who had made his movie debut in *The Cool Ones* (1967). Robert Duvall, filling the boots of Lucky Ned Pepper, was also a refugee from television (*The Outer Limits, The Fugitive, Combat*) although he had delivered a memorable performance as Boo Radley in *To Kill a Mockingbird* (1962) and had risen to third-billing for Francis Ford Coppola's *The Rain People* (1969).[7]

Hathaway, a former child actor, had directed 60 movies beginning in 1932. But he had learned about direction at the feet of Josef von Sternberg and Victor Fleming, both hard taskmasters, and only made the move into megging at the third attempt. First, he had spent nine months touring India with the idea of making a film in the style of the silent documentaries *Grass: A Nation's Battle for Life* (1925) and *Chang: A Drama of the Wilderness* (1927).[8] He managed to attract the interest of producer Irving G. Thalberg, but then Thalberg died before funding materialized. Next, Paramount intended to hire him when the studio planned an early 1930s investment in color. But they got cold feet and the idea was dropped.[9] Finally, when Paramount decided it was going to make its own westerns, rather than buying them, Hathaway was hired to direct *Heritage of the Desert* (1932) starring Randolph Scott. He was paid $100 a week for his first two westerns and then $65 a week for the next two after the Depression bit.[10] Hathaway hit pay dirt with the adventure *The Lives of a Bengal Lancer* (1935) with Gary Cooper and the comedy *Go West Young Man* (1936) with Mae West. When Paramount finally embraced three-color Technicolor, they chose Hathaway to direct the adventure *The Trail of the Lonesome Pine* (1936) starring Sylvia Sidney and Fred MacMurray. "It cannot be merely accidental that he was selected," commented historian Kingsley Canham, arguing that Hathaway had "more than just an aptitude for freshening familiar material through technical resourcefulness."[11] And like John Ford, he was economical with the camera. "I only shoot what can be used so the producer has no choice.... I always cut in the camera, the cutter just has to put the ends together," he said.[12] Determined to achieve verisimilitude, instead of using studio handmade locusts for the biopic *Brigham Young* (1940), he travelled to Nevada where there had been a big invasion of the insects.[13] Except for this film and *The Shepherd of the Hills* (1941), starring Wayne, Hathaway steered clear of westerns, preferring action and drama. However, he was instrumental in helping Wayne extend his acting style. For *The Shepherd of the Hills*, Hathaway "added new subtleties to the already characteristic western hero persona—the roiling gait and economy of dialog were still very much in evidence but his acting was more mature, more sensitive, and more assured."[14]

Hathaway was called upon to demonstrate further technical mastery in the first of Twentieth Century–Fox's semi-documentary dramas, *The House on 92nd Street* (1945). This was followed by the film noirs *The Dark Corner* (1946) and *Kiss of Death* (1947). He made his first western in a decade with *Rawhide* (1951) toplining Tyrone Power and Susan Hayward, and only two other westerns in the 1950s, *Garden of Evil* (1954), teaming Cooper and Hayward, and *From Hell to Texas* (1958) with Audie Murphy, the twist in this one being the hero rather than the villain subjected to a manhunt. He was so impressed with the acting skills of Marilyn Monroe in *Niagara* (1953) that he purchased Somerset Maugham's *Of Human Bondage* intending to team her with Montgomery Clift, but nothing came of the concept.[15] He worked with Wayne again in *Legend of the Lost* (1957).

Like Wayne, Hathaway returned in triumph to the western in the 1960s, all bar two of his movies in this decade in this genre. The first four of the decade starred Wayne: *North to Alaska* (1960), *How the West Was Won* (1962),[16] *Circus World* (1964) and *The Sons of Katie Elder*. He had finished up on *5 Card Stud* when Hal Wallis invited him to direct *True Grit*. He had only received one Oscar nomination, four decades previously, for *The Lives of a Bengal Lancer*, and no avant-garde French film critic was reassessing his work, but he was known to bring movies in on time, and had his own distinct style if anyone could be bothered looking for it. Certain themes did reappear, revenge for one; it was central to *The Trail of the Lonesome Pine*, *Kiss of Death*, the historical adventure *The Black Rose* (1950), *Prince Valiant* (1954), *The Sons of Katie Elder* and *Nevada Smith* (1966).[17] He also focused on disruption within the family, and situations where an older man aids an impetuous youngster, both instrumental to *True Grit*.[18] Kingsley Canham observed, "He is the only director I know to have specialized in films about backwoods and mountains."[19]

Screenwriter Marguerite Roberts was also old-school, born in 1905, with over 30 screen credits. She sold her first script while working as a secretary at Fox, and had her first screen credit in 1933 for *Sailor's Luck*. By 1939 she was earning $2500 a week at MGM and turned out *Honky Tonk* (1941) with Clark Gable and Lana Turner, *Sea of Grass* (1946) with Katharine Hepburn and Spencer Tracy, the *Gunga Din* remake *Soldiers Three* (1951) and the big-budget historical adventure *Ivanhoe* (1952) with Robert Taylor and Elizabeth Taylor. She fell out of favor with Hollywood for her left-wing sympathies and was black-

Steve McQueen in *Nevada Smith* (1966) adopts the "crucifixion" pose made famous by James Dean. A new edition of the Harold Robbins bestseller *The Carpetbaggers* was printed with "Nevada Smith" credits on the front and back. Exhibitors Showmanship Manual (Hannan Collection).

listed for nearly a decade, until *The Main Attraction* (1962) with Pat Boone, *Diamond Head* (1962) with Charlton Heston and *Rampage* (1963) with Robert Mitchum. She had been working for Hal Wallis on *5 Card Stud* before receiving the commission to adapt the Portis book. Roberts was familiar with the Old West, since her father had been a Colorado lawman.

Screenwriter Wendell Mayes, who wrote *From Hell to Texas*, commented, "Henry Hathaway is very easy for a writer to work with."[20] Hathaway said, "When a screenplay is finished, I go through it and work on it. I worked on *True Grit* with Marguerite Roberts because there was a great deal of repetition in the book and I eliminated a lot of things."[21] John Wayne felt that Hathaway "never got the creative credit I think is due him.... He was sort of a story doctor ... a fine, instinctive creator."[22]

Her first problem was how to translate the book's distinctive first-person style onto the screen without the entire movie sounding too archaic. Although many speeches were lifted verbatim from the book, it was Roberts who established Mattie Ross as an authority figure from the outset by introducing the teenager as her father's "bookkeeper" and inventing the argument about the type of horses he intended to buy. The result is an unusual composite of tight storyline, exuberant characterization and wonderful dialogue. The movie was filmed mainly in Colorado—Ouray, Owl Creek Pass, Ridgway, Canon City, Montrose, Bishop and Gunnison—as well as Durango, Mexico, and Inyo National Park in California, where Hot Creek was used along with Sherwin Summit.

John Wayne Meets His Match

I watched all these films in the order that they were released in order that I might come to them as fresh as an audience of the period might have done, and I am sure that I experienced the same sense of unalloyed joy as those moviegoers on first viewing *True Grit*, an old-style western with a modernized anti-hero in Rooster Cogburn (John Wayne), nearly as "rapaciously brutal" as *The Wild Bunch*, a script with language that captured the period, a heroine Mattie Ross (Kim Darby) in the robust Barbara Stanwyck-Maureen O'Hara mold, humor and action in equal measure, and an unfussy director (Henry Hathaway) who loved the panorama even more than John Ford. Although critically *True Grit* has always been in the shadow of *The Wild Bunch*,[23] and still mostly disdained by academics, I would argue that it has been grossly underrated and is fully deserving of a re-evaluation.

Despite directing very much in the old school, Hathaway exhibits many stylistic flourishes, not least the very long shot which has rarely been used to such effect. He also utilizes the shaky-camera point-of-view in a much more effective manner than *Mackenna's Gold* to record Cogburn's charge at the outlaws; there is even a zoom to pick out the villain Tom Chaney.[24] Also, you know exactly where you are in a Hathaway picture, not just in the narrative sense, but in terms of how people lived and where the towns and farms were in relation to each other (the Ross farm is 70 miles from Fort Smith, the hamlet of McAllister 60 miles from the villains' hideout). He liked to show many aspects of a town, so we see where the courthouse is in relation to the jail and the stable by the simple expedient of having the characters walk past them. And the movie is littered with sound effects of the most ordinary kind (blacksmith's hammer, train whistle, footsteps). The film is as much about progress as *Once Upon a Time in the West* and *The Wild Bunch*.

The name of the town where much of the initial action takes place, Fort Smith, indicates it was once a frontier town. Rooster Cogburn feels crowded out by a new generation of lawyers challenging swift justice, and Mattie Ross is well schooled in argument, winning many a confrontation with apparently more experienced and wily men by being more adept at negotiation and like a chess player always one move ahead. The aftermath of the Civil War lingers in the background, demonstrated by Mattie's weapon and Cogburn's antipathy to the Texas Ranger (Glen Campbell). But the story strikes an even balance: No matter how assured Mattie Ross comes across in civilization, she almost comes apart in the wilds and without the protection of Cogburn would have met the kind of fate at the hands of men undergone by female characters in *The Stalking Moon*, *Mackenna's Gold* and *The Wild Bunch*.

The entire credit sequence consists of three shots in the classic manner of an opening sequence. We see the Ross farm from above surrounded by countryside with the mountains in the background. This shot is held for about 90 seconds. Then the camera cuts to a closer view and finally closer still to the porch where Frank Ross is saying goodbye to his young son with his wife standing holding a baby. The wife wants him to take the train (the first sign of progress). Ross calls out, "Where's Mattie?" and she immediately appears in the window, framed slightly off-center. She looks like any other young, eager, not especially attractive teenager. Her father goes inside and treats her with considerable respect, calling her his "little bookkeeper" as she doles out funds for the trip (and his lucky gold pieces) and, clearly a different kind of youngster again, not just arguing with her father the way young women are apt to do with either parent, but with spirited purpose and a hint of authority, insisting he is buying the wrong sort of horse. He packs a long-barreled pistol, of sentimental value, dating back to the Civil War. The first of Hathaway's trademark lingering shots ends the sequence, as the father and ranch hand Tom Chaney ride away from the camera. Mattie turns to her mother and says of Chaney: "Now there's trash for you.... Poppa took him in when he was starving and gave him a home."

We cut to a camera peering in through the window of a Fort Smith saloon: Chaney being hauled away from a poker game by Ross, dragged outside, and in a moment of abrupt violence, after a brief argument, Ross is killed (without Peckinpah bloodshed) and his remaining money stolen.

This would be Mattie's first time in Fort Smith, probably her first visit to a town of any size, and Hathaway does not take the Sergio Leone route of heralding the arrival of Claudia Cardinale in *Once Upon a Time in the West* with operatic music and a crane shot of the new town. Instead, we hear the clanging of the train bell before we see Mattie and Poindexter, an African American, emerging, along with a flood of passengers, from a side street onto the Fort Smith main street. Nor is she dressed as glamorously as Miss Cardinale: She wears a simple long smock-dress, a hat clamped on her head, belongings in a leather bag. She asks directions to the undertaker's and is directed "round the corner from the courthouse," which provides the character with reason to go there. It should be said here that the movie is full of audience direction: We are always told where Mattie will go next or where Cogburn is intending to go, with accompanying plausible reason, especially when later Cogburn calls off the hunt for the outlaws. There is no exploration of mystery, the characters are always upfront, and where characters express regret, it is minus the self-pitying of *The Wild Bunch*. Nobody is defined by something they should have done instead, so, in that respect, the narrative is as clear as the overall direction.

Mattie cannot understand why the town is so busy but the more experienced Poindexter points out that there is a hanging. From her point-of-view, we see in long shot through a crowd the hanging stage. Hathaway presents the hanging as an everyday event, with a crowd materializing. Although the children gather round and push each other on swings hanging from the trees, or sell food, such (justified) violence is as clearly a part of their lives as that of the children of *The Wild Bunch* and without recourse to torturing scorpions. There is no focus on the children, who are merely shown within the general shots. When Mattie discovers that the undertaker went to the hanging, she decides, "I'll go along," knowing it is something she will not want to tell Mother about. There is an inherent humanity in Hathaway because as she makes this decision, we hear people singing a hymn, as though the men and woman out for a day's entertainment understand the solemnity of the occasion and are willing to afford the men facing death a good send-off.

As she returns to the hanging area, not set in a dusty main street but a central location of grass and trees probably most commonly used for picnics and celebration, we see that the crowd is much bigger now. Hathaway has no shots of other people rushing to the hanging, or any close-ups of expectant, bloodthirsty faces, just a shot of more people. A bystander tells Mattie that Judge Parker[25] watches hangings from his veranda "out of duty." Mattie responds, in the first of her pithy wise remarks, "Who knows what's in a man's heart?" Nor is there any close-up of the terrified men awaiting death. Hoods are placed over their heads. Poindexter tries to shield Mattie's eyes but she pushes his hand away, proof this is not your normal prissy, hysterical teenager, but a woman in a girl's body. She does not flinch, her response limited to the words, "My goodness." But, as we shall later discover, the hanging has made its mark, and not in the way we might expect, for she wants exactly the same justice meted out to Tom Chaney. Perhaps that is her consolation as she views her father's corpse at the undertaker, shedding no tears and refusing the invitation to kiss her beloved father.

Hathaway shows some of the town by virtue of Mattie and her companion walking to the courthouse where a man reads a paper on the steps. The sheriff knows Chaney as Chambers and imparts the information that he is riding with Lucky Ned Pepper and is in the Indian Territory, over which only a U.S. marshal has jurisdiction. Asked to name the best marshal, the sheriff suggests three, of whom the second, Rooster Cogburn, is the meanest: "a pitiless man, double tough, fear doesn't enter into his thinking." She learns that he will be at the Federal Court this afternoon bringing in a load of prisoners, though whether Chaney is one remains unknown.

The sheriff hands over her father's gun and directs her to Col. Stonehill's for her father traps and the boarding house for the rest of his stuff. She dispenses with Poindexter, and with a complete lack of sentimentality, instructs him to take her father's body back home and "put him in a better coffin," meaning she will not be back in time for the funeral, and also to make sure her mother signs no contracts in her absence (making Mattie the "man of the house"). Hathaway holds the shot of the pair departing the courthouse as they walk along the corridor until they are down the steps. The trademark shots serve to separate story developments, slowing down the pace, rather than achieving something similar through a more filmic device like a dissolve.

The next shot has the prisoner cage reversing into view, from the left of the screen. A small crowd has gathered and we hear Cogburn's voice before we see him, as if the director is preparing us for a different John Wayne. This is the actor in a new timbre, the

***True Grit* broke all records at New York's Radio City Music Hall with the biggest four days ($177,393), biggest holiday ($52,194) and biggest Saturday ($50, 610). Trade press advertisement (*International Motion Picture Exhibitor*, July 16, 1969).**

usual slow drawl replaced by a raucous bark. And it is a different Wayne, one eye covered by a black patch, giving him a piratical look. He hustles the prisoners out, viciously kicking one straggler in the butt. It is worth mentioning the director's attention to detail: This scene occurs next to a general store and we see an advertisement ("Staples to Fancy Grocers Fruit and Vegetables" painted on the exterior, at whose foot is a stack of logs). Wayne walks differently, too. Instead of the famous slow walk, Cogburn is a man in a hurry, pushing forward with purposeful strides, ignoring Mattie as she comes racing after him, slamming the basement door in her face while she rages, "If Mr. Cogburn thinks I'm going to be put off by a locked door, he does not know me." But she is mollified when informed Cogburn is due to testify before the judge.

We cut to the dining table at the boarding house, other men in the background sitting in chairs, Mattie disdainful of the plain fare (dumplings) and of the charge ("Can't see 25 cents in a little flour and grease"). Hathaway gives La Boeuf[26] (Glen Campbell) a proper director's introduction, none of the over-the-top Leone stuff. By that, I mean he does it all inside the camera. The landlady and other customers turn to look when he arrives and his arrival is framed within their onlooking heads and, like Cogburn, the audience gets a sound cue, this time the clanking of spurs on the wooden floor. The landlady is clearly smitten, leaping up to greet him, although she makes him remove his spurs for fear of the damage they will wreak on her chairs. Mattie treats him to a frown, this initial disgust not explained until much later (when she reminds him of the havoc spurs inflict on a horse's flanks). When he asks her name, she leaves the table, but he already, mysteriously, knows who she is. Learning she is sharing a room, on account of demand for beds as a result of the hanging, Mattie demands she pay half price. The landlady warns her about Cogburn ("He loves to pull a cork"). But in the privacy of the room, her emotions at last seep out, crying as she holds her father's watch to her face.

We have to make up our own minds about Cogburn as, under interrogation in the courthouse by defense counsel, he appears to play fast and loose with the law, unable to give a straight answer to the number of deaths he has caused in his not-quite four years in the job. He says 12 to 15 "stoppin' men in flight and defending myself" when the true number is 23. In the current instance, he has killed two and wounded another of the Morton family, clearly with little regard for their rights. This is another Wayne. His head lurches to one side and he uses his arms more freely to make points and witty remarks, and is defiant without due cause. He's not the noble defender of justice as in previous films, but a twisty, sly man who defines the law from his point of view. Dismissed, he pauses only to collect his holster at the door (another sign of civilization that guns are removed before entering a courtroom). He is caught on the stairs by Mattie, who proceeds, to his consternation and the audience's delight, to show him how to properly roll a cigarette ("Your makings are too dry"). When she jams the finished product into his astonished mouth, she might as well be saying, "I'm not afraid of no man."

And there is something else at play: pride, status ("My family has 440 acres of good bottomland"[27]—the kind of detail that directors tend not to bother audiences with). Cogburn dismisses her father's Colt Dragoon pistol that she intends to use to kill Chaney "if the law fails to do so" (in other words, take the law into her own hands) and sees her as "no bigger than a corn nubbin." But she begins to win him over with the prospect of money, not just the State pay for capturing Chaney but her reward of $50. We see more of the town as they walk from the courthouse to Chen Lee's store, hear the hammering on an anvil from the stables. He is definitely interested in Lucky Ned Pepper, who he shot in the lip. "Baby sister," he calls her as he takes her to his room at the back of the store run by Chen Lee ("my grandfather") and inhabited by a lazy cat ("my nephew, Gen. Sterling Price"—a reference to the soldier who fought in the Mexican-American War and on the Confederate side in the Civil War). He is a sloppy eater and when finished he slings the dishes to one side to start a card game with the Chinaman. He wants $100—$50 in advance—since it will not be easy "smoking old Ned out." Offered a drink of whiskey (that he has "confiscated," meaning he loots whatever he can from men he arrests), she produces the best of her pithy remarks: "I will not put a thief in my mouth to steal my brains."

We are already warming to both these characters far more than in any western of the year bar *Support Your Local Sheriff.* (Sam Varney in *Stalking Moon* has admirable qualities, but likability is not among them, creating a distance between character and audience.) They have different responses to a rat: She shouts "Scat!" and he shoots it, leading to the only heavy-handed exchange in the entire film, with Cogburn complaining "we had a good judge until the lawyers moved in" not realizing, as Mattie will soon demonstrate, how recourse to law provides relief for those who would otherwise be easily bullied.

At the boarding house, La Boeuf is waiting. He's a Texas Ranger but another dreamer, a "nobody yet" but aiming to "marry well," in this case "a well-placed young lady in Waco" who would "look with favor" on him for bringing back Chaney, who has also killed a Senator. His charm fails to convince her to join forces. She sees right through him: "I have no regard for you but I'm sure you have enough for yourself to go around."

Then comes a four-minute Mattie *tour de force* as she confronts Col. Stonehill (Strother Martin) and demands $300 in reparation for the loss of her father's saddle and for selling him dodgy horses. She threatens him with the law in the shape of Daggett, her secret weapon, and she knows enough about legality to beat Stonehill at his own game. Even better, this is no meek woman. It is one thing to be able to score points off an old lawman like Cogburn, who would have been putty in the hands of any capable woman of the Stanwyck-O'Hara variety, but another to outwit a wily old horse dealer like Stonehill (his title a hangover from the Civil War and one which ensures a measure of respect). Even better again, she knows she will win, so confident that she has already drawn up the papers to sign. Now neither Cogburn nor La Boeuf are witness to this demonstration of her capability, so they will, naturally, treat her as a young girl, "baby sister" in Cogburn's dismissive term. But Hathaway is setting a trap for the audience. Having witnessed this display, we think she will be able to hold her own in the wilderness, mistaking her willfulness for sagacity, and so are on her side in her attempts to win over the two men, when, in fact, she will prove to be so out of her depth as to endanger herself and others. She is ready, too, for Cogburn, finding him still fast asleep in a "Chinese rope-bed torture," concluding a deal for the $100 he demands, but wisely broken down into $25 in advance, another $25 on departure and the rest on completion. He determines to set off for the ferry (audience alert) next morning. She then returns to complete her triumph over Stonehill, convincing him to sell her back a horse she had sold him earlier for $25 for less than half that price. "How did you light upon that greasy vagabond?" inquires the colonel of Cogburn. She replies, "They say he has true grit."

But having purchased herself a horse for the expedition, she finds herself the victim of a double-cross when La Boeuf offers Cogburn a share of the $2000 reward offered in Texas for Chaney.[28] Mattie is outraged that Cogburn has refused to honor their contract in favor of the larger deal. Although Cogburn has sanctioned Mattie's participation, it is clear they have left without her, but she turns up at the ferry ("Freight Depot") and has paid her ten cents "for horse and rider" to cross.

LaBeef has other plans, immediately informing another man that Mattie is a runaway with a $50 reward, this leading to her being seized. Mounting a horse, she evades her captor and rides off. Hathaway holds the shot of Cogburn ringing the bell of the ferry

Taking aim, John Wayne in *True Grit* (1969). The character of Rooster Cogburn was probably the most bloodthirsty he—or any other mainstream western actor with the exception of Clint Eastwood, of course—ever played with over 20 notches on his belt. (Hannan Collection)

and the ferry pulling off. We cut to Mattie in the water on her horse. Cogburn catches sight of her. "She reminds me of me," he says. It never enters their heads to attempt a rescue. The whole episode of Mattie crossing the river is done in long shot, Hathaway ignoring the temptation to show Mattie's face in close-up as she battles the current in her attempts to stay afloat. But it is clearly a deliberate stylistic choice for on several occasions when others would have resorted to close-ups, the director resolutely sticks with the long shot. In this case, one of the byproducts of this choice is showing how effortlessly Mattie achieves her aim. Still she is unwelcome, the other two racing away without her. When she catches up, she is knocked to the ground, LaBeef seizing her, holding her down while he whips her with a switch until Cogburn calls on him to halt because it looks like he is enjoying it "too much." When LaBeef continues, Cogburn pulls a gun on him. Freed, Mattie asks, plaintively, if it is "dinner time," to which the reply is a gruff "Get on your horse."

They make an odd triangle, not of course close to a *ménage a trois*, but LaBeef's sexual inclinations are clear, in part because he expects every woman to fall at his feet, and in part because since she so clearly opposes him, she needs to be dominated in the old-fashioned way, which usually involves physical oppression of some kind. Cogburn's feelings are clearly mixed, no sexual wish at all, but the "baby sister" jibe is intended to put her in her place, and every time something in her stirs his admiration, he quickly follows up with a retort that tones it down. Although no harm is done except to Mattie's pride, the switching scene serves to remind the audience how vulnerable a young girl is away from civilization, a helplessness that will be further exposed by those with considerably less self-control than La Boeuf. Throughout, they adopt different alignments, Cogburn initially on LaBeef's side until the Texan starts to niggle him, Mattie dead set against the young man until she, too, changes allegiance, Cogburn's paternalism twisting from good to bad father at the drop of a hat.

There follows a very long shot both in time and distance as they traverse the country, which is now full of trees, and later very tall grass, with mountains in the distance. This is classic composition, the screen divided into three, the riders at the bottom, the countryside beyond, and the top third reserved for the mountains and sky. Where in *The Wild Bunch*, on their long journey through much bleaker landscape into Mexico, we have little idea where they are at any given point, or how close to their destination, here we are kept well-informed—60 miles to McAllister, with only corn dodgers to eat. Not that Cogburn relies on food for sustenance; he has his whiskey. Mattie offers to tell them the story of the Midnight Caller, acting out all the parts, if Cogburn will stop drinking. Needless to say, this lacks appeal. Meanwhile, LaBeef has shot a turkey, but his marksmanship is called into question by both Mattie and Cogburn, almost as if they are siding against him, the first time they have formed any such alliance. They take shelter in a dugout. This sequence ends with a tracking shot lasting about a minute with the characters again in long shot, tiny figures in a huge terrain, almost, in that sense, a nod to Hitchcock.

But when they reach the dugout, in a valley next to a creek, they see from the smoke coming out the chimney that the dugout is occupied. As Cogburn crosses the river, a face appears at the door, asking who they are and what they want. They smoke the inhabitants out, LaBeef climbing onto the roof and covering the chimney so the men inside suffocate and come tumbling out. They are captured; one, Moon, is shot in the melee. Cogburn cajoles and threatens the other man, Quincy, seeking information on Ned Pepper, telling the injured man he will bleed to death, setting the two men against each other. Moon starts to blab only to be knifed by his companion, whom Cogburn shoots. As he lies dying, Moon says that Ned Pepper is coming to the dugout that night. Mattie finds one of her father's gold coins. Cogburn dumps the bodies outside, hiding them under scrub, and instructs LaBeef to pick a vantage point on the other side of the river, and tells him, "Don't shoot until I do." His plan is to let the villains enter the dugout and then "I'll shoot the last man" as he goes through the door "and we'll have 'em over a barrel." LaBeef is taken aback, "You'll shoot them without a call?" Cogburn grudgingly agrees to stick to the letter of the law: "I'll holler down after I shoot."

But Mattie and LaBeef oppose his plans to kill them as they come out, wanting Chaney alive. Cogburn points out, "There are a lot of them and only two of us." I should also point out that we have so trusted everything that Cogburn has said about what he will do and what will happen that it comes as a shock to discover that this does not work out according to plan. As LaBeef goes to leave, Mattie says, "I go where Rooster goes."

It is darker now, almost twilight, as LaBeef, in long shot, crosses the river and goes up the hill opposite. After taking up their position, Mattie wants to watch. "Haven't you seen enough killing?" chides Cogburn. She refuses his offer of corn dodgers because some of them might be bloodstained. At Mattie's prompting, we hear Cogburn's mostly unvarnished, but never maudlin, history. He lost his eye in the war, committed a robbery to fund the purchase of an eating place that had a billiard table, married a grass widow until she left him for her first husband, taking their son Horace, hiding his sorrow at the boy's departure in a grumpy "He never liked me anyway" and berating him as "clumsy." He does not consider his crime "stealing" and tells of how he turned on the pursuing posse with the reins in his teeth and charged them, a gun in each hand. When she lies down to sleep, he gazes at her fondly for the first time, perhaps prompted by memory of his loss. We dissolve to the morning.

In a very long shot, we can just about see riders approaching the dugout. Cogburn wakes. We cut to the six outlaws lined up in medium shot across the screen like the Magnificent Seven. Pepper (Robert Duvall) and the Original Mexican Bob (Carlos Rivas) cross the creek. Pepper calls out for Quincy and Moon. On hearing no reply, he discharges his pistol in the air to attract their attention. LaBeef mistakes it for the signal from Cogburn and starts firing. The entire battle is shown in long shot. Ned's horse is shot from under him and when someone goes back to help, he unhorses the man and steals the horse, leaving the man to die. Mattie is shocked: "That man gave his life for him and he didn't even look back." Cogburn produces his own aphorism for the occasion: "Looking back is a bad habit." Two men are dead, one of them "not much older" than Mattie. Mattie arouses Cogburn's ire when she starts binding a wound on LaBeef's hand.

Now Cogburn abandons the hunt for Chaney, planning instead to return the dead men to McAllister for any reward. Along the way, Cogburn and LaBeef needle each other. The dead boy turns out to be "from a good family." Cogburn reneges on his promise to send Moon's "traps" to his brother and tries to wheedle out of his agreement until the stern face of Mattie fixes him. This is probably the best scene in the film, core to Wayne's performance, a true definition of Cogburn's character. When Cogburn tells Mattie to stay behind, LaBeef leaps to her defense: "She's won her spurs." Mattie refuses to let the decision be made by either of them. "I'm going and not because you say I can and not because you say I can't. I paid good cash money to be here. Now we'll have no more talk about it." While she appears at last to be an equal partner in the enterprise, this is again misleading because she does not yet possess the necessary survival instinct.

Resuming the hunt, Cogburn is convinced he knows where Pepper will "go to earth." But it is the marshal who shows his failings, mocked at every turn by LaBeef until he falls off his horse drunk, and in an attempt at recovering the situation, taps the ground with his whiskey bottle and announces, "We'll camp here." In the morning, Mattie, wanting to wash herself, is sent downhill to a stream rather than using valuable drinking water. She slips on the way down and lands at the edge of the water. In the background is a man. The camera zooms in on Chaney. When Mattie spots him, she does not react with the traditional scream of a lady in distress. Instead, she removes the gun from the bag she has toted all the way from Fort Smith: "I'm here to take you back to Fort Smith and hang you." Chaney is amused: "You better cock your piece … all the way back till it locks." She pulls the trigger and is thrown back by the recoil. He is wounded and shocked. He whines, "I just didn't think you would do it.… Everything happens to me and now I've been shot by a child." But he is not so badly wounded that he cannot attack her. When Ned Pepper intervenes, she tries to bluff her way out, telling him 50 officers are in the hunt. "Tell me another lie and I'll stove your head in," he replies. He stands over her, pushing down with his foot, calling out to Cogburn. When Pepper asks if he should kill Mattie, Cogburn replies, "You do what you think best, Ned."

During this exchange, the camera does not focus on Mattie's response, but on the two negotiators. When LaBeef strides into the shot to remonstrate with Cogburn, he is struck down by the marshal. In return for letting Pepper and his men go, and giving them time to get away, Cogburn asks for Chaney and the girl in exchange. Pepper responds by telling Cogburn he has five minutes to get over the hill. Pepper hisses at the girl, "It's enough that you know I'll do what I have to do," which clearly includes rape. In long shot we see Cogburn and LaBeef riding away. There are only four horses for the five outlaws, so Chaney is detailed to stay behind with the girl. When they have gone, Chaney threatens to throw her into a pit of rattlesnakes. Realizing her situation, Mattie tells Chaney that if he molests her, he won't get paid by Pepper. But Chaney knows how ruthless Pepper is, aware he has been left behind to be caught. Mattie attempts to negotiate: "Let me go and I'll keep silent about your whereabouts for two days." Chaney answers, "I can shut you up forever." She throws boiling water in his face, but that is not enough. He chases and catches her. Suddenly, there is a shot: LaBeef to the rescue. He collects Mattie, explaining Cogburn is "watching the front door."

The Pepper gang members race out of the wooded slopes onto the plain where Cogburn, in long shot, is waiting. LaBeef and Mattie watch from the hill. Cogburn gives the others the chance to flee, he only wants Pepper. When they do not disperse, in a "classic image to set beside the tracking shot that introduces him as the Ringo Kid in *Stagecoach*,"[29] he twirls his rifle, yelling an insult, and charges "like a medieval jouster with a lance," first in long shot, then from his point of view with a shaky camera. He has the reins in his teeth and fires two-handed. He kills two but Pepper shoots his horse from under him and Cogburn, in a sign of his age when otherwise traditionally cowboys leap free of a falling horse, is trapped on the ground under the weight of the animal, unable to reach his gun. The wounded Pepper advances. He towers over Cogburn until LaBeef, whose marksmanship had previously been in question, saves his life.

And that should pretty much have been the end of the picture, roll credits with Chaney being hung, but there is still nearly 15 minutes to go. Returning to collect Chaney, LaBeef is cracked on the head by a rock by an ambusher. Mattie shoots Chaney but the recoil sends her into the snake pit. Cogburn arrives in time to kill the wanted man, also sending him into the pit. She has damaged her shoulder and cannot pull herself up on a rope so Cogburn has to descend. He shoots a rattlesnake but another bites her. She still has enough presence of mind to demand he first collect her fallen gun and her father's gold piece from Chaney's corpse. As he hauls himself up, a dazed LaBeef, mounted on a horse, pulls on the rope to ease their ascent, but the effort is too much, and he keels over and dies. Mattie strokes his head, the first sign of her changed feelings towards him. Alternatively, this could be guilt because it was her wrong-headedness that caused his death, but that seems unlikely; she is not one to covet regret. Cogburn slaps saliva on the wound (rather than, as we might expect from watching other westerns, sucking out the poison), puts her arm in a sling and sticks her on Blackie, her horse, despite her protests about the little horse carrying such a weight. Cogburn is ruthless, riding the horse so hard it dies. Then he carries her and finally steals a buggy. Where previously most of the journey had been rendered in long shot, now Hathaway reverts to medium shot and close-up of the haggard Cogburn racing desperately to save the girl's life. When we cut to Cogburn and Chen Lee, instinctively we know she has been saved. The lawyer Daggett appears and pays Cogburn what he is owed plus $200 for saving her life, though, typically, she has prepared a receipt for him to sign.

Then she is home. It is winter. Snow lies on the ground. Cogburn explains there was no woman waiting for LaBeef, though the marshal has collected the reward. She shows him her father's grave and wants Cogburn, the father she has adopted, to be buried in the same burial ground. She gives him her father's gun and in a final triumphant moment the "fat old man" gloriously rides over a four-bar fence waving his hat in the air.

Critical Reception

The critics, who had slaughtered *The Green Berets* the previous year, and been largely indifferent to many of his previous westerns during the 1960s, virtually gave him a standing ovation. *Variety* called it a "top adventure drama.... Wayne towers over everything in the film—the actors, script and even the magnificent Colorado mountains."[30] Vincent Canby of the *New York Times* called it "a triumph ... one of the major movies of the year." The *New York Daily News* said it was "John Wayne's finest moment." The *New York Post* came closest to defining its appeal: "Few westerns will come along this or any other year that can be as fully enjoyed by as many people of varying ages and sex." Vernon Scott of United Press was not alone in predicting "Wayne should win the Oscar."[31] Joyce Haber of the *Los Angeles Times* said, "Come Oscar time Wayne will be a leading contender." Norma Lee Browning of the *Chicago Tribune* informed readers that "there's already talk that he may, at long last, get an Oscar nomination." Charles McHarry of the *New York Daily News* held the same view.[32] *Time* called the movie "a flawless portrait of a flawed man."[33] *International Motion Picture Exhibitor* found it "the perfect vehicle for Henry Hathaway's directorial style. He approached the simple western story in the most straightforward manner ... garnished it with a delightful humor that springs right out of the vagaries of the homespun characters ... and [gave] it a rhythm that carries the viewer along despite its lengthy running time."[34] Allen Eyles in *Focus on Film* summed up the film's appeal:

Aramis produced as a *True Grit* tie-in a new type of cleansing cream for men, which came in a small crock. Pressbook (Hannan Collection).

> That *True Grit* could end up being the best western of the year is a tribute to old Hollywood—to a producer, director, star, cameraman and others who've been at the top of the film business for more than three decades. Their solid, unpretentious professionalism enables them to meet the challenge of filming a first-rate novel with pleasing assurance and directness ... [I]t is far superior to ...

the poorly shaped but occasionally striking *The Wild Bunch* from Peckinpah.... [It] is not innovatory in style but the details are communicated with a freshness that is appealing.[35]

Box Office

Unusually, for a film of the period, the movie repeated a single image in all of its advertising, Wayne's face dominating the composition, with below him Mattie Ross standing gun in hand and Glen Campbell behind him. That Campbell sang the title song over the credits led to the release of a record, and there was a New American Library book tie-in.[36] Ancillary promotional items included a T-shirt embellished with the words "This Man Has True Grit,"[37] buttons announcing "I Have True Grit" and, alternatively, "Give Me a Man with True Grit."[38] Stetson created a special hat called "The Duke," with a special one costing $1500 to be presented to Johnny Carson on his show, with an advertising campaign that included *Playboy* and *Esquire*.[39] Aramis created a special line of "Grit Soap."

Time magazine raised expectations for the picture by putting Wayne on the cover on August 8, although this was in part retaliation to *Life*'s joint cover story on Wayne and Dustin Hoffman which ran in the July 11 issue,[40] and Paramount took a gamble opening it in New York at the Radio City Music Hall, partly a ploy to boost European revenues. It was the first western to be so honored, although the theater covered itself by claiming the movie was an "outdoor adventure" rather than a western per se.[41] The picture broke all sorts of records there and went on to conquer America, shattering Dallas records, for example,[42] and then it was helped along by the *Time* cover story.[43] For a few months it looked set to become the best performing western of all time, but was soon overtaken by the release of *Butch Cassidy and the Sundance Kid*. Even so, it took $11.5 million in rentals to finish sixth on the annual chart. It was reissued after Wayne's Oscar triumph the following year in an unlikely double-bill with the Oscar-nominated *The Sterile Cuckoo* and grossed $3.7 million in the 12 days. But Paramount, trying to offset calamitous losses, prematurely sold off the western to television so its reissue value was sharply curtailed.

9

Bloody to the Bone

The Wild Bunch

Starring William Holden, Ernest Borgnine, Robert Ryan, Jaime Sanchez, Warren Oates, Ben Johnson; directed by Sam Peckinpah; screenplay by Walon Green and Sam Peckinpah; Warner Brothers; 139 minutes

A Long Time Coming

Don't say Hollywood does not recognize talent. Between 1961 and 1965, Sam Peckinpah had made three westerns, *The Deadly Companions* (1961)[1] starring Maureen O'Hara, *Ride the High Country* (1962) with veterans Joel McCrea (in one of his last films) and Randolph Scott (his final movie),[2] and *Major Dundee* (1965)[3] starring Charlton Heston and Richard Harris. They all flopped. The first two had been low-budget affairs, *The Deadly Companions* funded in peculiar fashion: Half of the $300,000 total was provided by Motion Picture Investors which had been set up by exhibitors to provide more product.[4] MGM intended *Ride the High Country* as a program filler, playing on the lower half of double bills, the film only receiving more attention after winning a prize at a film festival. However, Columbia's *Major Dundee* represented a major investment of $3.8 million. But the studio was not happy with Peckinpah's 152-minute cut and reduced it to 136 minutes and then 123 minutes.

Peckinpah got his break from Don Siegel on *Riot in Cell Block 11* (1954) and worked as a "dialogue director," a Hollywood euphemism for personal assistant,[5] on the director's next four low-budget pictures[6] for mini-major Allied Artists. He was often called upon to play bit parts, four in *Invasion of the Body Snatchers* (1956) alone.[7] Peckinpah graduated to writing scripts for *Gunsmoke*, churning out 30-minute episodes in eight-hour bursts,[8] as well as for *Have Gun—Will Travel*, *Tales of Wells Fargo* and other western series. After writing five episodes of *Broken Arrow*,[9] an offshoot of the 1950 feature film, when *Gunsmoke* turned down one of his efforts, he reworked it and pitched it as a stand-alone series called *The Rifleman*, the pilot airing in 1958. Another failed venture, *Winchester*, was turned into the successful series *The Westerner* for NBC in 1960; he acted as producer and directed five episodes.[10] When the series was canceled, he had developed such a good relationship with star Brian Keith that when the actor was hired for *The Deadly Companions* by independent producer Charles B. Fitzsimons, brother of the picture's star Maureen O'Hara, "he took me along with him."[11] Peckinpah considered the script "bull-

This is the story of Major Dundee of the Union Army and Captain Tyreen of the Confederacy...of the regiment of regulars and renegades they fought with and battled over... and of the most incredible valor and violence in all the legendry of the Great Southwest!

COLUMBIA PICTURES
presents
A JERRY BRESLER Production
Major Dundee
starring
CHARLTON HESTON · RICHARD HARRIS
JIM HUTTON · JAMES COBURN
and MICHAEL ANDERSON, JR.
co-starring
MARIO ADORF · BROCK PETERS · and SENTA BERGER

Screenplay by HARRY JULIAN FINK, OSCAR SAUL and SAM PECKINPAH · Story by HARRY JULIAN FINK · Produced by JERRY BRESLER
Directed by SAM PECKINPAH · Music Composed by DANIELE AMFITHEATROF · FILMED IN PANAVISION® · COLOR
HEAR ORIGINAL SOUNDTRACK AND MITCH MILLER'S "MAJOR DUNDEE THEME" ON COLUMBIA RECORDS!
from COLUMBIA!

Exhibitors showing *Major Dundee* were urged to arrange an opening day parade of buglers and to decorate their lobbies with collections of battle flags. Charlton Heston reputedly concocted his own recipe for "Major Dundee Chili." Pressbook (Hannan Collection).

shit" but his efforts to change it were thwarted by the producer ("He wanted someone he could push about"[12]); alterations were slipped in during production, though not to improve O'Hara's role since the director was forbidden to talk to her.[13] In this revenge tale, a Union soldier (Keith) seeks vengeance on the man who scalped him during the Civil War.

Peckinpah was not the initiator of *Ride the High Country*, the package being put together by first-time producer Dick Lyons on an $800,000 budget and a 24-day shoot, money so tight that art director Leroy Coleman resorted to stealing sails from *Mutiny on the Bounty* to make tents for the mining camp scene.[14] After signing Joel McCrea and Randolph Scott, Lyons recruited Peckinpah, who rewrote the original script by N.B. Stone.[15] His major contributions was that he asked the two stars to swap roles[16] (an idea repeated in *Butch Cassidy and the Sundance Kid*) and killed off the good guy at the end rather than the bad guy. As director, Peckinpah hired cinematographer Lucien Ballard, who would be instrumental in achieving the "look" of *The Wild Bunch*, and developed his own skills as an editor.[17] But MGM boss Joseph R. Vogel hated the movie and it was sent out on the bottom half of a double bill[18] with either *Boys Night Out* (1962) starring Kim Novak and James Garner or the Italian production *The Tartars* (1961) with Victor Mature. *Cinema* magazine was impressed and when its interview[19] with Peckinpah appeared, the movie was booked into the Los Angeles art house Los Feliz, after which it was properly reviewed and received good notices and improved receipts, though hardly setting the box office alight.[20] Released in Europe to fulfill a booking commitment, but now with proper critical assessment, the movie found a more responsive audience.[21] By the time *The Wild Bunch* appeared seven years later, *Ride the High Country* was "already considered by many to be a classic."[22]

Major Dundee was a substantial step up, with a major star in Charlton Heston and a rising one in Richard Harris. Austrian Senta Berger, whom Peckinpah considered "totally wrong" for the part of Teresa Santiago,[23] was cast to bring in the foreign audience. It was made on a budget of under $3 million.[24] Jerry Bresler was an experienced producer, having shepherded onto the screen films as diverse as the film noir *The Mob* (1951), *The Vikings* (1958), *Gidget Goes Hawaiian* (1961) and *Diamond Head* (1962), the latter with Heston, and he had on his plate the drama *Love Has Many Faces* (1965). The *Major Dundee* screenplay by Harry Julian Fink centered on a combined group of Union and Confederate cavalry soldiers pursuing Apaches into Mexico, but Peckinpah, concerned about too many subplots, rewrote it to focus on the rivalry between Dundee (Heston) and Capt. Tyreen (Harris). Rewrites delayed shooting but when the movie did go into production, the screenplay was not complete. Bresler and Peckinpah fell out over the director's choice of impractical locations.[25] There were arguments over costumes,[26] and the producer was infuriated by the slowness of the shoot. But mostly they fell out because Bresler cut 15 days out of the schedule with just two days to go before shooting began.[27] The amount of footage being shot indicated that the film was going to be longer than anticipated—correctly, as it turned out, Peckinpah's cut running to 161 minutes, long enough for a roadshow. Alarm grew over rising costs with Heston sacrificing his $200,000 salary to save Peckinpah from being fired, and the movie ending up $1 million over budget.[28] In theory at least, Peckinpah's tribulations on *Major Dundee* had no effect on his career: He had already lined up his next picture, *The Cincinnati Kid* for MGM. Four months were spent on production before the cameras rolled,[29] shooting it in black-and-white. But he was fired after four days. He was reduced to helming the teleplays *Noon*

Wine (1966) and *The Lady Is My Wife* (1967) and lecturing at university. To tide himself over, he did manage to sell his screenplays for the western *The Glory Guys* (1965), from the Hoffman Birney novel, and *Villa Rides* (1968), although star Yul Brynner hated the script and brought in Robert Towne to rewrite it.[30]

Kenneth Hyman, who had made his name as producer of *The Dirty Dozen* (1967) and taken over as vice-president of worldwide production for Warner Brothers-Seven Arts the same year, hired Peckinpah to write the adventure *The Diamond Story* with the implicit agreement that Peckinpah would direct if the picture received the go-ahead. However, the studio dumped that idea in favor of *The Wild Bunch*, an original screenplay by Walon Green from a story by stuntman Roy Sickner, with Peckinpah on board as director. As usual, Peckinpah reckoned the screenplay was in need of some work, so refreshed the dialogue, added the preacher's speech and the idea of leaving Crazy Lee behind during the attempted hold-up, extended the Mexican village sequence and introduced the farewell song, plus flashbacks to deepen the characterization of the two principals.[31]

Hyman and Peckinpah were in agreement over Lee Marvin for the leading role of Pike Bishop. Marvin had headed up *The Dirty Dozen*, and the actor was very interested until offered $1 million for *Paint Your Wagon*. Although William Holden had been the number one global star for several years in the 1950s and an Oscar recipient for Billy Wilder's *Stalag 17* (1953) and nominated three years previously for the same director's *Sunset Blvd.*, his box office appeal had drastically dimmed by the mid–1960s. His last four films—the African adventure *The Lion* (1962), the romantic comedy *Paris When It Sizzles* (1964), the post–World War II drama *The Seventh Dawn* (1964) and the western *Alvarez Kelly* (1966)—had brought in shockingly low receipts, generating total domestic rentals of just $4.2 million. Despite the better-performing war film *The Devil's Brigade* (1968), his box office viability had been questioned by the industry trade paper *Variety*.[32] But, recalling his performance in *Stalag 17*, Peckinpah sensed the toughness required for Pike Bishop.

In fact, counting Holden, the movie had no stars of any significance. Robert Ryan had last received top billing in the 1965 low-budget thriller *The Crooked Road*, Ernest Borgnine the year before in the comedy *McHale's Navy*. The cast was filled out by character actors Strother Martin (*Cool Hand Luke*, 1967), Ben Johnson (*Major Dundee*), Edmond O'Brien[33] (*Seven Days in May*, 1964) and members of Peckinpah's stock company such as Warren Oates and L.Q. Jones (both in *Ride the High Country* and *Major Dundee*).[34] Outside of Holden, probably the most famous member of the cast was Emilio Fernandez (*Return of the Seven*, 1966), a legendary Mexican actor-director who knew all about revolution and exile from personal experience. Fernandez provided Peckinpah with the idea for the children setting ants on the scorpion.[35]

In setting up the film, director and cinematographer Ballard aimed to achieve the "arid, dusty feel of a scorched land" that they had witnessed in footage of the Mexican Revolution of 1913.[36] Editor Lou Lombardo was hired partly because of his experience of shooting a slow-motion death scene for television's *The Felony Squad*. Peckinpah lured out of retirement wardrobe man Gordon Dawson.[37] Shooting of the 81-day schedule was set to begin on March 25, 1968. Locations included the Durranzo Arroyo, El Rincon del Montero, El Romeral and the Hacienda Cienga del Carmen. The citizens of Parras de la Fuente, in the foothills of the Sierra Madre Occidental Mountains in the state of Coahuila, voted to postpone the installation of television reception in order to accommodate Peck-

When William Holden contracted salmonella, the entire production of *Alvarez Kelly* (1966) had to be shut down. Trade press advertisement (*Box Office*, August 15, 1966).

inpah's need for an antenna-free location, although, ironically, the director was forced to scour the area looking for telephone poles to make the point that civilization had reached even this remote area in 1913 when the movie was set.[38] Art director Edward Carrere, an Oscar winner for *Camelot* (1967), transformed the cobblestoned Parras plaza, dating from the 17th century, into a red clay-dirt town square with the addition of a false-front hotel, railroad office, saloons and gunsmith's shop. The town was itself of historical important, having been the center of the Mexican Revolution of 1910, home to Francisco Madero, the first independent president after the fall of the dictator Diaz.[39] Five cameras were utilized for the final shoot-out but soldiers were being killed so fast that bloodied uniforms were simply painted khaki.[40] The railroad bridge cost $100,000 to construct and was named the "P. & F. R.R." (i.e. the Peckinpah and Felding Railroad) in order to satisfy a condition laid down by the government that the railway could not be identified as Mexican.[41] For the opening scene, the red ants and their deadly enemy the hairy scorpions were imported by insect specialist James Dannaldson. As long as the ants supplied did not contain a queen, it would prevent a colony from being established. The vultures in a later scene were equipped with "Vulture Boots," weighted shoes attached to the birds' claws to prevent them flying away.[42] Jerry Fielding, who had scored *Noon Wine*, was brought in to provide the music. Although the composer had been responsible for films like *Advise & Consent* (1962) and *McHale's Navy*, the bulk of his work in the 1960s was for television. *The Wild Bunch* was his first movie score in four years. However, Fielding was at odds from the outset with the director's concept of using just two guitars, and even after Peckinpah had conceded the point, they had a huge falling-out over the music for the post-battle vulture scene when the idea for the two guitars was resurrected.[43] During the editing, 81 minutes were taken out of the rough cut. An average picture at that time had 600 cuts but *The Wild Bunch* had 3642.[44] Peckinpah was meticulous about looping and following the first preview totally redubbed the sound track.[45]

Although the ratings board had passed the film as R, requiring only some minor cuts and one line of dialogue, the final obstacle was public and media reaction to the violence. At the preview, audiences had either raved or hated the film. There were walkouts at the press junket held in the Bahamas, and Rex Reed, who wrote for the *New York Times*, showed his true feelings when he hissed at the director during the subsequent press conference.[46] But the makers defended the picture. Producer Phil Feldman commented: "The era of escapism is over, the era of reality is here." Holden asked: "Are people surprised that violence really exists?" Peckinpah originally envisaged the film as being "about the betrayal of friendship,"[47] but, forced to defend the violence, told reporters that "the film speaks for itself … my idea was that it would have a cathartic effect."[48]

The One Question

The overriding question facing Peckinpah in *The Wild Bunch* was how to make us care for a group of savage, amoral, bloodthirsty, drunken, whoring, lawless renegades. These are all Men with No Name, except on a wanted poster, with no relationships, who chase money with more venal ruthlessness than any character in the *Dollars* series, kill women and children without pity, show no remorse, and live by what appears to be a code of honor they make up as they go along. Why should an audience care a jot for this bunch of thugs? These are among the worst bad guys in the history of the movies, and end up "heroes" by sparking the worst massacre ever put on screen. The only difference between themselves and the evil Mexican self-appointed general is that they do not hang anyone. It is hard to argue that they even do good in the end since, with their multiplicity of murderous skills, they could have assassinated Mapache or affected some other rescue of Angel from the ragged, ill-disciplined Mexican army. So just how does Peckinpah do it? How does he turn the most violent movie ever made into one of the most critically (if not so fulsomely at the time) adored? A haunting score is not enough, the elegiac tone is not enough, the sense that these men are living on borrowed time and that they will forever be on the run, hunted down by an equally ruthless railroad baron, is not enough.

He does it by making *The Wild Bunch* human. And human in a way that had never been shown before on screen, not romanticized humanity where they carry out minor good deeds, or bad guys with a heart going to the rescue of a defenseless widow as in *Once Upon a Time in the West*, but filled with squabbles and tensions, only too ready to score a point over one of their own, to goad and taunt and challenge at any opportunity, too quick on the draw, needing to purchase female companionship, and, largely, stupid to boot. Peckinpah takes all these deficiencies that another director would have let alone, and shines a bright light on them. And somehow, in their magnification, he makes us enjoy the company of, at least empathize with, at least understand, these wild men of the west. The lives they live are starker than anything portrayed in the realistic world of *Once Upon a Time in the West*, their dreams long turned to dust, hiding out in country so barren and inhospitable most men would not bother pursuing them. But *The Wild Bunch* is, in some senses, a sequel to the idealistic *Once Upon a Time....* Gunmen are pursued relentlessly. Railroad magnates, every bit as ruthless as Morton, can harness the forces of the law to pursue with relentless vigor with whatever lawless means at their disposal anyone who threatens their operation. The railroad barons can buy the law, override the objections of upright citizens, and their trains do not convey progress so much as weaponry, to be used by either side to bring unwarranted death to innocent people. There are echoes of Vietnam in the horrors that are visited upon the innocent, in America and Mexico alike, by those with greater force of arms, demanding to make the world in their image, the seizure of what they consider theirs. The carnage that results from the ill-advised rescue of Angel is akin to the destruction hundreds of villagers faced in Vietnam simply by being in the wrong place at the wrong time when the soldiers, unwilling to distinguish between enemy and innocent, arrived.

Were it just in part a fable of Vietnam, *The Wild Bunch* would carry visceral power. Although Americans were exposed to the impact of Vietnam on television news every day of the week, they were spared close-ups of the atrocities committed, that *The Wild Bunch* showed in a detail—something that *The Green Berets* (1968) avoided. Setting aside any political overtones, any film has to stand alone in its portrait of the human condition, and there is hardly a single film that made its name in relation to Vietnam that stands up, not so much to the test of time because all still bear testament to a specific period of American history, but to the fickleness of audience taste. If *The Wild Bunch* still evokes strong feelings among moviegoers and critics alike, it is because of the warts-and-all depiction of the outlaws.

There is nothing particularly magnificent in the scenic sense in *The Wild Bunch*, no evocative Monument Valley brought into play to pay homage to the western gods, no conscious attempt to mimic or rewrite the genre, no self-conscious references to movie history, no grandstanding of violence with carefully choreographed standoffs, no deliberate point to make. The renegades inhabit a grubby, muddy, dirty, dusty world and this is enhanced by cinematography that never seeks an outstanding visual image. There are few close-ups, most scenes playing out in two-shots or small groupings, and no remorse or angst. A sense of loss and multiple examples of aging are not the same as critical self-analysis. What the film captures instead is an understanding of what it feels like for men without home or family to enjoy the discipline and camaraderie of a tight unit, to be able to do one thing well even if that specialty is killing. Nor does Peckinpah cheat by isolating the rivals so that the climax can be a glorious one-to-one shootout where visuals and music can be brought to bear. If anything, the director is the master of the crowd scene, especially when the principals are few among many, and where consequence is as much on his mind as how to frame and focus the main characters. From the shots Peckinpah chooses to include, this is as much a picture about collateral damage as about how the cowboys escape from a situation of their own making.

From the outset, Peckinpah suggests violence is inbred, that even the very young will take pleasure from watching the innocent suffer. While a scorpion is seen as a dangerous creature to encounter, and therefore a subject for justifiable extermination, there is deliberate cruelty in the opening scene where, while the outlaws pass disguised as soldiers, small boys and girls set a nest of ants on two scorpions trapped in a tiny arena and enjoy the resulting torment. More children appear as onlookers and participants in *The Wild Bunch* than in any comparable film, and they are rarely of the cute Disney variety. They are usually dirty, sometimes fearful, occasionally hiding, but as often, like here, acting as mini-savages. Later, having not tortured the scorpions enough, the youngsters set fire to them. Virtually the only cute kids we see in the entire movie are the boy and girl, brother and sister perhaps, holding onto each other during the first shootout. Thereafter, as much as they jump into rivers and nibble away at food and play, they take on other malevolent guises: from the young boy, dressed in uniform, who brings the telegram to Mapache, delighted to be so close to the general, who later graduates to shooting Pike Bishop in the back, to the children sitting above the entrance to Mapache's encampment dropping stones on people as they arrive. Even the striking shot of the baby at the bare breast reveals a moment later that the mother is wearing a bandolero, the bullets almost as close to the child's face as the nipple.

Riders, dressed as U.S. soldiers, enter the sleepy town of San Rafael, women holding parasols saluting men they take to be soldiers. Although the town is clearly civilized, many of its citizens are already corrupt, fallen victim to the evils of alcohol, so much so that, as the cowboys ride past, a temperance meeting is underway in a tent. The Gorch brothers, Lyle (Warren Oates) and Tector (Ben Johnson), sent along ahead to get the lay of the land, get up from a bench and tell the leader Pike Bishop (William Holden) that all is quiet. "Let's fall in," says Pike, using military terminology. As they march up the street, Pike, bumping into a woman who drops her parcels, courteously takes her arm.

We cut to Deke Thornton (Robert Ryan) being wakened. He is on a rooftop with other gunmen. This is an ambush and the ambushers are not of the stolid variety awaiting Harmonica's arrival in *Once Upon a Time...*, but jumpy, edgy, whiny, contentious, dirty. The cowboys invade the railroad station office, efficiently rounding up everyone inside. Pike instructs Lee (Bo Hopkins), a too-smiley youngster, "If they move, kill 'em." The temperance band strikes up and the preacher leads them, mostly women with kids trailing

Unlike its competitors, *The Wild Bunch*'s (1969) marketing team did not come up with a stack of promotional ideas or gimmicks for exhibitors beyond an illuminated counter display for the refreshment stand. Pressbook (Hannan Collection).

behind, up the street singing "Shall We Gather at the River." Looking out the window of the bank, Angel (Jaime Sanchez) catches sight of a rifle barrel over the top of the parapet. Tector, guarding the horses, also spots the rifles. One ambusher, Coffer (Strother Martin), kisses his rifle. The band music gets louder as the temperance march approaches. Pike intends using them as cover. He kicks one of the tellers out the door with the same brutality that Frank in *Once Upon a Time...* kicks the laundryman out of the train. As the innocent man tumbles out, he is shot to pieces by the ambushers. The battle ensues without, as is usually the case, the trapped men able to form any plan, just running for it, shooting as they go, and with no time, as is usually the case for westerns, as if by osmosis, for the public area to be cleared. A horse crashes in slow motion through a window, but most of the violence, the spurting blood, happens fast. The sequence combines speedy cuts with the luxury of slow motion. Inside the bank, Lee licks a terrified woman's face and demands his three hostages sing the hymn. Both sets of gunmen shoot at anything that moves. The noise is deafening, the bounty hunters refusing to stop shooting. At one point Deke has Pike in his sights but a tuba gets in the way. A woman is trampled to death by a horse, the boy and girl hold on to each other for dear life. We cut to the young children setting fire to the straw surrounding the ants and scorpions, killing indiscriminately in the fashion of the adults, as the escaping outlaws race past on horseback.

While the ambushers begin looting the dead, the camera focuses on the sad face of Deke. Coffer squabbles with T.C. (L.Q. Jones) over the spoils. Deke turns on his employer Harrigan (Albert Dekker), who is equally angry with him for not shooting Pike "when you had the chance." Lee kills the hostages and in turn is killed. Angry citizens (who foolishly believe they are living in the civilization predicted in *Once Upon a Time...* and cannot imagine what kind of mind would use their small town to stage an ambush), burst into the bank, blaming the railroad for the slaughter. Deke looks more desolate. Out in the streets, kids run around, using their fingers as pistols, shouting *bang bang, bang, bang*.

As the Wild Bunch escapes through the hills, one man falls from his horse. Blinded, he insists he can ride, but then concedes, "I can't ride. Finish it, Mr. Bishop," the first indication that these men live by their own code. They began as nine, now they are down to seven, with Tector wounded. The first crack in solidarity shows when they argue over whether to bury the dead man, clearly a difference of opinion over the code. A different argument flares up back in town, Deke demanding better men, furious that Harrigan can kill wantonly "with the law's caring arms around you." Now we discover that Deke is not a bounty hunter like the others but a convicted criminal and faced with going back to jail within 30 days if he does not catch Pike. A flashback shows Deke being whipped in Yuma Prison. Although the deadline is brought up here (not quite as immediate as the deadline in *Once Upon a Time...*), it is used sparingly, only one further mention, as it becomes clear that, relentlessly though Deke pursues Pike, something else binds the two men, and reminders of the penalty Deke faces should he fail would only get in the way of that deeper emotion. The Wild Bunch crosses the Rio Grande into the safety of Mexico but the bounty hunters are in pursuit and find the corpse of the blinded man.

And what has a life of crime brought the criminals? Not the money, cigars, whiskey, clothes and fine lifestyle, nor the possible transformation into a businessman, promised to Frank in the Leone picture. This not even a decent hideout, just a broken-down ranchero where old man Sykes (Edmond O'Brien), who "once did his share of killing," awaits.

Immediately, they are striven by enmity. The Gorch brothers complain that neither Angel nor Sykes deserve their share. Pike barks, "Either I lead this group or end it right now." But all the stolen bags contain is washers, "a dollar's worth of steel holes," and now it's Angel's turn to gloat, resulting in a stand-off between him and the brothers. "We got to start thinking beyond our guns," says Pike. But the gang manages to laugh off the upset and soon are all laughing together, their default mode of resilience. Deke is morose, eating his plate of food several steps away from the men he despises. We learn he "rode with Pike." At night, as the outlaws settle down, Angel plays a sad song on his guitar. For most of the philosophical scene that follows, Pike and Dutch (Ernest Borgnine) lie down beside the fire drinking whiskey and coffee. For Pike, as with the Gorch brothers, this had been intended as his last big job before he would "back off." Dutch retorts, "Back off to what?" Even the leaders are unable to plan for the future. They discuss possible projects, perhaps stealing a garrison payroll. There is a flashback of Deke and Pike with whores, living the good life, interrupted by a knock on the door that results in Deke being shot twice and arrested. He appears to share this memory at this precise moment with Deke. The outlaws are aware of being the subject of vengeful pursuit, not so much from Deke, but Harrigan. Despite this, neither would "have it any other way," as if resigned to their lives and what they are, seeking neither redemption nor pity. Angel is singing to a young girl and two kids.

Their ordinary life consists of a lot of riding and just as with the three *pistoleri* in *Once Upon a Time...*, much of their time is spent being bored. These routes are arduous, steep inclines, or sand dunes, or hard, rocky roads, or bridges that give way under pressure. Traversing them takes up a good chunk of the picture. Peckinpah could have delivered a leaner movie, eliminating many of these boring journeys, but they give a sense not only of time passing but of the nature of the life. Few journeys are without incident and now as they ride through the desert, the horses slip and tumble down the slopes in slow motion, a situation for which Sykes, who plans their routes, is blamed. Again, tempers are short. Tector threatens Sykes. Pike intervenes, invoking the code, "When you side with a man, you stay with him and if you can't do that, you're like some animal; you're finished; we're finished; all of us." But as they remount, Pike's stirrup breaks and he falls to the ground, causing Tector and Lyle to gloat. Pike's difficulty in getting back onto his saddle is noted by Dutch. Peckinpah holds the shot of Pike on horseback heading off, in the center of the frame, moving slowly, and that shot dissolves into a longer-held long shot of the group riding over desolate land. That violence passes down the generation is instanced when Sykes tells Pike that Lee is his grandson and Pike recalls, in flashback, that he sacrificed the boy to ensure their escape.

The hard-riding horsemen are Deke and the bounty hunters, strung out along the screen like the Magnificent Seven. They reach the river, the border, but that is Mapache territory and Deke turns back. Angel takes his colleagues to his village, pillaged by federal troops, cattle and corn stolen, full of hungry dogs and fearful children. There is nothing romantic about this village, just hard work, poverty, women making tortillas, containment, trying to survive, not the Hollywood version of a Mexican village with bright white walls, an effervescent, smiling population, cantinas and fiestas. Even so, it is touching to see the contentious Tector and Lyle easily pleased ("We all dream of being children again," observes the village elder), learning to do a trick with rope while making the acquaintance of a local girl. The elder, Don Jose (Chano Urueta), tells Angel that Mapache killed his father and stole his woman, and adds, in tones of disgust, as if betrayed, that "she went with them because she wished to, she became the woman of Mapache." Nothing changes for women, whether white or Native American or Mexican, they are plunder, chattels, and can be taken by force or give in gracefully, hoping to escape poverty or death. There is a simplicity to this village where people enjoy the simple pleasures, children diving into the river, food being roasted over fires, and singing and dancing (Tector, Lyle and Sykes join in) and drinking and, for Pike, just watching. Peckinpah does not encumber the storyline with romance sparking between Tector or Lyle and one of the village girls.

Revenge now drives the plot. Angel wants to avenge his woman. Pike reacts, "Either you learn to live with it or we'll leave you here." In other words, he will be banished. But, in fact, it's the Wild Bunch who are being abandoned, of their own volition. They have found a home, been welcomed unconditionally in this village by virtue of being friends of Angel. They could easily stay; Deke could not legitimately cross the border to take them prisoner. And, unless it is local custom, they are serenaded[49] as they leave, villagers waving goodbye as they sing, Dutch presented with a flower, Angel, who now dresses like a rebel, with a parcel by his mother. It is a long scene, elegiac for sure, but moving all the same.

Cut to a baby on a naked breast and the mother wearing a bandolero. This is Aqua Verde, a small town requisitioned by Mapache. Troops march past. The gate opens and a car drives in carrying Mapache. Most of the outlaws are amazed at the machine, but Pike is familiar with the automobile and the airplane. Mapache's men have commandeered the steps of a public building or church and he sits at a table with a lace tablecloth with candelabras getting drunk. The cowboys take seats at a table below Mapache. A young woman makes eyes at Pike. Two girls go up to Mapache and we cut to Angel (but in a two-shot, not a close-up) and he stands up and calls out, "Teresa." She turns and the camera zooms in on her face. Close-up of Angel. Then we see Angel and Teresa on either side of the screen, separated visually by Tector in the background. She turns to go but he seizes her arm. Sensing danger, Pike steps up. In Spanish, she vents her fury on Angel and shows she adores Mapache. Although her words are not translated on screen, she tells him, "I left the village so I wouldn't starve. But now I'm happy." You don't need to hear the words to understand their meaning. As Pike leads him away, Angel laments, "She was my woman." Then we have a close-up of Teresa's anguished face, tears forming. Then she laughs hysterically and goes up and sits in Mapache's lap. Unable to resist, Lyle goads Angel who reacts, in close-up, by shouting out. Pike, also in close-up, shouts, "No!" Angel shoots and kills Teresa. Pike seizes Angel while Tector punches him.

The Mexicans automatically think this is an assassination attempt. All guns are pulled as Pike tries to defuse the situation, pointing out, "He was after the girl." And, as if this is the common language of pacification, they all laugh. As the situation calms down, the German adviser notices they are carrying American army-issue weapons. With interest established, the outlaws are invited inside. We cut briefly to Deke and his men. When we return to Aqua Verde, we can hear mournful chanting and women are carrying Teresa's corpse on a slab of wood. The German offers Pike $10,000 to steal an arms shipment. Once the deal is concluded, Pike and Dutch maneuver around to collect Angel, who is under guard, but they are stopped by Mapache. "If you don't mind, general, we need him," says Pike. There is another brief stand-off while the general gives way. From now on, Mapache is mostly drunk, and it is possible this is his modus operandi. But before when he was drunk, he was in full spirits; now he is drunk and morose, as if the death of Teresa is affecting him badly and he, too, is human after all. Lyle has been eyeing a woman but when three whores are wheeled in, she sticks out her tongue at him, much to the man's puzzlement. Tector and Lyle get drunk with the women in the wine cellars, shooting holes in the barrels, ending up in a vat of wine. In a rudimentary sauna, Pike massages the bullet scar on his thigh. When Angel declares that he is "not going to steal guns for that devil to rob and kill my people again," Dutch suggests they give Angel one of the 16 cases of guns they are planning to steal, paid for out of the Mexican's share of the loot.

Tector and Lyle enter, arms draped around the women, and Lyle solemnly announces, "Boys, I want you to meet my fiancée." Once again, the camaraderie is spelled out in a mantra of laughter. Deke knows that Pike is going to attack the train and asks Harrigan for 20 trained men. Harrigan snaps, "You've got 24 days." There is a flashback

For Award Books, Brian Fox wrote a novelization of the *Wild Bunch* screenplay, priced 60 cents. "They wrote their own epitaphs in the blood of friend and foe alike," ran the blurb. Pressbook (Hannan Collection).

to how Pike was wounded in the thigh, shot by the husband of a Mexican woman with whom he was having an affair. The husband's first shots, however, were reserved for the wife, another example of how Mexican men treat women they believe have betrayed them. "Never caught up with him?" asks Dutch. Although Pike says not a day goes by without thinking of him, he has not been as relentless in pursuit of the murderer, as if he has learned, as he told Angel, to live with it. There is no sense of Pike feeling betrayed by women, but his weakness for them has cost him.

The train hijack is one of the movie's set pieces. It also shows that it is not only Leone who is the master of the sound effect as a vehicle for tension. Inside the carriage are Deke, his men and a troop of young soldiers hired by Harrigan. The train stops at a water tower beside a bridge (reflecting the importance of the water towers and the Sweetwater well to railroads in *Once Upon a Time in the West*, and also how prone they are to ambush as shown in *100 Rifles*). Hiding in the water tower sluice is Angel with a shotgun. He commandeers the engine while other men slip out from hiding places under the bridge. Climbing onto the flatcar containing the weaponry at the front of the train, Lyle forces the guards there to drop their weapons. Dutch climbs up behind the stacked ammunition and, like Cheyenne in *Once Upon a Time...*, uses a tap to get the attention of the astonished guards. Pike takes over in the engine while Angel uncouples the carriages. There are successive close-ups of Deke, Pike and Angel reacting to the clank as the train backs up. Alerted by the sudden noise, Deke looks out the window just as the sluice is raised. As the train sets off minus the passengers, Deke walks to the back of the carriage and sees what is happening. "Let's go," he commands.

In long shot we see a front view of the train departing and in the same shot a flap going up from the abandoned carriages. Close-up of Dutch. Long shot of horses emerging. Another close-up of Dutch and then we see Deke in pursuit. As the train speeds up, Dutch slips between the carriages and guards start shooting at him. Pike, echoing treatment of the laundryman on the train, kicks the driver out. Angel and Lyle kill the guards and the train outpaces the pursuers while the raw recruits are still struggling to get mounted. Sykes is waiting further up the line and the ammunition is transferred to a wagon. Pike puts the train in reverse. The runaway train is a Cinerama ploy, seen most recently in *Mackenna's Gold.* The bounty hunters avoid the danger but the train smashes into the carriages where the recruits are still trying to get on their horses. The outlaws reach the border bridge where Angel immediately lights fuses. Deke catches up and starts shooting at the robbers. The wagon wheels break through the bridge's timber and it is briefly trapped while the lit fuse races along. When the recruits arrive, the bounty hunters start shooting at them. Clearing the bridge, Pike stops to wave his hat in triumph. Deke halts in the middle of the bridge to take aim at Pike but the bridge blows up and in slow motion horses and men tumble into the water.

There is no time to savor the triumph. Sykes warns Pike that Deke "will be along and you know it." As ever, humor takes the sting out of the tension. A whiskey bottle is tossed from man to man, deliberately missing out Lyle. On the shore, Deke upbraids his men for being distracted by the recruits while Coffer and T.C. quarrel among themselves. Coffer and T.C. share a similar relationship to the Bunch, often squabbling, irritating each other, then making up with a mild slap, and they are certainly in the same league as Tector and Lyle when it comes to stupidity. Both the Gorch brothers and this pair exhibit childishness when thwarted. But Deke hates his gang which, with the exception of Coffer and T.C., shows no signs of camaraderie.

Although Mapache previously is seen in the ascendancy, he is not all-conquering now, in retreat from revolutionaries flooding down the hills. Mapache has his own train, where women sing in the face of danger. A small boy in uniform, already schooled in the glamour of battle, races to take a telegraph to the general, receiving a solicitous smile in return. The train is now a tool of flight, a speedy method of escaping consequence, for had Mapache's men been forced to fight they would have been overrun. Pike watches the pursuers through binoculars. Peckinpah cuts to Deke, incensed his men think they are not being watched. "I could point to them right now," says Deke. "They know what it's all about and what do I have? Egg-sucking, chicken-stealing gutter trash.... We're after men and I wish to God I was with them. Next time you make a mistake, I'm going to ride off and let you die." No code of honor there, then. Pike does not trust the Mexicans not to steal the load and kill them. They find the machine gun and mount it atop the wagon. At a hideout they are surprised by stealthy rebels, come to get the case promised to Angel. Lyle takes the opportunity to moan about Pike. But they are ready for the Mexicans, booby-trapping the wagon, and calling the Mexicans' bluff. At Aqua Verde, Pike appears with one quarter of the weapons in returns for $2500 and gives the machine gun as a present. Meanwhile, Tector tosses dynamite at Sykes when the old man is using the toilet. Mapache is delighted with the machine gun and, ignoring the German's instructions to mount it on a tripod, holds it in his hands and starts firing, causing as much devastation as the ambush at the bank. The greater the weapons at their disposal the more irresponsible men become.

Dutch and Angel arrive with the last of the weapons. Dutch explains, "We lost one." Mapache points the finger at Angel: "He stole it." Angel makes a run for it but is lassoed and caught. Dutch says, "He's a thief. You take care of him." Opinions are divided back at the camp. Dutch says Angel "played his string right out to the end" but, as if this inflexible code of honor is now flexible, Sykes believes they should go after him. Later, Sykes, alone with the string of horses, is shot by Coffer. Pike remains over-philosophical about Angel: "He gave his word." Dutch argues, "That ain't what counts. It's who you give it to." But at last they are trapped, lacking the water to stay put, and knowing they would be followed to the border by Deke. "I'm tired of being hunted," says Pike. He understates the case: He is plain tired. Weariness shows in his face and he is getting old in other ways, twice taken by surprise, ambushed by Deke and by the rebels, slipping from his horse when the stirrup breaks. Ironically, the safest way to go is the most dangerous, Aqua Verde, where they reckon Deke will not go. They bury the gold except for one stash to "pay their way" and cold-bloodedly abandon Sykes. Deke has also given up on the wounded Sykes, believing the buzzards will get him anyway, and the old man is surprised by the rebels. At Aqua Verde, fireworks are going off in celebration, and Angel is being dragged around behind the car. Pike is unsuccessful in his attempts to buy Angel back.

Dutch, who appears abstemious where women are concerned, sits outside whittling on a stick. Inside, Pike is getting dressed. A girl, whose baby is asleep, is washing her face and neck with water. Next door, Lyle and Tector argue with the girl they have shared about the price. Pike appears: "Let's go." Lyle responds, "Why not?" Along with Dutch, they collect guns and rifles from their horses and begin walking into town. The same haunting tune as accompanied them leaving the village plays in the background, with the gentle addition of a drumbeat. Peckinpah covers the march mostly in long shot. Facing Mapache, Pike demands Angel. Mapache's response is to slit his throat. There is a short stand-off, similar to the earlier one when Angel shot Teresa. But now the silence is ended by Pike shooting the German. Lyle shoots women. Tector seizes the machine gun and starts spraying bullets, this time with blood exploding everywhere. They toss grenades. Pike aims at a woman but shoots her reflection in a mirror instead. Dutch takes a woman as hostage, shooting from behind her. Lyle takes over at the machine gun. The woman Pike tried to kill now shoots him in the back and he blasts her with his rifle. Pike and Dutch take cover behind an overturned table. Pike turns to Dutch and says, "Come on, you lazy bastard." Now it is Pike at the machine gun. The small boy in uniform shoots him. Dutch dies, crying out, "Pike, Pike, Pike."

Deke, who has been watching the massacre in his binoculars, rides in with his men, who begin to loot. Deke takes the pistol from Pike's corpse. An exodus of people begins, a long thin trail stretching out past the town. Deke waits while the other bounty hunters leave with corpses strapped to horses. We hear gunfire in the distance and presently Sykes

It's not mentioned in *The Wild Bunch* but there was a bounty on each gang member's head; for the likes of Bishop and Tector, it was $1,125, working its way down to $100 for Angel. Pressbook (Hannan Collection).

arrives with the rebels. Sykes and Deke share a laugh, the unifying principle, and Deke takes up the invitation to join them. The picture ends with a reprisal of the Wild Bunch being serenaded as they leave the village and individual shots of them all laughing. The frame freezes as the credits roll. Then the camera dollies back to make the frame smaller and smaller until the freeze frame is replaced by **THE END**.

Critical Response

The major critics were split, four to three in favor. Vincent Canby of the *New York Times* called it "the first truly interesting American western in years." *Time* was also positive, asserting that the director belonged to "the best of the newer generation of American filmmakers." Judith Crist in *The New Yorker* took a negative view while William Woolf in *Cue* damned it as a "pointless, disgustingly bloody film."[50] *Variety* foresaw "solid box office potential" but claimed the "scripters lost sight of their narrative" and that the overlong film "should be tightened extensively, particularly in the first half."[51] *International Motion Picture Exhibitor* had no such qualms, declaring that "the wonderfully-directed and acted western ... should win critical and box office acclaim."[52]

Box Office

Lacking the promotional gimmicks that Paramount, for example, produced for *True Grit* and *Paint Your Wagon*, Warner Brothers concentrated on traditional methods, such as making the complete score available on WB-7A Records[53] with copies available at a special low price for exhibitors. In marketing to the trade, the company boasted to exhibitors of the expected reach—37 million circulation—of its advertising campaign, a technique much employed in the 1940s and 1950s but largely fallen out of use.[54] Using a key motif of shadows spreading out behind the nine men, with different core art, the movie, unlike *True Grit*, employed several different taglines. "Nine men who came too late and stayed too long" was the most memorable and this was buttressed by: "Born too late for their times, uncommonly significant for ours"; "Unchanged men in an unchanging land, out of step, out of place, and desperately out of time"; "Suddenly a new West had emerged, suddenly it was sundown for nine men, suddenly their day was over, suddenly the sky was bathed in blood"; "The land had changed, they hadn't, the earth had cooled, they couldn't."[55] Perhaps the most significant sign of WB's optimism and belief in the picture was the size, and weight, of the pressbook sent to exhibitors. It was a whopping 32 pages in A3 format with extra-thick covers,[56] compared to, for example, the 14-page pressbook for *Once Upon a Time in the West* and 12 pages for *True Grit*.

In terms of box office and partly as a result of heavy advertising coupled with media-stoked controversy, *The Wild Bunch* was solidly received in first-run theaters in the major cities, but struggled in the hinterland and finished the year below *The Undefeated* and *Support Your Local Sheriff* but above *100 Rifles* and *Mackenna's Gold*. It did comparatively better abroad where it had many 70mm engagements, but, according to Warner Brothers it never turned a profit on original release.

10

The Good, the Bad and the Burt

Young Billy Young • The Good Guys and the Bad Guys

Young Billy Young starring Robert Mitchum, Robert Walker, Angie Dickinson; directed by Burt Kennedy; screenplay by Burt Kennedy, based on *Who Rides with Wyatt* by Will Henry; United Artists; 89 minutes

Picking Up the John Ford Mantle: Candidate Number One

Since 1961, Burt Kennedy had directed eight films, all but one (*The Money Trap*, 1965) westerns. Prior to picking up the megaphone, he had been a writer, again primarily in the western genre, beginning with *Seven Men from Now* (1956), directed by Budd Boetticher and starring Randolph Scott, the first of four films he wrote for the pair, the others being *The Tall T* (1957), *Ride Lonesome* (1959) and *Comanche Station* (1960). After making his directorial debut with *The Canadians* (1961), he stepped sideways into television, working on *Lawman*, *The Virginian* and *Combat!* before returning to the big screen as a writer-director with the comedy western *Mail Order Bride* (1964) starring Buddy Ebsen. Along with Sam Peckinpah and Andrew V. McLaglen, he was the 1960s director most steeped in westerns, sometimes a hyphenate, other times only director. *The Rounders* (1965), an offbeat western with Glenn Ford and Henry Fonda as aging cowhands, predated the more widely acclaimed *Will Penny* (1968) in that it concentrated primarily on the job of the lowly cowboy. But it received good reviews[1] and did decent box office. He followed up with the sequel *Return of the Seven* (1966), then another gritty effort, *Welcome to Hard Times* (1967), again with Fonda, based on the E.L. Doctorow novel. He hit the big time budget-wise with the John Wayne-Kirk Douglas *The War Wagon* (1967), which yielded his biggest box office returns to date, ranking 15th for the year. There was a two-year gap before the release of his next picture *Support Your Local Sherriff* (see Chapter Four) but then his westerns came thick and fast, two within the space of a month, both starring Robert Mitchum. *Young Billy Young* debuted in September 1969, *The Good Guys and the Bad Guys* in October.

Like Ford, Kennedy believed in cutting in the camera, so as to leave a producer little material to tamper with. "I've never lost a sequence in a picture," he boasted. "My cut of *The War Wagon* was only 18 seconds longer than the final release."[2] This placed a heavy duty on the director to get it right first time around, rather than shooting mountains of material that he could shape and reshape in the editing room, as George Stevens did with

Max Evans, author of the novel on which *The Rounders* is based, was an actor-writer-producer-director. He acted in *The Ballad of Cable Hogue* (1970) and wrote, produced and directed *The Wheel* (1973). He also wrote the novel *The Hi-Lo Country* which was filmed in 1999. Trade press advertisement (*Box Office*, March 15, 1965).

Shane: Stevens produced three quite different versions of the movie from three different perspectives before he found one that worked, a working method only possible because of the amount of film he had exposed.[3]

Kennedy was also very specific when it came to determining the outfits characters would wear: "I'm awfully aware of wardrobe. I always see the fittings of any of the characters in the picture."[4] And like Peckinpah, he was an avid editor. "I find myself spending time in the cutting room with the cutter when the picture is over and I won't let anybody see the picture until I've made my final cut."[5]

Kennedy was ranked as "one of the top directors in his genre and one of the most interesting creative talents on the scene today [and] developed into a top-rate cinematic stylist who shows a deft visual skill as well as a shrewd knowledge of pacing."[6] His three new films of 1969 could not have been more different: *Support Your Local Sherriff*, an out-and-out comedy, *Young Billy Young*, a psychological revenge western, and *The Good Guys and the Bad Guys*, halfway between an affectionate parody and a meditation on growing old.

The Mitchum Conundrum

Robert Mitchum was a typical Hollywood anomaly, still regarded as a star but currently lacking the box office figures to support that contention. You would have to go back to Fred Zinnemann's *The Sundowners* (1960) to find his last genuine hit. Since then, there had been one flop after another: *Cape Fear* (1962),[7] *Rampage* (1963), *The Winston Affair* (1964), *Mister Moses* (1965) and *The Way West* (1967). Then his career enjoyed a revival in Howard Hawks' *El Dorado* (1967).[8] Although *5 Card Stud* (1968) generated reasonable numbers, that was sandwiched between the flops *Villa Rides* (1968), the war picture *Anzio* (1968) and the drama *Secret Ceremony* (1968). Yet he remained, on paper at least, a star of two decades standing.

Mitchum reportedly turned down *The Wild Bunch*. So the question facing Mitchum and any producers was whether the star was a star in name only or whether he could still pull in the public. He was still a star of some caliber and it was in some measure due to westerns that he reached that kind of pinnacle. Although John Wayne, after the debacle of *The Big Trail* (1930), had spent the best part of a decade relegated to B-westerns, Mitchum had spent the early part of his career beginning in 1943 in the same budgetary league in the same genre but much further down the cast list. An idea of how low down the pecking order he came can be gauged from the fact that he appeared in 20 pictures

Robert Mitchum played a preacher in *5 Card Stud* (1968) and then another in *The Wrath of God* (1972), Ralph Nelson's screen version of the Jack Higgins novel (Hannan Collection).

in 1943. Credited as Bob Mitchum, he made his debut in a small part in the Hopalong Cassidy western *Hoppy Serves a Writ* (1943) and followed up with tiny roles in six more: *Border Patrol* (1943), *Leather Burners* (1943), *Colt Comrades* (1943), *Bar 20* (1943), *False Colors* (1943) and *Riders of the Deadline* (1943). There was also one with Johnny Mack Brown, *Lone Star Trail* (1943), and *Beyond the Last Frontier* (1943) in which he rose as far as fourth billing. Away from westerns, he had an uncredited role in the Laurel and Hardy comedy *The Dancing Masters* (1943). So he certainly could argue that, in terms of the western, he had paid his dues.

The following year, his star began to rise when he received third billing behind Dean Jagger and Kim Hunter in the drama *When Strangers Marry*. He reached his first career peak, top billing, in the routine B-westerns *Nevada* (1944) and *West of Pecos* (1944). But he was already beginning to diversify into the two other genres with which he would also be commonly associated, war and film noir. For the former he was second-billed in William Wellman's *The Story of G.I. Joe* (1945), for which he was nominated in the Best Supporting Actor category. This breakout performance made his name. For the latter, he was third-billed behind Katharine Hepburn and Robert Taylor in Vincente Minnelli's *Undercurrent* (1946). Although Teresa Wright was ostensibly the star of his biggest-budget western to date, a genuine A-picture, *Pursued*, he stole the acting plaudits as the orphan Jeb Rand, haunted by nightmares about the night his family was murdered and endangered by the family which has adopted him.

For the next few years he alternated between second billing, to Greer Garson in *Desire Me* (1947), Robert Young in Edward Dmytryk's *Crossfire* (1947), and to Myrna Loy in *The Red Pony* (1949), and even third billing behind Loretta Young and another rising star William Holden in *Rachel and the Stranger* (1948). He had top billing in *Out of the Past* (1947) and *Blood on the Moon* (1948). Thereafter, apart from *The Lusty Men* (1952) and *White Witch Doctor* (1953) where he played second fiddle to Susan Hayward, his name always topped the cast lists. Female stars now took second billing to him: Faith Domergue in *Where Danger Lives* (1950), Ava Gardner in *My Forbidden Past* (1951), Jane Russell in *His Kind of Woman* (1951) and *Macao* (1952), Jean Simmons in *She Couldn't Say No* (1952) and *Angel Face* (1953) and Marilyn Monroe in Preminger's *River of No Return* (1954). When reteamed with Teresa Wright in *Track of the Cat* (1954), he was the undisputed star. While he was making a name for himself in film noir and drama, he interspersed these films with a healthy dose of westerns: *Rachel and the Stranger*, *Blood on the Moon*, *The Red Pony*, *Track of the Cat*, and then later in the decade *Man with a Gun* (1955) and *The Wonderful Country* (1959). But it would be another six years before he strapped on a holster for Andrew V. McLaglen's *The Way West*, which proved a disappointment, not only for its box office, but because, suddenly, after nearly 15 years of being the star, he was back to second billing, this time behind Kirk Douglas. For the next three films he was not the first name on the film posters, giving way to John Wayne in *El Dorado*, Yul Brynner in *Villa Rides* and Dean Martin[9] in *5 Card Stud*. There was a brief career revival in Edward Dmytryk's *Anzio*, once a roadshow contender, where he was once again the major player. But after that, he stumbled at the box office. And he dropped down the pecking order in *Secret Ceremony* (1968) with Elizabeth Taylor and Mia Farrow outranking him on the credits.

So the question facing Mitchum as the decade drew to a close was whether he was a star in name only or whether he was still a name to draw the crowds. In order to tip the scales in his favor, and since film noir was long out-of-date, he returned to the genre where had once enjoyed great success—the western.

Jim Morrison, the lead singer of The Doors, watched *Pursued* (1947) on the night he died. Trade press advertisement (*Box Office*, February 8, 1947).

Young Billy Young—*A Film in Search of a Story*

Kennedy adapted Will Henry's novel *Who Rides with Wyatt*, having previously written a screenplay, *Yellowstone Kelly* (1959), based on one of the author's books.[10] The film opens superbly. Two young Americans, Billy Young (Robert Walker, Jr.[11]) and Jesse (David Carradine), are loafing in a Mexican village awaiting the arrival of a troop train. A general gets off the train and walks past the dozing pair as a firing squad lines up. As the condemned men are herded out, the young men stroll to the train and climb aboard to hide in the carriage full of horses. After the men are shot, the general re-boards, the train sets off and the general in his private quarters at the rear celebrates with champagne. The Americans slip past the horses, pull the chain to stop the train, burst into the rear coach and massacre the occupants. Escaping on horseback, they are pursued across the plains but when one falls the other continues on. Except for a few orders barked in Spanish, the entire sequence has taken place without a word being spoken.

Billy Young staggers over the inhospitable landscape until he stumbles across a mule. While riding it, he encounters Ben Kane (Robert Mitchum) camped at the side of a river. Kane suggests the boy not try to cross. Ignoring this advice, the boy soon sinks into swampy water. Emerging sodden, he asks Kane to help him catch the drowning animal. Kane's reply: "Nope." The boy pleads, "You can't leave me out here." Kanc: "Can't I?" and rides off. Now we abandon the boy and follow Kane to a town where he is offered the job of cleaning up another town, Lordsburg. Disgusted, Kane walks out on the meeting, but then takes the job on hearing mention of the name Boone. So now it becomes a mystery. Who is Boone and what does he mean to Kane?

We cut to a poker game in which Young in involved. When he loses, he accuses an opponent of cheating. The accused man takes umbrage, demanding the boy retract the slur. In the stand-off, the boy outdraws the older man and kills him. Enter Kane, informing Young that he has just killed the sheriff. Nonetheless, for reasons not yet explained, Kane scoops up the boy's $300 winnings, minus a small sum to cover the dead man's funeral, and they ride off, pursued by a posse only seen as distant dust. Kane sends the boy away on his own to outrun the posse but agrees to meet him later. The boy turns up and attempts to surprise the sleeping man, but instead is surprised himself and knocked out. When the boy wakes, he asks, "How come you let me get away?" Kane retorts, "I ain't. I'm taking you in." Despite this, he hands the boy a rifle, which the boy tries to fire, except it is jammed. Kane sorts out the jam and hands it back, again to the boy's consternation. Kane explains that he will sort out the murder charge against the boy later on. They make their way across hard terrain until they come across a stagecoach whose aged driver Charlie knows Kane and asks him to ride shotgun since he is expecting to be robbed on the road he calls Thieves Highway. Kane dumps the boy inside where the sole passenger is Miss Cushman. Where Henry Hathaway covered any journey by means of the long shot, Kennedy shoots the ride every which way: long shot, medium shot, tracking shot, close-up, reverse point of view, overhead. After nearly two minutes of this, you can see the sense in Hathaway's technique.

In due course, they are ambushed by six gunmen, led by Jesse. Kane and Young beat them off and that night they arrive in Lordsburg where Kane discovers the sheriff's office is not only empty and abandoned but boarded up. As he enters, he endures a flashback to when a prisoner shoots a young boy and Kane, running towards the jail in the rain, discovers the corpse.

Enter John Behan, who informs Kane that the town "is not ready for the law." Kane retorts that the town has "until daybreak tomorrow to get ready." When the man protests, Kane slugs him. Across the street in front of the Gaslight Saloon, Billy Young is getting the worst of a fistfight. Saloon manager Lily (Angie Dickinson) breaks it up, Kane locks up Young and returns to the saloon where he briefly watches Lily join other girls on stage before sneaking up the back stairs to a room where he switches off the lights. When Lily enters, he puts them back on. She knows who he is and warns him of the danger he is in from Frank Boone. She reveals that Behan owns the saloon and, effectively, her as well, but plaintively adds that she has "never had a man the way a woman wants one" before explaining that she was in Dodge City the night the boy was killed. She gives him the key to a shack she owns behind the jail, refusing to take payment because he is "the first man in a long time to take his hat off to me." But in her house, Kane suffers another flashback, to being in bed with a woman while the boy was shot. Lily returns with a bleeding lip, the result of Behan finding out she had gone behind his back. "He had a right to get mad at me, the way he saw it," she says. He lights a fire and makes her take a bath, but resists her blandishments, which she accepts with resignation. "You know a decent man who'd look twice at a girl like me?"

In the morning, Billy Young explains about Jesse and their mercenary mission to Mexico. Kane lets Billy go on condition he becomes his deputy but Billy refuses. Later, Billy meets Miss Cushman who says Kane has a "love of killing." Kane comes across Behan beating Lily with a belt, thumps the aggressor, then tends the woman's wounds. Billy Young and Jesse make up. Outside, Doc Cushman tells Kane he was also in Dodge that night, "working all night to keep your boy alive and he had no more chance than you." Suddenly, there is the sound of gunfire. Cushman is shot dead. Kane accuses Young of the killing but on learning that Jesse had borrowed his rifle locks him up instead. At this point, Young knows why the sheriff has followed this course of action: "because Jesse is Boone's son" and this will draw Boone out into the open. During Cushman's funeral, with an original touch of an organ being played on the back of a wagon, men started arriving in town. Lily tells Behan she is leaving him and quitting town. He scoffs, "If it isn't me, it'll be another like me."

Boone has arrived. He complains to Behan that Jesse should not have been allowed anywhere near Kane and shows regret for shooting Kane's son although he acknowledges, "There's not one damn thing I can do to make up for it … ever." Lily tells Young that Kane let his son help out at the jail but the night Boone was in custody, Kane had skipped over to the Birdcage Saloon to meet a woman (not Lily).

Next morning, gunmen line the rooftops. Young charges along the street, attracting fire and taking refuge in the jail, where he knocks out the sheriff and releases Jesse. Misguidedly, Young thinks that will resolve the situation. "It's over," he declares. But the minute he goes outside, the firing continues. The battle begins in earnest, Young and Kane cowering in the jail under a hail of bullets. In the hotel, Jesse wants to tell his father to call it off. When Behan tries to stop him, he gets killed. When the shooting stops, Young says he will accept Kane's offer of a badge, but Kane, in a surge of paternalism, knocks out the boy and locks him up to keep him from danger. Kane continues the battle out in the street but then the stagecoach arrives in the nick of time and Kane swings aboard and starts shooting the assailants until at the end of the street, Boone stands. He is shot. The movie ends with Jesse in jail and Young as a deputy. Kane, minus his badge, goes into the saloon and sweeps up Lily from the stage, carries her out over his shoulder and dumps her, fishnet tights and all, in the stagecoach so they can leave and get married.

All in all, a tale of relentless revenge and regret. The younger men attempt to stop the older ones repeating the past. The whore, while lacking the essential heart of gold, demonstrates something more potent, a strong sense of law and order, and resignation to her way of life. Power corrupts the powerful and they treat women as playthings, resorting to physical violence to keep them in check. Like Rooster Cogburn, Kane has his own sense of morality, and understands the hypocrisy he must endure in his work. Revenge is his only way of expiating his sin, although he does find some redemption from treating all women with respect.

You have the impression this is a film of two halves which do not quite merge. Billy Young's story of crossing the line from hired gun to upholder of the law would have been a strong enough tale on its own; so would the story of Kane's relentless pursuit and feelings of guilt. Especially given the quite brilliant opening, when the movie appeared to be about Billy, a bad guy doing a good deed, in the manner of the final actions of *The Wild Bunch*, it seems almost perverse to change tack and go down the psychological western route. The characters are well drawn for the most part, but the direction lacks direction, and while the story never meanders, it could have done with more time to let it settle rather than being an over-trim 89 minutes long.

Critical Response

Variety considered Mitchum "quietly effective" in what was otherwise a "fast western."[12] *International Motion Picture Exhibitor* hailed it as "highly effective" and befitting from "fine performances, vitality and humor"; the *Exhibitor* also praised Mitchum's "easygoing performance."[13]

Box Office

It was a flop, failing to place in the annual rankings, which means it brought in rentals of less than $1 million. At best estimate, *Young Billy Young* generated less than $300,000.[14]

The Good Guys and the Bad Guys: Starring Robert Mitchum, George Kennedy, Martin Balsam and David Carradine; directed by Burt Kennedy; screenplay by Robert M. Cohan and Denis Shryack; Warner Brothers; 91 minutes

The Western That Could Not Make Up Its Mind

Despite Burt Kennedy's penchant for comedy and his success earlier in the year with *Support Your Local Sheriff*, *The Good Guys and the Bad Guys* suffers from overemphasis on comedy at the expense of action and believable characters. In one sense, the movie is a homage to the passing west: The story is set in the early 1900s where motor vehicles predominate, and like *The Wild Bunch* and *Butch Cassidy and the Sundance Kid*, it features characters who have outlived their time. But in one critical sense, it is all over the place.

Did I mention that the movie stops every now and then for a song? The writers were the producers and it is possible that their vision of the movie, as seen on the page, did not coincide so easily with what was achievable on screen. A story constructed around how difficult it is for aging lawmen and lawbreakers to come to terms with the passing of the years might have worked reasonably well. But that story is buried under misfiring comedy, a satire on political abuse, ambition and hypocrisy.

The story is simple enough. Mayor Wilker (Martin Balsam in scenery-chewing mode), wanting to clear the decks before an election, and in an echo of *Death of a Gunfighter*, pensions off Marshal James Flagg (Robert Mitchum) because the lawman suspects the new bank is about to be robbed and the politician does not wish such gloomy thought intruding on his campaign. Meanwhile, the once feared, now aged outlaw McKay (George Kennedy) suffers humiliation of a similar kind when he is belittled by the gang he has joined. After a few mishaps and a fistfight, outlaw and lawman realize they are on the same side and join forces to thwart the robbery by hijacking a train that is due to be robbed.

The movie, like *Young Billy Young*, begins with aerial shots of a train going through ravines with Mitchum, on a hill, watching before going to see an old man, Grundy (Douglas Fowley), who tells him he overheard talk of McKay and a planned robbery. We cut to the modernized town where Mayor Wilker, as an election ruse, is closing down the whorehouse, despite carrying on an affair with Carmel (Tina Louise), whose husband is so involved in his motor that Wilker deems her "a victim of internal combustion." Cue garters tossed into the crowd starting a riot. Flagg, who has "tamed the town for 20 years," wants to get up a posse, but the mayor resists the idea and soon pensions him off, and hands the job to an incompetent younger man. Unperturbed, Flagg tracks down the gang, gets the drop on McKay, but is slugged from behind. McKay is told to kill Flagg if he wants to remain in the gang, of which he is clearly not the leader. Fighting in the river, they are both clearly too old for the rough-and-tumble. Having arrested McKay, Flagg takes him not to jail but to his boarding house, where his landlady Mary has carried a torch for the lawman for years. We learn that McKay had married a Quaker gal in Canada after the "Red River job" but she died and he has not seen his son for five years. All members of the Red River gang are

Robert Mitchum in *The Good Guys and the Bad Guys* (1969), which was advertised as "the last of the Wildest Bunch" (Hannan Collection).

now dead, as are Flagg's contemporaries. In a saloon squabble, Grundy is killed by outlaw leader Waco (David Carradine). When Wilker discovers there is trouble afoot, he goes to Flagg for help. Flagg and McKay resolve to prevent the train, carrying money for the new bank, from stopping in the town. We are treated to yet another song while the two old guys pursue the train and board it, but they are arrested on board because Flagg has no badge to prove his credentials. They escape out a window and climb onto the carriage roof. Guards shoot at them. There is one visually effective scene when the train goes through a tunnel and gunfire illuminates the darkness. The outlaws wait patiently at the station and in what must be an homage to *High Noon*, the station clock is shown at various times. A motor car stalls on the railway track with the driver assuring his wife they are in no danger because the approaching train will halt at the station. When the train smashes through the car, the outlaws give chase and they, in turn, are pursued by a convoy of cars. Meanwhile, McKay turns the fire hose on the guards and separates the coaches from the engine while Flagg tosses sticks of dynamite at the outlaws. Up ahead, the railway line is twisted so they have to jump off the train. The outlaws are ambushed by Flagg and McKay as they retrieve the money bags from the train. In the shootout, the good guys advance in unison. The outlaws are defeated and the car convoy arrives. The mayor, puffed up with pride, considers running for governor.

There are some nice touches, but neither sufficient story nor laugh-out-loud humor. There is a running gag about McKay preening himself, and delighted to be recognized as a famous bank robber, but it is mostly a waste of the talent of all concerned.

Critical Reception

Variety recognized the end result as a confused product, determining that the producers "had a time of it trying to figure out what makes a film a comedy or a drama with the result that it is a mixture with a decided accent on comedy."[15] David Austen in *Films and Filming* believed it was Burt Kennedy's "ability to combine excitement and humor that makes many of his films a pleasure."[16] *International Motion Picture Exhibitor* found it "amusing" and "well acted" with Burt Kennedy directing "this one at a leisurely clip."[17]

Box Office

This also failed to register in the annual rankings, which meant rentals of under $1 million. At best estimate, *The Good Guys and the Bad Guys* returned about $600,000.[18]

11

One Step Ahead of the Audience

Butch Cassidy and the Sundance Kid

Starring Paul Newman, Robert Redford, Katharine Ross; directed by George Roy Hill; Screenplay by William Goldman; Twentieth Century–Fox; 110 minutes

Nobody Knows Anything

Screenwriter William Goldman[1] is most famous for the Hollywood axiom "Nobody knows anything,"[2] a phrase that could be easily applied to his most celebrated work, Twentieth Century–Fox's *Butch Cassidy and the Sundance Kid*.[3] Setting aside his record-breaking fee, there was nothing particularly auspicious about this picture as it went into production apart from the fact that it was ever made at all, after Fox had suffered staggering losses on the roadshows *Doctor Dolittle* (1967) and *Star!* (1968). The former brought in just $6.2 million in rentals out of a budget of $16-$18 million and the latter $4.2 million from $14 million.

These reverses had hit Fox to such an extent that in the first eight months of 1969 it had green-lighted only nine movies. But when revenues from *Planet of the Apes* (1968) and *Valley of the Dolls* (1968) helped balance the books,[4] the studio put into production six movies in the ninth month of the year.[5] Of these, the western was far from the most expensive, its budget of $6.8 million trailing by some considerable margin the $10.2 million laid out for *The Only Game in Town* (1970), much of that cost swallowed by stars Elizabeth Taylor and Warren Beatty[6] and director George Stevens, and still behind the $7.8 million allocated to *Justine* (1969), helmed by George Cukor and primed at that point as a roadshow, and the $7.1 million invested in another western, *The Undefeated* (1969), pairing John Wayne and Rock Hudson. It was not that much more than the budget for Martin Ritt's *Hombre* (1966), also starring Paul Newman, made by Fox three years earlier.[7] And, of course, it was only a fraction of the combined $62 million being gambled on the roadshow trio *Tora! Tora! Tora!* (1970), *Hello, Dolly* (1970) and *Patton* (1970).[8]

The movie raised some publicity juice when Steve McQueen was attached to the project. The Newman-McQueen combination was guaranteed to raise audience interest. McQueen walked away because he could not get top billing.[9] Others considered were Jack Lemmon, Marlon Brando and Dustin Hoffman.[10] The selection of future superstar Robert Redford as Newman's co-star did not attract much media attention, certainly not in comparison to the coverage given when McQueen was attached, for there were question marks about Redford's marquee capability. Although the actor had scored a hit in the adaptation of Neil Simon Broadway success *Barefoot in the Park* (1967), Jane Fonda, hot after *Cat Ballou* (1965), had received top billing. Rather than cashing in on his good fortune, Redford had fallen foul of Hollywood after breaking his contract on the Paramount western *Blue* (1968).[11] A sure sign of how little power Redford enjoyed was that when Newman was set to play the role of the Sundance Kid, the movie was entitled *The Sundance Kid and Butch Cassidy*, only reverting to the actual title when Newman changed his mind and swapped roles.[12]

But when, after an auction involving Columbia, Warner Brothers and Universal, Fox had paid a record $400,000 for Goldman's original screenplay, that made the news, and for good reason.

For a start, it was $100,000 above the previous record, to William Rose for the Stanley Kramer roadshow comedy *It's a Mad Mad Mad Mad World* (1963). More importantly, it indicated a shift away from investment in bestselling novels and hit plays and musicals to which Hollywood was more disposed because they came with a "pre-sold" audience (i.e., readers and playgoers). Out of the #1 films in each year of the 1960s, only *Cleopatra* (1963) had not been based on a novel or Broadway product. Hollywood would happily fork over $1 million to novelist Irving Wallace for two books and $3 million for the rights to *My Fair Lady* (1964) while at the same time spending a fraction of those sums on original scripts which came with no in-built audience.[13] Studios were in the business of buying expectation, not ideas that required substantial marketing. The original screenplay was "considered by many an orphan in a domestic film industry which tends towards properties allegedly pre-sold in other media." Unlike actor salaries, for example, fees for original screenplays did not go up and up. When a record $100,000 was paid to Ring Lardner Jr. and Michael Kanin for *Woman of the Year* in 1941, it was not followed by ever-increasing payments. In fact, screenplay salaries went down as much as up. *The Defiant Ones* (1958), another major original script purchase, was bought for just $75,000 and when William Rose sold *Guess Who's Coming to Dinner* (1967) to Stanley Kramer for what was considered a sky-high fee, the amount handed over was $100,000 less than for *It's a Mad Mad Mad Mad World*.[14]

The *Butch Cassidy and the Sundance Kid* sale was notable for one further reason: It was for a complete script. The reason you see so many names attached to a script and the reason why there are so many disputes over credits is that Hollywood has a nasty habit of taking an idea (the "story" in screenplay parlance) from one writer and handing it to another to complete the script, in effect discouraging any writer from spending two or three years developing an idea into enough of a story to attract the funding to finish the script. The Goldman deal was significant for a third reason: He was paid all the money[15] at once rather than, in the normal way, in dribs and drabs, so much for the story, so much for the first draft, so much for second draft, so much for revisions and so on, which meant an author could be endlessly tied to a project without any guarantee it would go into production, rather than being paid so much immediately that the studio had no option but to get it off the ground as soon as possible to recoup its investment.

***Opposite*: Renowned novelist William Goldman resisted the idea of turning his *Butch Cassidy and the Sundance Kid* screenplay into a novel. Instead, in an extremely unusual move for the time, the complete screenplay was published by Bantam Books. Even more surprisingly, it became a bestseller (Corgi Books, 1969).**

CORGI BOOKS

THE BRILLIANT NEW SCREENPLAY BY

WILLIAM GOLDMAN

AUTHOR OF "BOYS & GIRLS TOGETHER"

BUTCH CASSIDY AND THE SUNDANCE KID

At a time when scripts could take years to get into production, the Goldman effort took ten months.[16]

Twentieth Century–Fox did not simply pay up and then hire the principals. It was the other way around. The principals were the reason the studio bid for the script. Most top-name actors from Burt Lancaster, John Wayne and Frank Sinatra to Paul Newman and Jack Lemmon[17] had their own production companies which would have first-look deals with particular studios. Typically, the studios covered the overhead of these independent companies in return for star participation. Newman would not put up $400,000 of his own money for the Goldman script,[18] or if he did, it would be with a guarantee of reimbursement by Twentieth Century–Fox, but more likely would intimate his interest (and commitment) and leave the rest up to Fox.[19] In the event, it was Fox executive Paul Monash who carried out the negotiations with the writer's agent, for which he was rewarded an executive producer credit.[20] Goldman had some connection with both Newman and McQueen, the former having enjoyed first-hand experience of Goldman's skills, after essaying private eye *Harper* (1966) from the writer's adaptation of the Ross Macdonald novel *The Moving Target.* Normally, a writer would be required to do revisions to a script once leading actors had been assigned, adapting the words to suit a star's particular needs. But in the case of *Harper,* director Jack Smight put out a last-minute call to the writer to create a sequence to cover the opening credits and Goldman came up with the brilliant idea of showing Harper waking up and retrieving used grounds from the refuse to make his coffee, a scene that generated laughter from audiences and made them warm to the character.

Goldman had published his first novel *Temple of Gold* (1957) at the age of 26, following it up with *Your Turn to Curtsey, My Turn to Bow* (1958) and *Soldier in the Rain* (1960), which was later made into a film (starring Steve McQueen), as was *No Way to Treat a Lady* (1964) with Rod Steiger.[21] But he benefited from the paperback boom of the 1960s, when big fat novels like *Boys and Girls Together*[22] (1966) were turned into "beach" and later "airport" reads by the addition of attractive covers and marketing. By then he had already dabbled in screenwriting, originally with *No Way to Treat a Lady* and very quickly experienced the problems outlined above, brought into the film *Masquerade* (1965) starring Cliff Robertson to rewrite the screenplay by Michael Relph, and then jettisoned from *Charly* (1968) after delivering the first draft, and seeing screenplays such *The Spring the War Ended*, originally set to star Newman, fail to reach the screen.

Goldman first approached Newman with the script while the actor was making *Hombre* (1967). Goldman had first encountered the Butch Cassidy story in the 1950s and researched it for many years. Unlike most westerns where villains are generally killed after a chase or a confrontation, Butch and Sundance escaped to South America for eight years and became more famous than they had ever been in America. Goldman was attracted to the story because it counteracted the famous F. Scott Fitzgerald aphorism "There are no second acts in American lives." To turn his original story idea into a novel would have required considerably more research into historical detail, and so the screenplay was published as the movie tie-in.[23]

King of Hollywood

Hollywood had a simple, age-old method of deciding who was, at any given time, the biggest actor or actress in the business. It was who commanded the largest fee. That

Yugoslavian Sylva Koscina belonged to the second generation of European actresses imported to Hollywood. She also starred in *Three Bites of the Apple* (1966) with David McCallum, *Deadlier Than the Male* (1967) with Richard Johnson and *A Lovely Way to Die* (1968) with Kirk Douglas. Trade press advertisement (*Box Office*, April 29, 1968).

honor belonged to Newman, who had collected $1.1 million for the racing car drama *Winning* (1969). The actor had taken control of his own career since buying his way out of his Warner Brothers contract in 1959 for $500,000 when it still had three years left to run, a hefty gamble since his fee at the time was only $200,000. Left to his own devices, Newman proved not just an astute businessman but in a class of his own in picking scripts that both suited his talents and developed his acting chops. His production alliance with director Martin Ritt had resulted in films as diverse as *Hud* (1963) and *Hombre.* When that relationship ended, Newman set up shop on his own account to develop his directorial debut *Rachel, Rachel* (1968) and then hooked up with producer John Foreman to produce *Winning* and, subsequently, *Butch Cassidy and the Sundance Kid.* Newman was a bona fide global star with a superb track record and over the last four years a virtually unbroken string of hits: *Harper*, *Torn Curtain* (1966), *Hombre*, *Cool Hand Luke* (1967) and *Winning*, the only blip being the comedy *The Secret War of Harry Frigg* (1968).

Its failure had slightly unnerved him and he was initially daunted by the idea of taking on another picture where humor was a major element.[24] For a box office star, Newman was unusual in that the quality of his acting was appreciated by critics and contemporaries with four Best Actor nominations (*Cat on a Hot Tin Roof*, 1958; *The Hustler*, 1961; *Hud* and *Cool Hand Luke*)[25] and one (*Rachel, Rachel*, 1968) for direction. Although Newman primarily specialized in drama, he had starred in two critically acclaimed westerns, as Billy the Kid in Arthur Penn's *The Left Handed Gun* (1958) and as the raised-by-Indians hero of *Hombre.* (*The Outrage*, Martin Ritt's 1964 reworking of Akira Kurosawa's *Rashomon* [1950], had been less well-received.) Although Newman relished taking on new roles and subverting his public image, such decisions had not always worked to his advantage, examples being the romantic comedy *A New Kind of Love* (1963) with his wife Joanne Woodward and another ill-fated comedy, *Lady L* (1965) with Sophia Loren. Not only did *Butch Cassidy and the Sundance Kid* burden him with comedy, which so far in his career had not proved his best suit, but he was going to play an outlaw who could not shoot, did not win the girl, and died at the end.

Katharine Ross was lined up for the role of Etta Place, although her romance with director of photography Conrad Hall resulted in some conflict with director George Roy Hill.[26] She was 29 by the time the western appeared, having made her small screen debut at the age of 17 in the TV production *The Trial of Lizzie Borden* (1957); it was another five years before her next television part. She appeared on *The Alfred Hitchcock Hour*, *The Virginian* and *The Big Valley.* She was in *Shenandoah* (1965) and *The Singing Nun* (1966), fourth-billed in *Mister Buddwing* (1966) and third-billed in *Games* (1967) before her breakthrough in *The Graduate* (1967), for which she was nominated for a Best Supporting Actress Oscar, and followed with a starring role opposite John Wayne in *Hellfighters* (1968). Fox opposed the hiring of Hall, who had lensed *The Professionals* (1966), on the grounds of expense but was overruled.[27] Strother Martin, who had impressed Newman on *Cool Hand Luke*, played the Bolivian mine manager, thus ensuring the actor appeared in three of the most iconic westerns of the year.[28] To write the score (if it could be called that, given how minimalist it turned out), Burt Bacharach, better known as a songwriter ("Make it Easy on Yourself," "What's New, Pussycat?," "This Guy's in Love"), was hired to write the musical interludes. As a stopgap, Hill had used Simon and Garfunkel's "Fifty-Ninth Street Bridge Song" ("Feeling Groovy"), but was taken with Bacharach's "Raindrops Keep Falling on My Head," although the scene was shot in bright sunshine, and against the objections of the studio board of directors.[29]

The Oscars counted most with the public, but exhibitors had their own way of bestowing accolades. Winning the main annual award from the National Association of Theater Owners (NATO) helped a star's movies get booked into movie theaters. Trade press advertisement (*Box Office*, October 16, 1967).

King of the Hill

George Roy Hill was part of a generation of directors including Martin Ritt, John Frankenheimer and Arthur Penn who had made the successful transition from live television in the 1950s to the big screen. Over a five-year stint, beginning in 1954, on *Ponds Theater*, *Lux Video Theater*, *Kraft Theater*, *Kaiser Aluminum Hour* and *Playhouse 90* he directed a number of teleplays that later were translated to the big screen such as *A Night to Remember*,[30] *The Helen Morgan Story* and *Judgment at Nuremberg*.[31] He spent three years honing his skills on and off Broadway and after directing Tennessee Williams play *A Period of Adjustment* was hired to direct the screen version in 1962 with rising stars Tony Franciosa[32] and Jane Fonda. He followed up with an adaptation of the Lillian Hellman stage play *Toys in the Attic* (1963) starring Dean Martin and Geraldine Page. Thanks to Peter Sellers' breakthrough Hollywood performance in *The Pink Panther* (1964), his comedy *The World of Henry Orient* (1964) reached a wider audience. He had a formed a partnership, Pan Arts, to make *The World of Henry Orient* and that should also have seen Hill take on *A Fine Madness* (1966) starring Sean Connery, but that job went instead to Irvin Kershner.[33] Although his critical stock increased after his first and third films were nominated for Golden Globes, he was an unlikely choice for the big-budget blockbuster *Hawaii* (1966) after original choice Fred Zinnemann[34] had quit the adaptation of the James Michener bestseller starring Julie Andrews and Max von Sydow.[35] After being appointed director, Hill was briefly sacked and replaced by Arthur Hiller,[36] but soon proved equal to the task and pulled the unwieldy $14 million production into decent shape and into profit. His next venture was equally unusual, the musical *Thoroughly Modern Millie*, again with Andrews. This success tempted Hill to try his hand at a Broadway musical in 1967, *Henry, Sweet, Henry*,[37] based on *The World of Henry Orient*, but it failed to click with audiences. Nonetheless, he came to *Butch Cassidy and the Sundance Kid* buoyed with success and immediately clashed with Goldman who, believing that since Fox had spent so much on the script and widely publicized the purchase,[38] they would adhere to his vision. Goldman was furious when changes were made without his consent, not realizing that, no matter how much was paid for a property, the screenwriters came much further down the power chain than the director.[39] The published screenplay provides many examples of where Hill diverged from the screenwriter's intentions, the director eliminating many of Goldman's more elaborate instructions. One good example: the superposse arriving to interrupt the second train robbery.[40] Unusually, the actors were granted a two-week rehearsal period[41] followed by a 12-week shoot, largely on location in Utah, New Mexico, Colorado and Mexico (standing in for Bolivia). The famous cliff jump took place at Animus River George near Durango in Colorado.[42] Some ad-libbing was permitted in the scene with Butch and Agnes the prostitute (Cloris Leachman), though most was ultimately cut.[43] A recurrent back problem forced Hill to direct for ten days from a stretcher, and problems with the weather during the Newman-Logan fight scene put production back two days.[44]

A New Genre Is Born

Directors making their western debuts had a habit of turning the genre upside down (examples: Howard Hawks' *Red River* [1948] and Fred Zinnemann's *High Noon* [1952]).

This still showing Robert Redford and Paul Newman from *Butch Cassidy and the Sundance Kid* (1969) appeared on the cover of the October 1969 edition of British magazine *Films and Filming* to kick off its "Westerns" special edition (Hannan Collection).

With *Butch Cassidy and the Sundance Kid*, George Roy Hill brought a fresh pair of eyes which resulted in a number of stylistic innovations, not least the musical interlude, the black-and-white opening and ending and the freeze frame climax.[45] It sparked a whole new subgenre—the "buddy" movie or what would be called these days a "bromance."

But despite these new ideas, most of the credit for the picture's success must go to Goldman, who realized that to circumvent audience expectation, he had to keep one step ahead of the moviegoer. So although he adopts certain traditional western sequences (the player accused of cheating in a card game, a gang leader facing challenge, train robbing, pursuit by a posse, the outlaw's lover), he does so with a twist, so that instead of provoking confrontation at the poker game, the heroes try steadfastly to avoid it. The challenge to Butch's leadership is resolved without bloodshed, the robberies are littered with both humanity and humor, the posse remains a mysterious, distant threat, the anticipated shoot-out does not materialize and Sundance's lover does not spark jealousy between Butch (the love triangle[46] element was the director's invention). To Goldman, too, goes credit for the movie structure. It comprises, effectively, the classic three acts, each separated by a musical interlude. The relatively small number of sequences quickly pushes the story along as the heroes, if that is what they are, find their world increasingly under threat.

We go from one of the best character introductions ever written, for the Sundance Kid, to a challenge to Butch's leadership, to the introduction of schoolteacher Etta Place (Katharine Ross) and the realization that she has an unusual relationship with the two men, the train robberies, doubts creeping in about their chosen lifestyle, pursuit, escape, flight to Bolivia, more bank robbing, the suspicion someone is still on their tail, and climactic shoot-out. Goldman also deals with other problems inherent in a main character having a love interest, that resolution usually a distraction from the main story, by having Etta Place display as much obvious affection for Butch Cassidy as her ostensible lover Sundance (an unexpected twist for audiences would have expected Newman as the bigger star to get the girl) and having her play a more significant role in South America. But Goldman's greatest contribution is to have the heroes living in the present. Their camaraderie does not conceal bitterness, they are not laden with regret, even if (like Butch) they have abandoned wife and children along the way, so the past cannot bite them nor bring them down. No flashbacks are required to illuminate their lives, the writer introducing details about their past (their real names, birthplace, etc.) into the narrative, sometimes at moments of high drama (we learn Butch cannot shoot at the one moment when he needs to). What we see is what we get. Unusually, too, they are amiable characters for the most part, though deadly when confronted. Paul Newman (Butch) delivers a self-effacing performance, although his seeming generosity to his co-star obscures the reality that he had all the best lines in exchange for allowing gunslinger Sundance to steal the action scenes and experienced enough to understand that the most romantic scene in the picture is Butch and Etta on a bicycle. Still, only a star comfortable in his own skin would take on a role where he was continually mocked by his co-star ("You just keep thinking, Butch, that's what you're good at"). The screenplay offers the leading actors a film without angst, allowing their personalities to gel, to present such an amiable on-screen partnership, comrades without any bitterness or back-biting, a relationship unlikely to fracture under stress, men without a past, not haunted by regret, that it created the "buddy" movie.

Uncontainable Reality

Like *The Wild Bunch*, which beat it into theaters by a few months, *Butch Cassidy and the Sundance Kid* depicts the end of the road for the western outlaw. However, audiences are substantially more sympathetic to this pair than Pike Bishop and his gang simply because Butch and Sundance are eminently more likable, not given to self-pity. Butch in particular generally abhors violence. It helped that the movie is studded with humor, but also that, to some extent, they initially escape their expected fate. That this is going to be quite a different type of western is immediately apparent, the credits rolling as the screen shows a silent movie depicting the exploits of the Hole-in-the-Wall Gang[47] and their demise.[48] This opening is accompanied by a plaintive piano and the first of many distinctive uses of sound effects, in this case the operation of a movie projector. Music will be used sparingly and sound effects spectacularly.

For the opening two sequences, the director employs a sepia tint, reminiscent of what you might find in an old daguerreotype print. We begin with the camera zooming into a bank and then dissolving to Butch examining the building from a window. He stares at its bars and walks around before entering. From his point of view we are given close-ups of modern deterrents, a buzzer and a bell, and then the sounds of windows being closed and latches coming down on doors. As the bank closes and whatever little light there *is* fades, this first scene could almost be a hint at what will follow, darkness falling on a lifestyle that is fast going out of date. There is a punchline to lift the audience's mood but, interestingly, Hill does not afford Newman a close-up as he complains, "That's a small price to pay for beauty."[49] These words are delivered with Butch's back to the camera, so it is almost a voice-over. Instead, it is Sundance who gets the close-up, and continues getting it, all through the next scene, the camera focusing entirely on his face, filmed over the shoulders of two card players, with the dialogue being spoken by characters whose faces remain out of shot.[50] We do not know Butch has entered[51] until his face appears over Sundance's shoulder, and, contrary to audience expectation, not adding to the conflict but trying to defuse it. Even when Sundance is accused of cheating, the normal trigger for a stand-off, negotiations continue between the pair, with Sundance,

The advertising used as *Butch Cassidy*'s main promotional tool was the iconic image of the two heroes trying to shoot their way out of the Bolivian ambush, but a surprising number of promotional images were devoted to relaxed shots like this. Pictured: Robert Redford, Paul Newman (Hannan Collection).

pushing Butch aside, insisting on being "invited to stick around."[52] Only when Butch utters the immortal words, "Can't help you, Sundance," does the director cut to a two-shot showing the card player, and then a three-shot but with, unusually, so much space on the right that the left hand side of the screen is constricted, Sundance almost in the middle of the picture.

There's a cut to another three-shot as Sundance leaves, until the card player foolishly asks how good Sundance is and the gunslinger provides a vivid demonstration. Given that audiences have seen hundreds of displays of virtuoso gunslinging usually involving shooting coins in the air (sometimes several times before they land), this sticks in the memory as Sundance's bullets detach the man's holster and send it spinning across the floor. However, instead of allowing the audience to react with awe, the scene is immediately undercut with a laugh line, Butch muttering, "Like I been telling you—over the hill." Although this is given a humorous spin, it is nonetheless indicative, although neither of them know it, of their present situation.

Nor does Hill succumb to triumphalism, no surging score at this point, as the scene turns to color and they ride, mostly in medium shot, not the classic extreme long shot preferred by Henry Hathaway in *True Grit*, although the traditional framing is often maintained of the sky taking up the top one-third or one-quarter of the screen. They do a lot of riding, through riverbeds, across canyons.[53] There is no music, just the sound of hooves. Their easy camaraderie and their different characters are spelled out during the short piece of dialogue when Butch suggests going to Bolivia, the latest in a long line of ideas, that Sundance as easily bats back, in a way that never appears to compromise Butch's authority as leader: "You just keep thinking Butch, that's what you're good at." Butch's retort, "I got vision and the rest of the world wears bifocals," puts him square in line with the other outlandish dreamers of the 1969 generation of westerns— for example, Omar Sharif in *Mackenna's Gold*, visualizing Paris. Although in *The Wild Bunch*, Pike Bishop faces some threats to his authority, they are primarily the result of mild infirmity and inefficiency, but now Butch faces a real threat from a real he-man, the stripped-to-the-waist. muscular Logan (Ted Cassidy), who wants to rob trains, not banks. Interestingly, Hill has also peopled the hideout with more characters than the screenwriter and in the background we see old men and females of various ages and someone carrying a bucket of water and other aspects of domesticity and an unexpected degree of impoverishment. There are remarkably few characters in the picture, but News Carver (Timothy Scott) gets a line that justifies his name. During the confrontation, Sundance shows no signs of intervening, another twist since generally sides are swiftly taken in westerns. When Logan, wielding a knife, is distracted by Butch's insistence on discussing the rules, Butch has enough time to kick him in the balls. Even more surprisingly, Butch takes up Logan's idea of hitting the Flyer on both its journeys.[54]

Although Goldman would probably have been unaware of the details of the competing western *The Wild Bunch* and its plot pivot of a railroad king hiring mercenaries to hunt down the outlaws, the screenwriter initially misleads audiences and the two main characters about what they are up against by having as representative of the Union Pacific railroad the pipsqueak Woodcock rather than the menacing professional Deke Thornton (played by a grizzled Robert Ryan). There has already been one twist, the passengers intrigued by coming so close to the famous outlaws rather than being terrified out of their wits. And when they blow up the carriage, Butch's first reaction is a humane one, to make sure Woodcock is safe, an action at odds with Peckinpah's outlaws who will gun down everyone in sight. From now on, the twists come thick and fast. While Butch and Sundance enjoy a drink at the whorehouse, down below the marshal (Kenneth Mars) attempts, without success, to rouse a posse until the gathering is commandeered by a bicycle salesman ("Meet the future"). Butch suggests they sign up for the war against the Spanish, and proceeds to announce his real name, as does Sundance, both names Robert

Leroy Parker and Harry Longbaugh hardly a patch on their nicknames.[55] This sequence also serves to provide a historical background, the modernization of the west via wheels and the time stamp of the 1898 war against Spain, the banner "Remember the *Maine*" a reference to the sinking of the battleship *Maine* in Havana in February of that year.[56] And it also shows Butch's inflated sense of his own importance that he would instantly qualify to become a colonel and his colleague a major. When Sundance begins to recite the requisites he desires in a woman, Hill's direction takes over from Goldman's screenplay. Goldman simply lists the qualities, but Hill has Redford mention them in a dreamy manner, and slowly, as though coming upon each word for the first time, and it immediately adds a romantic dimension to his character.

At the outset, the Etta sequence seems more like rape than seduction. At this point, we do not know who she is,[57] and only see her outline until she lights a lamp. She starts to undress in the dark until catching sight of Sundance. He motions with a gun for her to continue. She lets down her hair on his instruction. He cocks his gun to tell her to open her blouse. The scene ends on a laugh that she wishes "he would get here on time." If she appears an unlikely companion for a gunslinger, what occurs next refutes all laws of the western. Butch turns up on a bicycle. And a song—I bet nobody in the audience expected that or expected it to work. Not only does she accept a ride, but she is delighted to see him, and clearly enjoys his company, and in a more physical manner than suggested in the screenplay,[58] with hugs and light kisses. A star never likes being landed with exposition, least of all about his own character, and so it is left to Etta to explain that he never has any money because he is a soft touch and a "rotten gambler." (All his deficiencies are undercut by his charm—though why Sundance, with as little money, is a better bet is never explained.)

During the second train robbery, they encounter a defiant Woodcock, arm-in-a-sling defiant, an indication, had Butch been alert to such things, that Mr. E.H. Harriman was more capable of inspiring confidence in his employees than the outlaws are in scaring them. This time, Butch does display his intelligence, tricking the employee into opening up, although disappointed that the railroad has installed a stronger safe. The resultant blasting of the safe, and the entire carriage, produces the movie's outstanding line, "Think you used enough dynamite there, Butch?" And while the outlaws race around gathering the dollar notes raining down from the sky, the audience is alerted by a sound cue—a train in the distance—and then a sight cue of smoke and an engine with just one carriage. A close-up of the train as it stops is followed by a close-up of Butch and Sundance.[59] There is no music, just the sound of the train whistle, then the carriage door opening and horses leaping out.

And what mostly we hear, as will hear for most of the next 40 minutes, are hooves, drumming at this stage as the Superposse appears, some gunshots as they pick off Logan and News. And in a foretaste of what is to come, the Superposse will not be deterred, nor tricked into following the other members of the gang when Butch and Sundance split off. Relentless pursuit has been a theme of the 1969 westerns, but nobody has ever been as relentless as this. The posse always appears in long shot, a threat, but inescapable.[60] "Who are those guys?" will become one refrain, "I think we lost them," another. Believing they are safe, Butch and Sundance hole up in the brothel, detailing an old man, Sweetface (Percy Helton), to misdirect the posse. Butch, overconfident as usual, enjoys the attentions of Agnes. It is possible to take at face value Agnes' protestations that she likes Butch for more than his money; "You're the only real man I ever met" echoes Angie Dickinson in

Young Billy Young. Although some clients at a whorehouse will be nicer than others, it is their money that makes them clients. This plan fails to dupe the posse, nor will the posse's horses scatter as horses usually do. Butch and Sundance ride through woods and mountains and even at night lanterns reveal that pursuit remains constant. When our protagonists try the old wheeze of using the same horse, sending the other off in the hope it will at least split the pursuing force (which it does, temporarily), there's a great shot of the lanterns in the night going one way and then returning. The posse takes on "a phantom quality."[61]

The Bledsoe sequence produced one of the only real disagreements between Hill and Newman. The actor argued that the scene belonged at the end of the pursuit section, not in the middle.[62] Butch thinks he can talk his way out of the situation, another crazy notion of enlisting, hoping he can negotiate when the opposition has closed down that option. But Sheriff Ray Bledsoe (Jeff Corey) apprises them of the truth: "It's over, and you're both gonna die bloody and all you can do is choose where." And it's back to trying to outrun and outthink the posse. The soundtrack is hooves. When they identify, from a distance, the posse leaders as Lord Baltimore and Joe Lefors, they refuse to believe it, even Sundance joining in the self-delusion.[63] Butch and Sundance are worn down, sweating, scratched, and as a final throw of the dice, chase their horse away and climb a steep slope, but once they reach the top and go down the other side, they are trapped on a cliff edge over a gorge. Now we see the figures of the posse as they come over the top of the rocks. Sundance wants to shoot it out but Butch has an even more audacious plan: jump into the river. Sundance strenuously objects because he can't swim. Interestingly, Hill shoots this scene as a two-shot rather than focusing on Butch at his most persuasive or Sundance when making his admission. The entire pursuit sequence runs on for about 40 minutes, and as extraordinary as it is to keep the whole thing maintain pace and tension, at the same time as giving us a closer insight into the main characters, and their togetherness in time of trouble, it is also extremely audacious of the director to stick pretty closely to the screenwriter's intentions, when the temptation must surely have been to trim it by a good ten minutes and give more distinct coverage of the pursuers. Hill's boldness results in probably the best chase sequence ever filmed.

The waiting Etta, who believed them dead, hugs both on their return rather than picking out Sundance. It is Etta who has a clearer view of the endgame. While Butch moans about what he sees, like a child, as "unfairness," Etta informs them that the posse will stick together not just for a few days but until the outlaws are dead. Sundance at last succumbs to one of Butch's zany ideas, "wherever the hell Bolivia is," and, in the macho man's inability to communicate his feelings, decides that Etta accompanying them will be "good cover." Etta gets her longest speech, happy to admit that Butch and Sundance (rather than, interestingly enough, not just Sundance) are "the only excitement" she has ever known. And pretty much contrary to the rules of westerns where schoolteachers are bide-at-homes who protect tough men from themselves and act as moral compasses, she agrees to go, but with one proviso: "I won't watch you die"—as if she is far more prescient than they are, or the only one of the three willing to admit it.

For the New York sequence, Hill requested use of the *Hello, Dolly* sets which were on an adjacent soundstage, but this was refused since Twentieth Century–Fox did not wish to give audiences a sneak preview of sets which had cost millions. Instead, Hill sneaked the three principals onto the set and took some photographs which he merged with period photographs.[64] This is another interlude, an intermission between the acts, and although it shows moments of high delight (dressed up to get their photographs taken, enjoying meals in fancy restaurants, Butch with his head in Etta's lap, a trip to Coney Island), the tone of the music changes once they board the ship, and it becomes an echo of the opening plaintive theme. And where we have mostly seen them together in the first part of this sequence, now we see the two outlaws separated, Sundance dancing with Etta, Butch staring wistfully at them or into space. While the screenplay[65] has blamed this sadness on their departure and emphasizes instead a "feeling of elegance" at having the time of their lives, the director makes much more emotional bounty from it. Goldman also has them just arriving in a stinking pit of a town in Bolivia, but Hill gives the ironical addition of a train, Nacionales de Bolivia, and places them first in a broken-down railway station.[66]

The dynamics of their relationship change dramatically in Bolivia. Sundance becomes more outspoken, questioning Butch's leadership ("How do you know?"), while Etta becomes more central, much more than the traditional girl who has come along for the ride but stays in the background emerging only as romance and instruction demand. More importantly, Butch is out of his depth, his boast that he can speak Spanish, and that robbing banks will be easier in South America, revealed as hollow on their first job when we discover he does not understand a word of the language. When Etta, in her element as a patient schoolteacher with unwilling pupils, attempts to teach them Spanish, Sundance sulks, believing that words are Butch's territory. Etta is mother, too, refusing Sundance's advances until he learns words by rote while praising Butch, next door, for getting them right, not realizing that he is cheating by using a crib sheet. Butch is not as clever as Sundance: At their next robbery, it is Sundance who knows the Spanish commands, Butch still relying on a crib sheet.

Goldman clearly has too much material that he is trying to cram into a picture with a running time of under two hours and I remain unconvinced by the final musical interlude, which does not act as a transition between narrative development, but serves as a crude method of stitching together several robberies, while at the same time as making fun of their pursuers, considerably less stoic than the Superposse. These pursuers turn tail at the first gunshots. It is a shame because there is development here. Robbing is more difficult than in the United States and Butch, presumably, has to dream up more imaginative ways to steal, setting off an explosion as a distraction or the ploy of Etta as a reluctant depositor inducing a bank manager to take her and Sundance down into the cellar and opening the safe to show how secure her money will be.[67] It also serves to underplay Etta's involvement: She looks after the horses, shoots at pursuers and plays the part of the reluctant depositor. Since they are not caught, we probably do not need to see any pursuit, and more important, dramatically, is Etta becoming one of the gang. But the illusion soon comes crashing down when Butch thinks he spots Lefors with his distinctive white straw hat. Sundance is dejected, but Butch comes up with his best idea yet: going straight.

Cue Strother Martin in another memorable role as tobacco-spitting[68] mine manager Percy Garris. Cue our first doubts about Sundance the gunslinger. Asked to prove his credentials as a payroll guard, Sundance cannot hit the target, Butch staring at him in astonishment, until he is allowed to move. Butch and Sundance, the shoe on the other foot as they attempt to work out where an ambush might occur, are revealed as "morons" for not realizing they will not be attacked when they are carrying nothing of value. But it is Garris who is overconfident and while the outlaws expect attack in an area of rocks, the mine manager believes he is safe. He is not. He is shot. Now come two major story developments, but one of them has been edited from the film or never shot in the first place. As Butch and Sundance hide behind rocks, Butch says that he has been an outlaw "since I was 15 and my wife left me on account of it and she took our kids on account of it."[69] This is a sensible elimination for two reasons: firstly, it retains much of the mystery surrounding Butch; and secondly, the second revelation has much more emotional impact. Having survived further shooting by the simple device of chucking the bandits the payroll, Butch and Sundance later confront them as they are dividing the spoils and ask for the money back, in order to fulfill their contract as hired guards. When the bandits laugh in their faces, Sundance resorts to violence only to discover that Butch has never shot anybody. However, between them, they gun down the bandits. The Bolivians fall in slow motion not with blood pumping from their chests as in *The Wild Bunch*, but as a visual expression of Butch's shock at seeing so many men dying so quickly and his part in it.[70]

Later, by the campfire, in close-up, with a recurrence of the plaintive music, Etta says she might leave "ahead of you."[71] In the scene as written, Butch seeks assurance that she is not leaving just so she will not see them die, but the director eliminates this.[72] At this point, too, the director eliminates a scene of Etta watching them die, as she views a silent film about the Hole-in-the-Wall Gang.[73] In Hill's version, there is no farewell scene. Etta just disappears.

After reverting to their former ways and robbing another payroll,[74] they enter a village to eat. The boy tying up their ponies notices a brand mark on the mule they have stolen. For the first time, the director moves away from the central characters and shows the audience action that Butch and Sundance cannot see as the boy races to police headquarters to explain the mule belongs to the mine.[75] But when the first shot rings out, we revert to their point of view, although now the director alternates between their point of view and what they cannot see, of the forces being brought to bear against them, as cavalry men arrive to reinforce the policemen.

True to the end, Butch and Sundance live in a world of illusion, imagining that there are not many soldiers. They are pinned down by gunfire, only emerging to get ammunition from the mule. Sundance is in his element, like he was an entire Magnificent Seven, picking off soldiers from rooftops, spinning and whirling and firing instinctively. There is still time for humorous banter between the pair, Australia being Butch's latest dream. But the audience knows the game is up as more soldiers take up position on rooftops and behind walls. Butch is wounded so badly Sundance has to press a gun into his hand. There is time for one last quip. On being reassured there is no sign of Lefors, Butch says, "For a minute, I thought we were in trouble." As they rush out, guns blazing, the screen freezes and reverts to sepia.[76] They could almost have been disappearing into the sunset.

Apart from the stylistic innovations, the most obvious element that springs from watching the picture is George Roy Hill's control. He keeps the focus on the two main characters, and Etta Place when she becomes more prominent, mostly by the simple device of two-shots and three-shots so that the main players are rarely seen apart. He steers away from the screenplay in order to maintain tension and emotion. In a movie where there is no overt declaration of love, it is a surprisingly potent picture. The action scenes are shot with bravura and, except for News Carver, incidental characters appear only to punch up the narrative or to let the viewer know what Butch and Sundance prefer

Twentieth Century–Fox believed it had a program of Christmas winners with *Butch Cassidy and the Sundance Kid* and these other three movies. Apart from promoting individual movies, studios liked to think that they could provide exhibitors with virtually everything they needed in the way of programming—a kind of one-stop shop. Trade press advertisement (*International Motion Picture Exhibitor*, December 10, 1969).

to avoid. Even the lengthy chase sequence works very well thanks to the interplay between the outlaws, as confidence gives way to fear. And, of course, the nuggets of humor, character-related rather than situational as in *Support Your Local Sheriff*, add not just to the audience enjoyment but also frame hidden feelings. The audience's final memory, rather than the Butch's quip or the freeze frame, might well have been the image of them tenderly bandaging each other's wounds.

Release Jitters

Twentieth Century–Fox was not as confident of the end result as it later claimed. By early 1969, it was clear that *Dr. Dolittle* and *Star!* were unmitigated disasters while Hollywood was beginning to worry about foreign receipts in the light of a box office slump in Europe. Overseas generally accounted for 50 to 55 percent of rentals, but in terms of the reception of American films, Germany was now considered a "disaster area" with France not much better.[77] There were concerns, too, that *100 Rifles* had not done as well as expected. *Butch Cassidy and the Sundance Kid* was originally scheduled to open on Memorial Day[78] (when it would have faced *Winning*) and then July[79] (when it would have run into *The Wild Bunch* and *True Grit*), but Fox got cold feet. This made little sense as, traditionally, summer was a peak period for westerns. William Holden had long-ago lost his box office cachet and Sam Peckinpah had none to speak of, and, although John Wayne was redoubtable at the box office, Newman was every bit as strong. Nonetheless, the movie was shifted to late September.[80] Then as now, that period was not considered a highpoint of the movie calendar. In fact, September was believed to be such a box office black hole that three years before an all-industry campaign, "National Film Month,"[81] had been launched to try to perk it up. Even then, the studio had built-in some protection against the possibility that *Butch Cassidy…* would struggle in first run and had blanketed it in for a wide release for Christmas.[82] But this was also a sign of low expectation: *Romeo and Juliet* (1968) had taken nine months from first-run to wide release, *Easy Rider* (1969) and *Goodbye Columbus* (1969) five, and even a low-budget picture like *Daddy's Gone A-Hunting* (1969) a clear four. However, having chosen a late September launch, Fox could not risk pushing the western out wide around Thanksgiving, where it might be swamped by more obvious attractions, nor could it afford to wait until January, a dead period.

Critical Reception

Roger Ebert in the *Chicago Sun-Times* called *Butch Cassidy…* "slow and disappointing," Pauline Kael in *The New Yorker* gave the picture the thumbs-down because it glamorized outlaws while *Time* magazine criticized the dialogue as straight out of a *Batman* episode. Few reviews were unilaterally positive, but *International Motion Picture Exhibitor* described it as a "directorial tour de force … [T]he ever-changing mood and pace are constantly refreshed and revitalized."[83] It was nominated for seven Oscars, including Best Picture and Best Director, and won four: for Goldman's screenplay, Bacharach's score, the Bacharach–Hal David song and sound. In Britain it cleaned up, winning in nine out of ten BAFTA categories including Best Film, Best Director and Best Actor for Robert Redford. The only nomination it did not win was for Newman as Best Actor. The Writers Guild of America placed the screenplay 11th in its list of the Top 101 Screenplays.

Box Office

The picture did not race out of the traps, but it did show legs.[84] Although it finally pulled in rentals of $40 million, that was not on the first go-round. The first year of release accounted for a mere $15 million, making it the fourth best film at the box office in 1969, but it continued to play well into the following year, bolstered by a double bill with *The Prime of Miss Jean Brodie*, collecting another $11 million plus $13.8 million on reissue in 1974.[85]

12

A Roadshow Too Far

Paint Your Wagon

Starring Lee Marvin, Clint Eastwood, Jean Seberg; directed by Joshua Logan; screenplay by Alan Jay Lerner; Paramount; 164 minutes (including intermission)

That Old Hollywood Trick

At one point, you had to be able to sing to star in a Hollywood musical. But with a dearth of singers who had screen charisma and audience acceptance of stars in the current decade such as Rex Harrison (*My Fair Lady*, 1964) and Richard Harris (*Camelot*, 1967)[1]—one of three non-singers in the cast[2]—who were not genuine singers in the idiom of Frank Sinatra or Bing Crosby and compensated by "speaking" a tune[3]—it appeared that you could throw almost any actor into a musical and get away with it. And whereas Julie Andrews sang most of the numbers in *The Sound of Music*, Yul Brynner had only three solos and one duet in *The King and I* (1956).

Nonetheless, with budgets for movie musicals going through the roof, Warner Brothers spending $17 million on *My Fair Lady*, including $5.5 million on the rights, you could not generally risk such colossal sums on unknowns, although *Oliver!* (1968) had managed it. In the wake of the surefire hits which had dominated the first part of the decade (*West Side Story* [1961], *Mary Poppins* [1964], *My Fair Lady* [1964] and *The Sound of Music* [1965]), they were seen as an essential element of a studio's output. In 1967, a total of 16 musicals were put on the starting blocks including movies by studios who had not made one for several years such as Universal (its first since 1961),[4] United Artists (also its first since 1961)[5] and Columbia (first since 1962).[6] The roster included *Thoroughly Modern Millie* from Universal, *How to Succeed in Business... Without Really Trying* (United Artists), *Camelot* and *Finian's Rainbow* (Warner Brothers), *Goodbye Mr. Chips*[7] and *Say It with Music*[8] (MGM), *Doctor Dolittle* and *Star!* (Twentieth Century–Fox), *The Happiest Millionaire* (Disney), *Oliver!* (Columbia) and *Paint Your Wagon* and *On a Clear Day You Can See Forever* (Paramount).[9] Interest in musical subjects continued for the next couple of years, Paramount leading the way by ponying up $2.25 million for *Coco* before it had even hit Broadway[10] and planning a musical out of the 1942 cult book *The Little Prince.*[11] "As the heated acquisition of stage musicals continued apace," CBS Films invested in the 1959 musical *Fiorello* and United Artists in *House of Flowers*[12] while Cinema Center aimed to make the seventh screen adaptation of Robert Louis Stevenson's *Treasure Island* a $15 million Jules Styne (*Funny Girl*)[13] musical.

Some of these tuners fell into two other booming sub-categories—period pictures[14] and musicals made in Britain.[15] Musicals were deemed as essential vehicles to meet roadshow demand and Paramount, the "sleeping giant" awakening a year after its 1966 takeover by Gulf & Western[16] and now, under the command of head honcho Robert Evans, pledging to spent $150 million on pictures, had taken the lead in the roadshow market with *Paint Your Wagon* on a $7 million original budget and *Darling Lili* on $6.5 million[17] plus high-end products like *The Adventurers* ($5 million) and *Catch-22* ($4.5 million) which had roadshow potential.[18] And even when *Dr. Dolittle* and *Star!*[19] hit the buffers, optimism about musicals remained high, studios continuing to pump huge sums on existing productions, both Paramount tuners adding $10 million to their original budgets.

Paint Your Wagon was the fifth movie collaboration between Alan Jay Lerner and Frederick Loewe, who had also written *Brigadoon* (1954), the Oscar-winning *Gigi* (1958),[20] *My Fair Lady*, also a multiple Oscar winner,[21] and *Camelot*. It was hardly a recent hit demanding speedy transference to the screen; it originated on Broadway in 1951 and ran seven months. But it had originally appeared at a point when westerns had provided a golden seam for musicals. *Annie Get Your Gun* (1950) ranked fifth at that year's box office, *Calamity Jane* (1953), *Seven Brides for Seven Brothers* (1954) and *Oklahoma!* (1955) were other hits. Crooner Eddie Fisher, ex-husband of Elizabeth Taylor, had acquired the rights to *Paint Your Wagon* from the Louis B. Mayer estate[22] and sold them to Paramount, which had entered into a multi-picture deal with Alan Jay Lerner.[23] Oscar-winning screenwriter Paddy Chayefsky (*Marty*, 1955) had beefed up the original stage concept, turning it into a "sexy morality tale" known during filming as "Sodom in the Sierras,"[24] so much so that Lee Marvin "jumped at" it,[25] although James Stewart, former roommate at Princeton of director Logan, had been an early contender.[26] Marvin's interest might have been spiked by the prospect of a $1 million payday (plus $20,000 per day in overtime).[27] Co-star Clint Eastwood was on $750,000 plus a percentage of Italian takings,[28] but was planning to abandon the acting style that had brought him adulation in the first place, "his absolute fixation," according to director Don Siegel, "as an anti-hero."[29] Female lead Jean Seberg was on substantially less.

At the time, both male stars were in the ascendancy, Marvin establishing his acting credentials by winning the Best Actor Oscar for *Cat Ballou* (1965) and polishing his box office halo in the action hits *The Professionals* (1966) and *The Dirty Dozen* (1967), while Eastwood followed the *Dollars* trilogy with the Don Siegel thriller *Coogan's Bluff* (1968), his first American western *Hang 'Em High* (1968) and the expectation of a further financial bounty in MGM's war picture *Where Eagles Dare* (1968). Seberg had no great marquee credentials, her biggest successes coming at the start of her career in Otto Preminger's *Saint Joan* (1957) and *Bonjour Tristesse* (1958) and Jean-Luc Godard's French film *Breathless* (1960). Director Joshua Logan had both box office cachet and critical acclaim with Oscar nominations for *Picnic* (1956), *Sayonara* (1957) and *Fanny* (1961), Of more relevance was that he had shepherded the Rodgers and Hammerstein musical *South Pacific* (1958) onto the big screen and at the time of being hired for *Paint Your Wagon* done the same for Lerner and Loewe's *Camelot*.

And if only the budget had not nudged ever upwards—$17 to $22 million the final estimate (although others reckoned it was $24 million[30])—the movie might have brought in a decent profit.[31] As well as the upfront money for stars and director, the production spent $2.4 million on building the mining camp set in Baker City, Oregon, a location so remote ("in the middle of nowhere as you can get") that it cost Paramount $80,000 a day for five months to ferry cast and crew 60 miles from the nearest town on roads it had

Coogan's Bluff (1968) was the first of five pictures director Don Siegel made with Clint Eastwood. The others were *Two Mules for Sister Sara* (1970), *The Beguiled* (1971), *Dirty Harry* (1971) and *Escape from Alcatraz* (1979) (Hannan Collection).

cost the studio $10,000 a mile to repair.[32] The first August rainfall in 35 years put the movie behind schedule[33] and rumors persisted that Logan would be fired.[34]

By the time the movie appeared, several industry reversals had taken place. Musicals were no longer in vogue, unable to attract audiences in the numbers required to compensate for the huge budgets. Along with *Doctor Dolittle* and *Star!*, flops included *Half a Sixpence* (1967), Logan's *Camelot*, *The Happiest Millionaire* (1967) and Francis Ford Coppola's *Finian's Rainbow* (1968); only one musical was planned for 1970 release, *Song of Norway*.[35] Even then, star appeal might have overcome these setbacks, but here *Paint*

Lee Marvin made two films back-to-back with British director John Boorman: *Point Blank* (1967), pictured, and *Hell in the Pacific* (1968). (Hannan Collection)

Your Wagon was in some difficulty. Lee Marvin's marquee quotient had dropped like a stone: Neither *Point Blank* (1967) nor *Hell in the Pacific* (1968), both directed by John Boorman, had justified their expense, and Paramount was worried that *The Dirty Dozen* might have proved a flash in the pan and that Marvin had no true following. Nor had MGM's teaming of Eastwood with Richard Burton in the much-trumpeted *Where Eagles Dare* brought in the expected business. In a nutshell, Paramount was set to release its most expensive-ever movie in a format (roadshow) that was fast losing favor, with two stars who had failed to hit the box office mark in their last outing, with a director whose previous picture had hit the skids, with the first roadshow to receive an "M" rating (for mature audiences) rather than a "G,"[36] a decision ratified at appeal,[37] and at a time when the industry was in a "panic right now about musicals."[38]

The Two Husband Trick

The plot of *Paint Your Wagon*, although different in many ways from the stage production,[39] is simple. During the gold rush, the brother of prospector Pardner (Clint Eastwood) is killed when their wagon topples down a hill. Overseeing the funeral, Ben Rumson (Lee Marvin) discovers gold in the grave (a similar plotline to *Support Your Local Sheriff*). The pair become partners and live in No Name City which is devoid of women until Mormon Jacob Woodling (John Mitchum), appearing with two wives, is willing to auction one, Elizabeth (Jean Seberg), to the highest bidder. This turns out to be a drunken Rumson. When Pardner and Elizabeth fall in love, the situation is resolved Mormon-style with the woman acquiring two "husbands." Although the town booms, the gold dries up and Rumson hatches a plan to tunnel underground and steal the gold dust hoarded under the flooring of various hotels and saloons. At one point, the need for putting on a respectable face threatens to break up the cozy threesome but the real damage is done when the tunnels undermine the town's foundations and it collapses. After this, Rumson, defined as the "Wand'rin' Star," leaves Elizabeth and Pardner behind. There's not much in the way of subplot to leaven the meager story, the hijacking of a party of French whores to bring respite to the women-hungry men, and a young man from a good family whom Rumson tries to lead astray finding he takes to drinking, smoking, whoring and gambling.

It attempts to be a serious musical without much to say beyond the reversal of the gender stereotype. The sets are authentic enough, the ramshackle town, bedraggled men living in a tent city at the mercy of the weather, torrential rain and so much wind the men have a song for it ("They Call the Wind Maria"), streets as muddy as those of *Support Your Local Sheriff*, basic emotions—jealousy, greed, and general cantankerousness—barely held in check. There is some exploration of male melancholy and human need: When a baby arrives, men queue up to pay $50 to hold it and come for 15 miles away to get a glimpse of the first woman, Elizabeth, they have seen in months, treating her with a respect that is at odds with the way they regard later arrivals such the French ladies. The central plotline focuses on Elizabeth refusing to be treated as a chattel, owned by her husband under mining law, and forcing him to treat her with respect ("I was bought for a wife not a whore"), build her a proper cabin, and then, turning dominant-male tradition on its head, insisting that if she was "married to a man with two wives," she can equally be married to two husbands. But most of the emotion is of the cartoon variety, as is much of the comedy, especially in the hands of the bewhiskered Lee Marvin, who has clearly never labored in the mines of subtlety. Apart from the opening scenes of a wagon train wending its way in traditional western long shot across the country, a runaway wagon filmed in Cinerama-style point of view, an elaborate tracking shot that pulls back to reveal No Name City, including a tree being felled on cue, some vigorous camerawork when the coach arrives with the whores, and the climactic collapse of the town, Joshua Logan directs the picture as if he is shooting a stage play. The camera might as well have been nailed down. This is especially true in the musical numbers, most of which are shot in a static style, the camera simply sitting in close-up or medium shot on the singer's face. Occasionally, the singer moves with purpose, Marvin walking slowly through the town for "Wand'rin' Star"[40] and Jean Seberg as she takes ownership of her new cabin, or symbolic purpose, Eastwood ambling through the trees while intoning "I Talk to the Trees." But virtually all the songs are delivered without the slightest nod in the direction of choreography and when the dancing begins, it is so clumsy you wish nobody had bothered. Of course, Logan clearly intends to put distance between himself and the old-style musicals which perhaps were over-dependent on choreography. But when the setting is as bleak as No Name City and few of the characters can muster a

A Lurex fashion tie-in was one of the "cornerstones" of *Paint Your Wagon*'s merchandising campaign with a four-page advertising spread in *Vogue* and Lurex hosting in-store fashion displays. Pressbook (Hannan Collection).

smile, you soon wish for a touch of the old-fashioned to shake things up a bit. It is possible, as one critic put it, that the director simply held to the perhaps wrongheaded view that "the youth of America are once again manifesting a fascination with American history particularly the frontier era ... college youth should be intrigued with the marital situation ... primitive commune ... hippy-like garb."[41]

The biggest problem is the singing. It is indicative of the difficulties of the project that eight of the movie's 14 songs are sung in whole or in part by a chorus composed of, needless to say, trained singers. It is not so much that Marvin and Eastwood cannot carry a tune but that they fail to bring any emotion to their songs, fall short of extracting from the lyrics what any proper singer would have detected. While it is fortuitous that Marvin's gravelly tones suit "Wand'rin' Star," he is out of his depth with anything else. Eastwood does not have a voice you would pay to hear. Ironically, Jean Seberg, whose voice is dubbed, generates far more emotion in "A Million Miles Away Behind the Door"[42] by her facial expressions, as if she genuinely understands the words she is singing. She does not have the picture's standout song but looks as if she does.

While Marvin does not stretch himself to play drunken oaf Rumson, Eastwood is badly miscast. Unable to narrow his eyes and look mean, Eastwood seems clean out of ideas, and charisma, and audiences expecting the tough guy of his earlier pictures would have been dismayed to see him coming across as a tenderfoot. Seberg, on the other hand, steals the picture with self-awareness, determination and tenderness. Far from the tough frontier woman in the Barbara Stanwyck mold, she nonetheless proves adept at negotiating a better future for herself, initiating the tradition-shattering changes to which the two men meekly succumb. She is believable not just in delivering the plot twist that she loves both men (especially when one is the generally disreputable Rumson) but in accepting the need for respectability even when it ruptures their relationship. She is also capable of some very subtle acting. When Rumson rips off her top to reveal her cleavage, and then, in the face of her anger, says, "I admire your spirit," with a glance down at her body, she replies, softly, "Is that what you admire?"

The film wanders after the intermission, by which time the threesome has been established and now must be undone come what may. This is achieved by the arrival of a family rescued from the harsh winter who are the instigators of the need to honor respectability, and by the bizarre idea of the two men planning to steal the gold dust by tunneling under the town. Despite the movie's flaws, many of the songs are excellent, especially the title song, Marvin's "Wand'rin' Star," "They Call the Wind Maria," "I Talk to the Trees" and Seberg's theme. But all in all the music would have been better served by a better quality of singer, stronger story and improved direction. In particular, both principals shift so far out of their comfort zones as actors and far away from their personas that it is asking too much for the novelty factor to fill the gaps. Although Marvin played as rancorous a drunk in *Cat Ballou*, he would not have achieved the heights of stardom had he continued in that vein. He had won audiences over to his type of character by the tough guys he portrayed in *The Professionals* and, in particular, *The Dirty Dozen*, and it was asking an enormous amount from the audience to go along with such a dramatic sea change without giving them anything in return. It did not help the picture that both United Artists and MGM decided to undermine the musical by reissuing movies that showed the actors in their best box office light, UA bringing back Eastwood's entire portfolio of westerns, the *Dollars* trio plus *Hang 'Em High*, while MGM revived *The Dirty Dozen* in a spectacular near–five-hour double bill with *Grand Prix* (1966). In effect,

Lee Marvin established his marquee credentials with *The Dirty Dozen*, the top film at the U.S. box office in 1967, ahead of two quite different James Bond adventures, *You Only Live Twice* and the spoof *Casino Royale*. Pressbook (Hannan Collection).

audiences were offered the choice between the personas which the actors had utilized in order to climb the Hollywood tree and indulging them in a piece of whimsy.

Critical Reception

Hardly anybody had a good word to say for *Paint Your Wagon*. *Variety* was the first to point out the obvious: "uphill fight to be a blockbusting box office hit." *International Motion Picture Exhibitor* averred that it should have "general audience appeal."[43]

Box Office

To help boost interest in the picture, Paramount provided exhibitors with a tabloid herald newspaper, "No Name City Gazette" ("The Hell-thiest City in the West, Population: Drunk"). Among its fake advertisements was one for "lessons on the pianoforte" from Alan Jay Lerner. There was a novelization of the film by George Scullin—in those days, free-standing book displays were arranged around bookstores so whether anyone bought a copy or not, they provided an extra area of promotion. Copies of the soundtrack album and the sheet music were promoted in record stores. There was a Study Guide aimed at American history classes in high school. Paramount took advantage of the trend for tie-dyeing with a list of fashion ideas from Rite Dye and Butterick Patterns which was inserted as a nine-page feature in *Mademoiselle* magazine plus a booklet on *Paint Your Wagon* tie-dyed ideas, with both companies placing shelf-talkers in supermarkets to promote their items.[44]

However, little of this energetic promotional work resulted in moviegoers racing to the theaters. Box office was filed under "disastrous." By year's end, there was only $2.2 million in the till, mostly from roadshow release (45th in the annual rankings) and not much more thereafter. The movie did better in some foreign countries, in London running for 79 weeks in a roadshow presentation at the Astoria. It had no chance of recovering its massive budget and was a major factor in Paramount's financial crisis at the end of the 1960s.

13

Pedigree Is Not Enough

The Undefeated

Starring John Wayne, Rock Hudson; directed by Andrew V. McLaglen; screenplay by James Lee Barrett, adapted from a screenplay by Stanley Hough and Casey Robinson (on the film, only Hough received a "Story by" credit); Twentieth Century–Fox; 119 minutes

Man of the West

Like Burt Kennedy and Sam Peckinpah, Andrew V. McLaglen was one of the decade's most prolific exponents of the genre. The son of actor Victor McLaglen (*The Informer*, 1935), he got his first break as assistant director on John Ford's *The Quiet Man* (1952) in which his father co-starred with John Wayne. It was Wayne who provided the financial guarantee four years later for Andrew to make his first foray into direction, the western *Gun the Man Down*, produced by Wayne's Batjac company and starring James Arness and Angie Dickinson. Two crime dramas followed, *Man in the Vault* (1956), with a screenplay by Burt Kennedy, and *The Abductors* (1957) toplining his dad Victor. Following these, however, the director made a bigger name for himself in westerns of the television variety. Between 1957 and 1963, he helmed over half the 200-plus episodes of *Have Gun—Will Travel*, the most by any director, and between 1959 and 1965 over one-sixth of the 600-odd episodes of *Gunsmoke*. He also contributed to *Rawhide*, *The Virginian*, *The Travels of Jamie McPheeters* and *Wagon Train*. Mostly, these took precedence over movies but Andrew still managed to churn out the remakes *Freckles*[1] (1960) and *The Little Shepherd of Kingdom Come*[2] (1961), the latter about a Civil War Union hero who returns to his Kentucky girlfriend. His career moved into higher gear when he was selected to direct the comedy western *McLintock!* (1963) starring John Wayne and Maureen O'Hara and followed up with a James Stewart pair, *Shenandoah*[3] (1965), also about the Civil War, and *The Rare Breed* (1966), also starring O'Hara. He dipped his toe into more straightforward comedy with Disney's *Monkeys, Go Home!* (1967) with Maurice Chevalier in the leading role. Kirk Douglas and Robert Mitchum headed up *The Way West* (1967)[4] and Doris Day comedy western, *The Ballad of Josie* (1967). Andrew then directed William Holden in the war epic *The Devil's Brigade* (1968) and from there was reunited first with James Stewart for *Bandolero!* (1968) and then with John Wayne for the oil rig adventure *Hellfighters* (1968).

Prior to *The Rare Breed* (1966), Maureen O'Hara and James Stewart had worked together on the comedy *Mr. Hobbs Takes a Vacation* (1962). Trade press advertisement (*Box Office*, December 20, 1965).

McLaglen was the victim of two erroneous assumptions. The first was that he was happy to be typecast as a director of westerns. He refuted this notion in an interview for *Conversations on Film*[5]: He claimed that "it's the way my course was laid out for me," suggesting that, in the early days at least, he had little control over the kind of projects for which he was deemed most suitable. Secondly, he was unfairly called a "journeyman" director, an unworthy successor to John Ford, although Christopher Frayling put it more kindly when he asserted that McLaglen was a "figurative painter when everyone else had gone abstract," indicating that the director was out of step with the times. However, this was equally unfair, since in the 1960s, until Sam Peckinpah produced *The Wild Bunch*, there had been no real contenders for the Ford throne apart from a critic-driven revival of the 1950s films of Budd Boetticher long after he had stopped making them and Anthony Mann's decade-long love affair with the western which had ended with the dismal *Cimarron* in 1960. The spaghetti western upsurge had not produced any worthy successors with the exception of Sergio Leone, recognition of whose talents was slow in coming at the end of the decade.

Other directors considered as candidates for the western pantheon such as John Sturges (*Gunfight at the O.K. Corral*, 1957; *The Magnificent Seven*, 1960) proved too erratic, while the likes of Henry Hathaway had only consistently turned to the genre in the 1960s. McLaglen was underrated as a director of westerns: *McLintock!* was hugely enjoyable, *Shenandoah* belonged close to the top rank, and, as I shall attempt to prove, *The Undefeated* a far better movie than given credit for.

The Rise of the Double Act

Two top male stars were always, in Hollywood's eyes, better than one, especially in a western, Gary Cooper and Burt Lancaster in *Vera Cruz* (1954), for example, or Lancaster and Kirk Douglas in *Gunfight at the O.K. Corral.*[6] John Wayne had cruised through most of the 1950s without the need for such topline support until Howard Hawks signed Dean Martin[7] for *Rio Bravo* (1959) and John Ford lassoed William Holden for *The Horse Soldiers* (1959). The former made a bundle, the latter, saddled with $1.5 million in fees to the actors, not so. Following Wayne's battle with cancer in 1964, most of his westerns came with a top co-star: Dean Martin in *The Sons of Katie Elder* (1965), Robert Mitchum in *El Dorado* (1967) and Kirk Douglas in *The War Wagon* (1967). Such solidarity was not confined to Wayne, James Stewart and Dean Martin teaming for *Bandolero!* and Martin with Mitchum in *5 Card Stud* (1968). Wayne had gone solo in *The Green Berets* (1968) and *True Grit* (1969), but for *The Undefeated* he was assigned Rock Hudson.

Hudson's career had faded since the heady days at the start of the decade as the country's number one star thanks to a series of light comedies with Doris Day. The star's comedy persona had obscured the fact that he was a fine dramatic actor, having been nominated for a Best Actor Oscar for George Stevens' *Giant* (1956). In fact, what was probably more extraordinary was that he had switched to comedy at all since his forte appeared to be drama, having appeared in five Douglas Sirk pictures in successive years, *Magnificent Obsession* (1954) with Jane Wyman, *All That Heaven Allows* (1955) with Wyman, *Written on the Wind* (1956) with Lauren Bacall, *Battle Hymn* (1957) and *The Tarnished Angels* (1957). The first three were female-centered, the second pair male-oriented, one about a pilot swapping bombs for Bibles in the Korean War, the other about male friendship. On top of which, Hudson starred opposite Jennifer Jones in *A Farewell to Arms* (1957), a remake of the Ernest Hemingway novel. The drama-to-comedy switch was not the first sharp about-face in the actor's career since, prior to aligning with Sirk, he had been known for westerns (*Tomahawk*, 1951; *Bend of the River*, 1952, *Horizons West*, 1952, *The Lawless Breed*, 1952, *Seminole*, 1953) and tales of adventure (*Sea Devils*, 1953, and *The Golden Blade*, 1953).

Barbara Hale, Rock Hudson's leading lady in *Seminole* (Universal, 1953), became more famous as Della Street on television's *Perry Mason*. Lee Marvin had a small part in the picture, as did Hugh O'Brian (television's *Wyatt Earp*). Trade press advertisement (*Box Office*, February 7, 1953).

So if he had switched genres with such style and success throughout his career, why could he not do so again? Except that he felt he had to recapture the imagination of the public, which had perhaps grown tired of his diet of comedies, science fiction was certainly a departure. And *Seconds* (1966) proved a riskier proposition than the kind of 1950s sci-fi, with monsters and alien invasion, to which audiences were accustomed. In the 1960s, prior to *2001: A Space Odyssey* (1968) and *Barbarella* (1968), the genre rarely attracted A-list talent, either in putting the picture together or acting in it. The special effects–driven *Fantastic Voyage* (1966), also heavily reliant on a "what if" scenario, did not attract top-of-the-line stars either. And Hudson, with his lightweight comedy baggage, was hardly director John Frankenheimer's first choice. Kirk Douglas, who had snapped up the rights to the novel by David Ely[8] on which the film was based, had envisioned himself in the leading role. When he ducked out, Laurence Olivier was considered long before anyone thought of taking a look at Hudson. The plastic surgery concept, revolutionary at the time, would hardly attract a second glance today, and while the idea of someone seeking a change of identity was hardly novel, this one came with enough of a twist to make it stand out. Frankenheimer, a director associated with risks that had initially come off including *Birdman of Alcatraz* (1962), *The Manchurian Candidate* (1962) and *Seven Days in May* (1964), had taken a risk too far with *The Train* (1965),[9] although its box office failure was not entirely his fault since he had stepped in after original director Arthur Penn was fired. *Seconds* was a riskier proposal in other ways. Frankenheimer planned to shoot the film in black-and-white, which guaranteed the film would be viewed as an "arty" number. He also intended to show a substantial amount of nudity,[10] both male and female, perhaps as a publicity device to attract the wrath of the censors since there was no way it would be permitted in U.S. theaters at the time. On top of that, the movie employed three formerly blacklisted actors in John Anderson, Will Geer and Jeff Corey. However, the biggest gamble was hiring Hudson, since Frankenheimer had previously been associated with actors of greater range and depth such as Douglas and Burt Lancaster. In so doing, he risked alienating his core audience who would disdain the prospect of watching a film in which Hudson starred, as well as putting out the wrong message to the legion of Hudson fans. Even if the movie had piqued the curiosity of Hudson fans, they would have been alarmed to find their hero's face encased in bandages for much of the picture. If Rock Hudson was looking for an acting challenge, he certainly had come to the right place. However, the fine acting done in the picture was ignored, partly because critics hated the film and because nobody went to see it. Frankenheimer, who believed he had broken new ground with this picture, was shocked by the reaction it received at the Cannes Film Festival. Instead of being applauded as he had expected, it was derided. Although it has since become a cult classic, that was not much use to promoting Hudson's career, as cults usually only spring up long after a film's original release.

Despite *Seconds*' poor box office reception, it certainly did it no permanent damage to Hudson's career in the eyes of Hollywood producers, otherwise he would not have been recruited for the thriller *Blindfold* (1966) with Claudia Cardinale, the war picture *Tobruk* (1967), a second crime comedy with Cardinale, *A Fine Pair* (1968), and then persuaded to head up MGM's big-budget Cinerama *Ice Station Zebra* (1968). However, those choices turned out to be as big a gamble, and went to show that Hudson had reached a career impasse for his last five pictures had pulled in a total of just $8.5 million in rentals.

The rest of the cast was composed of newcomers Michael (later Jan Michael) Vincent and Melissa Newman, pro football players Merlin Olsen and Roman Gabriel of the Los

***Seconds* (1966) was the first screenplay of Lewis John Carlino, who went on to write *The Mechanic* (1972) and wrote and directed *The Sailor Who Fell from Grace with the Sea* (1976). Advertisement (*Films and Filming*, December 1966).**

Angeles Rams, John Ford stock company members Ben Johnson and Harry Carey Jr., and Mexican actor-singer Antonio Aguilar. The movie was filmed on a 1600-acre plantation in Louisiana and in and around Durango, Mexico.[11] Nonetheless, with a bigger budget than *Butch Cassidy and the Sundance Kid* and of the studio's two biggest non-roadshow hits *Valley of the Dolls* (1967) and *Planet of the Apes* (1968),[12] a director in top form, one star (Wayne) at a box office peak, a movie that promised rousing adventure, battles and personal conflict, plus a couple of interesting subplots, there was considerable optimism about the outcome.

What Is Style?

Style in the late 1960s had come to mean change. Directors intent on using new techniques (Arthur Penn on *Bonnie and Clyde* [1967], Dennis Hopper on *Easy Rider,* [1969]) or exploring dangerous subject matter (John Schlesinger on *Midnight Cowboy* [1969]) had come to define style as far as the critics were concerned. By this token, the most stylish westerns of the year were *Once Upon a Time in the West* and *Butch Cassidy and the Sundance Kid*. To include *The Undefeated* on this list appears the most foolhardy of notions. However, in the wider sense, style could comprise any number of elements or a combination of them all. It could encompass subject matter, such as the encroachment of civilization on the traditional gunfighter or outlaw as in *Once Upon a Time in the West, The Wild Bunch* and *Butch Cassidy and the Sundance Kid*. Or it could be the treatment of women either in a historical context or by Hollywood itself in the case of *The Stalking Moon, 100 Rifles, Once Upon a Time in the West, Mackenna's Gold, True Grit, Paint Your Wagon* and *Tell Them Willie Boy Is Here*. Or it could be changing attitudes to Indians (*The Undefeated*) or African Americans (*100 Rifles*). It could be expressed through new techniques—visual or aural operatics, slow motion, fast cutting, sepia tinting and freeze-framing—or old ones like the long shot. And it could also take the form of discipline, of sticking rigidly to a method of presentation, consistency of framing and composition, a method of making the audience see the movie the way the director particularly wants them to view it—of which *The Undefeated* is a classic example.

Look at the Sky

I don't usually begin a discussion of a film by examining its composition but I will make an exception with *The Undefeated.* I had come to this picture with vague memories of having seen it at my local theater on original release in second- or possibly third-run. I do not recall being particularly impressed, although at that age, 16 or 17, I had not formed any critical faculties for the evaluation of the western, nor any movie for that matter. As a result, I did not hold out much hope for the movie when it came to the current re-evaluation, in part because it lacked the critical status of *The Wild Bunch* and *Once Upon a Time in the West*, which I had viewed many times since their original release, and in part because it had not been a box office hit and therefore subject to theatrical reissue or the continuous television programming that had accompanied *True Grit* and *Butch Cassidy and the Sundance Kid.*

It would not be fair to say that I was blown away—the picture has a number of flaws which prevent any representation of it as an undiscovered masterpiece. But I found so much to admire that I sat down and watched it straight through again. (This was similar to my response to previous pictures which had blown me away such as *Badlands* [1973] where at the conclusion of one performance I had headed straight back to the box office to buy another ticket, which meant also sitting through *It's Alive* twice.)

What struck me most was how Andrew V. McLaglen constructed the movie on screen. A substantial number of scenes were in long shot but, unlike say, *True Grit*, the director made more consistent use of the divisions between background, center and foreground. Most often by using the 3000 horses as the long distance focal point in the middle of the screen, or a line of cavalry, he achieved a fine separation of elements that, to me, at least appeared to show a mastery of composition. The screen, lengthways, was consistently divided into three, or four. Sometimes the entire action took place in the bottom half of the screen, the upper part reserved for sky or sky peering through mountains. Like a traditional landscape painter, McLaglen worked with the horizon line, sometimes with a vanishing point. It seemed to me that an artist, in the most ordinary sense of the word, was at work. This conceptual approach is apparent from the very start. When a rider arrives to announce to the Union troops that the Civil War is over, half the screen is sky.

What does let the movie down is the story. The basic concept—the reconciliation of deadly enemies—is intriguing and more than enough to carry the picture, but the plot is overly complicated and the ending, while in one respect emotionally satisfying, is an anticlimax. In post–Civil War America, a group of ex–Union soldiers and a contingent of former Confederate soldiers (plus families) converge on Mexico, but for different reasons. The Unions soldiers are intent on selling a herd of 3000 wild horses to the Mexican Army, while the Confederates are taking their weapons and money in the same direction but in the hope of setting up a second front in order to continue the fight against the Union. On the way, both groups encounter double-dealing: The Mexicans attempt to renege on the agreement to buy the wild horses, while the rebels are taken hostage by, ironically enough, forces in opposition to the existing Mexican government. The Union men come to the rescue of the Confederates twice, once in a rousing battle against bandits and, at the climax, by trading their horses (and their futures) for their former enemies' lives. But this is an unsatisfactory conclusion since, to complete the circle, it should have been the Confederates bailing the Union men out of trouble, and therefore, honors even, they can come to a peaceful accommodation.

The movie opens with a battered Confederate flag. The camera tracks left along lines of gray-uniformed soldiers waiting for an attack. Almost immediately, their ranks are decimated by cannon fire followed by a Union cavalry charge, sabers cutting the defending soldiers to ribbons. Col. John Henry Thomas (John Wayne) is in the thick of the action, a Confederate flag abandoned on the ground. As a rider brings news of the cessation of hostilities, the camera, from Thomas' point of view, lingers on the dead. Thomas seeks out the enemy to accept their surrender. To his astonishment, the Confederates already knew that peace had been agreed when they continued fighting and, as far as the rebel commanding officer is concerned, the war is not over. "Are you telling me," asks an incredulous Thomas, "that you intend to keep fighting?" The officer replies, "Haven't we just proven it?" A few minutes into the picture, the entire concept is established, emotional sides taken, a Union soldier exhibiting disbelief, a Confederate soldier appearing resolute.

Mustachioed and resplendent in a Southern uniform that incorporates a cape and a hat with a feather in it, the dashing Col. James Langdon (Rock Hudson) spells out his postwar secret mission to his troops: a 2000-mile trip to Mexico, arms and ammunition and uniforms hidden at the bottom of wagons, their rendezvous, 500 miles south of the border, in Durango leading to being escorted by representatives of Emperor Maximilian to the country's capital. Meanwhile, Langdon's wife Margaret (Lee Meriwether) and sister-in-law Ann (Marian McCargo) are being assailed by a carpetbagger, accompanied by an equally grasping African American ("Who is going to pick your cotton?") offering 50 cents an acre for their plantation. Dismissing the man, Langdon sets fire to their grand mansion. McLaglen introduces what appears to be the romantic subplot featuring two juveniles, Langdon's daughter Charlotte (Melissa Newman) and the slightly older Bubba Wilkes (Jan Michael Vincent).

Thomas hands in his resignation, explaining that the ten men remaining out of the 75 he recruited three years prior take priority over continuing as a soldier. "Those left deserve more than a pat on the back from some newspaper editor and I'm gonna see they get it," he snaps, as he leads his men away on their mission to round up 3000 horses to sell to the U.S. Army. What do men do while they wait around, capture flies as in *Once Upon a Time in the West*, or bicker as *The Wild Bunch*? Like Peckinpah's squad, these men like to make fun of each other and, reminiscent of the scene when Warren Oates is teased over a bottle of whiskey, the ex-soldiers toss a chew of tobacco around until one stops after catching sight of approaching Indians. In a mild twist, these are not enemies, but a group led by Blue Blood (Roman Gabriel), who, in another twist, is Thomas' adopted son—a major twist, in fact, given *The Searchers* (1956) where Ethan Edwards is dedicated to hunting down and killing Debbie (Natalie Wood) simply because she lived with Indians after being kidnapped. The arrival of the riders is typical of McLaglen's compositional skills: the men appear in long shot below the horizon. The screen, in reality, is divided into two—sky at the top, land at the bottom. Crammed into the middle is a tiny stretch of men.

BATTLING IT OUT TOE TO TOE AND SIDE BY SIDE
ACROSS 2000 MILES OF THUNDERING ADVENTURE!

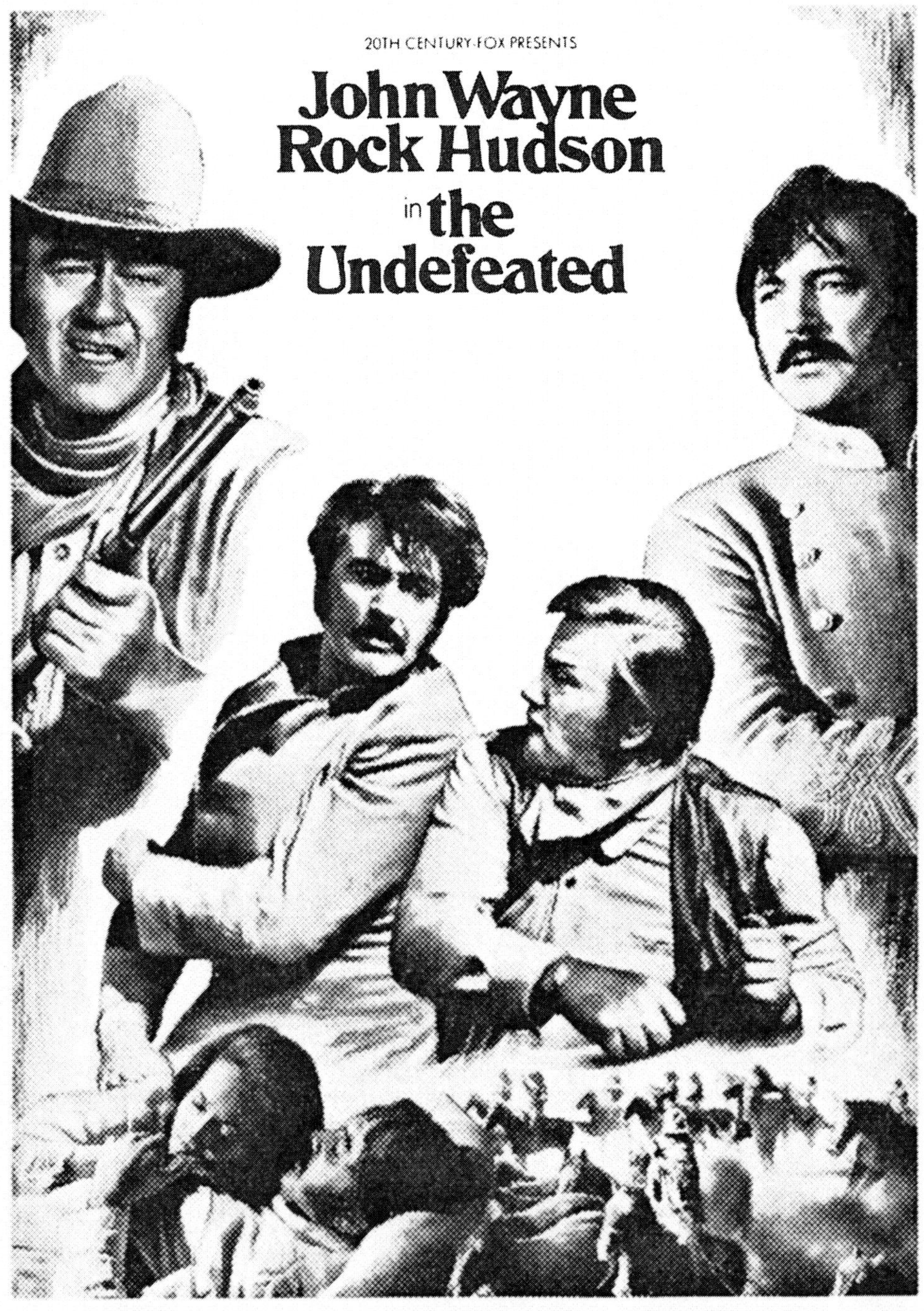

They feared no one—Juarista rebels, cut-throat Banditos, the armies of Maximilian... as they challenged an angry land—and each other!

The first rousing adventure is a two-minute scene of the lassoing, capture and breaking-in of thousands of horses, the screen filled with images of the racing animals. As Col. Langdon's wagon train sets off, Charlotte tells her beau that she is "looking for something more substantial" in a man than this lovelorn youth, as if she has quickly grown up during the war. Thomas and Short Grub (Ben Johnson) head off to a staging post for a meeting with the agents who buy horses for the government but instead they come into contact with a "couple of popinjays" representing Emperor Maximilian and willing to buy the entire herd. The loyal Thomas rejects their offer out of hand until, in an attempt to defraud him, the government agents offer him $10 less per horse than the going market rate, and for a fraction of the herd. Summary justice, in the form of a punch, is meted out to the agents. In the middle of a fog we learn that the Confederates are being pursued by Union cavalry intent on turning them around. When Langdon hears the Union horses, he orders his wagon train to race the enemy to the Rio Grande. Once across, there is a close-up of the Confederate flag and McLaglen pulls back to reveal the train of wagons which takes up only the bottom half of the screen, the upper half entirely sky. Thomas faces the same dilemma and only a massive stampede of the horses sees them safely across. As 1969 westerns are filled with dreamers (Butch Cassidy filling his head with ideas of Bolivia and, later, Australia; Omar Sharif's bandit in *Mackenna's Gold* dreaming of Paris), there is a short scene of Thomas' men talking about what they will do with the money they will earn. Most of their notions are relatively mundane but one entertains a vision of a small library under a big elm. Thomas is in no mood for such frivolities, going to sleep with his guns cocked, telling his men, "We're Americans in Mexico taking horses to a very unpopular government."

Blue Blood, who has been scouting ahead, returns the next morning to inform Thomas that in a box canyon four miles ahead, there is forage and water for the horses. But he also warns that he came across two trails, the first of wagons and horses, and the second, following the first, about 40 riders. "I'd suspect an ambush," says Thomas. When Blue Blood and Thomas investigate, they find the Confederates. In a nod to the opening shot, McLaglen gives a close-up of the rebel flag, this time in pristine condition. Approaching the wagon train, arranged in a circle, they explain the situation to Langdon, who asks what the bandits could be after. "Gold, horses, women," replies Thomas, at which point Margaret and Ann look up. This is another twist, or will be, for what happens to captured women has been a constant theme of westerns, especially in 1969, the treatment of white women at the hands of Indians forming a central plank of *The Stalking Moon* and *Mackenna's Gold,* and any women taken by any men in *100 Rifles*, *The Wild Bunch* and *True Grit*. Hatred for an enemy being subsumed by Southern hospitality, Langdon offers the visitors a bed for the night and invites Thomas to join him on his rounds, accompanied by a soldier who provides a bottle of whiskey at appropriate moments to head off the Confederate's incipient rage. The whiskey bottle adds a comedic element to what is an emotional scene, as we learn that Langdon's son was killed at Shiloh, an engagement in which Thomas participated. "Why did you come clear out here to continue a war that ended months ago?" asks Thomas. "Let's just say," replies Langdon, "we haven't seen the end." Meanwhile, Blue Blood has been making eyes at young Charlotte until Thomas beckons him close and sends him away on an errand.

***Opposite*: Before shooting *The Undefeated* (1969), John Wayne had to lose the weight he put on for the role of Rooster Cogburn in *True Grit* (Hannan Collection).**

The next day, in anticipation of an attack, Langdon sets up his defenses, ignoring Thomas' suggestion to "arm the women" until the night picket returns, dead, strapped to his horse. As Thomas and Langdon confer, they are interrupted by Capt. Anderson (Edward Faulkner), who suspects Blue Blood of being involved in the man's death. Thomas reveals that Blue Blood is his adopted son, information that receives a glance from Ann as she cocks her rifle. As Thomas gives her some advice ("Windage and elevation"), we suspect this may be the beginning of a romance. Thomas and Langdon ride out to parley with the Mexican bandit leader who tells them, bluntly, "We want everything. We want wagons, horses, guns and gold and you also have some women." Bearing in mind that Thomas is a soldier rather than a frontiersman or a citizen of the west who, in confrontation, would not, in the grand Hollywood tradition, shoot first, it still comes as a surprise when Thomas simply kills the Mexican in the way of a soldier understanding the importance of the element of surprise. Back at the wagons, Thomas is upbraided by Ann: "Why did you have to shoot him." His dry response, "Conversation kind of dried up," would not have been out of place in *Butch Cassidy and the Sundance Kid*, and while there are many other funny quips, and while McLaglen has an eye—and ear—for comedy as demonstrated in previous films, there is a big difference in audience response between lines delivered by the amiable Butch Cassidy and those uttered by the no-nonsense Thomas.

Maintaining compositional discipline, the battle begins with McLaglen creating a shot that places the wagons horizontally in the bottom quarter of the screen, the line of charging bandits above them but still below the screen's halfway point, with the rest of the picture taken up with two huge rocks on either side of the screen with the sky peeking through them. This is followed by, in the context of this particular film, an unusual framing, the attackers seen from underneath a wagon. Thomas pushes Ann down out of the way. In the subsequent battle, three women—Ann, Charlotte and Margaret—are seen shooting together, although the wife is more reluctant than the other two. The bandits are beaten off. Ann says to Thomas, "Tell me they're leaving." If any romance is brewing between these two, McLaglen's shorthand method of showing it is simply to put them in the same frame without resorting to anything more intimate. "No, ma'am," replies Thomas, "they're reforming to charge again." He pauses, then adds, "At least that's their plan."

What follows is easily the picture's best action scene, especially as it is entirely done in long shot and not, as others would be tempted to do, with lots of close-ups of individual pieces of action. Racing away to re-form, the bandits head for the shelter of rocks where they are ambushed by the rest of Thomas' outfit. When they twist away to escape the relentless gunfire, Blue Blood leads his band of Indians in a charge against them and the Mexican bandits are routed. The symmetry of the action as the bandits race from one side of the screen to the other, encountering conflict at every turn, is stunning.

Following the battle, Thomas confides in Langdon that he was at the battle where Ann lost her husband. In part, this is further shorthand, Thomas expecting such a revelation, which clearly he expects the Confederate to pass on, to kill off any incipient romance. But in the wider emotional context, it binds the former enemies together, not in conflict, but in sadness for what they have all lost. Winners and losers, McLaglen appears to point out, all suffer the same losses.

Charlotte and Blue Blood are getting closer, the Indian having waved his hat in her direction on his triumphant return, the girl's eyes lighting up at the sight, and when, on their departure, Blue Blood states that he wants Charlotte; Thomas responds in typical Hollywood western hero style that "nobody knows what's on a woman's mind," Blue Blood tersely rejects such drivel with "Well, she wants me."

No sooner has Thomas returned to his own camp than his men are invited back to join the Confederates to celebrate the Fourth of July. One of the reasons for Thomas to grow closer to Ann is a technical one, so that he can unburden himself. Romance, if it is that, is not advanced one iota except for the way the woman listens to the man, who recounts his tale without prompting and without being accused of being uncommunicative and without it being beaten out of him. It turns out that Thomas was once married but his wife left him: "She was so busy being a lady that she forgot to be a woman." She objected to him going off hunting but, most of all, she did not want children so he adopted Blue Blood and is "as proud of him as if he were my own blood." The adoption of the Indian is not as odd as all that in the current western iteration: Glenn Ford was brought up by Indians in *Smith!* (1969) and, two years before, in *Hombre* (1967), Paul Newman's character was brought up by Indians. But those were matters of chance not individual decision; a child has no say in who brings it up, but for an adult male to choose to adopt an Indian boy is a different story. Nothing more is made of Blue Blood's adoption but, as loyal viewers of many westerns over many years, audiences will have grown accustomed to romances between an Indian and a white woman hitting the skids, objections from the less liberal usually leading to violence. When Blue Blood tells Thomas that he wants Charlotte and she wants him, the audience is inclined to believe he is somewhat misguided. However, at this point, the relationship does flourish. Charlotte tells him, with all the sweetness of young love, that "nobody ever looked at me the way you do."

But just as the movie clicks into gear, with two incipient romances and bandits thwarted, the question of the Confederate dream still unresolved, issues regarding the acceptance of Indians into society under discussion, former enemies halfway to reconciliation by fighting together against a common foe, both groups still to conclude their missions, the script almost destroys the fine work so far by introducing one of the most stereotypical elements of the traditional western: the fistfight. As usual, there is no good reason, plot-wise, for it, and it has been largely missing from the 1969 contingent excepting a spoof mud-bath fistfight in *Support Your Local Sheriff*. This one springs up in the aftermath of some good-natured leg wrestling when the Confederate Little George (Merlin Olsen), a giant of a man, is forced into taking on the Union man Mudlow (Big John Hamilton). "Biggest Reb I ever saw," says one man. "Biggest anything I ever saw," says Thomas as the ensuing fight kicks off a brawl. Thomas and Langdon are dragged in, until the unnecessary fracas (with the usual side helping of low comedy) is halted by Ann firing a rifle.

As Thomas and his men take their leave the next day, Langdon notes the look on his daughter's face. The horses are shown in another classic composition, the screen horizontally divided into four, the bottom quarter comprising land, the herd filling the next quarter up, hills the third quarter above that, sky at the top of the screen the fourth. When the whole screen is filled with sky, it is also filled with buzzards and the birds are scavenging on the corpses of a brigade of French troops[13] that Thomas deduces were the ones sent by Emperor Maximilian to meet the Confederates. As he is wondering who to send back to warn them, Blue Blood ups and offs. Having delivered his message, Blue Blood is invited to stay the night, and when he kisses Charlotte for the first time, she wants him to take her away with him "now, tonight." But they have been spied upon by Bubba Wilkes and he and Capt. Anderson beat up Blue Blood, stick him on his horse and send him away. Later, recovering at a river, the Indian spots Mexican troops.

Thomas, awaiting a rendezvous with the Mexican agents, is annoyed that his team has lost 500 horses on the journey (none of this has been dramatized) and worried that Blue Blood is three days late. There is a nice exchange worthy of the self-delusion exhibited in *Butch Cassidy and the Sundance Kid* between Thomas and Short Grub. The latter says, "I'd be thinking that he's made off with that little Reb girl and he'd be just about by Rio Grande by this time." Thomas replies, "That's what I'm thinking." Short Grub continues, "He wouldn't do that." Thomas agrees, "He wouldn't do that," while his expression and tone of voice shows the opposite. On arriving, the Mexican government representatives explain that payment is on its way. Thomas' calculation of losses has been accurate, when the herd is counted: They are down to 2505 horses.

Langdon's party reaches Durango as the Confederate flag is being raised and a local band plays Dixie. Host Gen. Rojas (Antonio Aguilar) lays out a welcoming banquet. But it is a trap: As they eat, they are surrounded by gunmen on the rooftops. "Consider yourselves prisoners of the revolution," says Rojas, forcing Langdon to witness the execution of "invaders of my country," French mercenaries hired by Maximilian. Now Langdon's men plus 32 women and 17 children are held hostage until Thomas' herd is brought in exchange. This is the worst possible dilemma for a Southerner. "I'm not asking any Yankee for anything," blusters Langdon, at which point one of the Confederates is dragged in front of the firing squad, and Langdon has no option but to capitulate. Rojas sets a deadline: horses delivered "by noon tomorrow" or all will be shot. Within this scene, there has been a shot of Blue Blood in the crowd, and when, at night, Charlotte wanders away from the group and is set upon by Mexicans, he rushes to her rescue.

At the cowboy camp, Langdon explains the situation. Some humor defuses the sour mood: Langdon tells McCartney he makes good coffee, apparently the first compliment the cook has ever received, and Short Grub tells a joke to Thomas' men as they try to decide whether (implied rather than stated) to give up the money they would have received from the sale of the horses and their futures, to help a man who, by his own definition, remains their enemy. The Union soldiers agree to help.

Unbeknownst to them, there is an unexpected obstacle in their way. The Mexican government has no intention of paying for the herd when they can as easily steal it by force of arms. A regiment of cavalry will do the enforcing. McLaglen lines up another beautiful shot. In long shot, a diagonal line of cavalrymen limber up. Below them on screen are Thomas and the herd. But here's the kicker: Mexicans and Union men both take up only the bottom third of the screen. Seizing the initiative as he had done when faced with the bandits, Thomas sets the herd on a collision course with the Mexicans. Leading the stampede are two wagons bristling with guns. The attack takes the Mexicans by surprise, the wild horses punching through the cavalry line, rifles picking off the enemy, Langdon slashing with his saber. One wagon topples over, killing McCartney and his beloved cat. McLaglen cuts to Rojas' watch. With seven or eight minutes to go to the deadline, the general has begun selecting Confederates to face the firing squad to the sound of a drum beat. As the firing squad members take up their positions, Rojas hears the sound of approaching hooves and in a moment the herd appears. All are saved. Blue Blood kisses Charlotte. Thomas, Langdon and Rojas drink to Juarez, the Mexican rebel leader.[14]

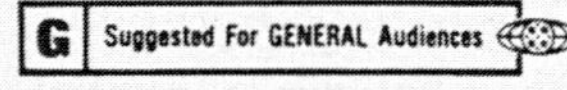

Royal Dano who played the small part of Major Sanders in *The Undefeated* (1969), was one of the quirkiest character actors in the business. And one of the hardest-working, with 193 credits by the time he stopped. Pressbook (Hannan Collection).

Now comes the final twist for students of the American western of 1969. Many of the key pictures of the year had involved escape of one kind or another. The Wild Bunch take refuge in Mexico, Butch Cassidy and the Sundance Kid in Bolivia. All the refugees have no intention of returning home. Only in *The Undefeated* do the would-be escapees return home, having resolved their differences, rather than running away from them.

While that is an intriguing ending—Langdon resolving to run for the House of Representatives, Charlotte determined to go with Blue Blood to his home, the romance between Thomas and Ann remaining, unusually for a western, unresolved—the incidents leading up to this are, for many, anti-climactic. I do not know whether the ending has been truncated for reasons of running time or because McLaglen believed a longer scene showing the herd racing towards Durango and the clock ticking away was redundant. As it stands, the ending convinces me, although to Hollywood, the idea of Americans helping foreigners overthrow their government always provides an easy get-out clause, and, as I mentioned, in order for the picture to run full circle, it should be the Confederates who save the Union men's skins. Nonetheless, it is a bold decision to end the picture in this fashion. The movie is not seen as having a political point to make, but what could be more political, at the height of the Vietnam War, than of finding a way for bitter enemies to put aside their enmity and resolve to work together? The film ends in compromise: Riding out, returning to the U.S. as companions not enemies, they play "Yankee Doodle Dandy" instead of the divisive "Battle Hymn of the Republic" or "Dixie."

This is another impressive performance from John Wayne, especially as his character is fully formed by his experiences in the Civil War, where, unlike the traditional western, the good guy does not need to wait for the other fellow to draw first. In fact, the astute commander will take every opportunity to undermine the enemy whether by use of surprise or by knocking out their leader at the first opportunity. This is Wayne in a more thoughtful register, looking after his adopted son and the soldiers he has equally "adopted," able to speak openly about regret and accepting the part he played, courtesy of the war, in inflicting grief on others. Gung ho is long gone. The actor cracked a couple of ribs during filming so for some weeks could only be filmed from one camera angle, but that appears to have been no limitation on his performance, which is considerably more rounded than in the past.

Had there been no *True Grit* between this and *Hellfighters*, his performance might have been praised. For a country still mired in bigotry and inflamed by race hatred at the end of the 1960s, Wayne, taking on a role where he espoused racial appeasement and where he accepted the sadness war inevitably inflicts on families regardless of which side they are on, sounds like the opposite of the character in *The Green Berets*. Rock Hudson is a shade over-the-top in his portrayal of Col. Langdon but movies work best with opposites and it would not do if he was as reflective as Wayne. Nobody came within a mile of Oscar consideration but spare a thought for Marian McCargo's quiet dignity as the widow.

But, as I mentioned at the outset, what impressed me most was McLaglen's cinematic handling, the consistent way in which he used the screen, a discipline he maintained right up to the end when the screen is divided in two by the Rio Grande with (in the bottom half) the wagon train itself splitting the screen by going up the its middle. Should anyone decide to celebrate the 50th anniversary of *The Undefeated* by showing it on the big screen, then take advantage of the opportunity and see why Andrew V. McLaglen should not be denigrated as a "journeyman" director.

Critical Response

Roger Ebert in the *Chicago Sun-Times*[15] was far from impressed, complaining that McLaglen is "never able to draw the threads together," taking a "panoramic theme" and then losing sight of it in the various subplots, the conflict not helped by a "wooden and uninteresting" Rock Hudson; Blue Blood "looks about as Indian as one of the Beach Boys." *Variety* had similar doubts, concerned about the "uneven mood ... [N]either Wayne nor Hudson seem to know whether they are in a light comedy or a serious drama."[16] But *The Showmen's Servisection* was positive: "Plenty of action, stylish direction."[17]

Box Office

The movie world-premiered in New Orleans. "Together for the first time," referring to Wayne and Hudson, was one of the taglines used in the advertisement campaign.[18] In keeping with most movies of the period (*The Wild Bunch*, for example), *The Undefeated* had a series of different taglines: "Battling it out toe to toe and side by side across 2000 miles of thundering adventure"; "They rode where no one dared, they fought when no

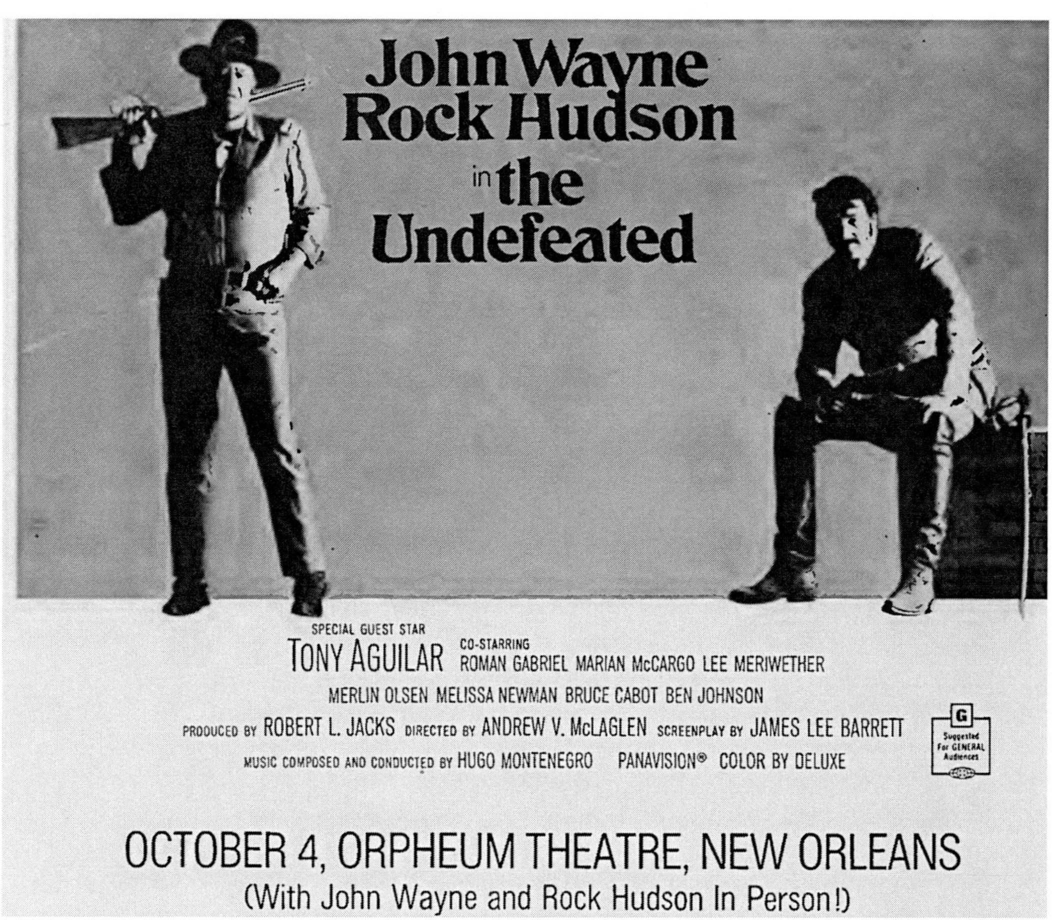

The world premiere of *The Undefeated* (1969) was broadcast live on prime-time television in seven states with an estimated four million viewers across 37 markets. Its stars John Wayne and Rock Hudson were in attendance before embarking on a two-week promotional tour. Trade press advertisement (*Box Office*, September 22, 1969).

one else could, across 2000 miles of savage wasteland, they lived for adventure"; "They lived a thundering adventure that rocked two nations"; "Pitted against each other ... Battling savage Juarista rebels ... Facing the blazing guns of the Mexican Army ... and driving 3000 wild horses in the greatest stampede ever filmed"; and "They feared no one—Juarista rebels, cut-throat Banditos, the armies of Maximilian ... as they challenged the angry land—and each other." Each advertisement featured photographs of Wayne and Hudson on either side of the frame, with the central image varying between the two principals knocking seven bells out of each other, the stampede, and Hudson and wife in a romantic clinch.[19]

Twentieth Century–Fox had stolen a march on Paramount's release of *True Grit* in the summer by persuading *Life* magazine to run a cover story on July 11 featuring its oldest and newest stars, John Wayne in *The Undefeated* and Dustin Hoffman in the contemporary drama *John and Mary*.[20] However, the publicity may have been too far in advance, for *The Undefeated* fell considerably short of its financial targets, not covering its expense in U.S. rentals, not so surprising in retrospect, since it appeared so quickly after the company's *Butch Cassidy and the Sundance* which took a revolutionary approach to the genre, and was celebrated in accordance with the director's new kind of style, while McLaglen was ignored for his traditional approach.

14

Cause Célèbre

Tell Them Willie Boy Is Here

Starring Robert Redford, Robert Blake, Katharine Ross, Susan Clark; directed by Abraham Polonsky; screenplay: Abraham Polonsky, based on the book by Harry Lawton; Universal; 98 minutes.

The Talent Hollywood Denied

Tell Them Willie Boy Is Here was bookended by real-life tragedy that in some respects has overtaken appreciation of the picture itself. Firstly, director Abraham Polonsky, who had fought in the O.S.S. in the Second World War, became a victim of the anti–Communist hysteria of the 1950s and was blacklisted in Hollywood for refusing to testify to the House Un-American Activities Committee in 1951.[1] Secondly, star Robert Blake was arrested in 2002 for the murder of his wife Bonnie Lee Bakley[2] but found not guilty in 2005 although eight months later a jury in a civil case brought by his wife's children found him guilty of "wrongful death" and ordered him to paying $30 million in compensation.[3]

Polonsky came to Hollywood by a circuitous route, having first worked as an attorney. After impressing one of his clients with his writing skills, he was hired for the radio show *The Goldbergs*[4] in 1937, but eschewed show business for labor organization. Writing novels on the side brought him to the attention of Paramount but the war intervened. Postwar, he fell out with Paramount[5] and joined Enterprise Productions, run by actor John Garfield along cooperative lines. There he wrote the Oscar-nominated film noir boxing drama *Body and Soul* (1947) starring Garfield (also Oscar-nominated)[6] and Lilli Palmer and directed by Robert Rossen. As well as writing the screenplay, adapted from the 1940 novel *Tucker's People*, he moved into the director's chair for *Force of Evil* (1948), again toplined by Garfield, and these days considered one of the finest examples of the noir genre. His only other work to reach the screen was the romantic drama *I Can Get It For You Wholesale* (1951) starring Susan Hayward and directed by Michael Gordon, before his career was upended by HUAC. He continued writing for television using other writers to front for him (several episodes of *Danger* [1952–53] and *You Are There* [1953–1955]) before completing Robert Wise thriller *Odds Against Tomorrow* (1959) which was also fronted.[7] Following Otto Preminger's championing of Dalton Trumbo, the most famous of the blacklisted screenwriters, for his screenplay of *Exodus* (1960), general

After 1969's *Tell Them Willie Boy Is Here* (pictured), Robert Blake turned down parts in *The Wild Bunch* (1969) and *Midnight Cowboy* (1969)—and, in turn, *he* was passed over for *The Rockford Files* TV series in favor of James Garner (Hannan Collection).

antipathy towards blacklisted writers began to fade and Polonsky was able to operate under his own name for his television creation *Seaway* (1965–66), for which he also contributed the scripts for three episodes.

Getting back into Hollywood after such a long absence proved difficult, though persistence was finally rewarded with Universal's tough thriller *Madigan* (1968), directed by Don Siegel and starring Richard Widmark. When the picture became an unexpected success, Universal not only green-lit *Tell Them Willie Boy Is Here* (initially known as just *Willie Boy*[8]) but awarded Polonsky a multi-picture contract.[9]

Robert Blake began his Hollywood career under real name Mickey Gubitosi at the age of six with a small part in MGM's *Bridal Suite* (1939) before winning a regular spot in the studio's *Our Gang* series of shorts from 1939 to 1944. By '44 he was the lead character and had changed his name to Bobby Blake. He graduated to playing Little Beaver, a Native American, in the *Red Ryder* western series from 1944 until 1947.[10] The transition to more adult roles was not helped by reejecting the part of Joe Cartwright in the TV western series *Bonanza* in 1959. He had second billing in the low-budget crime drama *The Purple Gang* (1960) but mostly existed on the fringes of television until larger parts beckoned in *The Richard Boone Show* (1963–64). Even then it was mostly television like *Rawhide* and *The F.B.I.*, although he had a small part in *This Property Is Condemned* (1966) where he met Robert Redford. His breakthrough role was as one of the killers[11] in Richard Brooks' 1967 adaptation of Truman Capote's bestseller *In Cold Blood*. As a result, Columbia signed him to a six-picture contract,[12] but this was a non-exclusive deal and his next picture was for Universal with third-billing in *Tell Them Willie Boy Is Here*.

Universal, buoyant after the roadshow success of *Thoroughly Modern Millie*[13] (1967) and the John Wayne western *The War Wagon*[14] (1967), had embarked on its biggest movie production spree in 11 years.[15] *Tell Them Willie Boy Is Here* was made on a modest budget, Polonsky only too delighted for the chance to direct again. Neither Robert Redford nor Blake had the marquee clout to demand a large fee. Katharine Ross[16] was a graduate of Universal's star school, the so-called "stable system," and after being loaned out to MGM for *Mister Buddwing* (1966) and *The Singing Nun* (1966) and Avco Embassy for a pivotal role in *The Graduate* (1967), she was only now in receipt of a "revised" contract which required her to make two pictures a year for the studio for seven years. Before being selected for the pivotal role of Etta Place in *Butch Cassidy and the Sundance Kid*, Ross had been billed below star John Wayne in *Hellfighters* (1968). She was promoted on *Hellfighters* posters as "the sensation of *The Graduate*" even though she played a relatively undemanding role as Wayne's daughter.

Canadian Susan Clark was another rising star. Unusually, although her early parts were, as you might expect, in television, this was not in the U.S. but in Britain and Canada, with parts in the U.K. in *The Plane Makers*, *Emergency Ward 10* and *The Benny Hill Show*, and then on to her native country for *Festival*. She had worked with Polonsky before, on *Seaway*, and made her movie debut in *Banning* (1967), several rungs below stars Robert Wagner and Anjanette Comer. Then she was billed sixth in Don Siegel's detective drama *Madigan*, and rose to third billing as the probation officer in the same director's *Coogan's Bluff*. She played another significant role in the western teleflick *Something for a Lonely Man* (1968) opposite Dan Blocker of *Bonanza* fame.

In short, five careers very much hung in the balance on the outcome of this film, for it went into production in May 1968, several months before Twentieth Century–Fox put *Butch Cassidy and the Sundance Kid* before the cameras. Those careers remained very much in the balance once shooting had completed for the movie was on the shelf for over a year, even avoiding cashing in on the sixtieth anniversary of the incidents it portrayed.[17] Possibly it would never have seen the light of day except for the extraordinary success of *Butch Cassidy*, which turned Redford into a star and reignited interest in Ross. The role of Deputy Cooper in *Willie Boy* was something of a role reversal for Redford since a few years previously he had played the target of a manhunt, as prison escapee Bubber in Arthur Penn's *The Chase* (1966). In the early days it looked as though Redford's career would never catch fire. Starting with a bit part in *Maverick* in 1960, he spent his early years in television (*The Untouchables*, *The Twilight Zone*, etc.), and once he broke into films it looked as it would never take off and that he would become yet another "nearly man" in Hollywood, stuck in a rut of being the leading man to much more successful leading ladies. He made his movie debut with a bit part in *War Hunt* (1962) and you would have to ask what possessed him, beyond desperation, to head for Germany for *Situation Hopeless...Not Serious* (1965) where he would be up against Alec Guinness, one of the greatest actors of all time, in a film that made little sense on screen, and carried little appeal to audiences. He generated some kind of chemistry with the female stars for after being third-billed to Natalie Wood in *Inside Daisy Clover* (1965), he was second-billed to her in *This Property Is Condemned* (1966). The same thing happened with Jane

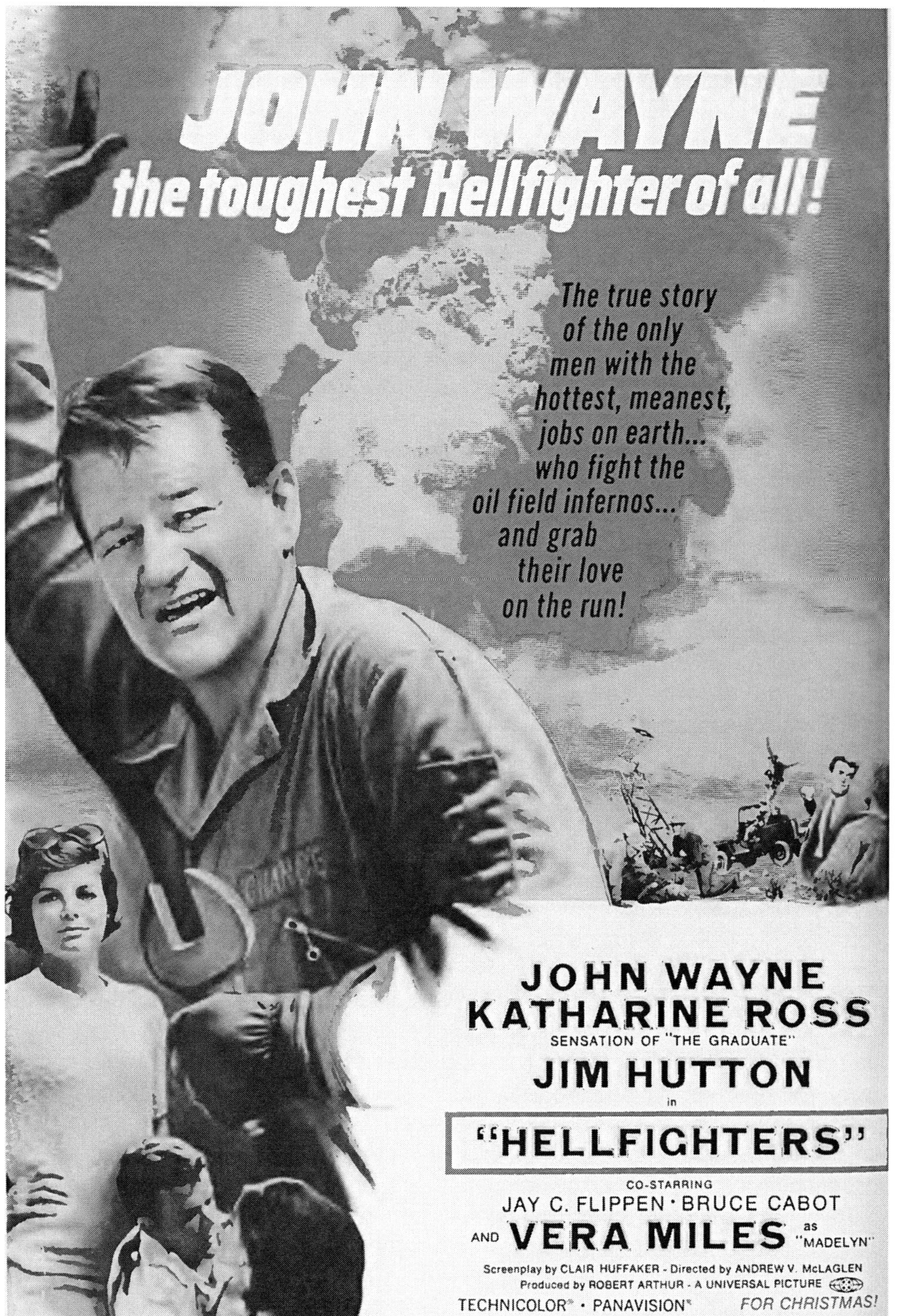

Hellfighters (1968) was based on the exploits of "Red" Adair. Stars John Wayne, Jim Hutton and Bruce Cabot had worked together on *The Green Berets* (1968). Trade press advertisement (*Box Office*, October 14, 1968).

Gary Cooper and Montgomery Clift were paired in an early attempt to get *The Chase* (1966) off the ground. Steve McQueen had also been mooted for the Arthur Penn film. Advertisement (*Films and Filming*, October 1966).

Fonda: He was billed below her in *The Chase*, which belonged to Marlon Brando, and then again in the comedy *Barefoot in the Park* (1967). But after the debacle of *Blue*, he did not appear on the screen for another two years, Universal clearly of the opinion that he was not yet star material and that releasing the Polonsky picture within a normal timeframe following completion was too big a risk. Universal held back, waiting to see how much interest there actually was in Redford. They delayed the release of *Willie Boy* until Redford's next film *Downhill Racer* was safely ensconced at the Baronet Theater in New York,[18] generating good reviews, prior to letting moviegoers see for themselves the film the new star had made long before the fuss began. And, of course, audiences, being susceptible creatures, opened up to the suggestion that the new film would find Redford and Ross in another romantic entanglement.[19]

Hollywood's Treatment of the Native American

In the movies, hardly anyone killed Native Americans any more and they barely feature as the enemy in the 1969 crop of westerns, apart from the lone wolf in *The Stalking Moon*, outlaws in Omar Sharif's gang in *Mackenna's Gold* and those, in the same film, trying to prevent disaster befalling a sacred ground, and the eponymous "hero" of *Tell Them Willie Boy Is Here*. The kind of cruel Indian who dispatches a white woman by stuffing pearls down her throat in *Shalako* (1968) or staked a man out to die in *Day of the Evil Gun* (1968) is nowhere in sight. Before the 1950, "the noble redman provided target practice for countless cowboy heroes and cavalrymen."[20] Delmer Daves, who had spent a lot of time with real Native Americans in his youth, began to change attitudes in *Broken Arrow* (1950), for which Jeff Chandler, as Cochise, won the Best Supporting Actor Oscar. He went on to play the Indian chief in *War Arrow* (1953) and, briefly, *Taza, Son of Cochise* (1954). Robert Taylor starred in Anthony Mann's first western *Devil's Doorway* (1950) as an educated Shoshone deprived of his land. In Edward Dmytryk's *Broken Lance* (1954), Katy Jurado is the "Indian princess" who breaks up a cowboy family. The theme of the half-breed or the man or woman brought up by Native Americans predominated. Charlton Heston in *The Savage* (1952) is a white man raised by the Sioux who has to choose sides. In *Arrowhead* (1953), Heston has an Native American mistress and a half-breed blood brother (Jack Palance); Natalie Wood in John Ford's *The Searchers* (1956) is the girl snatched in childhood but now happy to be a chieftain's wife, which infuriates her uncle Ethan (John Wayne). Audrey Hepburn's life in *The Unforgiven* (1960) is turned upside down when she discovers she was born a Native American; Elvis Presley is a half-breed in *Flaming Star* (1960), torn by split loyalties.

Or the films focus on people from one group trying to fraternize with the other. Ex-Confederate Rod Steiger in Sam Fuller's *Run of the Arrow* (1957) joins the Sioux in order to continue the war; in *Reprisal!* (1956) it is prejudice against a half-breed trying to live as a white man; in *Hombre* (1967), half-breed Paul Newman protects a stagecoach against bandits; while the half-breed title character in *Nevada Smith* (1966) beds a squaw.[21]

However, even with movies that set out with revisionist intent such as John Ford's *Cheyenne Autumn* (1964) and *Hombre*, seen by one historian as "a plea for tolerance and understanding,"[22] something vital was missing. It was salutary to realize that "although Hollywood uses Negro actors to play Negroes, Mexicans to play Mexicans, etc., an important Indian role is usually played by a white man."[23] With the exception of Jay Silverheels' portrayal of Tonto and of Geronimo in both *The Battle at Apache Pass* (1952) and *Walk the Proud Land* (1956), and Iron Eyes Cody of Crazy Horse in *Sitting Bull* (1954) and *The Great Sioux Massacre* (1965), there was not a single instance of a major Native American character in a film being played by a Native American. Even when the films concerned famous tribal leaders, Hollywood was unable to find a Native American to act the parts. Just as Cochise was essayed by Jeff Chandler and John Hodiak (*Conquest of Cochise*, 1953),

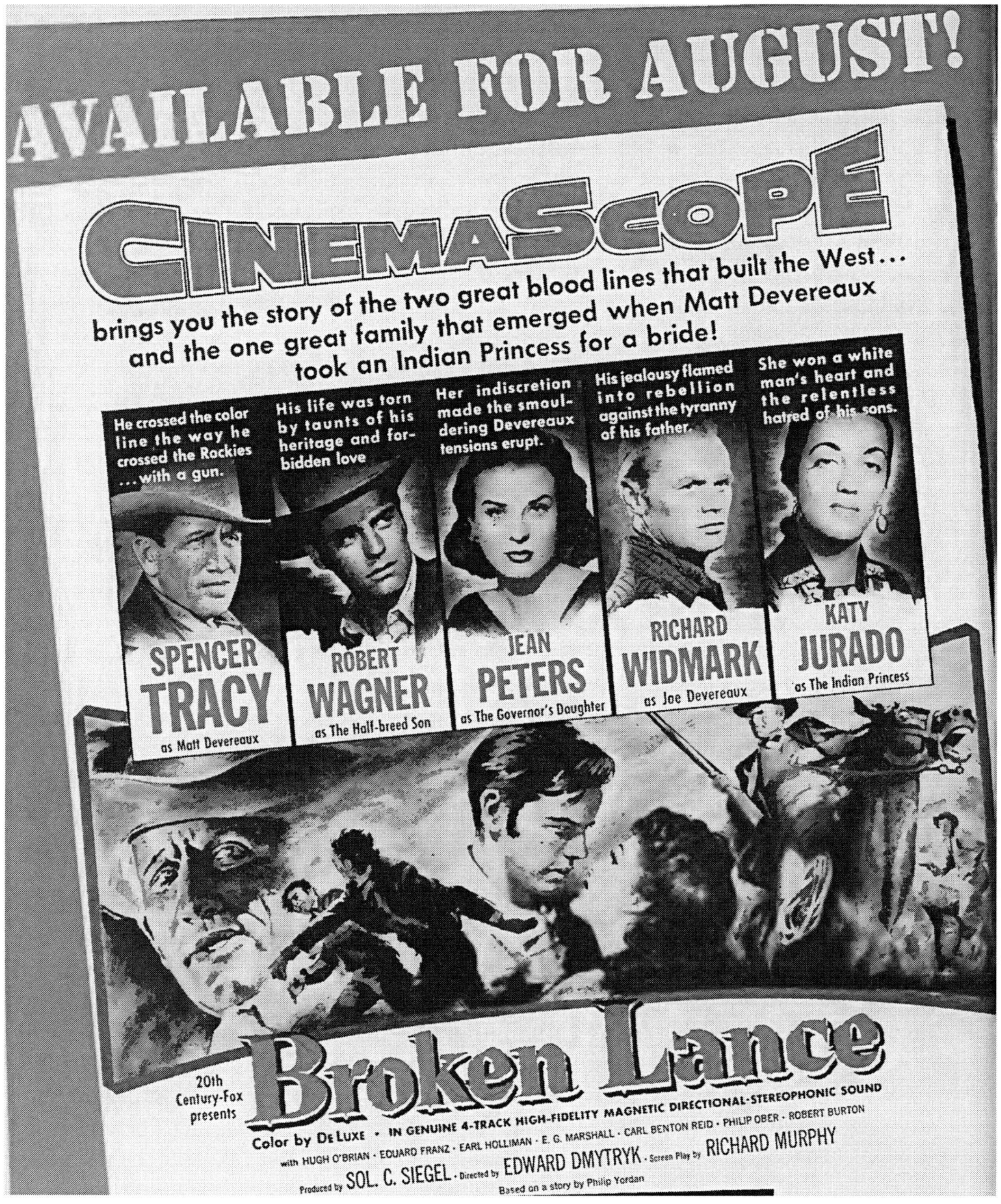

The grandson of Geronimo, Chief Geronimo Kuthlee had a small part in director Edward Dmytryk's *Broken Lance* (1954). Trade press advertisement (*Box Office*, July 10, 1954).

so was the part of *Geronimo* (1962) taken by Chuck Connors. Monte Blue played him in *Apache* (1954). Victor Mature was *Chief Crazy Horse* (1955) and the role was given to Mexican Anthony Quinn in *They Died with Their Boots On* (1942). J. Carrol Naish depicted the eponymous *Sitting Bull* (1954) as he had in *Annie Get Your Gun* (1950), while Michael Granger played the chief in *Fort Vengeance* (1953) and Australian Michael Pate in *The Great Sioux Massacre*.[24] Katy Jurado of *Broken Lance* was Mexican. John Ford cast Mexicans Ricardo Montalban, Gilbert Roland and Dolores del Rio and white man Victor Jory to play the Native Americans in *Cheyenne Autumn*, a move that was "as dishonest as almost any other Indian western."[25] Ford had cast Native Americans in small parts in both *The Searchers* and *Cheyenne Autumn*, but he used Navajos to play Comanches in the first and Navajos to play Cheyenne in the second.

Conversely, the Native American with the biggest impact on westerns of the 1950s and 1960s was gun expert Rodd Redwing, a Chickasaw, who taught Glenn Ford, Henry Fonda, Burt Lancaster, Dean Martin, Gary Cooper and a host of others to do the quick draw. His clap-hands trick was stolen for a scene in *The Magnificent Seven* (1960).[26] In 1969, Chief Dan George and Jay Silverheels had parts in *Smith!* and Rudy Diaz in *Mackenna's Gold*, but when Abraham Polonsky came to cast *Tell Them Willie Boy Is Here* he did not think it untoward to give the main Native American roles to Robert Blake and Katharine Ross.

"The Story I Wanted To Tell"

In essence, *Tell Them Willie Boy Is Here* is a manhunt, a chase, and bearing in mind that pursuit plays a dominant role in *Butch Cassidy and the Sundance Kid*, you have to wonder what is so difficult about this film that Universal did not want to release it. Like *In Cold Blood*, it was based on a true story[27] and addressed issues of racism, if you substituted Native Americans for African Americans, that had been commercially and artistically explored in films like *In the Heat of the Night* (1967). Mistreatment of Native Americans had been explored in many films, perhaps most poignantly in *Cheyenne Autumn* and *Hombre*. Equally, there was considerable public focus on the plight of the Native American, President Lyndon B. Johnson having signed in March 1968 Executive Order 11399 which set in motion the National Council on Indian Opportunity as a way of bringing civil rights pressures to bear. In addition, a new pressure group, the independent American Indian Movement, was founded in July 1968 to address economic issues affecting Native Americans.[28]

The facts behind *Willie Boy* are that on September 16, 1909, Willie Boy, a Chemehuevi-Paiute Indian living in Banning, California, killed William Mike (also known as Old Mike Boniface) after being denied permission to marry his daughter Carlota. Willie Boy went on the run with Carlota, who was subsequently killed in a shootout with his pursuers, and ended up 600 miles away in the Mojave Desert where he was reportedly shot dead two weeks later. The manhunt coincided with President Taft's visit to the area; Taft was followed by a posse of hard-bitten newspapermen desperate for a story, so the Willie Boy incident made nationwide headlines thanks to the journalists inflaming incipient racism by suggesting Taft could suffer the same fate from the murderous Native American as President William McKinley, assassinated eight years earlier, and that a party of Native Americans was planning insurrection.[29] The publishers of the book presented Willie Boy as someone who had "achieved immortality" by his stamina-defying run on horse and foot.[30]

The problem with the truth is that it too easily gets in the way of a good story—and Abraham Polonsky felt no obligation to stick to the known facts: "I just used the historical background, but, as a storyteller, put in anything I felt like. I invented all that stuff, it has nothing to do with history. ...I changed everything to fit the story I wanted to tell."[31] To

Richard Boone and Anthony Quinn, who had some Native American blood in their genes, were considered for roles in *Cheyenne Autumn* (1964). Fifteen minutes were cut after the premiere. Pressbook (Hannan Collection).

create a classic tale of pursuit, and investigate other issues of personal concern, Polonsky invented Coop (Robert Redford), a deputy sheriff of Indian descent, an amalgam of several real-life characters including the lawman who led the chase, Sheriff Frank Wilson. He gave Coop as romantic interest his boss Liz (Susan Clark), supervisor of the Paiute reservation and an agitator for human rights for Native Americans. Lola Boniface (Katharine Ross) is presented as someone wanting to better herself by becoming a schoolteacher, but subservient to her father and then Willie Boy, as much his property as Elizabeth is Jacob Woodling's property in *Paint Your Wagon*. Polonsky has Willie Boy killing Old Mike in self-defense, the Native American going on the run because he fears unfair treatment by the American judicial system and because of his previous experience of incarceration. For dramatic purposes, the domestic lives of the Native Americans, political background and the actual posse size are heightened but the story ultimately comes down to a one-to-one cat-and-mouse chase between Coop and Willie Boy, who are alike in many ways, especially in their contempt for their superiors and their attitudes toward women.

The picture opens with Willie Boy returning home after working as a foreman on a ranch. He jumps from a moving train and hitches a lift in a wagon to the Morongo River Estate where the camera picks out Native Indians involved in various traditional pursuits. He is immediately confronted by Lola's father and brothers. In the past, he and Lola have run off and been forcibly returned. Coop enters the reservation on horseback and is detailed by Liz to investigate white men selling whiskey from the back of a wagon. Willie Boy, who has purchased some of the whiskey, goes to a billiard room where he is taunted by white men: "Why don't you get back on the reservation where you belong?"

After Willie Boy physically retaliates, Coop is called in. One of the assaulted men complains, "He tried to kill me," to which Coop replies, "If he tried, you'd be dead," giving us our first true measure of the man.

At night, when Coop turns up at Liz's door, she initially refuses him entry. Meanwhile, Lola, dressed in white as if a virginal bride, looks for Willie Boy, kissing him intensely. Liz hates herself for being attracted to such a boorish man as Coop and they trade insults. "How can I resist you?" Liz asks sarcastically, the question directed as much to herself as him, calling him, "cold, brutal." He snaps, "I use you the way you use me." But she is as contemptuous: "You can make yourself into a man-killing Indian like your father."

We cut to Willie Boy and Lola naked and she dreams of a different life together: "I could teach school and you could have your own ranch." But Willie Boy does not believe they will be able to fulfill such dreams. He has asked for her hand in marriage "the white man way and the Indian way," and her father has chased him away with a gun. As they begin to make love, men appear out of the darkness, and Willie Boy kills her father. (There is, noticeably, neither now or in the future, any lament on her part for her father's death.) But when Liz is informed that the couple has vanished, she says that Lola "doesn't want to be a desert squaw" and believes this is a "wedding by capture." Willie Boy thinks the lawmen will not come after him as "nobody gives a damn what Indians do." Even so, he ties her up to prevent her from leaving, but then cuts her loose, the fugitives walking all through the night before taking refuge in a cave and evading the pursuing posse.

Polonsky takes an unusual approach in filming the chase. Both pursuers and pursued crisscross the screen, running and riding in different directions rather than consistently taking the one path, as for example in *Butch Cassidy and the Sundance Kid.* According to the director, this was a deliberate ploy to confuse the audience with a view to having them more involved in the hunt, but it as easily simply ends up being an irritation because we never know exactly where we are. Unlike *True Grit* where Henry Hathaway lets the audience know virtually every inch of the way where Mattie Ross must go or where Rooster Cogburn is headed, *Willie Boy* moviegoers are completely mystified as the hunt takes in different types of terrain, never knowing, except vaguely, where anyone is going, never enjoying the tension when they fail to reach a destination or when a plan falls through as with *Butch Cassidy*.

At this point, we are given some insight into Coop's character. He is the less successful son of a famous lawman who died "while it was still good," that is, at a time when marshals and sheriffs could take the law into their own hands and were not constrained by legalities or the long arm of civilization. The exhausted pair enjoy some respite beside a pool. Willie Boy says he doesn't want to die "in a white man's prison" and asks, "What's wrong with us? Nothing. Just color." Lola is more realistic: "You can't beat them." The posse men have arrived minus Coop, only to be ambushed by Willie Boy, who proves deadly with a rifle, killing horses and men alike. Coop is in town awaiting the arrival of President Taft, expecting to protect him against an assassination attempt. Liz, dressed in finery, pours scorn on the hunt. "You mean a dozen armed and mounted men can't catch one Indian on foot?" Coop is immediately possessive and predatory. When he asks what room she is in, she dismisses him, with disparaging reference to his position: "Good night, *deputy* sheriff." But when later she goes to her room, he is waiting. She orders him out. He refuses. She leaves and shortly after returns and begins to cry as she strips for him, humiliated at his treatment of her. As if to complete her degradation, he leaves without sleeping with her. In an echo of her pain, we cut to Lola crying in her sleep, both women trapped out of love or lust with men largely indifferent to their feelings.

In the morning, Liz's mortification is complete. Hoping to have made contact with the president to press for improvements in the Native Indian conditions, she has been told a "man would be better suited" for her line of work. Coop reveals that the posse has been ambushed and there are now fears of an Indian uprising. They arrive by motorcar at Whitewater to rendezvous with an enlarged posse. Willie Boy's bunkmate Charlie tries to excuse the ambush, claiming Willie Boy, intent on killing the horses to hold up the pursuers and gain time, killed men by accident.

Another insight into the lawman: Prompted by nothing at all, Coop volunteers, "One time I had a job to do and didn't do it," suggesting he has been a failure in his profession. But he does believe he knows where Willie Boy is headed. In an abandoned village, Willie Boy finds a hidden pistol, $15 in cash and his father's shirt. In the dark, Willie Boy's attempt to steal horses is thwarted by Coop and at one point he has the lawman in his sights. Coop reveals that his brother was killed by a horse thief who was half-Indian. Aware that she is slowing him down, Lola, encouraged by Willie Boy, leaves him, only to change her mind, and in ironic contrast to Etta Place decides, "I'll never leave you, I'm your wife." However, when Coop arrives at the empty village, he finds Lola dead

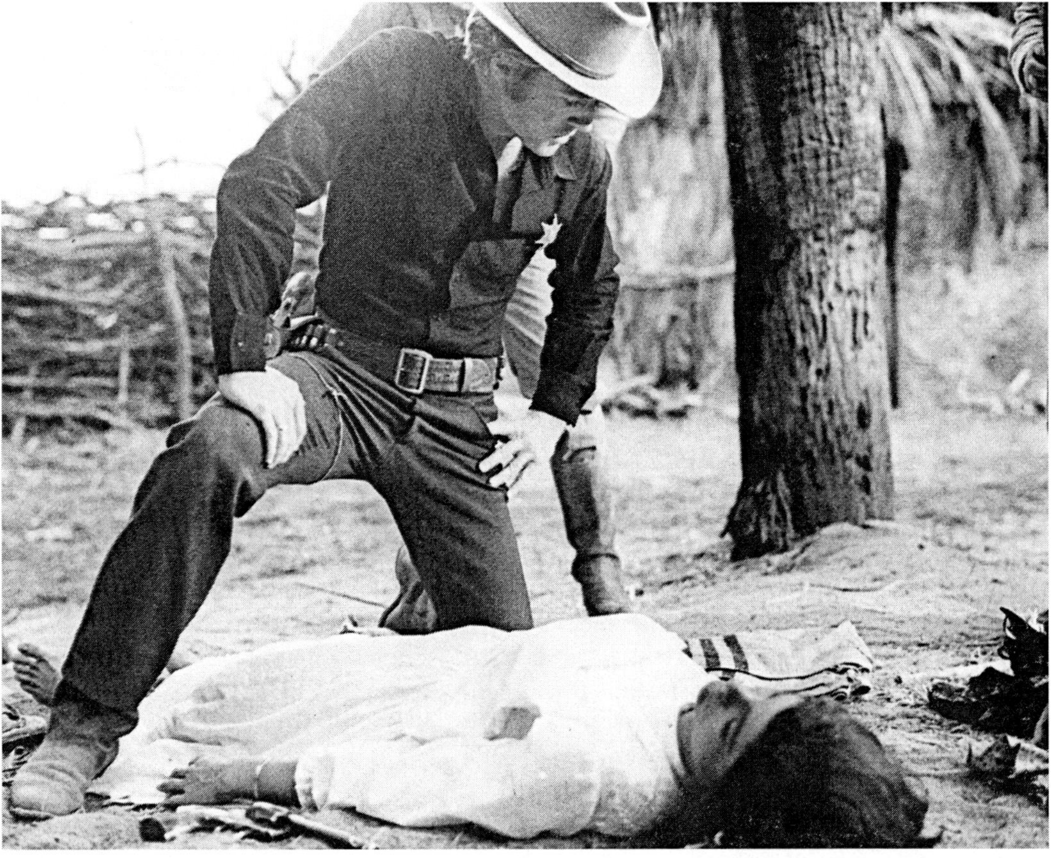

Coop (Robert Redford) kneels down over the corpse of Lola in *Tell Them Willie Boy Is Here* (1969) (Hannan Collection).

with a gun at her side. While it is implied that she could have killed herself, the wound in her stomach suggests she did not.

Coop on horseback pursues Willie Boy on foot. Rather than cover the pursuit of Willie Boy with consistent long shot, Polonsky cuts between close-up, medium shot and long shot as the Native American twists this way and that. Liz does not believe Lola has committed suicide. (Although not mentioned in the film, Liz would know such an action would be contrary to tribal law.) She is told Willie Boy would not want to let his woman "fall into the hands of the enemy" (reversing the genre tradition where many white men believe their womenfolk should kill themselves rather than be captured by a Native American) but it is also pointed out that she could have taken her own life to help her husband escape. To detect Willie Boy's position, Coop puts up a dummy and now, briefly, the hunter becomes the hunted, Coop narrowly escaping being shot. He climbs the mountain, coming up above Willie Boy, whom he shoots. Then Coop discovers that the man had no bullets in his rifle, leaving open the idea that Willie Boy effectively committed suicide. Coop carries him down the mountain, washes his bloodied hands in sand, and tells Liz, "I gave him his chance. He didn't want it." He gives instructions for the body to be burned.

Apart from trying to keep track of the geography of the situation and being sidetracked into understanding how the manhunt obsessed a nation, the picture's biggest problem is that none of the characters are remotely sympathetic. Willie Boy's plight obviously strikes a chord as an example of the bigotry and racism prevalent at the turn of the century (and not much improved since then), but the character is often repellent in his treatment of his fellow Native Americans (although, again not mentioned in the film, Lola's father had sound reasons for trying to prevent the marriage) and especially of Lola, effectively dragging her to her death because she belongs to him, tying her up to prevent her escape and then killing her. Ostensibly, he believes her murder is justified to prevent her from being sent to prison, but it is equally possible that she was killed for more selfish reasons, that she was slowing him down. Coop is not much better, dogged by a sense of failure, and treating Liz as if she too is a chattel, available for his pleasure when and where he wants her. The various revelations about his character are just dumped into the story with none of the narrative skill with which William Goldman enlightens us, often in times of crises, about deficiencies in the characters of *Butch Cassidy and the Sundance Kid*.

Lola and Liz share similar characteristics, both in thrall to misogynists. Liz attempts to create a wider role for herself in a man's world, but she is belittled and dismissed. She would be rather more sympathetic if she did not relish the prospect of putting Coop in his place, reminding him that, outside of the bedroom, she is in charge and accusing him of taking too much pleasure in his job. Lola is rendered unsympathetic for largely technical reasons. Every moment Lola is on screen, it is impossible to ignore the ridiculous makeup and the fact that her face is obscured most of the time by a shock of hair. These deficiencies make it difficult to assess her acting, although it is interesting to compare the actress in this film with her portrayal of Etta Place. In *Butch Cassidy*, she appears much more confident about her acting.

Bearing in mind that it is Redford's first starring role, he also appears uncomfortable, with little of the charisma he exhibited in the George Roy Hill western. Robert Blake is the acting standout: dour, tense, unpredictable, indefatigable, making a worthy adversary. His was the only acting rewarded, nominated for Best Supporting Actor by the New York Critics Circle. But Susan Clark as Liz runs a close second, with a rounded performance as the sharp-tongued, passionate woman. The humiliation of her strip scene is perhaps the best moment in the picture. Audiences came expecting a tense, modern western, but that was not what the director delivered, the core manhunt too fragmented. But he never set out to do so. According to a later report, Polonsky said: "*Willie Boy*, as far as I am concerned, is not about the West, it's a very personal picture about something else entirely.... I was making a picture about what happened to me during the blacklist."[32] And while thematically, this is probably correct, as he was hounded for perceived wrongdoing, and knew what it was like to be treated as an outcast, this particular outlet did not do his experience justice, nor did it chime sufficiently with moviegoers. A leaner tale, limiting the historical background, concentrating on the hunter and the hunted, would have produced a better result.

Critical Response

Variety called *Willie Boy* "the most complex and original [film] since *Bonnie and Clyde*" but pointed out that it lacked "entertainment value" which placed a question mark over its commercial future. However, it was a western in disguise: "America is what the film is all about."[33] It appeared to personify a "new class of oater [using] the oldest of film genres for new purposes."[34] Generally, the reviews were positive with only Richard Schickel in *Life* and one of the other seven major critics reacting negatively.[35] It was named in three of the year-end Top Ten lists—by the *New York Times* (by its secondary critic Roger Greenspan), *Holiday* magazine (the influential Rex Reed) and *The Los Angeles Times*.[36]

Box Office

Box office response was tepid to disappointing. Its year-end release meant it did not qualify for the 1969 Annual Rankings, but in the 1970 listings it finished forty-third.

15

Reissue Fever

A Fistful of Dollars • For a Few Dollars More • The Good, the Bad and the Ugly • Hang 'Em High • Return of the Seven • The Stranger • The Stranger Returns

Box office–wise, the best of the rest of the westerns released in 1969 were not new movies at all, but old ones. Reissues—also known as "reprints," "encore triumphs" or "masterpiece reprints"[1]—had formed a regular part of the moviegoer's diet since the 1940s, and generally appeared when the industry was short of product. After World War II when companies such as Film Classics and Astor[2] specialized in releasing old pictures, many films (e.g., *A Rage in Heaven*, 1941)[3] earned more on their revival than they had on first release. In 1952 and 1954 when Hollywood production had been cut to the bone, it was the likes of *King Kong* (1933)[4] and *Duel in the Sun* (1946)[5] that came to the rescue of beleaguered exhibitors. Although most studios dipped their toes in the reissue pond on a periodic basis, the companies with the biggest revival arsenals were MGM (*Gone with the Wind*, 1939,[6] and its "Perpetual Product Plan" in the 1960s[7]) and Disney with its animated treasures and family-friendly pictures like *Swiss Family Robinson* (1960)[8] and *Darby O'Gill and the Little People* (1959).[9]

In the 1960s, United Artists dramatically changed the reissue dynamic. Instead of waiting the traditional seven years or so for the next generation of moviegoers to come along, UA, on the back of its James Bond blockbusters, invented a new revival business model, whereby the latest iteration in a series (James Bond, *The Pink Panther*, the Beatles) was preceded or followed by a double bill of previous films. The 1965 twin-bill *Dr. No* (1962) and *From Russia with Love* (1963) became the biggest reissue up to that point with $8 million in rentals (the previous record holder was *Gone with the Wind* in 1961 with $7 million), enough to take fifth place in the annual box office chart.[10] Perhaps the most astonishing part of the first Bond double bill was that the movies earned far more on their second outing than they had on initial run.

So even though the first two *Dollars* films had not met box office expectations, neither making the Top 40 in the annual rentals chart,[11] it was no surprise when in 1969 UA brought out the Clint Eastwood double bill *A Fistful of Dollars* (1967) and *For a Few Dollars More* (1967)[12] less than 18 months after the second film had finished its run. UA had two other good reasons for making a revival play at this particular point. Firstly, it was piggybacking on what it had hoped would be the success of *Once Upon a Time in the West* (1969) and the Eastwood vehicles *Where Eagles Dare* (1968) and *Paint Your Wagon* (1969). Secondly, and more to the point, there was little chance of selling these pictures

United Artists bought the rights to *A Fistful of Dollars* partly because the management felt American audiences would respond to a new kind of hero at a time of social upheaval. Pressbook (Hannan Collection).

to television[13] because of the amount of violence they contained and, therefore, the only way to generate any further income was by sending them back into theaters.

After one final western, *Hang 'Em High* (1968), Clint Eastwood had quit the company which had given him his big break. He moved to Universal for *Coogan's Bluff* (1968), MGM for the war adventure *Where Eagles Dare* (1968) and Paramount for *Paint Your Wagon* (1969). *Where Eagles Dare* had been launched in the U.S. first run with huge fanfare in March 1969 and Sergio Leone's *Once upon a Time in the West* was due at the end of May, so UA sneaked out its reissue double bill between both in early April. Unusually, and perhaps to test the waters, the picture did not go straight into wide release, but opened instead at a single first-run theater in Chicago, where it had a two-week start on the rest of the country. To everyone's surprise, especially given the near–four-hour running time which limited the number of performances, it cleaned up. Its gross of $58,000[14] would be the third-best opening week take for a western in Chicago over the entire year, beaten only by *100 Rifles* and *The Wild Bunch*. It continued to perform in a robust manner at the first run and showcase box office in April and June, and by the end of the year it had lassoed a very decent $2 million in rentals.[15]

Spurred by its success, and with both The *Wild Bunch* and *True Grit* now in theaters, UA followed up in August with *The Good, the Bad and the Ugly* (1968) and *Hang 'Em High* with a combined four hour–plus running time. This was a riskier venture since the final part of the *Dollars* trilogy had already enjoyed three reissues in the previous nine months. The double bill came close to its predecessor in Chicago, $51,000 in the till,[16] but was less fortunate elsewhere, ending up with $1 million in rentals.[17]

Reissues had long been one of the key methods of measuring the arrival of a genuine star. And so it transpired with Clint Eastwood, the quartet serving to attract a new audience (who had wondered what all the fuss was about) as well as bringing back existing fans for a second helping. For moviegoers, it was an opportunity to chart the development of the star's persona, in a way that James Bond never did for Sean Connery since that particular character interpretation did not vary much from start to finish. Eastwood quickly developed screen maturity and an appealing persona. Just as importantly, by the time of *Hang 'Em High* he was beginning to astutely manage his career, his Malpaso company having been involved in its production. For Sergio Leone, too, it brought his entire western oeuvre together and fans and cinephiles alike could check the director's progress from the quick-fire and bloody *A Fistful of Dollars* to the greater cinematic nuances, handling of a wider range of characters and complicated action scenes in *The Good, the Bad and the Ugly*, the other film in his canon that would continue to be reassessed and re-evaluated in the 50 years after its release. But his work was completely ignored in the seminal multi-volume *History of the American Cinema*,[18] and by the majority of critics until relatively recently, when the final part of the trilogy was set alongside such masterpieces as Nicholas Ray's *Johnny Guitar* (1954) and John Ford's *Wagon Master* (1950) in the *Sight & Sound* Top Ten Westerns of All Time.[19]

Nor was UA concerned about cannibalizing its own pictures and so programmed a revival of *Return of the Seven* (1966), with Yul Brynner reprising his role as Chris, leader of the Magnificent Seven, shortly after the opening of the third film in the series, *Guns of the Magnificent Seven*. Brynner was by now a faded force at the box office, his last western *Villa Rides* (1968) sinking without trace. But luckily, UA's timing proved spot-on for after the release of the reissue came three further flops, *The File of the Golden Goose* (1969), *The Battle on the River Neretva* (1969) and Bryan Forbes' *The Madwoman*

Composer Elmer Bernstein was nominated for an Oscar for *Return of the Seven* (1966) even though the music for the sequel was virtually the same as the music for *The Magnificent Seven* (1960), for which he had also been nominated. Trade press advertisement (*Box Office*, September 12, 1966).

of Chaillot (1969). If ever an audience demonstrated preference, it was here. Matching the original man in black with the new substitute proved an impossibility for George Kennedy. *Return of the Seven* not only made more money than *Guns of The Magnificent Seven*, it also came close to matching the sequel's original receipts, finishing 71st in the annual rankings with domestic rentals of $1.3 million.

The biggest attribute an actor could bring to the spaghetti western at this time was the ability to speak English like a native, thereby eliminating the need for the sometimes awkward dubbing. Virginia-born actor and sometime executive producer and writer[20] Tony Anthony moved to Italy in the early 1960s and was perfectly positioned, in part because of his native tongue, to take the lead in *A Stranger in Town* (1967)–aka *A Dollar in the Teeth*—co-produced by Primex Italiana and Taka Productions and distributed in Italy by Titanus, with MGM[21] snapping up a release deal in the U.S. The "Stranger" was more of a "man next door" than the lawless, money-grabbing, amoral "Man with No Name," but in the advertising he was either presented with his face concealed and wearing a poncho or blasting away with a four-barrel shotgun. MGM invested in the sequel *The Stranger Returns* (1968)—aka, covering all the options, *A Man, a Horse, a Gun, Shoot First...Laugh Last!*—in which he sported a pink parasol. Copylines veered from the straightforward "Trap him! Tease him! Try and shove him in a coffin" to the frankly perplexing: "Can he roll a cigarette? No. Is he interested in women? When he has time. Can he Kill? Only when necessary and it's always necessary when The Stranger returns." In a case of the piggybacker being piggybacked, two weeks before the second UA reissue, MGM brought out a double bill of *A Stranger in Town* and *The Stranger Returns*. It had a wild opening week in Detroit, the $50,000 gross the best single-cinema haul there for a western in the entire year. However, other results did not duplicate the majority of the UA western double bills and it closed out the year with rentals of under $1 million.

Few companies could resist the prospect of making more money from an old picture. On the back of *True Grit* (1969), Paramount released a John Wayne double of *El Dorado* (1967) and *The War Wagon* (1967). *Hombre* (1967) starring Paul Newman was the obvious revival play for Twentieth Century–Fox after *Butch Cassidy and the Sundance Kid* (1969). Paramount's *Will Penny* (1967) reappeared in the wake of the same director's *100 Rifles* (1969) and its *Nevada Smith* (1966)[22] because of the Steve McQueen hit *Bullitt* (1969). MGM ordered another roll of the dice for *The Rounders* (1965) which starred Glenn Ford and Henry Fonda. Fox's *Rio Conchos* (1964) was courtesy of Jim Brown's stint in *100 Rifles* while UA's *Duel at Diablo* (1966) starring James Garner was revived thanks to the success of *Support Your Local Sheriff*. But none of these showed much traction in first run and, although they came in handy for nabes and drive-ins faced with programming problems, none showed any distinction on reappearance.[23]

16

The Last Round Up

The Great Bank Robbery • The Desperados • Death of a Gunfighter • A Talent for Loving • Charro • A Time for Dying • Sam Whiskey • A Man Called Gannon • Journey to Shiloh • Death Rides a Horse • Day of Anger • A Bullet for the General • God Forgives ... I Don't • The Brute and the Beast • The Man from Nowhere • Ace High • Any Gun Can Play • Payment in Blood • More Dead Than Alive • The Ramrodder • Brand of Shame • Hot Spur

Death of a Star, Number One: Richard Widmark: Death of a Gunfighter *and* A Talent for Loving

Some actors began their careers in westerns, but it was also the genre where others were, effectively, laid to rest. Like Glenn Ford, Richard Widmark spent a significant part of his career in westerns, but he was in the Last Chance Saloon in *Death of a Gunfighter* and A *Talent for Loving*.

Widmark, whose career stretched back to 1947, had several outstanding westerns to his credit: *Garden of Evil* (1954), *Broken Lance* (1954), *The Law and Jake Wade* (1957), *The Alamo* (1960), *How the West Was Won* (1962), *Two Rode Together* (1961) and *Cheyenne Autumn* (1964). During the 1950s he was guaranteed top billing in a medium-budgeted picture but in the 1960s he lost his box office appeal. Of 11 pictures between 1960 and 1967, he received top billing in only two, the adaptation of the Alistair MacLean thriller *The Secret Ways* (1961) and the Cold War drama *The Bedford Incident* (1965). And he had followed those with big-budget flops, both westerns: second billing to William Holden in *Alvarez Kelly* (1966) and third billing to Kirk Douglas and Robert Mitchum in *The Way West* (1967). So it came as something of a surprise that he surfaced as the star (ahead of Henry Fonda) of the unexpected hit *Madigan* (1968), as a maverick detective. Its director Don Siegel had languished in television since 1962; *The Killers* (1964) was originally made for television. Following its success, Widmark was signed for the starring role of Marshal Dan Patch in *Death of a Gunfighter* (its original title *Patch* was deemed "too vague"[1]). Playing opposite him was singer Lena Horne, who had not been in a picture since 1956's *Meet Me in Las Vegas*, but in other ways it was her movie debut because mostly what Horne did was play herself. Inexperienced movie director Robert Totten, whose only previous credit was the low-budget war film *The Quick and the Dead* (1963),[2] directed 25 days of the 34-day shoot but after "creative differences" with Widmark, Siegel was invited to take over the shoot. Although Siegel now had marquee appeal after his "modern" western *Coogan's Bluff* (1968) and *Madigan*, he refused to take a credit, so an agreement was reached to credit as director the non-existent "Allen Smithee" (a name later adopted by the industry to solve similar problems). And that was a shame because *Death of a Gunfighter*, released by Universal with a trim 94-minute running time, addressed the same issues as *Butch Cassidy and the Sundance Kid*, *The Wild Bunch* and *Once Upon a Time in the West*, namely the passing of the Old West in favor of civilization, and also *100 Rifles* in that miscegenation was a core element.

Richard Widmark was nominated for a Best Supporting Actor Oscar in his debut *Kiss of Death* (1947). *Death of a Gunfighter* (1969) was his 45th picture. Trade press advertisement (*International Motion Picture Exhibitor*, April 16, 1969, 13).

At the turn of the twentieth century, a small town has decided it is time to move on from the old method of enforcing the law at the point of a gun: Marshal Patch has dispatched one villain too many, taking his total to 12. The town fires him but he refuses to quit and remains in conflict with the good citizens until, against all their law-abiding instincts, they hire someone to dispatch *him*. Nothing overt is made of Patch's marriage to Claire Quintana (Lena Horne), certainly none of the sexual fireworks that marked *100 Rifles*, and the fact that it is simply taken for granted is, in reality, a much better way of dealing with what could have been an inflammatory situation. There is a touching scene between Patch and his son when the pair go fishing and there is enough in the climax for action fans. Exactly what triggered the split with Totten is not clear from watching the film. It was considered by *Variety* to be "hefty exploitation material,"[3] and praised by *The Showmen's Servisection* for its attempts "with some success to get beneath the surface of its characters."[4] But it did not go down well at the box office, despite a world premiere in Chicago and Universal promoting a range of "pre-release engagements" in 12 cities between

May 9 and May 30.[5] Its poor financial performance—about $600,000 in rentals[6]—cast doubt on the marquee credentials of Widmark, in his first movie after the career-reviving *Madigan*.

By the time the film came out, Widmark was already onto his next film, also a western, but more of a comedic vehicle, *A Talent for Loving* (1969). Walter Shenson,[7] who had produced the Beatles vehicles *A Hard Day's Night* (1964) and *Help!* (1965), originally envisioned the script as the third film for the Fab Four,[8] to be directed by Richard Lester, but the pop stars backed out. Director Richard Quine[9] was a Hollywood veteran and the screenplay by Jack Rose (*Houseboat*, 1959) was based on a book by Richard Condon (*The Manchurian Candidate*). Its co-stars were international: Israeli actor Topol, being built up for future stardom after a leading role in *Before Winter Comes* (1968), and French actress Genevieve Page (*Grand Prix*, 1966; *Belle du Jour*, 1967). Independently released (by Walter Shenson Films), it had an overlong running time of 110 minutes. The story was a mess: A gambler marries a sex-mad Mexican and falls under an Aztec curse and there are way too many characters for an audience to keep up with, never mind untangling the various plotlines. If there was one thing worse for an actor than being in a flop, it was appearing in a film so bad it was denied a theatrical release. With studios in financial disarray, many had come to the conclusion that it was better not to throw good money after bad and not to waste marketing dollars on dubious propositions. *A Talent for Loving* was shelved, never shown in theaters and not screened until 1974 when shown on ABC television.

Death of a Star, Number Two: Elvis Presley: Charro

Career-wise, Elvis Presley was in a similar situation to Richard Widmark and the western *Charro* was virtually the last roll of the dice. While Presley had been making three films a year since 1963, demand for them had shrunk—*Stay Away Joe* (1968) had flopped—and his 29th picture was a change of pace and style from the usual cheap musical. In *Charro*[10] (1969), instead of singing, he grew a beard.[11] He had essayed the western genre before to considerable success in *Flaming Star* (1960) and believed he was stepping into the shoes, literally, of Clint Eastwood, who had previously been linked with the film. But the script was rewritten to soften up the action, and once Presley had taken his $850,000 cut out of the budget, there was only the same amount left for the rest of the production. Newcomer National General Pictures, which had made *The Stalking Moon*, backed the movie. Writer-director Charles Marquis Warren, the creator of the *Rawhide* television series, had not made a movie in 11 years, his last being the low-budget Foreign Legion adventure *Desert Hell* (1958). Although responsible for the western *Arrowhead* (1953) with Charlton Heston, most of Warren's work was in the low-budget range.[12] It was rather late in the day for Presley to be trying to redeem his movie career, given that his fans had become accustomed to routine comedy-musicals laden with pretty girls. Like *The Desperados* the same year, the main thrust of the story is an outlaw trying to go straight, rather than as in *The Wild Bunch* and *Butch Cassidy and the Sundance Kid* planning to continue their outlaw ways elsewhere. A simple storyline might have played to Presley's limited acting skills. Instead, the plot is overloaded.

The film opens with Jess Wade (Presley) arriving in Mexico for a rendezvous with Tracey Winters (Ina Balin) only to find himself walking into a trap set by his former

Charro! (1969) was originally titled *Come Hell, Come Sundown*. Barbara Werle had also appeared in *Seconds* (1966) and *Krakatoa, East of Java* (1968). Trade press advertisement (*Box Office*, February 10, 1969).

partners in crime. They have stolen a solid gold-and-silver cannon known as the Victory Gun and plan to frame him for the robbery by searing his neck with a red-hot poker so he resembles the only one of the gang, a man with a scar on its neck, on a WANTED poster. Wade makes his way to Rio Seco where he meets boyhood friend Sheriff Ramsey (James Almanzar), who believes he is innocent, and finally makes his assignation with Tracey. When one of the outlaws shoots the sheriff, Wade puts him in jail, at which point outlaw leader Vince Hackett (Victor French[13]) threatens to turn the cannon on the town unless the prisoner is released. Then Mexican troops, alerted to the existence of the cannon, turn up looking for Wade. French keeps his word and blasts the town, killing the sheriff. In retaliation, the lawman's wife Sarah (Barbara Werle)[14] exposes Wade. To save their town, the citizens urge Wade to free the jailed outlaw. Wade does so but sneaks up behind the outlaws and kills them all except the leader, who is jailed. Wade then departs to return the cannon to the Mexicans.

Presley is not strong enough to make the most of the material and it is hard to accept him as a former hard-bitten outlaw, never mind a reformed man looking to go straight. The scarring scene, while well done, should have carried more emotional punch but Presley does not rise to the occasion and instead the picture is stolen by the two main outlaws. Ina Balin makes no more of her second-billed role than she did in the Jerry Lewis comedy *The Patsy* (1964) and does not come close to fulfilling the promise she showed in *The Comancheros* (1961). She also seems too much woman for Presley, who is more accustomed to innocuous eye candy. Reviews were uniformly negative[15] although *Independent Motion Picture Exhibitor* imagined that Presley's presence might stir interest in a "routine western."[16] He turns in a better performance than the critics expected, but the film did little better than the musicals, taking 67th position on the annual chart, the $1.5 million rentals not covering the negative cost.

Death of a Star Director: Budd Boetticher: A Time for Dying

By the time Budd Boetticher made his last film—his first since 1960—he had not yet been recognized in the United States (although invited in 1969 to lecture at the British Film Institute and in France) as one of the great directors of westerns; otherwise his final effort might have attracted more attention. Many of his best-known westerns had starred Randolph Scott, seven in total including *The Tall T* (1957), *Buchanan Rides Alone* (1958) and *Ride Lonesome* (1959). *Horizons West* (1952) had starred Robert Ryan and *Seminole* (1953) Rock Hudson. Stars of that caliber were no longer available for a director who had never had a big hit and was now making a comeback, and for *A Time for Dying* he settled for unknowns Richard Lapp and Anne Randall with Audie Murphy, also producing, in his first picture in two years bringing some welcome marquee sparkle in a small part as Jesse James. Boetticher had directed Murphy at the start of his movie career in *The Cimarron Kid* (1952).

Originally called *Dying for Arizona*, the new film was produced by First Investment Planning Co. for somewhere between $750,000 and $1 million, and shot at Apache Junction near Phoenix, Arizona.[17] The story was more of a downbeat odyssey than a traditional western, with raw farm boy Cass (Lapp) leaving home post–Civil War to make a name for himself as a bounty hunter. He meets Nellie (Randall) and they are forced to marry by hanging judge Roy Bean (Victor Jory). Cass gets into a shooting match with a psychotic youngster and loses, dying prematurely. *Variety* praised it for its "pared down story" and for its "atmosphere"[18] Rated M (Mature),[19] it premiered in Dallas in September 1969 but failed to find a domestic distributor until the following year when it was taken up by Western International[20] after it had been shown at the Netherlands Film Festival.[21] But it was not more widely shown until 1971 and even then to no great public response. Boetticher and Murphy had planned a second film, *When There's Sumphin' to Do*, with the actor in the starring role, but it never materialized.

Birth of a Star, Number One: Burt Reynolds: Sam Whiskey

As a promising young actor, Burt Reynolds had seen westerns as his way out of the rut of television, heading to Italy to make his movie debut as the star of *Navajo Joe* (not released in the U.S. until 1967). After that failed to provide box office lift-off impact, it was back to TV as Detective Lt. John Hawk in the series *Hawk* (1966) and two made-for-television pictures, *Lassiter* (1968), a composite of failed TV pilots, and the modern western *Fade-In* (1968) which made enough of a splash to bring him third billing in *100 Rifles* and the starring role in *Sam Whiskey* (1969).

Arnold Laven was a hyphenate, producer-director of a score of television westerns including *The Rifleman* (1959–1963) and *The Big Valley* (1965–1969) and the big-screen westerns *Geronimo* (1962) and *The Glory Guys* (1965).[22] He also produced Sydney Pollack's *The Scalphunters* (1967) starring Burt Lancaster and directed *Rough Night in Jericho* (1967) with Dean Martin. *Sam Whiskey* fell into the comedy-western subgenre. Angie Dickinson and Clint Walker co-starred.

The plot is a twist on the caper movie, Sam Whiskey (Reynolds) being recruited by Laura Breckenridge (Dickinson) to return stolen gold to the government. Reynolds takes his fun-loving "good ol' boy" screen persona to a new level but cannot muster the aplomb of James Garner in *Support Your Local Sheriff*. In fairness, this is not a spoof, but a western built on a comic absurdity. And from the actor's point of view, it did not achieve the result of turning him into a mainstream star. *The Showmen's Servisection* commented: "Entertaining western benefits from lots of action and a sense of humor."[23]

Birth of a Star, Number Two: Michael Sarrazin: A Man Called Gannon *and* Journey to Shiloh

Anthony Franciosa had waited a decade for his first starring role in *Fathom* (1967) after an auspicious start to his career with an Oscar nomination for Best Actor (even though he was third-billed) in Fred Zinnemann's drug addiction drama *A Hatful of Rain* (1957). But he seemed destined never to take the leap to top billing, doomed to second fiddle to top-billed females such as Rita Hayworth in *The Story on Page One* (1959), Gina Lollobrigida in *Go Naked into the World* (1961) and Ann-Margret in both *The Pleasure Seekers* (1964) and *The Swinger* (1966). Even in his starring debut he was outclassed by co-star Raquel Welch. So he was hoping to use *A Man Called Gannon* to establish his credentials as a top marquee draw.

Unfortunately, he was up against rising star Michael Sarrazin, a mop-haired, soulful-eyed 29-year-old with only two films to his credit, a small part in the western *Gunfight at Abilene* (1967) and a larger one as George C. Scott's protégé in the con man caper *The Flim Flam Man* (1967) where his performance drew attention. Also seeking to make a name for himself was television director James Goldstone in his film debut. Sarrazin plays Jess Washburn, a tenderfoot taken under the wing of Gannon (Franciosa), who rescued him from being run over by a train and from being charged with a murder. The men sign on as cowboys at a ranch owned by young widow Beth Cross (Judi West) and Gannon teaches his protégé the ropes. But then it shifts into range-war territory as Cross falls foul of neighboring ranchers for having too large a herd (which require too much local forage). Initially, Gannon and Washburn fight on her behalf to protect her property. But when Gannon advises Cross, with whom he is having an affair, to sell some of her herd, and she refuses, he quits. This leaves Washburn to fill his boots and take his place in Cross' bed and back her in her fight. After Washburn kills an older man in a duel, he and Gannon end up on opposite sides. In a confrontation, Washburn shoots Gannon but the older man drags the younger man behind him on his horse until Washburn is nearly dead from exhaustion. Having taught him a lesson (and perhaps a lesson in life), Gannon then leaves. With a contemporary outlook in that there were no real villains and all the good guys had an element of badness, and a plot that settled down to a more traditional one of the apprentice trying to unseat his mentor, and with romantic tutoring from the young widow, this is a better picture than it was given credit for at the time. In *Will Penny* style, the rudiments of ranch life are well drawn and there are some standout scenes, such as Gannon tearing his hands to ribbons on barbed wire, and Washburn dragged to near-death at the climax. But of course it went against the grain in that no one died. Sarrazin fit the bill as a brash, young cowboy, and stood out on screen with his good looks and especially his eyes which drew in the camera. He had the stillness which all great screen actors require. *Variety* called it an "overly contrived western suitable for minor bookings"[24] while *The Showmen's Servisection* deemed it an "offbeat western with good performances but cloudy motivation."[25] *International Motion Picture Exhibitor* termed it "a trifle offbeat for a western … [It] provides some bloody fights and captures the rough atmosphere of the range."[26] Universal had high hopes for the picture, but it was a flop.[27]

Directed by Italian-born William Hale, another television specialist, *Journey to Shiloh* fitted into a different category, the coming-of-age movie, albeit in a western setting. It's reminiscent in many ways of *Shenandoah* (1965), of young people making their way in the world against the backdrop of the Civil War. The cast was full of rising talent, leading the way James Caan, who had already enjoyed top billing in *Red Line 7000* (1965), *Countdown* (1967) and *Submarine X-1* (1968) and third billing in *El Dorado* (1967). Sarrazin took second billing and also in the cast were Harrison Ford, Don Stroud and Michael Vincent (aka Jan-Michael Vincent). The picture could be called the "The Young Magnificent Seven" as it follows seven young men, dreaming of war glory, as they cross the country to join the Confederate Army. Their odyssey is effectively a lesson in life as they see racism at first hand and watch a lynching. Danger mostly comes from encounters with the townspeople they meet on their way, although there is the usual bickering you might expect from a group of young men. Their journey ends when they sign up in time to join the Battle of Shiloh where they finally realize the folly of war.

In some senses, it is really an anti-war film and in other respects suffers from lack of traditional western action until the bloody climactic battle. Sarrazin acquits himself well, though Caan has such a forceful screen personality that there is no danger of Sarrazin stealing scenes. But Sarrazin's soulfulness provides an excellent contrast to Caan's more muscular physique. Despite it being a bigger flop than *A Man Called Gannon*, Sarrazin came out of this film with the potential to become a star.

Birth of a Star, Number Three: Lee van Cleef: Death Rides a Horse *and* Day of Anger

The other major beneficiary of the re-release of *For a Few Dollars More* and *The Good, the Bad and the Ugly* was Lee Van Cleef. The New Jersey–born actor had been a staple of television series with a few minor roles in venerated westerns (*High Noon*, 1952, *Gunfight at the O.K Corral*, 1957, and *The Man Who Shot Liberty Valance*, 1962) until cast as Colonel Mortimer in *For a Few Dollars More*. Capitalizing on its success, he made four more Italian westerns, generally playing a character similar to the one that had brought him fame. None of these pictures did especially well in the U.S., not finding a spot in the annual rentals rankings, which meant they earned less than a million for their distributors. But, as with the reissues, they often found a spot in the schedules of the beleaguered exhibitors. In terms of box office, the pick of these titles was *Death Rides a Horse* (1967), a revenge picture with Bill Meceita (John Philip Law) seeking vengeance on the men who slaughtered his family and raped his mother and sister. He has common cause with Ryan (Van Cleef), just out of jail and wanting retribution against the same gang. The criminal refuses to assist and sets about taking his own kind of retribution, financial compensation for the time spent in jail. But mostly he ends up killing people. However, when Ryan is captured, he is saved by Bill and later repays the favor by snatching Bill from bandits who have trapped him. The ending is intriguing: Bell realizes Ryan is one of the murderers he is hunting, and the outlaw gives himself over to Ryan, who finds that he cannot kill Ryan because of the debt he owes him.

There is some decent direction (Giulio Petroni), especially in the opening scene in a rainstorm where the peaceful family is savagely attacked, Bill as a child of five hiding watches the obscenity. In spaghetti western fashion, the action and characters are generally over the top, Van Cleef taking the opportunity to stamp his authority on the picture, and not so much move out of the shadow of the *Dollars* pictures as paint an even blacker persona. John Philip Law is as wooden as he was in *Barbarella*. "A second-string western," opined *Variety*.[28] "[L]ittle besides violence in mediocre Italian western," posited *The Showmen's Servisection*.[29] *International Motion Picture Exhibitor* chipped in with "ludicrous dialog, poor dubbing, over-acting, a plot that lacks credibility and an exaggeration of the violence that becomes almost absurd."[30] *Films and Filming* decreed it "a worthwhile addition to the cycle of Italian westerns."[31] In first run it scored $29,000 in Chicago, $13,500 in Boston and $7000 in Cleveland[32] and finished the year with an estimated $646,000 in rentals.[33]

In *Day of Anger* (1967), Van Cleef took second billing to popular Italian star Giuliano Gemma, who had already made four spaghetti westerns; for the 1969 U.S. release, this billing was reversed. This is a variation on the tale of an old gunfighter tutoring a young apprentice, Frank (Van Cleef) the former, Scott (Gemma) the latter, although there were, in reality, only 13 years between them, and it comes across a bit like an Italian version of *True Grit* while borrowing from *For a Few Dollars More*. In true immoral fashion, Frank's first action after taking on the young man as his student is to steal his savings. The main plot driver is, ironically enough, Frank trying to recover money stolen from him, but he is ambushed, with Scott turning up in time to save him, and later returning the favor. In an echo of the later *High Plains Drifter* (1973), Frank takes revenge on double-crossing townspeople, burning down a saloon. The apprenticeship element is filled with twists (including a six-shooter belonging to Doc Holliday) that strain credulity. The film ends with a duel between the two men and although the younger one wins, he is so disgusted by the prospect of life as a gunfighter that he chucks away his weapons. One of the high points of the picture is a rifle duel between Frank and an assassin, but otherwise the gunplay is fast and bloody. Van Cleef cuts a striking figure, like Yul Brynner in *The Magnificent Seven* in terms of style, suggesting that he could have had a decent career in low-budget westerns.

It was reviewed in the trades primarily because it took the industry by surprise with "its unusual box office staying power" but was still dismissed as " a violent campy western as the Italians like to make them."[34] This hit the Los Angeles showcase circuit for a moderate $65,000 from 27 theaters,[35] but its annual take was an estimated $150,000.[36] Also appearing, in a brief repeat run, was *The Big Gundown* (1966), Van Cleef's first Italian western, directed by Sergio Sollima, which grossed $8000 in Boston,[37] but in total took in less than $50,000 in rentals.[38]

The Great Bank Robbery

Written by William Peter Blatty before he turned his hand to the horror masterpiece *The Exorcist*, this comedy, originally titled *O'Rourke's Robbery*, was set up at Paramount by independent producer Malcolm Stuart[39] in 1967. Stuart had six other potential pictures in various stages of production including the thriller *The Night of Camp David* to star Paul Newman and *Scalawag* with Kirk Douglas.[40] It was later moved to Warner Brothers. Shooting was due to start in March 1968[41] with Jules Dassin[42] in the director's chair and Rex Harrison and Dassin's wife Melina Mercouri as its stars.[43] Dassin was something of a coup because he had virtually invented the heist caper movie with *Rififi* (1955) and refined it with *Topkapi* (1964), which also starred Mercouri. But his recruitment pushed the start date back a month. When he pulled out, production of *The Great Bank Robbery*, as it was now known, was delayed until September 1968, by which time it had acquired two songs by Sammy Cahn and Jimmy Van Heusen, who had contributed Oscar-nominated songs to *Robin and the 7 Hoods* and *Star!*

Zero Mostel made his name on stage[44] in *A Funny Thing Happened on the Way to the Forum* and *Fiddler on the Roof*. He abandoned legitimate theater for movies in 1966, reprising his role in *A Funny Thing Happened...* and following up as the iconic Max Bialystock in *The Producers*, a "sleeper" hit. His next film, the detective spoof *Monsieur LeCoq* (1967), was abandoned, and *Great Catherine* (1968), a comedy based on the George Bernard Shaw play and starring Peter O'Toole, flopped, so he was not the marquee attraction he once had been. Kim Novak had been a bigger star than Mostel would ever be, in *The Man with the Golden Arm* (1955) with Frank Sinatra, *Picnic* (1956) starring William Holden, *Pal Joey* (1956) with Sinatra again and *Vertigo* (1958) opposite James Stewart; the majority of her pictures in the 1960s had been built around her name. In *The Notorious Landlady* (1962), her name took precedence over that of Jack Lemmon, in *Boys Night Out* (1962) over James Garner, in *Of Human Bondage* (1964) over Laurence Harvey, in *The*

British actresses Sylvia Sims and Kate O'Mara had the leading female roles in *The Desperados* (Columbia, 1969). Trade press advertisement (*Box Office*, April 21, 1969).

Amorous Adventures of Moll Flanders (1965) over Richard Johnson and in *The Legend of Lylah Clare* (1968) over Peter Finch. Clint Walker had never quite shaken off the title character in his long-running television character *Cheyenne* (1955–1962) and although he had been the star of *The Night of the Grizzly* (1966), *Maya* (1966) and *More Dead Than Alive* (1969), he had attracted more attention in a supporting role in *The Dirty Dozen* (1967). Director Hy Averback had a decent track record,[45] over a decade in comedy television, beginning his movie career with the low-budget *Chamber of Horrors* (1966) and quickly graduating to the Doris Day vehicle *Where Were You When the Lights Went Out* (1968) and the Peter Sellers comedy *I Love You, Alice B. Toklas* (1968), so at least he had the experience to helm the $5 million *The Great Bank Robbery*.

Where screenwriter William Goldman had recognized the need to stay one step ahead of the audience, William Peter Blatty interpreted this notion as "Hit them with so much they do not know whether they are coming or going." Keeping up with the plot is just one of the problems with *The Great Bank Robbery*, the other being lack of genuine laughs. It falls more into the mild humor category of *The Good Guys and the Bad Guys* than the laugh-out-loud *Support Your Local Sheriff*. In a twist on the caper movie and the standard western bank robbery theme, three separate groups intend to rob the same bank in the town of Friendly on the same day, the Fourth of July. The Reverend Pious Blue (Mostel) and Sister Lyda Kebanov (Novak) head one gang, planning to tunnel into it from the church and get away in a giant balloon. Mexican bandits led by Juan (Larry Storch) and his father (Akim Tamiroff[46]) lead the second team, aiming to smash their way in using a juggernaut. The third crew is led by a good guy, Ranger Ben Quick (Walker), also using tunneling, this time from the laundry, because he rightly suspects that the bank is a front for outlaws, and wants to find the ledgers proving this. On top of this, there is Slade (Claude Akins), another outlaw, who robs trains and generally gets in the way. As if there is not complication enough, Quick has the hots for Sister Lyda.

On the day of the robbery, in an echo of *100 Rifles*, Lyda appears as a vision of Lady Godiva, naked on a horse, to distract the guards. With just this simple story outline, you can imagine the farce that will unfold. There are shootouts and chases and everyone gets in each other's way. While in the vein of epic comedies like Blake Edwards' *The Great Race* (1965) and Stanley Kramer's *It's a Mad Mad Mad Mad World* (1963), it did not work out that way, or *any* way for that matter. Where previous Mostel vehicles had been tailored to fit his apoplectic style, in this picture he lacked a straight man, and seemed ill at ease, unable to dominate the screen, and he was outshone by the supporting cast. The comedy never sparks. The funny lines are not funny enough, the action verges on the ridiculous and the audience quickly guesses exactly what is about to transpire.

It is always hard to view comedy at home, away from a theater where often one person getting the joke will be enough to trigger hoots of laughter from the rest of the moviegoers. But where I laughed myself silly watching *Support Your Local Sheriff* on DVD, I watched most of this with the same straight face as, I imagine, did most of the audience in 1969.

It was filmed on location in the historic gold rush town of Columbia, in Sierra Nevada, California, and the balloon sequences were filmed over the Sonora and Placerita Canyons (site of the actual original gold rush); the production spent a considerable amount of effort on period details.[47] Costumes from previous pictures were reused: the shoes Errol Flynn wore in *Gentleman Jim* (1942), James Cagney's shirt from *The Oklahoma Kid* (1939), Clark Gable's suit from *Band of Angels* (1957) and Humphrey Bogart's shirt from *Virginia City* (1940). The locomotive used was built in 1884.[48] Marketing was old-school: the balloon touring Dallas, Houston, Austin, Fort Worth and San Antonio prior to the Texas launch,[49] a four-page tabloid herald handout called *The Desert News*,[50] gimmicks such as "Zero Dollars" given away to the public.[51] At the press junket held by Warner Brothers in the Bahamas to preview the film, Kim Novak was asked about appearing in the nude.[52]

All the major critics gave it a thumbs-down.[53] *Variety* added: "It limps more often than it flies.... *Maverick*-style humor attempts fall short.... Mostel has few moments of brightness but loses out for the most part.... Tamiroff, Storch and [Ruth] Warrick steal their scenes at every turn."[54] Given the poor critical response, it did better than expected with rentals of $1.5 million, though that still put it in the flop bracket.

The Desperados

Henry Levin had directed 48 films by the time he came to make *The Desperados*. He had turned his hand to virtually ever genre, most recently the Matt Helm spy spoofs *Murderers Row* (1966) and *The Ambushers* (1967) as well as the historical adventure *Genghis Khan* (1965) and MGM's Cinerama film *The Wonderful World of the Brothers Grimm* (1962). His career had kicked off with the horror film *Cry of the Werewolf* (1944) and he had handled swashbucklers such as *The Bandit of Sherwood Forest* (1946), adventure in *Journey to the Center of the Earth* (1959), comedies such as *The Corpse Came C.O.D* (1947) and *And Baby Makes Three* (1949), the musicals *Jolson Sings Again* (1949) and *The Farmer Takes a Wife* (1953), the Andrew Jackson biopic *The President's Lady* (1953) and the Pat Boone vehicles *Bernardine* (1957) and *April Love* (1957). Amidst this extensive portfolio, he had ridden herd on three westerns, *The Man from Colorado* (1949), *Three Young Texans* (1954) and *The Lonely Man* (1957).

For *The Desperados*, a post–Civil War story filmed in Spain and released in the U.S. by Columbia, he was reunited with *The Lonely Man*'s Jack Palance as psychotic preacher Josiah Galt, leader of a marauding Confederate unit that includes his three sons. It appeared as though top-billed Vince Edwards, playing David Galt, had dispelled his image as the title character on TV's *Ben Casey* (1961–1966) with the leading roles in *The Victors* (1963) and *Hammerhead* (1968), but he was third-billed in the war film *The Devil's Brigade* (1968) so this was an opportunity to reassert his marquee appeal. George Maharis and newcomer Christian Roberts played sons Jacob and Adam.

The Walter Clarke screenplay had an intriguing concept, a study of a doomed family, torn apart by violence. David Galt is condemned to death by his father in a kangaroo court after he has stood up against members of the gang when they attacked a small Kansas town, killing men and raping women. He escapes with his wife and flees to Texas where they live under an assumed name until, going straight, some years later, after the war is over, he spots his father's gang on the edge of town. When the outlaws hold up the bank, the townspeople are waiting and his brothers are arrested and jailed. Josiah frees them. Although Edwards and Marshal Kilpatrick (Neville Brand) head off in pursuit, David is hampered by refusing to use a gun against his family. When captured by Josiah, David is told to prove his loyalty to the family by killing the lawman. In the scuffle that follows, it is his brother Adam who dies. In revenge, Josiah kills David's wife and kidnaps his son. Foiling a robbery by the bandits, David kills his other brother Jacob. Jacob's mistress, a cripple, shoots Josiah and rescues the kidnapped child but when David confronts his father on a rocky cliff, they both fall to their deaths.

The end result should have been a satisfying study of a family that violence has turned in on itself, and of man renouncing the gun in order to seek a new life with his wife and child, their newfound freedom threatened by their old life. Instead, apart from the maniacal Josiah, none of the characters seem to come to grips with their inner turmoil

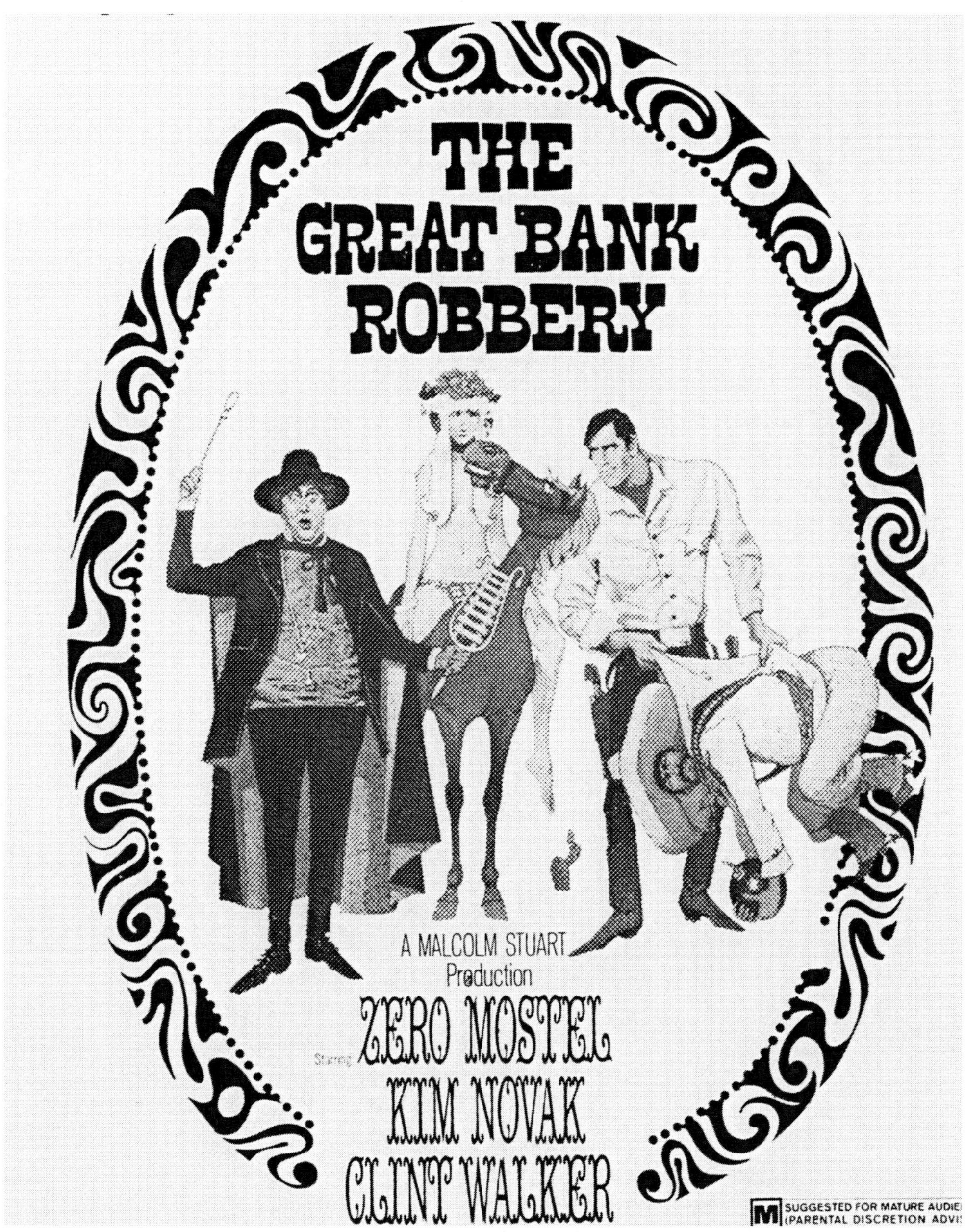

The balloon used in *The Great Bank Robbery* (1969) cost $45,000 and was the largest ever built at that time, at ten stories high and 130 feet around. Pressbook (Hannan Collection).

and there are so many plot twists, shoot-outs, robberies and attacks that it plays out like a poor man's spaghetti western, with none of the tragedy that the storyline should have invoked. The film was mostly dismissed as a trashy, over-violent western, but *Variety* considered it "okay for intended market."[55] *International Motion Picture Exhibitor* found that Palance was so over-the-top that the other characters paled in comparison.[56] By my estimation, it returned less than $250,000 in rentals. A resounding flop, in other words.

Limp Spaghetti

Demand for spaghetti westerns and low-budget westerns proved to be overrated in 1969, judging from the ten or so pictures released in that subgenre. (Note that spaghetti westerns were often released as many as three years after their initial Italian release—as had occurred with the original "Dollars" pictures.) Best results were garnered by 1967's *A Bullet for the General* ("unending explosive carnage" according to the *New York Times*[57]) starring Gian Maria Volonte (*A Fistful of Dollars, For a Few Dollars More*) and German

By the time *The Brute and the Beast* (1969) appeared in the U.S., Franco Nero was a considerable attraction after *Camelot* (1967) and his much-publicized affair with his co-star on that film Vanessa Redgrave. Trade press advertisement (*Box Office*, November 11, 1968).

Roger Gentry, star of *The Ramrodder* (1969), later turned to directing, making *Sleazy Rider* (1973) and *The Invitation* (1975). Trade press advertisement (*Box Office*, January 19, 1969).

cult figure Klaus Kinski. It was also accorded a New York showcase circuit release, but with poor uptake, just $73,000 from 23 houses.[58] *God Forgives ... I Don't* (1967) ("long on action but short on story line"[59]) introduced the team of Terence Hill and Bud Spencer and also starred Frank Wolff (Brett McBain in *Once Upon a Time in the West*) and picked up $20,000 in Chicago and $7500 in Boston.[60] *The Brute and the Beast* (1966), directed by Lucio Fulci (now better known for horror films), starred romantic idol Franco Nero and George Hilton and grossed $8000 in Boston, while *The Man from Nowhere* (1966) with Giuliano Gemma did not rate a first-run performance in any of the major cities.[61] *Ace High* (1968), "an uneven mixture of comedy and menace,"[62] also starred Spencer and Hill; it achieved a wider release primarily because it was dualed with the British crime caper *The Italian Job* (1969) starring Michael Caine. In New York, the pair took $217,000 from 31 theaters,[63] including one week in first run on Broadway. Television star Edd Byrnes (*77 Sunset Strip*) was top-billed in *Any Gun Can Play*[64] (1967), directed by Enzo G. Castellari, which grossed $5800 in Boston and $6000 in Cleveland,[65] and *Payment in Blood*[66] ("violence, cynicism and raw humor"[67]), again directed by Castellari.

The release of spaghetti westerns was not always straightforward and sometimes it would take over a year for them to play out. *Any Gun Can Play*, for example, earned rentals of around $383,000 in first run in 1968.[68]

Hardcore

Westerns were not excluded from the gradual encroaching of first-run theaters by hardcore porn. Three porn films set against a western background found their way onto first-run screens in 1969. The storyline of *The Ramrodder* (1969), "the naked west as you've never seen it before," centers on rape. Starring Roger Gentry and Kathy Williams, it grossed $6000 in Boston first-run and invaded small theaters elsewhere with nowhere to turn for product except this kind of film.[69] *Brand of Shame* (1968, aka *Nude Django*), an Italian-German co-production starring Steve Stunning in his only movie and Cara Peters (using the name Paula Pleasure), was from a screenplay co-written by David F. Friedman, one of the most prolific producers of porn (*Trader Hornee*, 1970, *The Budding of Brie*, 1980). The story concerned the attempts by foul means to force a schoolteacher to surrender the map to a gold mine. The highlight, if it could be called such a thing, was worse brutality than found in the blood-spattered spaghetti westerns, the whipping of a woman. It was directed by occasional television actor Byron Mabe (*The Virginian*) under his *nom de plume* B. Ron Elliott; he had previously been involved in such sex epics as *The Lustful Turk* (1968). The first week of first run in New York grossed $4700.[70]

Following close on its heels was *Hot Spur* (1968) starring James Arena, also his only movie credit, and Virginia Gordon and directed by Lee Frost (who later directed *Dixie Dynamite*, 1976, starring Warren Oates) under his pseudonym R.L. Frost. The "story" concerns kidnap and rape.[71] This had a slightly wider distribution and grossed $8000 in New York and $6700 in Boston. It was written and directed by Van Guylder (the pseudonym of Ed Forsyth).

Conclusion

My Western marathon (over 40 films) ended with a feeling of delight. All the westerns I had confidently placed in the masterpiece category—*Once Upon a Time in the West*, *True Grit*, *The Wild Bunch* and *Butch Cassidy and the Sundance Kid*—stood up to the test of time. *True Grit* I found especially rewarding, not just for the acting and direction, but because Rooster Cogburn was a character in keeping with the times, a shoot-first-ask-questions-later frontiersman in the mold of the Man with No Name.

Perhaps the most satisfying part of the exercise (if that is the correct word for such a pleasurable experience) was to look again at some westerns which had not been regarded as top-notch. Of these, *The Undefeated* was the stand-out, especially for the compositions and director Andrew McLaglen's treatment of landscape, and because, of all the fugitives in 1969, Rock Hudson's gallant Confederates returned home to explore reconciliation. The other three that ran it close were *100 Rifles*, woefully ignored in critical circles, *Support Your Local Sheriff* which is every bit as funny as Mel Brooks' *Blazing Saddles* (1974), and *The Stalking Moon*, which focuses on uncommunicative characters so much on the edge with each other that it is often painful to watch. And there should be a special mention for *Heaven with a Gun*, which, for two-thirds of its running time keeps you guessing. Some of the smaller films, especially from the spaghetti category, are also worth a replay.

No year in movie history has given us four western masterpieces. The films were not all recognized as such on initial release but have continued to grow in critical esteem. As I mentioned in my introduction, in 1969 audiences flocked to westerns at a greater rate than ever before. The year had the greatest number of westerns ever to make the annual box office rankings Top Ten, and the Top 100, while *Butch Cassidy and the Sundance Kid* went on to make even more money than its 1969 tally over the next five years. A decade that began with only two westerns in the top-ranked movies at the box office ended with more westerns hitting the target than ever before.

The demise of the western has been confidently predicted virtually every decade during the last century and still, though output has generally declined, it stubbornly refuses to die. The 1970s continued to mine a rich seam. The first year of the decade saw Arthur Penn's revisionist western *Little Big Man* with Dustin Hoffman, Peckinpah's *The Ballad of Cable Hogue*, Ralph Nelson's visceral *Soldier Blue* and Richard Harris in the title role of *A Man Called Horse*. The following year brought Sergio *Leone's A Fistful of Dynamite* with Rod Steiger and James Coburn, Burt Lancaster in Michael Winner's *Lawman*, Clint Eastwood in *The Beguiled*, Warren Beatty and Julie Christie in *McCabe and Mrs. Miller* and Raquel Welch as *Hannie Caulder*. Sydney Pollack's *Jeremiah Johnson* starring Robert Redford was the pick of 1972 along with Mark Rydell's *The Cowboys* and John Huston's *The Life and Times of Judge Roy Bean*. And on went the decade with Clint Eastwood (*High Plains Drifter*, 1973, and *The Outlaw Josey Wales*, 1976) firing on all cylinders and John Wayne[1] reveling in both action (*Cahill U.S. Marshal*, 1973, and *The Train Robbers*, 1973) and reflection (*The Shootist*, 1976), Peckinpah in top form with *Pat Garrett and Billy the Kid* (1973) and Robert Aldrich with *Ulzana's Raid* (1972). The genre survived critical and box officer disasters like *The Missouri Breaks* (1976), which failed despite the dream team of Jack Nicholson and Marlon Brando, and *Buffalo Bill and the Indians* (1976) despite Paul Newman. New directors breathing life into the genre included Robert Benton with *Bad Company* (1972) and Dick Richards with *The Culpepper Cattle Co.* (1972).

But the late 1970s, a decline set in, and from then on, westerns did not appear with the same frequency nor the same audience or critical approval. Nobody warmed to the idea of *Butch and Sundance: The Early Days* (1979) while Michael Cimino's budget-bloated *Heaven's Gate* (1980) buried United Artists. Clint Eastwood suffered a rare box office reverse with the modern western *Bronco Billy* (1980). Nonetheless, a handful of the new generation of actors and directors venerated the genre, most obviously Kevin Costner in *Silverado* (1985), his Oscar-winning and blockbusting *Dances with Wolves* (1990), *Tombstone* (1993), *Wyatt Earp* (1994) and *Open Range* (2003). The Brat Pack created renewed interest via such films as *Young Guns* (1988) and its sequel plus *Bad Girls* (1994) and *Texas Rangers* (2001). Just when you thought Clint Eastwood had forgotten about the genre that brought him international fame, he popped up with *Pale Rider* (1985) and *Unforgiven* (1992), for which he was named Best Director at the Oscars.

The new millennium has seen a variety of genre crossovers like the Eastern-Western *Shanghai Noon* (2000); the sci-fi westerns *Wild, Wild West* (1999) toplined by Will Smith and Kevin Kline and *Cowboys and Aliens* (2011) featuring Daniel Craig and Harrison Ford; and the horror western *Bone Tomahawk* (2015). New versions of old favorites included John Lee Hancock's *The Alamo* (2004) starring Dennis Quaid and Billy Bob Thornton, James Mangold's *3:10 to Yuma* (2007) with Russell Crowe and Christian Bale, the Coen Brothers' *True Grit* (2010) with Jeff Bridges as Rooster Cogburn, Antoine Fuqua's *The Magnificent Seven* (2016) with Denzel Washington and Chris Pratt, and Sofia Coppola's *The Beguiled* (2017) with Nicole Kidman and Kirsten Dunst. And let's not forget the outlandish reimagining of *The Lone Ranger* (2013) with Arnie Hammer and Johnny Depp. There was space for bold experiments such as Andrew Dominik's *The Assassination of Jesse James by the Coward Robert Ford* (2007) starring Brad Pitt and Quentin Tarantino's *The Hateful Eight* (2015) with Kurt Russell.

The Academy of Motion Picture Arts and Sciences has bestowed more Oscars on westerns, traditional and contemporary, since 2005 than in almost any other comparable period. Ang Lee was named Best Director for the modern western *Brokeback Mountain* (2005) while Heath Ledger was nominated for Best Actor. Two years later, *No Country for Old Men* (2007) and *There Will Be Blood* (2007) were in competition for the Best Picture gong, the former winning that category plus Best Director for the Coen Brothers, the latter taking home Best Actor for Daniel Day-Lewis. *True Grit* was nominated for Best Picture, the Coens for Best Director, Jeff Bridges for Best Actor and Hailee Steinfeld for Best Supporting Actress. Quentin Tarantino's *Django Unchained* (2012) was in contention for Best Picture and Christoph Waltz was named Best Supporting Actor. More recently, Alejandro Innaritu won Best Director for *The Revenant* (2015) and Leonardo DiCaprio Best Actor while the film was also nominated, along with Tom Hardy for Best

Supporting Actor. The contemporary western *Hell or High Water* (2016) was nominated in the categories of Best Picture and Best Supporting Actor (Jeff Bridges).

No single year hit pay dirt in the manner of 1969 which produced more westerns considered among the best movies ever made, two westerns in the top six in the annual box office rankings and a record number in the top 100. But there were still several good individual years. No doubt arguments will continue to rage over which year takes precedence for producing the best westerns, judged by both critical and audience approval. That 1969 was a year when old hands such as Henry Hathaway and newer ones like Sam Peckinpah, Sergio Leone, Andrew V. McLaglen and Burt Kennedy produced their best work, while genre newcomer George Roy Hill virtually single-handedly changed what audiences could expect from a western. It was a year when Hollywood recognized the value of the western screenplay, paying a record-breaking sum for *Butch Cassidy and the Sundance Kid.* And, at a time when the majors were crumbling under failed investments in big-budget musicals, westerns rode to the box office rescue. More westerns were honored in 1969 than in any other previous year. As importantly, the best westerns of 1969 have achieved more longer-lasting success, in terms of ongoing critical reappraisal, than in any other year.

Appendix A: City-by-City First Run Opening Dates

Film	*First Date*	*New York*	*Los Angeles*	*Baltimore*	*Boston*
The Stalking Moon	Jan-01	Jan-29	Jan-01	Jan-08	Feb-05
Hot Spur	Jan-22				Feb-05
Brand of Shame	Jan-15	Jan-15			
The Brute and the Beast	Jan-01				Feb-26
The Big Gundown	Feb-12				Jul-23
More Dead Than Alive	Feb-19			Feb-19	
Sam Whiskey	Feb-26	Jun-25	Mar-19		Apr-09
Ramrodder	Mar-05			Mar-05	Sep-03
Any Gun Can Play	Mar-12				
Payment in Blood	Mar-19			Mar-26	Mar-19
Support Your Local Sheriff	Apr-02		Apr-09	Apr-09	Apr-02
100 Rifles	Apr-02		Apr-02	Apr-16	Apr-16
Smith!	Apr-02		Apr-09	Apr-09	Apr-30
A Fistful of Dollars/For a Few Dollars More	Apr-16	Apr-30	May-07	Jun-04	May-07
Charro!	Apr-30	Sep-10			Apr-30
A Bullet for the General	Apr-30	May-07			
Death of a Gunfighhter	May-07	May-07		Jun-11	Jun-04
A Man Called Gannon	May-21				
Heaven with a Gun	May-21	Jun-18			Oct-29
God Forgives...I Don't	May-28			Jun-25	Sep-17
Once Upon a Time in the West	Jun-04	Jun-04		Aug-06	Jun-04
Guns of the Magnificent Seven	Jun-04	Jun-04	Aug-20	Jun-18	Jul-09
Mackenna's Gold	Jun-04	Jun-25	Jul-02	Jul-02	Jul-02
True Grit	Jun-18	Jul-09	Jun-18	Jul-02	Jun-25
Wild Bunch	Jun-25	Jul-02	Jun-25	Jul-23	Jul-02
Death Rides a Horse	Jul-02				Aug-20
The Great Bank Robbery	Jul-02	Sep-17	Aug-13	Jul-30	Jul-23
A Stranger in Town/The Stranger Returns	Aug-13		Sep-17		Oct-15
The Good, the Bad and the Ugly/ Hang 'Em High	Aug-27	Oct-15	Nov-05		Sep-10
Young Bily Young	Sep-24	Oct-22	Oct-22	Oct-29	Oct-15
Ace High	Oct-01	Oct-15			
Butch Cassidy and the Sundance Kid	Oct-01	Oct-01	Oct-08	Oct-08	Oct-08
Hombre	Oct-01				
The Good Guys and the Bad Guys	Oct-22	Nov-26		Nov-05	
Paint Your Wagon	Oct-22	Oct-22	Nov-05	Nov-05	Nov-05
The Undefeated	Nov-26		Nov-26	Dec-03	Dec-03
Desperadoes	Nov-26	Nov-26			
Day of Anger	Dec-10		Dec-10		
Tell Them Willie Boy Is Here	Dec-24	Dec-24			

Chicago	*Cleveland*	*Dayton*	*Denver*	*Detroit*	*Kansas City*	*Minneapolis*
Feb-12	Jan-22	Mar-12	Jan-08	Jan-08	Jan-01	
						Feb-05
		Jan-01				
		Feb-12		Sep-10		
					Feb-26	
Apr-30	Mar-26		Feb-26	May-28	Mar-26	
	Mar-12					
	Mar-19					
May-21	Apr-09	Apr-16	Apr-02	Apr-02	Apr-09	Apr-30
Apr-09	Apr-09		May-07	Apr-02	Apr-09	May-14
		Apr-16	Apr-09		Apr-30	May-21
Apr-16	Apr-30	Jun-04	Apr-23	May-07		May-21
		Jun-11	Oct-22	Jun-18		
May-07	Jun-04				Jun-11	
			Jun-04		May-21	
	Aug-13			Oct-29	May-21	
Jul-02				May-28		
Jun-04	Jun-04	Aug-06	Jun-04	Jul-23		Jun-18
		Jun-25	Jul-16	Jun-18	Jul-02	Aug-06
Jun-25		Aug-13	Jun-04	Jun-18	Jul-09	Jul-02
Jul-02	Aug-06	Jul-09	Jun-25	Jul-02	Jul-23	Jul-09
Jul-16	Jul-02	Jul-09	Jul-30	Jul-02	Jul-09	Jul-02
			Jul-02	Aug-06		Aug-06
		Aug-27	Aug-20	Aug-27	Jul-02	Jul-23
Oct-22		Oct-15		Aug-13		
Aug-27	Sep-24	Dec-17	Aug-27			Sep-03
		Oct-22	Sep-24		Sep-24	Oct-01
			Nov-12	Nov-05		Oct-01
Oct-15	Oct-08	Oct-15	Oct-08	Oct-15	Oct-08	Oct-08
		Nov-05	Nov-19		Oct-22	
Nov-05	Nov-19	Nov-26	Nov-05	Nov-12	Nov-19	Dec-17
Dec-03	Dec-03	Dec-03	Dec-03	Nov-26	Nov-26	Nov-12
						Nov-26

(Film)	*First Date*	*Philadelphia*	*Pittsburgh*	*Portland*
The Stalking Moon	Jan-01	Jan-01	Jan-22	Jan-01
Hot Spur	Jan-22			Jan-22
Brand of Shame	Jan-15			
The Brute and the Beast	Jan-01			
The Big Gundown	Feb-12			
More Dead than Alive	Feb-19			
Sam Whiskey	Feb-26	Mar-12	Mar-26	May-21
Ramrodder	Mar-05			
Any Gun Can Play	Mar-12			
Payment in Blood	Mar-19			
Support Your Local Sheriff	Apr-02	Apr-09	Apr-09	Apr-09
100 Rifles	Apr-02	Apr-02	Apr-09	
Smith!	Apr-02			Jun-25
A Fistful of Dollars/For a Few Dollars More May-07		Apr-16	May-21	Apr-30
Charro!	Apr-30			
A Bullet for General	Apr-30			Jun-11
Death of a Gunfighhter	May-07	May-21	May-21	Jul-02
A Man Called Gannon	May-21			Oct-01
Heaven with a Gun	May-21			
God Forgives...I Don't	May-28			
Once Upon a Time in the West	Jun-04	Jun-04	Jun-18	Jun-04
Guns of the Magnificent Seven	Jun-04	Jun-04		Jun-25
Mackenna's Gold	Jun-04	Jul-02	Jul-23	Jul-23
True Grit	Jun-18	Jun-18	Jun-25	Jul-02
Wild Bunch	Jun-25	Jul-02	Jul-09	
Death Rides a Horse	Jul-02			
The Great Bank Robbery	Jul-02	Aug-13	Aug-27	
A Stranger in Town/The Stranger Returns		Aug-13		Oct-01
The Good, the Bad and the Ugly/ Hang 'Em High	Aug-27	Sep-17		Sep-03
Young Bily Young	Sep-24			Sep-24
Ace High	Oct-01	Oct-29		Oct-15
Butch Cassidy and the Sundance Kid	Oct-01	Oct-08	Oct-08	Oct-08
Hombre	Oct-01			
The Good Guys and the Bad Guys	Oct-22	Nov-12	Nov-12	Oct-22
Paint Your Wagon	Oct-22	Nov-05	Nov-12	Nov-05
The Undefeated	Nov-26		Dec-03	Nov-26
Desperadoes	Nov-26			
Day of Anger	Dec-10	Nov-26		
Tell Them Willie Boy Is Here	Dec-24			

Providence	*San Francisco*	*Seattle*	*St. Louis*	*Washington*
Feb-05	Jan-08		Feb-05	
Jan-22				
			Apr-02	
Apr-02	Mar-26			Mar-26
				Apr-02
	Apr-23	Apr-09	Apr-09	
Apr-16	Apr-02		Apr-02	Apr-02
Apr-30	Apr-02		Apr-16	
May 21	May-21	May-07	May-07	
Apr-30				
				Apr-30
Jun-18	Oct-01			May-21
				Jun-18
Jun-18	Jun-25	Jun-04	Jun-18	Jun-04
Aug-06	Jun-18	Jun-18	Sep-17	Jun-11
Jul-02	Jul-02	Jul-09	Jul-02	
Jun-25	Jul-09	Jun-25		Jun-25
Jul-09	Jul-02	Jul-02	Jul-16	Jul-16
Aug-27				
Aug-06	Jul-02	Aug-13	Jul-16	Jul-30
Sep-03			Oct-22	Sep-24
Sep-03		Nov-05	Sep-03	Nov-12
Sep-24				
		Nov-12		
Oct-08	Oct-08	Oct-08	Oct-08	Oct-08
			Dec-10	Oct-01
Nov-12	Oct-22	Nov-19	Oct-15	Oct-22
	Nov-05	Nov-12	Nov-19	Nov-05
Nov-26	Nov-26	Dec-03	Nov-26	Nov-26

Note: These dates relate to when the box office figures were reported in *Variety*.

Appendix B: City-by-City First Run Box Office Earnings

Film	*New York*	*Los Angeles*	*Baltimore*
100 Rifles	$53,000		$30,000
Ace High	$13,000		
Any Gun Can Play			
The Big Gundown			
Brand of Shame	$4,700		
The Brute and the Beast			
A Bullet for the General	$73,000 - 23*		
Butch Cassidy and the Sundance Kid	$82,000 - 2	$42,000	$40,000 - 5
Charro!			
Day of Anger		$65,000 - 27	
Death of a Gunfighter	$23,500 - 2		$8,000
Death Rides a Horse	$34,000		$10,000
A Fisftul of Dollars/For a Few Dollars More	$39,000	$125,000 -23	$12,000
God Forgives ... I Don't			$6,000
The Good, the Bad and the Ugly/Hang 'Em High			
The Good Guys and the Bad Guys			$7,000 - 5
The Great Bank Robbery	$125,000 - 37	$175,000 -24	$11,000
Guns of the Magnificent Seven	$33,600	$130,000 - 26	$10,000
Heaven with a Gun			
Hombre reissue			
Hot Spur	$8,000		
Mackenna's Gold	$67,000 - 2	$27,000	$20,000 - 5
A Man Called Gannon			
More Dead Than Alive			$8,000
Once Upon a Time in the West	$68,000 - 2		$20,000 - 4
Paint Your Wagon		$42,000	$10,000
Payment in Blood			$17,500 - 5
The Ramrodder			$8,500
Sam Whiskey			
Smith!		$116,000 - 25	$15,000 - 3
The Stalking Moon	$59,000 - 2	$35,000	
A Stranger in Town/The Stranger Returns			
Support Your Local Sheriff		$82,000 - 23	$35,000 - 5
Tell Them Willie Boy Is Here	$16,000		
True Grit		$36,000	
The Undefeated			$37,000 - 4
Wild Bunch	$48,000 - 2	$39,000	$15,000 - 2
Young Billy Young			$6,000

*The number after the $ figure shows the number of theaters where the movie played. A movie playing in 8-12 theaters was one that went straight into showcase (wide) release

Boston	*Chicago*	*Cleveland*	*Dayton*	*Denver*	*Detroit*	*Kansas City*
$27,500	$72,000	$12,000		$18,000 - 3	$36,000	$13,000 - 3
			$17,500	$10,500		
$6,000		$5,800				
$8,000			$14,000 - 5			
$8,000			$3,000 - 3			
$34,000	$50,000	$17,500	$10,500	$23,000	$28,000 - 2	$14,000 - 2
$7,000			$51,400 - 7	$12,000	$110,000 - 8	
$17,000	$37,000	$7,000				$20,000 - 5
$13,500	$29,000	$9,000		$10,000	$23,000	
$8,500	$58,000	$14,500 - 2	$4,100	$18,000	$13,000	
$7,500	$20,000	$6,000			$25,000	
$3,000	$51,000	$11,000		$20,000		
		$3,400			$46,000 - 16	
$16,000			$16,000 - 3	$9,000	$30,000 - 4	$7,000 - 2
		$4,900	$13,000	$11,000	$25,000 - 7	
$4,000					$20,000	$12,000 - 4
$6,700						
$20,000	$48,000		$5,100	$17,000	$65,000 - 6	
		$19,200 - 7			$28,000 - 10	
					$13,000 - 6	
$17,200	$38,000	$9,000 - 2	$24,000 - 6	$20,000 - 2	$19,000	
$15,000		$10,5000	$14,500	$16,000	$30,000	$16,000
$6,000		$7,500				
$6,000						
$7,000	$22,000	$8,000 - 2		$13,000	$35,000 - 5	$5,000
$9,000			$24,500 - 7	$30,000 - 11		$24,000 - 12
$15,000	$36,000	$24,900 - 4			$6,500	$17,000 - 3
$6,500	$25,000		$2,900		$50,000	
$18,500	$30,000	$15,500 - 3	$5,300 - 2	$15,000	$6,500	$12,000
$18,000	$48,000	$23,500 - 2	$1,800	$20,000	$32,000 - 2	$28,000
$15,000	$50,000	$14,500 - 2	$7,800 - 2	$21,500	$7,000	$20,000
$30,000	$65,000		$23,800 - 6	$22,000	$58,000 - 7	
$4,000		$4,000	$2,400	$8,000		$6,500

(Film)	*Kansas City*	*Minneapolis*	*Philadelphia*
100 Rifles	$13,000 - 3	$12,000	$31,000
Ace High		$6,000	$4,500
Any Gun Can Play			
The Big Gundown			
Brand of Shame			
The Brute and the Beast			
A Bullet for the General			
Butch Cassidy and the Sundance Kid	$14,000 - 2	$19,000	$28,000
Charro!			
Day of Anger	$20,000 - 5		
Death of a Gunfighter		$10,000	
Death Rides a Horse		$5,000	
A Fisftul of Dollars/For a Few Dollars More		$12,000	$24,000
God Forgives ... I Don't			
The Good, the Bad and the Ugly/Hang 'Em High		$14,000	$17,000
The Good Guys and the Bad Guys	$7,000 - 2	$17,000 - 7	$12,000
The Great Bank Robbery		$7,000	
Guns of the Magnificent Seven	$12,000 - 4	$10,500	$24,000
Heaven with a Gun			
Hombre reissue			
Hot Spur			
Mackenna's Gold		$10,500	$19,000
A Man Called Gannon			
More Dead Than Alive			
Once Upon a Time in the West	$16,000	$26,000 - 4	$12,000
Paint Your Wagon		$13,000	$19,000
Payment in Blood			
The Ramrodder	$5,000		
Sam Whiskey	$24,000 - 12	$15,000 - 3	$8,000
Smith!	$17,000 - 3	$13,000 - 6	
The Stalking Moon		$12,000	$20,000
A Stranger in Town/The Stranger Returns	$12,000		
Support Your Local Sheriff		$15,000	$32,000 - 2
Tell Them Willie Boy Is Here	$28,000		
True Grit	$20,000	$21.000	
The Undefeated		$13,000	
Wild Bunch	$6,500	$11,000	
Young Billy Young		$8,000	

Pittsburgh	Portland	Providence	San Fran	Seattle	St Louis	Washington
18,000	$10,000	$3,500			$29,000 - 2	$17,000
	$3,800			$4,000		
			$2,100			
	$2,500					$4,000
$14,000	$7,500	$17,000 - 2	$31,000 - 2	$16,000	$52,000 - 4	$11,000
	$2,000	$6,000				
$11,000	$4,000	$3,500	$5,000 - 2			$8,000
	$5,000	$3,000	$15,000 - 3	46,000		$14,000
$10,000	$8,000	$5,000		$15,000	$23,000 - 3	$24,000
6,800	$5,100	$6,500	$6,000 - 2	$7,000	$22,000 - 3	$15,000
$6,000	$8,000	$5,000	$10,000	$5,500	$5,000	$7,500
$9,000	$5,700 - 2	$6,500		$12,000	$5,500	
	$7,500	$9,000	$17,000- 2	$7,000	$4,500	$14,000
	$3,000					$4,500
			$5,000	$2,000		
	$8,000					
$10,000	$4,500	$6,000	$18,000		$16,000 - 2	$15,000
	$5,000					
$4,000	$8,000	$2,200	$15,000 - 2	$11,600	$15,000 - 2	$12,000
$8,000	$15,000	$12,000	$14,000	$16,000		
	$20,000 - 3					
$6,500	$5,500	$5,000	$8,000		$4,500	$12,000
	$3,000	$4,000	$9,000 - 3		$10,000 - 4	
	$9,000			$9,000	$25,000 - 2	
	$5,000	$7,500			$7,000	$8,000
$10,000	$10,000		$16,000	$15,000	$29,000 - 2	$16,000
$7,500	$4,100	$5,800	$6,500	$12,000		$11,500
$8,000	$6,500	$4,000	$19,500	$12,400	$20,000 - 2	$12,000
	$7,700	$3,000 - 2	$23,000 - 4	$12,000	$25,000 - 3	$24,500
	$3,400	$8,500				

Appendix C: Annual Rankings of Westerns at the Box Office, 1960–1969

1960—*The Unforgiven* (20)*; *The Magnificent Seven* (38)

1961—*The Alamo* (5); *North to Alaska* (13); *One Eyed Jacks* (16); *The Misfits* (19); *Cimarron* (30); *The Last Sunset* (35); *Flaming Star* (45); *Two Rode Together* (55)

1962—*Sergeants 3* (17); *The Man Who Shot Liberty Valance* (27); *Merrill's Marauders* (50)

1963—*How the West Was Won* (5); *McLintock* (10); *Hud* (20); *Savage Sam* (35)

1964—*Rio Conchos* (30); *Mail Order Bride* (53); *A Distant Trumpet* (54)

1965—*Shenandoah* (7), *Cat Ballou* (13); *The Sons of Katie Elder* (15); *Cheyenne Autumn* (31); *The Outrage* (49); *The Rounders* (62); *The Hallelujah Trail* (70); *Old Yeller* (70)

1966—*Nevada Smith* (16); *Texas Across the River* (20); *Stagecoach* (27); *The Professionals* (29); *The Rare Breed* (50); *Return of the Seven* (62); *Alvarez Kelly* (67); *The Appaloosa* (75); *Viva Maria* (75)

1967—*Hombre* (10); *El Dorado* (13); *The War Wagon* (15), *For a Few Dollars More* (40); *A Fistful of Dollars* (46); *Waterhole 3* (50); *The Way West* (55); *Duel At Diablo* (57)

1968—*Bandolero!* (18); *Hang 'Em High* (20); *The Good, the Bad and the Ugly* (24); *5 Card Stud* (31); *The Scalphunters* (42); *Waterhole 3* (44); *Will Penny* (54); *The Shakiest Gun in the West* (56); *A Stranger in Town* (60); *Villa Rides* (74); *Firecreek* (76); *Shalako* (85)

1969—*Butch Cassidy and the Sundance Kid* (4); *True Grit* (6); *Support Your Local Sheriff* (20); *The Undefeated* (21); *The Wild Bunch* (23); *100 Rifles* (27); *Mackenna's Gold* (31); *The Stalking Moon* (38); *Paint Your Wagon* (45); *Once Upon a Time in the West* (47); *Charro* (68); *Return of the Seven* (reissue) (70); *A Fistful of Dollars* (reissue) (75)

Note: *Waterhole 3* did appear in successive years on the chart.
Source: *Variety* Annual Rentals Charts 1960–1969.

*Numbers in parentheses indicate position in the annual rankings chart.

Chapter Notes

Introduction

1. This was shown in France in December 1968 but not released in the USA until 1969 so it qualifies as a 1969 western because the whole concept behind the book is watching the films as they appeared in the American theaters.

2. Box office figures for the years before this are not available.

3. "National and Genre Top 10s," *Sight & Sound*, September 2012, 60.

4. "Directors Poll," *Sight & Sound*, September 2012, 62–71. These figures are based on my own calculations as there were no genre breakdown within the votes of the directors.

5. "AFI 10 Top 10s—Westerns," https://www.afi.com/10top10/category.aspx?cat=3.

6. "Greatest Westerns," AMC Filmsite, https://www.filmsite.org/greatwesterns.html.

7. "*Empire* Magazine's 500 Greatest Movies of All Time," dhttps://www.listchallenges.com/empire-magazines-500-greatest-films-of-all-time.

8. "Onassis Involved in MGM Takeover?" *International Motion Picture Exhibitor*, November 26, 1969, 3.

9. "Metro's Annual Report Discloses $35,666,000 Loss Vs. $9,409,000 Profit in '68; Aubrey's Stringent Economies," *Variety*, December 17, 1969, 3.

10. "*Tai Pan* Budget Now $10,000,000," *Variety*, August 6, 1969, 7. The original budget for the adaptation of the James Clavell bestseller had been $25 million. In the end it was canned. MGM was spending (so far) a reported $9.2 million on *Ryan's Daughter* (newspapers claimed it was more) and had already spent $9 million on *Ice Station Zebra*, $6.7 million on *The Shoes of the Fisherman* and $6 million on *Where Eagles Dare*—none of which returned a profit in domestic rentals.

11. "Okayed to Proceed in Production; Nat Gen Plans 12 Features," *Variety*, April 30, 1969, 4. *El Condor* was planned as a roadshow but that failed to materialize. *The French Connection* and *The Valdez Horses* were dropped only to be later picked up by Twentieth Century Fox and United Artists, respectively.

12. "Projects Scratched at Warners," *Variety*, October 29, 6. These included a musical about Shakespeare, *The Bawdy Bard*; two planned for Sam Peckinpah—*Diamond Story* and *North to Yesterday*; Sidney Lumet directing *99 and 44/100 Dead* (made in 1974 by John Frankenheimer with Richard Harris); *The Apple Tree* based on the John Galsworthy novel; *Heart of Darkness*; Mae West in *Sextet* (Ken Hughes directed this in 1978 as *Sextette*); and *Napoleon and Josephine* directed by Bryan Forbes. These were added to the previously shelved *The Well of Loneliness*, *The Frontiersman* and a musical version of *Tom Sawyer* (made by *Reader's Digest* in 1973).

13. "Merger Expenses on W7 and Kinney Reach $11,500,000," *Variety*, June 4, 1969, 3.

14. "Fox's Rental Comparatives," *Variety*, June 4, 1969, 3. The first quarter of 1969 was down nearly $10 million on the 1968 figure of $33.5million.

15. "Disney Sci Fi Feature Heading $33,000,000 Prod. Schedule," *Variety*, September 17, 1969, 17. *The Boatniks* and *The Aristocats* appeared in 1970. *The Newcomers* aka *The Wild Country*, *Bedknobs and Broomsticks* and *Scandalous John* showed up in 1971, but only half the planned budget was spent, with Jules Verne $6 million sci-fi *Lost Ones* and a $5.5 million western *Paniola* scrapped.

16. "Monaco's Sad Europe Figure Data," *Variety*, March 26, 1969, 19; "U.S. Fall Off," *Variety*, February 26, 1969, 4. A decade previously nearly three-quarters of the Top Ten movies in Italy originated from Hollywood, but now the position was reversed. Spain had an import quota and in Germany moviegoers preferred sex documentaries like *Helga*.

17. "Big Budget Bust Up," *Variety*, July 23, 1969, 3. All the studios had trimmed budgets, where 1968 had four $10 million pictures going into production, 1969 had only one.

18. "Court Hears NATO'S Case Vs Pay-TV," *International Motion Picture Exhibitor*, June 11, 1969, 5. NATO was the National Association of Theater Owners.

19. "Building Bridges of Understanding," *International Motion Picture Exhibitor*, November 20, 1968, 6–7. Exhibitors and church representatives met to discuss the place of movies in a time of social change.

20. "Sexless Cowboy of U.S. Westerns Goes to Boudoir," *Variety*, May 7, 1969, 35.

21. "Generally Favorable Reaction Greets Industry's Film Rating System," *International Motion Picture Exhibitor*, October 30, 1968, 3. The ratings system took effect from November 1, 1968. The "favorable reaction" was from exhibitors not the public. Some films were caught up in ratings controversies, most notably *Midnight Cowboy* (1969) which was the first movie from a major studio to be released with an "X" rating, and was a box office hit, but Robert Aldrich complained that confusion among the public about the new system damaged the box office for *The Killing of Sister George* (1968).

22. "Youth Slated Product Paces Summer," *Variety*, August 8, 1969, 8.

23. "Joe Solomon's Motorcycle Sagas," *Variety*, April

23, 1969, 19. *Hell's Angels on Wheels* had cost $210,000 and worldwide gross (not rental) was at $3 million, *Angels from Hell* costing $310,000 had generated $1.5 million gross.

24. "Universal Bathes in Youth Fountain," *Variety*, December 10, 1969, 3. It had three movies lined up: *Puzzle of a Downfall Child* starring Faye Dunaway, *Diary of a Mad Housewife* with Carrie Snodgrass and Dennis Hopper's *The Last Movie* which would, in the end, kill off any profits from the first two; "Taking Note of Youth-Slanted Clicks of Others, Fox Eager About Five Newbies," *Variety*, August 13, 1969, 6. These five movies were budgeted at a total of $4 million.

25. "Western Cycle Rolls Again," *Variety*, June 25, 1969, 5. "Circuit bookers are waiting with some wonder in light of alleged evidence that the younger crowd finds older oater stuff dated."

26. "Oaters Class and/or Parody, Future Aside, Fox Plots 400 Wayne Prints for Regional Saturation," *Variety*, November 5, 1969, 5.

27. Review, *International Motion Picture Exhibitor*, June 25, 1969, 8.

28. "Old Wine in New Bottles," *International Motion Picture Exhibitor*, July 16, 1969, 6.

29. Including the five major reissues examined in chapter 15.

30. Weekly box office is always reported in grosses rather than rentals. The gross is the amount of money earned at a particular theater in any given week before the money is divided up between exhibitor and studio.

31. Annual box office is always represented as rentals rather than grosses. Rentals represent the amount of money a studio receives back from its share of the gross taken at an individual theater.

Chapter 1

1. The film was shown in two theaters in December 1968 in a bid to win Oscar nominations, but NGC always planned for the movie to have a 1969 release.

2. Cook, David A., *Lost Illusions: American Cinema in the Shadow of Watergate and Vietnam, 1970–1979* (Berkeley: University of California Press, 2000), 400.

3. "National General Earnings Up 31 Percent," *Variety*, December 18, 1963, 11.

4. Hefferman, Kevin, *Ghouls, Gimmicks and Gold: Horror Films and the American Movie Business* (Durham: Duke University Press: 2004), 72.

5. "See Three-Year OK for Nat'l General to Produce and Distribute Films Under Trust Decree Modification," *Variety*, June 19, 1963, 3.

6. "National Circuit (217 Theaters) Readying to Produce Features," *Variety*, March 4, 1964, 5. *The Girl in the Turquoise Bikini* was also mooted, but never made.

7. "Nat'l General Producing Features Shuns Hazards of Live Concerts," *Variety*, Jun 30, 1964, 20. NGC dropped its live concert business.

8. "Carthay (Nat'l General) in 3-Film Deal with Fielder Cook's Eden Prods," *Variety*, July 28, 1965, 3.

9. "1st Feature Rolls Under Eady Plan for Carthay" (Nat'l General-Rank), *Variety*, October 20, 1965, 7. The picture would be a joint production with British company rank, which offered instant distribution in Britain. The other pictures covered in the announcement were: *Divorce-American Style*, *What Are Little Girls Made of* and *John Henry Goes to New York* (All Under the Tandem Aegis); Plus *Flight and Pursuit* and *Careful, They're Our Allies* from Charles K. Peck Films.

10. There was no great initial interest in the picture from distributors and it sat on the shelf until June 1967 when it was distributed by Columbia. It was a surprise hit at the box office, ranking 17th on the annual chart with $5.1 million in rentals—above in *Like Flint* and just below the John Wayne pair *El Dorado* and the *War Wagon*.

11. "NGC'S $10m Loan," *Variety*, January 12, 1966, 21. Half the money was going towards expanding the company's theater empire with the aim of adding another 100 houses to the chain.

12. "Greg Peck and His Corporate Shadow Comprise Nat'l General's 3d Feature," *Variety*, January 22, 1966, 5.

13. *Ibid.*

14. *A Dream of Kings* was the seventh.

15. "Circuit's Prod'n Arm Acquires 8th Story with Olsen's *Stalking Moon*," *Variety*, December 8, 1965, 11.

16. "Greg Peck and His," *Variety*, January 22, 1966, 5. To accommodate the picture, *What Are Little Girls Made of* was "temporarily" shelved, though it ended up never being made, and plans to make *John Henry Goes to New York* were dropped.

17. "Wendell Mayes *Hotel* Then *Stalking Moon*," *Variety*, Apr 13, 1966, 17. He was hired as writer-producer.

18. By the time the movie appeared, Brentwood was no longer involved.

19. "George Stevens to U for 3 Features," *Variety*, November 16, 1966, 11. In order to fulfill this deal, Universal had to become involved in *The Stalking Moon*.

20. "George Stevens to U"; "Doubling Starts, 'U Lines Up 19,'" *Variety*, January 8, 1967, 22. Universal planned to make 19 movies between January and May 1967 including *The Stalking Moon*. Incidentally, *The Green Berets* also formed part of this schedule but was later filmed at Warner Brothers.

21. "Inside Stuff—Pictures," *Variety*, March 29, 1967, 21.

22. *Ibid.*

23. "Nat'l Gen'l Prod, Again Party to Peck's *Moon* Which U Will Release," *Variety*, April 5, 1967, 15.

24. "16 of U's 24 in '67 Get Shooting Dates," *Variety*, February 1, 1967, 28.

25. "Nat'l Gen'l Again Party."

26. "Off-&-Ballyhooing at NGC," *Variety*, November 27, 1967, 3.

27. "NGC Pleas for Tenure in Its Film Production Calculations," *Variety*, February 19, 1969, 15. The company had been given a three-year extension in 1966 to the original deal.

28. Cook, *Lost Illusions*, 331.

29. "National's Chain: 263," *Variety*, May 27, 1968, 7.

30. Cook, *Lost Illusions*, 331–332. NGC won its case. The Pacific Coast Theater circuit had taken over Cinerama in 1963. ABC had 418 theaters, the largest in the country, and set up Circle Films. In 1967 Cinerama Releasing Corporation was established to distribute the films of both Cinerama and ABC Circle and, in fact, had been, at least in terms of output, more prolific than NGC, releases comprising *Custer of the West* (1967), *Hell in the Pacific* (1968), *Charly* (1968), *The Killing of Sister George* (1968), *They Shoot Horses, Don't They* (1969) and *Krakatoa East of Java* (1969). ABC Circle closed down in 1973 despite registering its biggest-ever hit *Cabaret* in 1972. In fact, most CRC releases were flops.

31. "NGC, WB-7 Merger Plans Unveiled; Industry Waiting for Details," *International Motion Picture Exhibitor*, August 21, 1968, 5; "NGC Will Tailor Deal to Fit Merger with WB," *Variety*, December 25, 1968, 3.

32. "Drop Carthay Center Tag for NGC Films," *Variety*, May 25, 1966, 13.

33. "NG Not Up to Intended Pic Per Month Release Rate for '68," *Variety*, March 20, 1968, 214. *Poor Cow*, *Twisted Nerve*, and *All Neat in Black Stockings* were British; *How Sweet It Is* was made by Cinema Center; *With Six You Get Eggroll* by Doris Day's production company; and *A Quiet Place in the Country* was Italian. And none boasted stars of the Gregory Peck caliber.

34. Peck also won a David as Best Foreign Actor in the Italian film awards and the film received a Special Award at the Cannes Film Festival.

35. The Production Code demanded the word "rape" be excised from the finished film and other changes made to the script. British censors demanded a total of 161 cuts, provoking co-star Polly Bergen to complain there was no point in her promoting the film in the UK since she was now hardly in it. The star was not perturbed. "An adult audience will understand the theme," he said.

36. "Box Office," *Variety*.

37. Hannan, Brian, *The Making of the Guns of Navarone* (Glasgow: Baroliant Press, 2015).

38. "Peck for Cinerama," *Variety*, February 19, 1964, 6; "Colony on Mars as U's Top Costing Feature to Date," *Variety*, July 22, 1964, 3; Hannan, Brian, *The Making of the Guns of Navarone* (Glasgow: Baroliant Press, 2015). With a budget of $10 million-plus, this would have been Universal's biggest-ever film.

39. "Walter Wanger's Return to Producer Activity," *Variety*, April 19, 1964, 4. Wanger and Peck had jointly bought the rights to the Burke Wilkinson book.

40. "Metro's 27 Finished Features Give It Exceptionally Long Market Slotting," *Variety*, Jun 16, 1965, 5; *Variety*, April 28, 1965, 17. There was no heading on this story. The picture was being scheduled for a summer 1966 release.

41. "Aussie Film Cameras to Turn Again This Month After Lengthy Layoff," *Variety*, October 13, 1965, 28. Michael Powell now held the directorial reins.

42. "Virna Lisi Signatured to Star in Germi's New Pic but Sans Glamour," *Variety*, July 7, 1965, 22. This was an old project. Peck had first been associated with it in 1950.

43. "Swiss Dewdrops O.O. the *Bells of Hell*," *Variety*, August 10, 1966, 7; "Mirisch's Bells Won't Peal Till 1967," *Variety*, August 24, 1966, 22. A total of 12 minutes were completed before filming ended. Peck played a British Army colonel charged in World War One of leading a team to ferry aircraft parts across Switzerland to Lake Constance and then reassemble them to bomb a Zeppelin base. Ian McKellen (*Lord of the Rings*), making his movie debut, began to correct Peck's American pronunciation of "lieutenant" only to be told by director David Miller that Peck could pronounce it any way he liked because "Britain was only five percent of the world market."

44. "After Navarone," *Variety*, April 19, 1967, 9. The sequel would reunite stars Peck, David Niven and Anthony Quinn with director J. Lee Thompson and was considered a possibility for the Cinerama treatment.

45. "Cinerama Rolls 1st Int'l Sales Meet in Link with London Bow of Custer," *Variety*, November 8, 1967, 2; "Cinerama Revs Up," *Variety*, December 6, 1967, 18.

46. Peck spent the downtime working for charity, work that was recognized when he was presented with the Jean Hersholt Humanitarian Academy Award in 1968.

47. "Peck in Africa," *Variety*, January 25, 1967, 27.

48. Advert, *Years of Lightning, Day of Drums*, *Variety*, April 19, 1967, 42.

49. Beaupre, Lee, "Today's Independent Actor," *Variety*, Jul 17, 1968, 3.

50. Published in 1965.

51. There are other parallels. Heston's career at this point was in as much of a downward spiral as that of Gregory Peck, having been in a string of flops—*Major Dundee* (1965), *The Agony and the Ecstasy* (1965), *The War Lord* (1965), and *Khartoum* (1966). The picture had a meager $1.8 million budget. Gries, who had written the screenplay, would only agree to sell it if he was allowed to direct.

52. *International Motion Picture Exhibitor*, December 18, 1968, 6; *Variety*, December 18, 1968, 26.

53. These reviews were culled from an advert promoting the film, *International Motion Picture* Exhibitor, Dec 25, 1968, 17.

54. Review, *The Showmen's Servisection*, November 19, 1969, 2.

55. *Chicago Sun Times*, February 11, 1969; *New York Times*, January 23, 1969.

56. I make no bones about including *The Stalking Moon* in this book of 1969 films since, as I have mentioned, were I a normal moviegoer, I would have in all probability only been able to see it in 1969 and also since the Xmas 1968 showings were an anomaly, simply fitted in for Oscar-nomination reasons when the movie had always been intended as a 1969 picture.

57. "Year's Surprise: Family Films Did Best," *Variety*, January 7, 1970, 15.

58. "Paris First Runs: Recent Months, '68–'69 Estimate," *Variety*, April 29, 1970, 76; "Swiss Pix May Top '68 Biz," *Variety*, January 7, 1970, 112.

Chapter 2

1. "Valenti's 36 Story Suggestions," *Variety*, February 5, 1969, 7. More African-American involvement was in the top five suggestions on his list.

2. "More Negro Actors in Big Films and Not Just Dixie or Riot Themes," *Variety*, July 24, 1968. 1.

3. He had small roles in both *Shalako* and *Once Upon a Time in the West*.

4. Gene Hackman was the co-star in both *The Split* and *Riot*. The movie's world premiere took place in a prison.

5. "Italo Hoss Opera Not on Sunset Trail," *Variety*, May 8, 1968, 44.

6. "Jim Brown Touts Films, 'Civil War Easily Avoidable," *Variety*, Oct 16, 1968, 4; "Jim Brown Sees Sidney Poitier Wise to Survival in Whitey's Biz," *Variety*, Dec 4, 1968, 2; "Jim Brown's Credo," *Variety*, March 26, 1969, 102.

7. "Unknowns Vs. Stars," *Variety*, January 8, 1969, 18. Other new stars for the year were Jacqueline Bisset, Dustin Hoffman, Mia Farrow, Vanessa Redgrave, Anne Heywood, Alan Arkin and Maggie Smith. It's not often these kind of predictions come true, but, in this case, *Variety* proved spot-on.

8. Solomon, Aubrey, *Twentieth Century Fox, a Corporate and Financial History* (Lanham, MD: Scarecrow Press, 2002,), 255. By contrast, *Bandolero*, with more established stars in James Stewart and Dean Martin had cost $4.45 million.

9. "Sex Goddess Is Human After All," *Los Angeles Times*, June 9, 1968, c12.

10. "Big Rental Films of 1968," *Variety*, January 8, 1969.

11. Huffaker's novels were: *Badge for a Gunfighter*

(1957), *Rider from Thunder Mountain* (1957), Cowboy (1958)—a novelization of the movie starring Glenn Ford, *Flaming Lance* (1958), *Posse from Hell* (1958), *Guns of Rio Conchos* (1958), *Badman* (1958), *Seven Ways from Sundown* (1959), *Good Lord, You're Upside Down* (1963), *Nobody Loves a Drunken Indian* (1967), and *The Cowboy and the Cossack* (1973). In addition, he published an autobiography *One Time I Saw Morning Come Home* (1974) and *Clair Huffaker's Profiles of the American West* (1976).

12. The novel was called *Flaming Lance.*

13. The novel was called *The Guns of Rio Conchos.*

14. MacLeod was a landscape artist and drew for the cowboy comic *Red Ryder and Little Beaver.* He wrote 10 western novels in all. The only other one filmed was *Appaloosa* (1966) starring Marlon Brando.

15. "Huffaker's New Case of Producer, Director Ignoring Writer," *Variety*, February 12, 1969, 17. In the event, Huffaker's name went on the credit.

16. "English Track—Filming in Spain," *Variety*, May 8, 1968, 157. Westerns scheduled to be shot in Spain in 1968 included *Shalako, Guns of the Magnificent Seven, Winchester Hill, Desperados* (then called *Marauders*), *Once Upon a Time in the West* and *Red Sun.* War films included *Play Dirty* and The *Battle of Britain.* Other films included *The Adventurers* and *A Talent for Loving.*

17. *Ibid.* There were now 70 pesetas to the dollar instead of 60. This was more important for British productions shooting in Spain because of the instability at this period of sterling.

18. "Spain's Realism Re Export," *Variety*, March 20, 1968, 20. The number of movies shot in 1967 had been a record 129 compared with 39 fewer lined up for 1968.

19. "Raquel on Cutting Floor," *Variety*, April 9, 1969, 30. Tom Gries retaliated that, although this has occurred, the scenes had not been cut by him.

20. "Raquel and Jim Brown," *Variety*, February 19, 1969, 30.

21. Solomon, *Twentieth Century Fox,* 162.

22. *Ibid.*, 255.

23. *Ibid.*, 231.

24. MacLeod, Robert, *The Californio* (London: Coronet Books, 1968), 58. When Yaqui Joe gives Steve a gun, he recoils, "Joe, I wouldn't know what to do with one of those" (52).

25. In the book, Maria returns home with Steve. She is pregnant, but Steve is unsure whether the child is hers, or her husband's or the result of her being raped. To complicate matters, he has a fiancée at home. We never find out if Steve is the father because Maria leaves before giving birth, disgusted at the way she is treated.

26. Anthony Quinn in *The Guns of Navarone* wore a red neckerchief so that he would stand out in scenes which contained multiple characters.

27. The sex scene was more likely to result in a ban, as occurred in Chicopee, Massachusetts ("Chicopee Bans *Rifles*," *Variety*, June 11, 1969, 44.) However, vice-president Spiro Agnew attended the Washington world premiere which benefited the Black Economic Union of which Jim Brown was president.

28. Review, *The Showmen's Servisection,* November 19, 1969, 3.

29. *Variety*, March 12, 1969, 6; *Chicago Sun-Times*, April 8, 1969; *New York Times*, March 27, 1969.

Chapter 3

1. It was originally known as *The Sheriff.*

2. Many of these were big hits. *The Paleface* ranked 13th, *Son of Paleface* 8th, and *Sergeants 3* 16th in their respective years.

3. Marlene Dietrich was the star of *Destry Rides Again*, directed by George Marshall. Hollywood veteran Raoul Walsh took charge of *The Sheriff of Fractured Jaw* which was filmed in Spain.

4. Steinberg, Cobbett, *Reel Facts, Revised Edition* (London: Penguin, 1981) 434–442. I have done the computation.

5. *Ibid.*

6. Unusually for the screenwriter, William Bowers' face is well-know to most moviegoers since he played the role of the Senate committee chairman in *The Godfather Part II* (1974).

7. "After 60 Screenplays, Bill Bowers a Producer for United Artists," *Variety,* May 22, 1968, 4.

8. First of all, apparently, Garner took it to Hilary Productions, which claimed it had made a deal with the actor in 1967 and promptly sued when it discovered Garner had also done a deal with United Artists ("Hilary Suit Alleges Bowers and Garner 'Dumped' Deal-Maker," *Variety*, August 20, 1969, 7).

9. *The Great Escape* was 13th and *Grand Prix* 7th in their respective years.

10. "Rising Skepticism on Stars," *Variety*, May 15, 1968, 78.

11. *Ibid.* Garner had to set up a meeting with MGM executives to plead his case, a humiliating exercise for a supposed star, for *The Little Sister* and the veto was overruled.

12. *Ibid.* The misjudged roles in question were deemed to be an amnesiac in *36 Hours* and *Mister Buddwing.*

13. "Review, *A Man Could Get Killed*," *Variety*, March 14, 1966, 6. Equally, he often came under criticism for his performance in comedies: "Garner plays like a romantic leading man who shouldn't be doing satire" ("Review, the *Art of Love*," *Variety*, May 12, 1965, 6). The trade paper had not always been so harsh on the actor. He was judged to "acquit himself handsomely" in *Duel at Diablo* ("Review," *Variety*, May 18, 1966, 6).

14. "Review, *Mister Buddwing*," *Variety*, September 14, 1966, 6.

15. "Garner's 150g for *Great Escape*," *Variety*, May 9, 1962, 19. However, other studios were unwilling to pay him what he thought he was due. When he demanded $200,000 for *Something's Gotta Give*, Twentieth Century Fox dropped him ("Garner as Lead Paid Higher Than Marilyn on Her Last Pic for Fox" *Variety*, February 7, 1962, 2). Monroe's unfortunate death meant the film was never made. Incidentally, his performance in *The Great Escape* was considered "his best screen work to date" (Review, *Variety*, April 17, 1963, 6).

16. "Promo Credo of Hollywood Actor," *Variety*, November 4, 1965, 15.

17. *Trapeze* was the most successful, finishing third in the annual rankings. By deferring his own salary, Lancaster was able to afford strong co-stars, Gary Cooper in *Vera Cruz*, Tony Curtis in *Trapeze* and *The Sweet Smell of Success*, Clark Gable in *Run Silent, Run Deep* and Audrey Hepburn in *The Unforgiven.*

18. It was Douglas in his role as producer who fired Stanley Kubrick from the project.

19. There were many instances of a star making films in which he was not the leading actor. Batjac films that did not star John Wayne included *Track of the Cat* (1954) with Robert Mitchum and *Goodbye, My Lady* (1956) and it also produced the television series *Hondo* (1967). Hecht-Hill-Lancaster had also produced *Marty* (1955),

The Bachelor Party (1957) and *The Rabbit Trap* (1959) Jack Lemmon's company Jalem Productions set up *Cool Hand Luke* (1967) starring Paul Newman. Kirk Douglas was involved in *Grand Prix*.

20. 'Break-even' was notoriously difficult to calculate and usually weighted heavily in favor of the studio, which tended to load up a production with all sorts of overhead and additional costs. But James Stewart had been one of the first to benefit from this method of making pictures, when he deferred his salary for *Bend of the River* for Universal, and went to recoup his biggest-ever salary.

21. "WB'S Suspension of Garner Triggers Suits and Counter Suits," *Variety*, April 20, 1960, 127; "Court to Release James Garner from Exclusive WB Pact; Token Damages," *Variety*, December 14, 1960, 22; "Echo of Strike: WB'S Appeal on James Garner," *Variety*, January 18, 1961, 25. The writer's strike of 1960 meant that Warner Brothers had run out of scripts for *Maverick* and so took Garner off the payroll. His objections were the basis of the court case, but there was a strong suspicion that he invoked the legal proceedings to force the cancellation of his long-term contract. He was also, at this time, heavily involved in the Screen Actors Guild, which had launched an Actor's Strike, causing production in Hollywood to shut down, as a result of which some films were permanently shelved.

22. "TV'S $1-Mil-a-Year Stars," *Variety*, August 10, 1966, 1.

23. "James Garner Moves from Actor Towards Future Producer Status," *Variety*, October 5, 1966, 5; "James Garner's Own Plot: Performer-to-Producer," *Variety*, November 1, 1967, 18.

24. "Promo Credo of Hollywood Actor," *Variety*, November 4, 1964, 15.

25. These traits had been attributed to him in reviews of *Grand Prix, Up Periscope, How Sweet It Is* and *The Pink Jungle* (*Variety*, December 28, 1966, 6; February 11, 1959, 6; June 26, 1968, 6 and July 24, 1968, 20).

26. Review, *Variety*, February 26, 1969, 6.

27. *Ibid.*

28. "*Support Your Local Sheriff* Wins April Blue Ribbon Award," *Box Office*, May 12, 1969, a3.

29. "NY Critic Gist," *Variety*, April 16, 1969, 28.

30. *Washington Post*, April 7, 1969, B6.

31. *New York Times*, April 9, 1969.

32. *Sight & Sound*, Summer 1969, 158. At this time *Sight & Sound* was a quarterly magazine.

33. *Monthly Film Bulletin*, January 1, 1969, 165; *New Statesman*, January, 1969, 812; *The Guardian*, May 30, 1969.

34. Picture Grosses, *Variety*, April 9, 1969, 12. See Appendix for details of first run box office.

35. "Big Rental Films of 1969," *Variety*, January 7, 1970, 15.

Chapter 4

1. Foreword to Ford, Peter, *Glenn Ford: A Life* (Madison: University of Wisconsin Press, 2011).

2. "Rising Skepticism on Stars," *Variety*, May 15, 1968, 1.

3. Ford, *Glenn Ford, a Life*, 151.

4. By comparison John Wayne averaged two a year in the 1950s and James Stewart was slightly more prolific but not in the Glenn Ford class.

5. Rising Skepticism, *Variety*.

6. "Zane Grey Tales Filming for TV in Mexico," *Variety*, January 17, 1968, 26. *Tappans Burro* was due to co-star Susan Hayward on a $1.25 million budget. Filming was to have begun in February 1968.

7. "Tell Metro Losses, Full Figures Due," *Variety*, Jul 23, 1969, 5. MGM had turned an $8.7 million profit the previous year into a $40illion loss over the first 40 weeks of the current financial year. Expensive films underperforming in the current year including *Ice Station Zebra*, *Where Eagles Dare* and even *2001: A Space Odyssey* which was expected to take in $5 million less in rentals because of the decision to quit 70mm roadshow in a bid to target the younger audience ("Metro's Sub-Zebra Cheer," *Variety*, July 9, 1969, 18). The cost of launching a film in roadshow was often the difference between break-even and healthy profit. MGM reckoned that had *Ice Station Zebra* gone straight into continuous performance, it would have done better, citing the $366,000 from 56 theaters in a Los Angeles showcased release and the $650,000 from 101 theaters in New York ("Gold in 'Abandoned' Films," *Variety*, July 19, 1969, 1). But *Where Eagles Dare* had not been held up in roadshow and its returns were less than expected, so the argument did not quite hold water.

8. The King Brothers were born Kosinsky.

9. "Kings Diversify to Mail Order Jewels," *Variety*, July 30, 1969, 21. They had acquired the Hollywood Diamond Exchange.

10. John Goodman played Frank Kozinsky in the film.

11. Blacklisted talent employed by the King Brothers included director Edward Dmytryk (*Mutiny*, 1952), and Dalton Trumbo (*The Brave One*, 1956) which earned him an Oscar. The brothers also employed rising talent such as Philip Yordan who wrote seven pictures for them before going on to *The Man from Laramie* (1955), *The Bravados* (1958) and *The Fall of the Roman Empire* (1964).

12. The episodes were *The Backshooter* and *The Incident of the Running Man*.

13. In the 1960s she had supporting roles in *Ice Palace* (1960), *Sail a Crooked Ship* (1961) and *How the West Was Won* (1962). She had played the female lead in *Baby Face Nelson* (1957) and *King Creole* (1958) and had supporting roles in *The Invasion of the Body Snatchers* (1956) and *The Man Who Knew Too Much* (1956).

14. There is some humor at Mormon expense. At one point Killian approaches Mr. Murdock who is standing with three women. Killian addresses the one he assumes to be Murdoch's wife. "And these must be your two lovely daughters." No, they are his other wives.

15. "Films Still Central with Disney; Plan 13 for 1970–71," *Variety*, May 28, 1969, 3. The other two movies were *The Horse in the Grey Flannel Suit* and *Rascal*. Although *The Love Bug* had been released at the tail end of 1968 and unexpectedly a huge hit, it was relying on reissues of *101 Dalmatians* and *Darby O'Gill and the Little People* to sustain theatrical income.

16. Ford's other charitable endeavors included chairmanship of the National See Eye Dog Foundation.

17. Pressbook, *Smith!* (Walt Disney Productions, 1969) 8. She married lyricist Alan Jay Lerner (*Brigadoon, My Fair Lady*) in 1950 and following their divorce in 1957 the president of Capitol Records Alan Livingston.

18. Pressbook, *Smith!*, 10. Note: many of the quotes from actors that most people would see in a national or local newspaper or in a film magazine originated in the movie pressbook. Studios printed extensive material in the pressbooks with the sole intention of giving the media free rein to chose whatever they wanted to publicize the picture.

19. The episode of *Festival*, written by Paul St Pierre, was called *How to Break a Quarter Horse* and was the original title of *Smith!*

20. Oddly enough, although the central theme is about injustice to Indians, there is no promotional mention of Chief Dan George in the movie pressbook where, normally, each actor would be allocated a few hundred words about their career and/or anything interesting about their general life. There are three articles on Ford, two on Olson, and one each on Wynn, Roger Ewing, Jagger, Wynn, producer Bill Anderson, director O'Herlihy, songwriter Bobby Russell (*Little Green Apples, Honey*), child actors Christopher Shea and Ricky Cordell, and even the Appaloosa horse used in the filming, but nothing on Chief Dan George or Jay Silverheels.

21. Will Henry's novel *From Where the Sun Now Stands* was based on the Nez Perce flight. John Ford's *Cheyenne Autumn* was based on a similar Indian flight.

Chapter 5

1. However, analysis of the film is based on the 159-minute DVD version which eliminates the shootout at the train and Cheyenne being mortally wounded.

2. Before Leone's masterpiece appeared, Argento had written or contributed to the screenplays of thriller *Every Man Is My Enemy* (1967), western *Today We Kill, Tomorrow We Die* (1968), *Comandamenti Per Un Gangster* (1968), war film *Commandos* (1968), and drama *La Rivoluzione Sessuale*, and afterwards worked on six films including western *Five Man Army* (1969) before directing his first film.

3. Frayling, Christopher, *Something to Do with Death* (Faber and Faber, 2000: London), 240.

4. *Ibid.*, 241.

5. *Ibid.*, 247–251.

6. Advert, *Variety*, May 7, 1969, 51. Euro-International, which put up half the production money, took out this advert to promote the "diptych" of *Once Upon a Time in the West* and *Once Upon a Time in America*, which it was heralding as a 1969 production.

7. *Ibid.*, 254, 255, 266, 267. Frayling counted about 30 references to, for example, *Farewell My Lovely*, *Murder Inc.*, *Ace in the Hole*, *Letter from an Unknown Woman*, and *High Sierra*. From other westerns came references to *High Noon*, *The Iron Horse*, *The Last Sunset*, *Union Pacific*, *Pursued*, *The Searchers*, *Run of the Arrow*, *Fort Apache*, *Winchester '73*, *Man of the West*, and *Rio Bravo*.

8. *Ibid.*, 265. Argento also claimed he wrote the fly sequence.

9. Pressbook, *Once Upon a Time in America*, 3.

10. Werba, Hank, "Am. Western Filmed by an Italian," *Variety*, July 17, 1968, 28.

11. "Italian Films 1967–68–69; Euro-Int'l Leading Italian Distributor," October 1, 1967, 30.

12. Werba, "Am. Western," *Variety*, July 17, 1968, 28, and "Leone Prepping $5,000,000 Saga," *Variety*, January 10, 1968, 7, both put the budget at $5 million. "Rome's Cinecitta Marks 500th Film with Leone's *West*," *Variety*, April 10, 1968, 27 claimed the film had a budget "Upwards of $5 Million" and "Leone Eyes $4,500,000 Italo Biz for His Latest Oater *Once Upon Time*," *Variety*, February 19, 1969, 39, also stated the movie was made on "A budget in excess of $5 million (how big the excess was not disclosed)." The film was made in association with Rafran Cinematografica, but Euro-International was, effectively, putting up half the budget in return for Italian rights. Paramount put up the other half. Leone, perhaps to save face, later insisted the picture had cost no more than $3 million including $1.5 million for the cast (Frayling, *Something to Do with Death*, 269, 293), although he had told a French news program in 1967 that the film would cost $4 million. Euro-International expected to make a killing because Leone was by far the most popular director in the country and it was confident that the picture would produce a record $8 million, nearly double the gross of *The Good, the Bad and the Ugly*.

13. *Ibid.*, *Variety*.

14. "Cigona in N.Y.; Serpre New U.S. Rep; Rand to Tout; Expect 28 Euro Pix," *Variety*, September 25, 1968, 5. The number of pictures appeared to be a misprint; it should be 18.

15. "Par O'seas Filming Peaks at Eight," *Variety*, April 10, 1968, 8; "Ornstein Denies Report of Drastic Cuts in Par's O'seas Production Set Up," *Variety*, October 16, 1968, 31.

16. While they were very profitable for United Artists, that was based on their relatively low budgets by U.S. standards and the fact that UA paid only $30,000 for the U.S. rights plus half of the subsequent rentals. *A Fistful of Dollars* finished 46th on the annual chart in 1967, the same year as *For a Few Dollars More* came 40th. *The Good, the Bad and the Ugly* claimed a more respectable placing when it finished 24th in 1968.

17. Simsolo, Noel, *Conversations avec Sergio Leone* (Paris: Stock, 1987, reprinted 1998).

18. You had to go back to the mid-1950s to find a sequence of films where Henry Fonda undisputedly received top billing—*The Wrong Man* (1956), *Twelve Angry Men* (1957), *The Tin Star* (1957), and *Stage Struck* (1958). Richard Widmark had top billing in *Warlock* (1959) and Leslie Caron in *The Man Who Understood Women* (1959). He spent most of 1959–1961 in the television series *The Deputy*. He was in supporting roles for *Advise and Consent* (1962), *The Longest Day* (1962), and *How the West Was Won* (1962). He received top billing on his next trio—*Spencer's Mountain* (1963) with Maureen O'Hara, *The Best Man* (1964) and *Fail Safe* (1964), but only the latter was a hit. Then he was back to third billing behind Tony Curtis and Natalie Wood in *Sex and the Single Girl* (1965) and second to Glenn Ford in *The Rounders* (1965). He had a minor role in *In Harm's Way* (1965) and was top billed for German-made *The Dirty Game* (1965) and top-billed among an ensemble cast for *Battle of the Bulge* (1965).

19. Wallach, Eli, *The Good, the Bad and Me* (Harvest, Orlando: 2006), 259.

20. Frayling, *Something to Do*, 269–270.

21. *Fonda: Dialog on Film* (American Film Institute Seminar, November 1973.); Fonda, Henry and Teichmann, Howard, *My Life* (New York: New American Library, 1981) 305–307. Leone claimed the transition was not as abrupt and was more gradual (Frayling, 270).

22. Peary, Danny, *Close Ups* (Galahad Books, New York, 1978) 535–536.

23. Schickel, Richard, *Clint Eastwood*, 184.

24. *Hang 'Em High* would be the second-best performing western at the 1968 box office, finishing 20th in the annual chart.

25. Werba, "Am. Western," *Variety*.

26. Frayling, 273.

27. *Ibid.* 274.

28. "Anglo-Gallic Versions for *L'Ami* Points Up Growing Int'l Practice," *Variety*, January 31, 1968, 14. The film, starring Alain Delon, had begun shooting in Jan-

uary on an eight-week schedule. The film was shot simultaneously in English and French to make it easier to sell to the American and British markets.

29. Simsolo, Noel, *Conversations Avec Sergio Leone* (Stock, Paris, 1978, reprint 1998), 139–141.

30. The other important aspect of his job was learning how to use and hold the harmonica and for this he received tutoring.

31. De Fornari, Oreste, *Sergio Leone* (Moizzi, Milan, 1977), 155–156.

32. Simsolo, 141–142.

33. He was billed third in *Once Upon a Time in the West*, above Charles Bronson.

34. Simsolo, 141–142.

35. De Fornari, 158–160.

36. Simsolo, 141–142.

37. Frayling, 277.

38. This description of Cardinale was attributed to David Niven, who worked with her on *The Pink Panther* (1964). Post Leone, you could amend it to "after spaghetti and spaghetti westerns."

39. Simsolo, 143.

40. The film was based on the 1946 play *Filumena* by Eduardo De Filippa. The play had been a huge hit in London in 1977 when directed by Franco Zeffirelli and was revived in 1998 with Judi Dench in the title role.

41. *The Pride and the Passion* had been ranked seventh in the annual box office chart, *Houseboat* 17th, *El Cid* 5th, and *Operation Crossbow* 20th in their respective years.

42. Incidentally, Frank Wolff who played Brett McBain was 39 in 1967.

43. "Claudia Cardinale into UA'S *Gerard* for $500,000 Fee," *Variety*, August 14, 1968, 2. This was the $4 million production of *The Adventures of Gerard* based on the stories by Arthur Conan Doyle.

44. "Behind or Below, Italo Production, There's an Authoritative Director," *Variety*, October 11, 1967, 32. One of the justifications for Leone's salary was that the picture would take two years of his life.

45. *Goha* won the Jury Prize at the Cannes Film Festival.

46. Frayling, 277.

47. She had won a Special "David" for her performance in *Girl with a Suitcase* (1961).

48. Frayling, 277.

49. Frayling, 261.

50. De Fornari, 155–156; Cardinale, Claudia (with Mori, Anna Maria) *Lo, Claudia—Tu, Claudia* (Edizione Frassinelli, 1995), 1560–152.

51. Over a 25-year period, beginning with *Stagecoach* (1939) John Ford shot a total of ten westerns in Monument Valley.

52. De Fornari, 155–156. This was the Goulding Trading Post, now a motel.

53. *Ibid.*

54. Frayling, 280–283. The prop man had a jar full of flies at the ready, but only required one. The water dropping on Woody Strode's hat took three hours to film. Morricone got the idea for the sound-effect score after watching a workman on stage at a concert making a stepladder creak for several minutes, to the consternation of the audience. Erroneously, someone tried to oil the windmill. Morricone recorded another 20 soundtracks that year.

55. "Rome's Cinecitta Marks 500th Film with Leone's *West*," *Variety*, April 10, 1968, 27.

56. "Italo Runaway in Reverse," *Variety*, January 3, 1968, 11. Italian producers had realized that it was easier to sell a movie in America if it was set in America.

57. Frayling, 287; De Fornari, 20–12. According to Hank Werba ("Am. Western," *Variety*), the nearest town of Gaudix was isolated with a population of 25,000 on the secondary Almeria-Granada Road although the stars were quartered a 90-minute drive away in Granada.

58. Frayling, 281.

59. *Ibid.*, 286–289.

60. "Rome's Cinecitta Marks 500th," *Variety*, April 10, 1968, 27.

61. Frayling, 286–290. Since the surrounding land was mostly desert, Simi also positioned a large tree stump in front of the house to give the suggestion that trees had been felled to supply the timber for the house. Most of the set has survived and is known as "Western Leone—*Poblado Del Oeste*." The logs had been used in Orson Welles' *Falstaff*.

62. *Ibid.*, 291.

63. *The Alamo* clocked in at 162 minutes, *Cheyenne Autumn* at 154 minutes, *The Hallelujah Trail* at 165 minutes and *How the West Was Won* at 164 minutes.

64. He committed suicide during shooting.

65. Palombi had bit parts in *For a Few Dollars More* and *The Good, the Bad and the Ugly*.

66. A reference to the opening of *The Searchers*.

67. "Filming Booms in Almeria, Spain," *Variety*, June 12, 1968, 31. Wolff did not even have to change hotels to join the picture as he was already in the area shooting *I Pray with Lead*.

68. A nod to *Shane*.

69. A classically-trained Italian actor, most notable for running a theater where Luchino Visconti trained. He made rare appearances in minor roles in Hollywood films, *Becket* (1964) the best remembered, and generally his relationship with Hollywood was limited to dubbing the voices of actors like Kirk Douglas.

70. Although one of Italy's biggest stars in the 1950s, he often took second billing to his leading ladies, for example to Gina Lollobrigida in *The Wayward Wife* (1953) and Valentina Cortese in *Adriana Lecouvreur* (1955).

71. "Leone Eyes," *Variety*.

72. *Isadora* (1969) faced a worse fate—nearly an hour chopped off its running time between its flop roadshow run and general release cutting it down to 128 minutes. The title was also changed to *The Loves of Isadora*. Neither tactic worked—it still flopped.

73. Review, *Variety*, May 28, 1969, 6.

74. Review, *Chicago Sun-Times*, June, 1969.

75. Review, *Time*, Jun 13, 1969.

76. "Euro's Accelerated Spread Out; *Helga* Smash B.O. Big Factor; Aims Biggest Distrib After U.S.," *Variety*, November 20, 1968, 42. The company had purchased the *Helga* rights for $30,000 plus a 50 percent share of rentals and the picture had already grossed $3.5million in two months. By now the company had also invested in John Cassavetes' *Husbands*, *Twinky* (retitled *Lola* in the U.S.) starring Charles Bronson, and *The Battle of Midway* (never made) as well as what it expected to be Leone's next picture *The Battle of Stalingrad*.

77. "Italo Hoss Opera Not on Sunset Trail," *Variety*, May 8, 1968, 44. Fears that the 'spaghetti western bubble had burst in 1967 proved wildly off the mark. Antonio Sabatoi in *Hate for Hate*, Lee van Cleef in *From Man to Man*, and Clint Eastwood in *Hang 'Em High* set the cash registers buzzing. The Eastwood picture, opening on Good Friday in 51 theaters, grossed $450,000 in a fortnight.

78. "Distribs Vie for Xmas B.O. Laurels in Italy with Top Product," *Variety*, December 11, 1968, 34.

79. "Leone Eyes $4,500,000," *Variety*, February 19, 1969, 39.It made $600,000 in 10 key cities between December 24, 1968, and January 6, 1969 and $2 million from 110 screens from Xmas to February. Ironically, *Coogan's Bluff* (1968) starring Clint Eastwood and with a much lower negative cost finished in the top ten for the Xmas-February period. "*Sick* Tops Italo '68–'69 Box Office," *Variety*, July 23, 1969, 31. *Once Upon a Time in the West* finished fifth for the year, behind box office champ comedy *Get Sick ... It's Free* starring Alberto Sordi, Monica Vitti as *The Girl with a Pistol* in second place, another comedy *Serafino* starring Adriano Celentano in third and *Where Eagles Dare* in fourth.

80. "Is There a Mass for Class," *Variety*, September 24, 1969, 5. Since the State 2 was a designated roadshow theater when the expected run of *Chitty, Chitty, Bang, Bang* closed six months early—next roadshow due being *Paint Your Wagon*—it left management with a big hole to fill and rather than looking around for another roadshow they opted for general first run.

81. "B'way Catching Breath for Holiday," *Variety*, May 28, 1969, 3. Other movies opening in two first run theaters in New York around this time were *Hard Contact, Those Daring Young Men in Their Jaunty Jalopies, April Fools, Popi* and *Che*.

82. "Five N.Y. Showcase Tracks," *Variety*, April 30, 1969, 7. The length of time between first run and multiple release was shortening with some movies omitting first run altogether. The five showcase operations were: UATC One, UATC Two, Loews-Century, UA (the distribution company), and RKO-SW. A new film broke on each of the circuits every week unless the film did well enough to be retained, usually for just one more week. Westerns made up a large proportion of the May-July schedule over the five circuits: *A Bullet for the General* opening April 30, *100 Rifles* and *Smith!* and *More Dead than Alive* all set for May 14, *Death of a Gunfighter* May 28, *Heaven with a Gun* Jun 11, *Sam Whiskey* June 18, *The Wild Bunch* July 9, *Once Upon a Time in the West* July 16, and *Mackenna's Gold* Jul 23.

83. "This Week's N.Y. Showcases," *Variety*, July 23, 1969, 8. *April Fools* came top with $361,000 from 37 theaters, *Romeo and Juliet* (in its fourth week) $223,000 from 26, *Hard Contract/The Boston Strangler* $200,000 from 33, *How to Commit Marriage* (in its second week) $192,000 from 30, *Once Upon a Time in the West* $168,000 from 29, *The Maltese Bippy/Grand Prix* $133,000 from 22 and "2" (in its third week) $82,000 from 18.

84. "Different Endings *Once Upon a Time* Stir Beefs in Paris," *Variety*, February 4, 1970, 29. The theater showing the English version in Paris had received over a thousand complaints about the ambiguous ending.

85. The only other westerns in the top 100 in the Admissions Chart were *Dances with Wolves* (74th) and *The Magnificent Seven* (87th).

86. "ABC Pays $20-Mil for Par Package," *Variety*, July 23, 1969, 8.

Chapter 6

1. Sheldon Hall has argued that the movie was never intended to be three hours long and that judging from a screenplay of 145 pages the film would have been roughly two-and-half-hours long. He identified a major sequence that was filmed but edited out—of another battle between the Apaches and the gold-seekers ("Film in Focus, *Mackenna's Gold*," *Cinema Retro*, Issue 43, 40).

2. "Foreman to Start *Gold*, Delays Churchill Pic," *Variety*, September 8, 1965, 4. The Churchill project would eventually become *Young Winston* made in 1972 for Columbia. The movie was originally postponed due to political unrest in the chosen movie locations.

3. Carl Foreman had originally worked on the screenplay for *The Bridge on the River Kwai*, but his version had been rejected by the director. The script can be viewed at the British Film Institute Library where it forms part of the Carl Foreman Collection.

4. David Lean had been nominated for *Brief Encounter* (1945), *Great Expectations* (1946) and *Summertime* (1955) and would win his first Oscar *For Bridge on the River Kwai*, a second for *Lawrence of Arabia* (1962) and further nominations for *Doctor Zhivago* (1965) and his final picture *A Passage to India* (1984).

5. At its most basic the term roadshow simply indicated a film shown with separate rather than continuous performances. At that time, advance booking was not obligatory. It had been used since the silent movie era from *Birth of a Nation* (1915) to *The Big Parade* (1925) and later for films as diverse as Wings (1927), *The Jazz Singer* (1927), *Gone with the Wind* (1939), *For Whom the Bell Tolls* (1943), *Joan of Arc* (1948) and *Quo Vadis* (1951). The introduction of widescreen and Cinerama revived roadshow and it was utilized for, among others, *This Is Cinerama* (1952), *The Robe* (1953), *The Ten Commandments* (1956) and *Giant* (1956). *Ben-Hur* (1959) was considered the picture that shoved the roadshow into the modern era.

6. The "little three" were Columbia, United Artists and Universal, which were largely exempt from the fallout of the Consent Decree because they did not own, or did not own very many, theaters. The "big five" were Paramount, MGM, Warner Brothers, Twentieth Century Fox and RKO, which would be so badly hit by the Consent Decree and mismanagement by owner Howard Hughes that it fell apart in the 1950s and disappeared off the Hollywood map as a production force.

7. "Third Roadshow Study: *Funny* Gets Special Sell to Party Agents; Columbia's Hard Ducat Thinking," *Variety*, August 28, 1968, 5.

8. Hannan, Brian, *The Making of the Guns of Navarone* (Baroliant Press, 2013), 103.

9. Schofield was primarily a stage actor and had played the leading role in *A Man for All Seasons* on stage in London and Broadway to enormous critical and financial acclaim. Schofield had only one major picture to his name, *The Train* in 1964 when he was billed second to Burt Lancaster.

10. "Third Roadshow Study," *Variety*. A change in the number of showings per week was also considered influential, the studio going from 10 showings per week to 16, in addition to carefully choosing which cities for roadshow.

11. Rentals amounted to $9.25 million putting it ahead of roadshow rivals *Thoroughly Modern Millie* and *Grand Prix* and other successes such as *Barefoot in the Park* and Matt Helm spy adventure *Murderer's Row*.

12. *Gone with the Wind* (1939) was the most famous example of this process, but was a huge success, so much so that it finished 12th in the annual rankings in 1967. Some films blown up in this fashion were only seen once or a handful of times as 70mm roadshows, or shown in continuous performance. These included *The Dirty Dozen* (1967), *Hellfighters* (1968), *Shoes of the Fisherman* (1968), *The Wild Bunch* (1969), *Winning* (1969) and *Marooned* (1969). Other films were released as 70mm roadshows abroad where demand for this kind of film had not diminished.

13. Filmmakers licensing the Cinerama name had to pay $500,000 upfront and Foreman was committed to spend $875,000 for Cinerama camera equipment. The cost might escalate because Columbia also had to agree to pay Cinerama 10 percent of the gross ("C'rama Sets Major Int'l Expansion as More Pix, More Theaters Use Process," *Variety*, November 15, 1967, 25).

14. "Junket for *Noon* Sparks Nostalgia," *Variety*, April 24, 1968, 31. Not only was the revival a critical success but it was a box office hit all over again in Paris.

15. "26 Probable Roadshows Due," *Variety*, January 17, 1968, 7. The full list, at this point, comprised: *Half a Sixpence, Custer of the West, 2001: A Space Odyssey, Finian's Rainbow, Funny Girl, The Charge of the Light Brigade, Star!, Sweet Charity, Oliver!, Chitty Chitty Bang Bang, Ice Station Zebra, Mackenna's Gold, Hello Dolly, Anzio, On a Clear Day You Can See Forever, Krakatoa—East of Java, William the Conqueror. The Shoes of the Fisherman, Patton, Tora! Tora! Tora!, Fiddler on the Roof, Man of La Mancha, Tom Swift* and *Goodbye Mr Chips*.

16. "10 for Cinerama in 2 Yrs," *Variety*, November 1, 1967, 3. So far, pictures announced were: *Mackenna's Gold, Anzio, Royal Hunt of the Sun, Custer of the West, Krakatoa—East of Java,* and *Song of Norway*.

17. "Leo Greenfield's Chore," *Variety*, May 31, 1967, 8. Wyler, of course, was the king of the roadshow, having directed *Ben Hur*. Reed had directed *The Agony and the Ecstasy* (1965) after an initial chastening experience with roadshow having pulled out of MGM's *Mutiny on the Bounty* (1962) after clashing with star Marlon Brando.

18. *Ibid.*

19. "C'rama Sets," *Variety*. There were 250 theaters in the U.S. and 2100 worldwide equipped to show Cinerama.

20. "13-Week $679,000 Contrast Year Ago," *Variety*, November 20, 1968, 14. The figures compared September 1967 to September 1968.

21. "News in Col Annual Report Is 'Solid Solvency,'" *Variety*, November 4, 1968, 3.

22. Switching of *Isadora* from Hard Ducat," *Variety*, January 15, 1969, 7.

23. "Third Road Show Study," *Variety*.

24. "Switching of *Isadora*," *Variety*. The film, which had opened on December 18, was set to close on February 8 and go straight into continuous performance.

25. *Ibid.*

26. "Col Bows *Gold* in Munich to Spark Lagging Box Office," *Variety*, March 26, 1969, 41; "*Mackenna's Gold* Launching Pattern," *Variety*, March 5, 1969, 28.. While it was true the studios were concerned about falling box office in Europe, the true reason for launching the picture in Europe ahead of America was because Foreman was so much better known there courtesy of his major marketing blitz for *The Guns of Navarone* and *The Victors*. It opened in Paris and Rome in March and in April in London.

27. Foreman may well have played a considerable part in the release delay. For *The Guns of Navarone,* he had insisted on holding back the release so that he could put into action a marketing strategy that involved visiting all the major countries in advance. Outside of the U.S., the roll-out was staggered so that Foreman could attend every national premiere (Hannan, *The Making of...*,100–102).

28. Sylvester Stallone got his big break by refusing to sell his screenplay for *Rocky* (1976) unless he was allowed to star in the film, Matt Damon and Ben Affleck repeating the trick with *Good Will Hunting* (1997).

29. Running a production company meant a person would be taxed as a company rather than an individual which could mean a reduction in personal liability and the potential to spread earnings over a number of years rather than being taxed for a big hit, for example, over one year.

30. Wilder rarely wrote a screenplay entirely on his own. He teamed up most commonly with Charles Brackett and I.A.L. Diamond and shared the credit for *The Spirit of St Louis* (1957) with Wendell Mayes and Charles Lederer.

31. By the end of his career, Olivier had produced 10 films and directed seven.

32. By the end of his career, Sinatra had produced or acted as executive-producer on seven films.

33. Gregory Peck was producer or executive-producer on eight films by career end.

34. The other downside was that production deals were rarely one-offs, producer or director finding that the profits from one big hit were wiped out by the losses on other films. Studios would not permit producers to take their share of profits until the complete program of movies had been finished and the total financial picture was clear. Producer Stanley Kramer, for example, found that any profits arising from *Not as a Stranger* (1955) were offset against losses from *The Pride and the Passion* (1957). John Wayne was nearly wiped out by the debts incurred on *The Alamo*. In addition, actors faced further loss by the amount of time a movie took to make. It could two years to get a picture from initial green light to exhibition and in that time the actor may have to turn down other more lucrative work.

35. Hannan, Brian, *The Making of the Guns of Navarone* (Baroliant Press, 2013), 74.

36. "Cash Advantages Motivate Foreman Not Europe's Authentic Locales," *Variety*, November 9, 1966, 4.

37. Later renamed *After Navarone*, it finally appeared as *Force 10 from Navarone*.

38. The book was actually called *MacKenna's Gold*.

39. Hannan, *The Guns of Navarone*, 98. Tiomkin received a record $50,000 for *The Guns of Navarone* and set other precedents for this picture. He forced Columbia to concede a share of publishing and performance rights, the first time the studio had ever given in to such a request, and he was able to choose which record company would release the soundtrack even though Columbia had its own label.

40. The film eventually appeared in 1970. His last movie composing credits were *The War Wagon* (1967) and *Great Catherine* (1968).

41. "Civil War OK-Now," *Variety*, January 26, 1966, 19.

42. *Santa Fe Passage* was a short story published in 1951 in *Esquire* magazine, *The Pillars of the Sky* was adapted from *To Follow a Flag* (1953), *Ten Tall Men* was published in 1954 and *Yellowstone Kelly* in 1957. Although he was also known as a prolific writer of screenplays, many of these were Tex Avery cartoons written between 1944 and 1955 which were considered some of the funniest ever made. He also worked on Woody Woodpecker and other cartoon characters. His novel *From Where the Sun Now Stands* (1960) won The Spur Award as well as The Saddleman Award while *The Gates of the Mountains* (1963) won The Spur Award.

43. By the time the movie came out, Tiomkin had given up composing and the score was done by Quincy Jones.

44. "Tiomkin-Foreman Partners for Col," *Variety*, April 21, 1965, 19.

45. *Ibid.*

46. "Cash Advantages," *Variety*.

47. *The Carl Foreman Tapes, Transcripts of Tapes Between Sidney Cohn and Carl Foreman*, Carl Foreman Collection, ITM—4408 (Tape V—A, December 20, 1977, British Film Institute, Reubens Library, London).

48. Avery, Kevin ed., *Conversations with Clint, Paul Nelson's Lost Interviews with Clint Eastwood*, 35 ; Neibaur, James L, *The Clint Eastwood Westerns*, 44.

49. Fishgall, Gary, *Gregory Peck, a Biography* (Scribner, New York, 2002), 264.

50. In her early films, she was credited as Julie Newmeyer.

51. *The Carl Foreman Tapes.*

52. *Ibid.*

53. Feliciano's version of The Doors' *Light My Fire* sold one million copies in summer 1968 and the artists won two Grammys.

54. *Appointment in Samarra* originated as a fable in ancient Mesopotamia and first appeared in the Babylon Talmud. In 1933 Somerset Maugham famously retold the story. American writer John O'Hara appropriated the title for his 1934 novel, which incorporated the Maugham tale in the introduction.

55. Agnew, Jeremy, *The Creation of the Cowboy Hero, Fiction, Film and Fact*, 180.

56. *Ibid.*, 176. The heroine dressed as a girl had been seen in *Riders of the Purple Sage* (1941) and *Border Legion* (1940).

57. *Ibid.*, 179. In *Day of the Evil Gun* (1968) this had happened to Owen Forbes (Arthur Kennedy).

58. *Ibid.*, 178.

59. *Ibid.*, 177.

60. *Ibid.*, 180. In Anthony Mann's *Man of the West* (1958), the Julie London character is forced to strip by the villainous gang.

61. *Ibid.*, 179.

62. Unless you count the likes of sexploitation pictures like *Hot Spur* (1968) which was advertised as "A Fistful of Flesh," *Brand of Shame* (1968) and *Ramrodder* (1969); Broughton, Lee, *Critical Perspectives on the Western: From a Fistful of Dollars to Django* (Lanham, MD: Rowman and Littlefield, 1969), 63.

63. Compare this narrator with the way information is given out in *True Grit.*

64. See "Film in Focus, *Mackenna's Gold*," *Cinema Retro*, Issue 43, 42, for further information on special visual effects.

65. Review, *Variety*, March 26, 1969, 6.

66. Advertisement, *International Motion Picture Exhibitor*, May 7, 1969, 12.

67. "Crix Boxscore on New Pix," *Variety*, June 25, 1969, 28.

68. Fishgall, *Gregory Peck*, 265.

69. *Sick* Tops Italo '68-'69 Box Office," *Variety*, July 23, 1969, 31. *Mayerling* ranked ninth at the box office for this period.

70. "Big Rentals.

71. "*Gold* Sets Madras Record," *Variety*, December 2, 1970, 26.

Chapter 7

1. Hannan, Brian, *The Making of the Magnificent Seven: Behind the Scenes of the Pivotal Western* (Jefferson, NC: McFarland, 2015), 183.

2. *Ibid.*, 207–208. It broke records in London, was the number one film for the year in Japan, in Germany among Hollywood pictures outranked only by *Ben Hur* and did exceptionally well in France.

3. *Ibid.*, 212. The cost was $400,000, small potatoes when placed along the $2 million generated the following year for *The Bridge on the River Kwai* (1957).

4. *Ibid.*, 211.

5. *Ibid.*, 212.

6. *Ibid.*, 214.

7. *Ibid.*, 215.

8. *Ibid.*,217.

9. *Ibid.*, 217.

10. *Ibid.*, 217.

11. Warren Oates and Jordan Christopher did go on to win top billing.

12. Fernandez played Mapache in *The Wild Bunch* (1969).

13. Hannan, *The Making of the Magnificent Seven*, 219;

14. Mirisch, Walter, *I Thought We Were Making Movies, Not History* (University of Wisconsin Press, 2008) 283.

15. *Ibid.*

16. "New York Sound Track," *Variety*, September 13, 1967, 20. A shortened version of this title was used for the third sequel.

17. He had just signed a multi-picture deal with Mirisch. ("New York Sound Track," *Variety*, February 28, 1968, 20).

18. Mirisch, *I Thought We Were Making Movies*, 284.

19. For Best Supporting Actor.

20. Actually, Hoffman was better known as director of sci-fi cult classic *The Invisible Boy* (1957) and television, which included nine episodes of *Sea Hunt* (1959–1960), 10 of *M Squad* (1959–1960), six of *The Asphalt Jungle* (1961), and one each of *Rawhide* and *Bonanza.*

21. Rey had played a priest in *Return of the Seven.*

22. Review, *International Motion Picture Herald*, August 27, 1969, 12.

23. "Hollywood Production Pulse," *Variety*, May 8, 1968, 215. While domiciled in Madrid, Wendkos and Kennedy shot a little documentary on local students ("New York Sound Track," *Variety*, May 29, 1968, 18).

24. Review, *Variety*, May 21, 1969, 6. It was reviewed in the same issue as *True Grit.*

25. Review, *International Motion Picture Exhibitor*, August 27, 1969, 12.

26. Hannan, *The Making of the Magnificent Seven*, 219; *Variety*, May 7, 1969, 6.

27. *Ibid.* However, overall rentals were still going downwards. *The Magnificent Seven* worldwide rentals had been $7.5 million, *Return of the Seven* $5 million and *Guns of the Magnificent Seven* $4 million. In 1968, a double bill of *The Magnificent Seven/Return of the Seven* was shown in London ("International Sound Track," *Variety*, September 11, 1968, 15), suggesting the issue of the new picture was more imminent than the following summer. *The Magnificent Seven* had opened at the beginning of the year in Britain.

Chapter 8

1. Although made in 1949, it was not released until too late in the year to qualify for the 1949 annual rankings and went into the 1950 list.

2. Nor for that matter did *Fort Apache* (1948) or *She Wore a Yellow Ribbon* (1949). However, *Red River* (1948), in a generally quiet year at the box office, came in third.

3. He did appear in a small role in *Cast a Giant Shadow* (1966) which was set in the late 1940s, not strictly contemporary but not historical either.

4. Filmed after *True Grit* with Glen Campbell.

5. Oscar-nominated for Best Picture. Wallis had previously been nominated for *The Rose Tattoo* (1955) and, long before either, twice winner of the Irving Thalberg Memorial Award, in 1939 and 1944. He would later be nominated for *Anne of the Thousand Days* (1969).

6. Neither Wayne nor Hathaway approved of Darby's casting.

7. Wayne did not like him either.

8. Nogueira, Rui, "Henry Hathaway," *Focus on Film*, Issue 7, 11–21.

9. *Ibid.*

10. *Ibid.*

11. Canham, Kingsley. "Hathaway's Films," *Focus on Film*, Issue 7, 22–27.

12. Nogueira, "Henry Hathaway."

13. *Ibid.*

14. Hall, Dennis John, "Tall in the Saddle," *Films and Filming*, October, 1969, 13–19.

15. Nogueira, "Henry Hathaway." He worked for only one day before quitting when the project finally got in front of the cameras in 1964 with Kim Novak in the lead.

16. Although he did not direct the segment that Wayne was in.

17. Kingsley, "Hathaway's Films."

18. *Ibid.*

19. *Ibid.*

20. Nogueira, Rui, "Writing for the Movies," *Focus on Film,* Issue 7, 36–42. Actors did not always take that view as Hathaway was known to be a hard taskmaster.

21. Nogueira, "Henry Hathaway."

22. Eyman, Scott, "John Wayne Looking Back," *Focus on Film*, Spring, 1975, 17–23.

23. Although these two films had their first showings in America on exactly the same day, *The Wild Bunch* opened earlier in New York and so jumped the gun on *True Grit* in terms of critical assessment, since all the critics who counted were based in New York and their reviews not posted until the film was about to appear in New York theaters.

24. I also noted that the music began before the credit came up, appearing the minute the Paramount logo was screened.

25. Based on the real Judge Isaac Parker known as 'the hanging judge.'

26. Real name Le Boeuf, pronounced Le Beef by the man himself.

27. "Bottomland" means low lying land near water, therefore likely to be more fertile.

28. All negotiations in this film are explained in detail. The Governor of Texas has put up a $500 reward for Chaney and the family of the man he killed another $1,500. If they bring him back alive, Cogburn will receive half the $1,500, if dead the sum reduces to $500.

29. Eyles, Allen, "*True Grit,*" *Focus on Film*, January-February, 1970, 5. This was the first issue of the venerated British magazine, with its unusual landscape format, which dealt more with historical films than current ones.

30. Review, *Variety*, May 21, 1969, 6.

31. Quotes taken from an advert, *International Motion Picture Exhibitor*, Jul 16, 1969, 2.

32. Advertisement, *International Motion Picture Exhibitor*, June 18, 1969, 3.

33. Hall, Dennis John, "Tall in the Saddle," *Films and Filming*, October, 1969, 13–19.

34. Review, *International Motion Picture Exhibitor*, May 21, 1969, 6–7.

35. Eyles, Allen, "*True Grit,*" *Focus on Film*, January-February, 1970, 5.

36. Pressbook, *True Grit*, 9. It is worth noting that, in this case, Paramount did not simply come up with a promotional idea and leave the exhibitor to get on with it, the pressbook supplied a list of distributors for the book, encouraging exhibitors to give away the novel as a prize on the day the film opened.

37. *Ibid.*, 9.

38. *Ibid.*, 10.

39. *Ibid.*, 9. It was suggested to exhibitors that they gave free tickets to people turning up wearing "the Duke Stetson" and give away a hat to local celebrities. A list of key Stetson dealers was supplied.

40. Advertisement, *International Motion Picture Exhibitor*, July 16, 1969, 5.

41. "What Radio City Booking Signifies to Europe: Wow!," *Variety*, September 10, 1969, 50. The ploy had worked for *Mayerling* which, despite poor grosses in the U.S., was expecting to gross $10 million in Europe.

42. Advertisement, *Variety*, June 25, 1969, 21.

43. "*Time* Raises Points Re Oscar for Wayne; a Grant Not a Win," *Variety*, August 13, 1969, 6.

Chapter 9

1. Strother Martin had a small part.

2. They had over 200 movies between them, Scott especially mostly making westerns, but had long lost their box office appeal.

3. Ben Johnson and Warren Oates appeared in *Major Dundee*.

4. Maureen O'Hara, her brother Charles Fitzsimons and writer A.S. Fleischman also put money into the film. Co-star Brian Keith earned $15,000, Peckinpah double that. Fleischman wrote a novelization of his script.

5. Simmons, Garner, *Peckinpah, A Portrait in Montage*, University of Texas Press, 1982, 25.

6. These were: *Private Hell 36* (1954), *Annapolis Story* (1955), *Invasion of the Body Snatchers* (1956) and *Crime in the Streets* (1956). Peckinpah was apt to exaggerate his accomplishment, claiming that he had written parts of *Invasion of the Body Snatchers*, which Siegel refuted (Simmons, Peckinpah, 26).

7. Cutts, John, "Shoot," *Films and Filming*, October, 1969, 4–8. He played a meter reader, a pod man and a member of the posse and another walk-on part.

8. Simmons, 27.

9. Elliott Arnold, author of the book on which the film was based, was a producer on the show.

10. Simmons, Peckinpah, 31. During this five-year period he also wrote *Villa Rides* which was not made into a movie until 1968 and the script for what became *One-Eyed Jacks* (1960).

11. Cutts, "Shoot."

12. *Ibid.*

13. *Ibid.*

14. *Ibid.*

15. *Ibid.*, 43. William Roberts (*The Magnificent Seven*) also worked, uncredited, on the screenplay.

16. Cutts, "Shoot."

17. *Ibid.*, 49–51.

18. In fairness, that was probably its destination all along given the size of the budget.

19. By Jim Silke.

20. Simmons, *Peckinpah*, 53. The *New York Times* called it a "dandy little western" and the *New York Herald-Tribune* a "superior western." It was released in Europe as *Guns in the Afternoon* and won the Grand Prix at the Belgium International Film Festival.

21. Cutts, "Shoot."
22. Review, *International Motion Picture Exhibitor*, June 25, 1969, 8.
23. *Ibid.* Interestingly, she was hired for *The Glory Guys* (1965), which Peckinpah wrote.
24. *Ibid.*
25. Simmons, *Peckinpah*, 59. Peckinpah wanted one shot of the cavalry in a location 100 miles away from another.
26. Simmons, *Peckinpah*, 60.
27. Cutts, "Shoot."
28. Simmons, *Peckinpah*, 69, 71.
29. Cutts, "Shoot."
30. *Ibid.*
31. Simmons, *Peckinpah*, 83.
32. "Rising Skepticism on Stars," *Variety*, May 1, 1968, 1.
33. O'Brien had won the Best Supporting Actor Oscar for *The Barefoot Contessa* (1954).
34. Oates had also starred in television series *Stoney Burke* (1962–1963). He had roles in *Return of the Seven* (1966) and *Smith!* (1969).
35. Simmons, *Peckinpah*, 87.
36. *Ibid.*, 84.
37. *Ibid.*, 85, 86. Dawson had quit the wardrobe business for writing but was tempted back by the offer of $750 a week.
38. Pressbook, *The Wild Bunch*, 4.
39. *Ibid.*
40. Simmons, *Peckinpah*, 97.
41. Pressbook, *The Wild Bunch*, 5.
42. *Ibid.*, 6.
43. *Ibid.*, 104. Fielding received one of the only two Oscar nominations.
44. *Ibid.*, 101. One of the most famous subliminal cuts, ironically edited out of the original U.S. version, was during a flashback that cuts between Holden and Ryan and you realize they are both remembering the same incident.
45. *Ibid.*, 102–103.
46. Hope, I.C., "WB-7 Fete Reaps World Word Harvest," *International Motion Picture Exhibitor*, June 25, 1969, 4. WB screened five other films—Francis Ford Coppola's *The Rain People* budgeted at $750,000, Luchino Visconti's *The Damned*, *The Learning Tree*, the $4.5 million *Madwoman of Chaillot* and *The Great Bank Robbery*.
47. Cutts, "Shoot."
48. "Press Violent About Film's Violence," *Variety*, July 2, 1969, 15.
49. The song is traditional, *La Golondrina* (*The Swallow*), written in 1862 by 19-year-old Narciso Serradell Sevilla, at the time exiled to France, and it became the signature tune for exiled Mexicans. The swallow represents a longing to go home. The English version is known as *She Wears My Ring*, made famous by Solomon King, but first recorded as a guitar instrumental by Chet Atkins in 1955. Versions of the song, sung by children, became number one hits in Germany, Sweden and Norway.
50. "New York Critics 4 to 3 on the *Wild Bunch*," *Variety*, July 2, 1969, 15.
51. Review, *Variety*, June 18, 1969, 6.
52. Review, *International Motion Picture Exhibitor*, June 25, 1969, 8.
53. Pressbook Supplement, *The Wild Bunch*.
54. Pressbook, *The Wild Bunch*, 9, 12–13. This comprised the circulation (not actual bought copies) of six major fan magazines plus a two-page advertisement running in the July issues (on the newsstands in mid-June) of *Playboy*, *Look*, *Sports Illustrated*, *True*, *Esquire* and *Sport*.
55. Pressbook, *The Wild Bunch*, 22–30. Please note I have taken the liberty of replacing periods with commas to make the words run more easily to the eye in this book. The original advertisements show the correct placing of the periods.
56. Pressbook, *The Wild Bunch*.

Chapter 10

1. "A complete delight" (*Hollywood Reporter*), "a gem" (*Seventeen*) were among the plaudits highlighted in an advertisement in *Box Office*, March 15, 1969.
2. Kennedy, Burt, "Our Way West," *Films and Filming*, October, 1969, 30–32.
3. Nogueira, Rui, "Henry Hathaway," *Focus on Film*, Issue 7, 11–21.
4. Kennedy, "Our Way West."
5. *Ibid.*
6. Review, *International Motion Picture Exhibitor*, September 10, 1969, 11.
7. Often touted as a hit, otherwise why would Martin Scorsese consider a remake? Nonetheless this was a flop at the time.
8. John Wayne was undoubtedly the star, however, of this one. It ranked tenth for the year.
9. Dean Martin had scored sensational business in the Matt Helm pictures so was again the bigger draw. It ranked 31st for the year.
10. This went out under the author's real name Heck Allen, who had shared the screenplay credit.
11. The picture featured the sons and daughter of major stars. Robert Walker, Jr., was the son of actors Robert Walker (*Strangers on a Train*) and Jennifer Jones (*Duel in the Sun*), Deana Martin was the daughter of Dean Martin, David Carradine the son of John Carradine and Mitchum's son Christopher had an unbilled part. Robert Mitchum sung the theme song.
12. Review, *Variety*, September 10, 1969, 48.
13. Review, *International Motion Picture Exhibitor*, September 10, 1969, 11.
14. "Box Office Charts 1969, Results," *Variety*, April 29, 1970, 26. By this time, *Variety* had introduced a computerized weekly box office chart that calculated about 30 percent of a film's gross. *The Good Guys and the Bad Guys* racked up $466,000 and *Young Billy Young* $222,000 by this method. I have arrived at my estimates by calculating what the total gross would be and then subtracting the amount that would be paid to the theaters. Such dire box office should have killed off Mitchum's career except, by then, he was signed up for David Lean's *Ryan's Daughter*.
15. Review, *Variety*, September 10, 1969, 48. It was reviewed on the same page as *Young Billy Young*.
16. Review, *Films and Filming*, November, 1969, 46.
17. Review, *International Motion Picture Exhibitor*, September 10, 1969, 10. The two films were reviewed on the same date.
18. "Box Office Charts 1969, Results," *Variety*, April 29, 1970, 26.

Chapter 11

1. Brother of playwright, novelist and screenwriter James Goldman (*The Lion in Winter*, 1968). They collaborated on a number of stage projects.

2. He coined this phrase in his groundbreaking study of how movies are made, *Adventures in the Screen Trade*, which he only wrote because, despite his enormous success, he had unexpectedly fallen out of favor with the Hollywood hierarchy.

3. In real-life Butch was every bit as amiable as shown on screen, but the film glossed over in large part Sundance's personality. He was a mean killer and very much a loner, Butch his only known friend. There is much debate over whether Etta Place was actually a schoolteacher, and was possibly more likely a prostitute.

4. Solomon, Aubrey, *Twentieth Century Fox, a Corporate and Financial History* (Lanham, MD: Scarecrow, 2002, 230–231, 254–256). Overall profit only dipped 5.5 percent for the year 1968 thanks in the main to the $15 million generated by *Planet of the Apes* on a budget of $5.8 million and *Valley of the Dolls* $20 million receipts on a $4.6 million negative cost.

5. "Fox's Sixshooter Month, September," *Variety*, July 24, 1968, 5. The others were *Staircase* (1969) starring Richard Burton and Rex Harrison, Omar Sharif as *Che!* (1969) and *The Chairman* (1969) with Gregory Peck. *The Only Game in Town* and *Staircase* were set to shoot back-to-back in Paris to suit Elizabeth Taylor and Richard Burton.

6. Frank Sinatra was the original male lead.

7. Solomon, *Twentieth Century Fox*, 255.

8. *Ibid.*, 256. Both *Tora! Tora! Tora!* and *Hello Dolly* cost $25 million, *Patton* $12 million.

9. O'Brien, Daniel, *Paul Newman* (London: Faber and Faber, 2004) 150–152. McQueen and Newman resolved the billing issue for *The Towering Inferno* (1974) when both were above the title McQueen first, but Newman higher up.

10. *Ibid.*

11. At this point, Redford had never received top billing, coming in third to Alec Guinness and Mike Connors in offbeat comedy *Situation Hopeless but Not Serious* (1965), third behind Natalie Wood and Christopher Plummer in *Inside Daisy Clover* (1965), third behind Marlon Brando and Jane Fonda in *The Chase* (1966), and second to Natalie Wood in *This Property Is Condemned* (1966). That he was toplined in *Downhill Racer* (1969) was due to the fact that his company Wildwood was making the film and he would take a smaller fee in lieu of a participation pay-off. Universal's *Tell Them Willie Boy Is Here* (1969) in which he also starred, was not in the same league budget-wise as *Butch Cassidy and the Sundance Kid*. He was replaced on *Blue* by Terence Stamp.

12. It was also rumored that Sundance's name came first because Steve McQueen was taking that role and he was purportedly the bigger star, but in reality the pre-*Bullitt* McQueen was not nearly as big a star as Newman.

13. "Original Sold to Fox for $400,000," *Variety*, November 15, 1967, 3.

14. *Ibid.*

15. Not quite, since he also had a share in the profits.

16. "Original Sold," *Variety*.

17. Jack Lemmon's production company Jalem was behind *Cool Hand Luke* (1967) which starred Paul Newman. Lancaster was part of Hecht-Hill-Lancaster which made *Marty* (1955) which did not star the actor and many of the 1950s films which did. Sinatra's company backed his directorial debut *None but the Brave* (1965). Wayne had been in the production business since *The Angel and the Badman* in 1947 and his output included *Hondo* (1953) and *The Alamo* (1960).

18. Although at one point Newman and McQueen discussed splitting Goldman's fee between them.

19. Stars and directors who did buy scripts usually sold them on to a studio for a hefty profit.

20. O'Brien, Daniel, *Paul Newman*, 150. Twentieth Century Fox president Richard Zanuck and vice-president David Brown (who later formed an independent company, making *Jaws*, for example) authorized the sale. Paramount had previously offered $200,000.

21. The novel was originally written as a screenplay and when it failed to find a buyer was turned into a novel, but even in that form it looked more like a treatment, very short chapters mostly filled with dialogue.

22. Goldman received a $100,000 advance, and although Goldman's earlier work had been well-received the book was slaughtered by the critics.

23. This was a highly original idea and it worked. The screenplay became a bestseller and was partly responsible for the growth of interest in screenwriting, since you could now purchase a genuine screenplay for less than a dollar.

24. O'Brien, Daniel, *Paul Newman*, 151.

25. By contrast Steve McQueen had one nomination for *The Sand Pebbles* (1966).

26. O'Brien, *Paul Newman*, 153, 155. Hall let Ross operate one of the cameras during the train robbery sequence, incurring the director's wrath.

27. *Ibid.*

28. Most character actors are largely hired to play the same kind of part each time but Strother Martin performed three distinct roles—as the whiny outlaw in *The Wild Bunch*, the wily horse trader in *True Grit* and now an authority figure as he had been in *Cool Hand Luke*.

29. Bacharach, Burt, *Anyone Who Had a Heart* (New York: Harper, 2013) 144–147. The song went to number one on the charts in January 1970 and won a Grammy. He had previously scored *After the Fox* (1966) and *Casino Royale* (1967) but mostly was called into to write theme tunes.

30. He won an Emmy for this.

31. *A Night to Remember* appeared as a two-parter in 1956 ahead of the British film starring Kenneth More two years later. Paul Newman co-starred in *The Helen Morgan Story* (1957) and Stanley Kramer directed the star-studded *Judgement at Nuremberg* (1961).

32. Known at this time as Anthony Franciosca.

33. "Hellman-Hill to Produce *Fine Madness*," *Variety*, June 23, 1965, 28. The partnership was dissolved in 1967.

34. The Zinnemann version was to star Audrey Hepburn and Alec Guinness. Realizing there was too much material for one film, even a long one, the director had wanted to make a two-part picture, each section two hours long. A sequel *The Hawaiians* (1970) starred Charlton Heston. Heston had been offered roles in the original.

35. Tom Courtenay turned down this role. For European release, von Sydow was billed first ("Billing Plot for *Hawaii*," *Variety*, August 3, 1966, 14).

36. "Hawaiians Partisan to George Roy Hill," *Variety*, August 11, 1965, 27.

37. "Report Robin Wilson for *Sweet Henry* Lead," *Variety*, April 12, 1967, 66.

38. Advertisement, "The Look Ahead from 20th," *Variety*, January 1, 1969, 10. This trumpeted the fact that the studio had "paid the highest price ever spent on an original screenplay."

39. *George Roy Hill Collection*, Yale University, Box 1, Folder 5.

40. Goldman, William, *Butch Cassidy and the Sun-*

dance Kid (New York: Bantam, 1969). This part of the sequence begins with the instruction "the longest traveling shot in history" and goes on to detail such items as "deafening" music whereas Hill shot this quite differently.

41. O'Brien, *Paul Newman*, 153. At Newman's insistence though Redford was less comfortable with this process believing it reduced spontaneity.

42. *Ibid.* 155–156. In reality, the actors jumped six feet onto a mattress. The river was too shallow and so the actual jump was completed at the Fox ranch in Malibu.

43. *Ibid.*, 154.

44. *Ibid.* Butch's real-life sister Lulu Betanson visited the set.

45. These elements are included in the screenplay, but there was no need for the director to use these ideas. He could have simply discarded them. It took considerable courage to include them, as they went very much against the way westerns were made.

46. The screenplay, for example, makes no reference to the way the couple hug and kiss on and off the bicycle. In addition, during the New York and ship sequence, Butch looks on forlornly at the couple, which is not written into the screenplay.

47. Butch's gang was actually called "The Wild Bunch" but the other moniker was adopted to distance it from the Peckinpah picture.

48. Goldman, *Butch Cassidy*, 1. This is not Goldman's opening. He has a scene much later (156–164) of Butch, Sundance and Etta watching a longer version of this silent movie in a makeshift theater in Bolivia. From the screenwriter's perspective, this constitutes a time stamp, establishing how much further we are away from the war in Spain which was the last notable date. It was also a deliberate counterpoint to Etta's determination not to "watch them die" as here she is shown their cinematic counterparts killed.

49. Goldman, *Butch Cassidy*, 3. Goldman treated this payoff in a different fashion. He had Butch walk away from the bank before turning round and yelling the line from halfway across the street. He also showed the saloon building.

50. Goldman, *Butch Cassidy*, 4–8. This is also contrary to the screenplay. Goldman gives the other card player John Macon a proper introduction ("A well-dressed, good-looking man in a rugged sort of way"—he is not presented as such in the film when we do see him, briefly) and indicates that the camera should cut between the two characters rather than remaining on Sundance.

51. Goldman, *Butch Cassidy*, 6. Again, contrary to Goldman, who has Butch "tearing up to the card table."

52. Goldman, *Butch Cassidy*, 8. The screenplay becomes overly-complicated at this point, Goldman providing half a page of directions that Hill just ignores in order to stay focused on Sundance.

53. Goldman, *Butch Cassidy*, 14. Hill ignores more of the writer's complications. Goldman has them come across a herd of deer and, to show the passage of time, has them sitting beside a dying fire.

54. Although this appears clever at the time, it is actually a massive underestimate of the forces ranged against him, and in leading his men into a second robbery he is walking into an ambush. We tend to accept at face value that Butch is "smart," partly because he plans the robberies and partly because he is not a gunslinger. But he is, actually, like most outlaws, pretty stupid, with a child's grasp of his situation, hoping he can twist it to his own end. Comparisons with these outlaws and *The Wild Bunch* show Butch and Sundance to be a rather sanitized version of villains, one with a proper girlfriend rather than committing adultery, the other welcomed into whorehouses because of his likeability without it ever occurring to him or anybody else why he is so lacking in a wife.

55. Goldman, *Butch Cassidy*, 40. Again, Hill cuts back on some of the detail in the screenplay to stick to the main characters.

56. It was a short war—ending in December.

57. Goldman, *Butch Cassidy*, 46. The screenwriter was much more explicit. In his version, there is nearly a full page of description of her at work in the schoolhouse before, hearing a noise, she leaves to go across to her house. Goldman also has her seen face-on at the start whereas the audience is introduced to her as a dark figure walking towards the house.

58. Goldman, *Butch Cassidy*, 52. "They are aware of each other" is as far as Goldman goes in explaining their physicality.

59. Goldman, *Butch Cassidy*, 63–64. The director ignores most of Goldman's highly detailed instructions.

60. *Ibid.*, 67. It was the director's decision to have the posse seen only from the perspective of the outlaws. Goldman suggests an alternative—"a camera shot from an enormous height. It is a s if two great black centipedes are racing."

61. *Ibid.*, 79. The night scene with the glowing torches is directed pretty much as written.

62. O'Brien, *Paul Newman*, 154.

63. Goldman, *Butch Cassidy*, 89. The screenwriter often asks for external shots of "blinding sun" but the director simply concentrates on the men, reacting to the heat, rather than showing its source in a clichéd manner.

64. *Ibid.*, 311*n*5.

65. Goldman, *Butch Cassidy*, 116–117.

66. Goldman, *Butch Cassidy*, 118. As part of the quarrel here, we learn that Sundance grew up in New Jersey.

67. Goldman, *Butch Cassidy*, 130–131. Goldman has Butch and Sundance doing this robbery rather than Etta and Sundance and the writer's scene is much shorter than the scene shot by Hill.

68. Goldman, *Butch Cassidy*, 137. Garris's habit of shouting "bingo" every time he spits is actually scripted, not an ad-lib by the actor.

69. Goldman, *Butch Cassidy*, 145.

70. Goldman, *Butch Cassidy*, 150–151. Goldman had written it quite different, though still in the interests of effect. He called for the action to freeze sixty times in sixty seconds and for the soundtrack to carry one enormous scream and with particular emphasis on blood.

71. Goldman, *Butch Cassidy*, 153–156. Goldman writes the campfire scene quite differently with the "Camera in Constant Motion, Moving Above the Three People Lying Below."

72. *Ibid.*

73. Goldman, *Butch Cassidy*, 156–164. This was shot but edited out.

74. Goldman, *Butch Cassidy*, 164–166. Hill eliminates all the dialogue in this film, as well as an essential plot point.

75. Goldman, *Butch Cassidy*, 167. In the script there is no boy. It is the restaurant owner who notices the brand and we cut to two policemen, from behind cover, checking this out.

76. Goldman, *Butch Cassidy*, 184. This idea was in the script.

77. "B.O. Slump in Cont'l Europe Spurs 20th Bally to Regain 'Lost Audience,'" *Variety*, March 19, 1969, 32.

78. O'Brien, *Paul Newman*, 159.

79. "Fox Lot Comes Alive, Roadshows Figure Very Much in Future," *Variety*, April 2, 1969, 4.

80. "Fox to Penthouse *Che*, *Staircase*, *Kid*, *Town*, Cover 1969," *Variety*, April 30, 1969, 5. The studio had concluded a deal with the Penthouse theater in Times Square in New York to launch its major productions there, starting May 29;. O'Brien, *Paul Newman*, 160, claimed that after a preview in San Francisco in August that Hill cut back on some of the comedy but a reading of the screenplay does not bear this out. O'Brien also claimed there was selected released in New York at the end of September with a wide release at the end of October, but in fact it was initially widely released in first run all over the country at the end of September with the showcase wide release in December.

81. Hannan, *Coming Back*, 182. In September 1966, the studios launched 13 movies including *Return of the Seven*, *Khartoum*, *Alvarez Kelly* and *Seconds* into this month, although none appeared to benefit. The following year this was expanded to "fall film fare" featuring *Point Blank*, *Rough Night in Jericho* and *Waterhole 3*, again without any specific success.

82. "Working on Myers New Sales Plan, Fox Pics Well Tracked on Showcases," *Variety*, May 28, 1969, 7. See *In Theaters Everywhere* (2019, McFarland, Jefferson) for a detailed history of the rise of the wide release. Although the use of the "Showcase" system had gained traction in the mid-1960s it had been largely abandoned by the beginning of 1969 following the success of films like *The Graduate* (1967) which first run houses kept playing for as long as possible. The moment a movie entered showcase it killed off its first-run prospects, this being important because although showcase generated receipts faster than first run they were rarely as profitable.

83. Review, *International Motion Picture Exhibitor*, September 10, 1969, 8–9.

84. Advertisement, "At Last! a Western with Legs," *Variety*, October 29, 1969, 25. In its first weekend at 98 theatres, it pulled in $542,000, in its second this dropped to $488,000 and in its third to $462,000 which were remarkably small drop-offs.

85. Hannan, *Coming Back*, 312, 313, Appendix B: Top Reissues 1970–1979.

Chapter 12

1. This extended to female stars as well. Deborah Kerr's singing was dubbed in *The King and I* (1956) by Marni Nixon. Audrey Hepburn in *My Fair Lady* was also dubbed or partially-dubbed by Nixon.

2. Holston, Kim R., *Movie Roadshows* (Jefferson, N Carolina, McFarland, 2013), 207. The others were Vanessa Redgrave and Franco Nero. Julie Andrews, who had played Guinevere on Broadway, was not invited to take part. Harris was signed up for his "dangerous" personality.

3. Technically, it was called "talking on pitch" and was used by stars with a limited vocal range. It was also known as "uttering."

4. When *Flower Drum Song* was released.

5. The date of *West Side Story*.

6. *Bye, Bye, Birdie* appeared then.

7. At that point to star Rex Harrison.

8. Never made.

9. "H'wood Hoppin' to Sound of Music with 16 Film Tuners Set by Majors," *Variety*, February 1, 1967, 1. The others were: *Half a Sixpence*, *The Family Band* and *A Funny Thing Happened on the Way to the Forum*.

10. "Paramount Back Stage *Coco* for $750,000; Screen Rights Command $2,250,000," *Variety*, December 20, 1967, 2. The studio invested in the actual stage production which was to star Katharine Hepburn and be written by Alan Jay Lerner and Andre Previn.

11. "*Little Prince* ('43) as Tandet-Lerner Paramount Film," *Variety*, March 22, 1967, 4. Shooting was to begin in 1968.

12. "CBS Films Buys *Fiorello* Rights," *Variety*, March 20, 1968, 69.

13. "*Treasure Island* No. 7, as Musical," *Variety*, July 30, 1969, 7.

14. "Period Films Due for New Surge; Count 25 Releases for 1969," *Variety*, December 4, 1968, 17. Period pictures, which had fallen out of favor after flops such as *The Agony and the Ecstasy* (1965) and *Lord Jim* (1965), were back in demand "After Almost Three Years of Almost Exclusive Concentration on Contemporary Subjects." There had been only nine period pictures set for 1966–1967 compared to the current boom which included, as well as musicals, *Waterloo*, *Mayerling*, *Women in Love And Krakatoa, East of Java*.

15. "Filmusicals O'seas Accent, Britain Blazing Tune Pix Trend," *Variety*, May 3, 1967, 5. *Half a Sixpence* would be the first American musical to be made entirely in Britain. Others included *Oliver!* and *Goodbye Mr Chips*.

16. "Evans 'Sleeping Giant Now Awake,' Par's Hollywood Product'n'Pep Rally," *Variety*, January 25, 1967, 3.

17. "Par's Big Roadshow Splash," *Variety*, June 25, 1969, 3. By 1969, it had four roadshows ready, more than any other studio—*Paint Your Wagon*, *Darling Lili*, *On a Clear Day You Can See Forever* and *Waterloo*. Roadshows took a long time to reach fruition, the first three pictures in the pipeline since as early as 1966.

18. "Par Exec Teams 'Vibrancy,'" *Variety*, November 8, 1967, 3. Other films on the slate included the never-made Steve McQueen starrer *The Cold War Swap* at $3.5 million.

19. And *The Happiest Millionaire* (1967) and *Half a Sixpence* (1968).

20. Written directly for the screen and winner of nine Oscars including Best Picture and Best Director.

21. It won eight Oscars including Best Picture, Best Director (George Cukor) and Rex Harrison as Best Actor.

22. "'Man' Passes to Fisher," *Variety*, November 15, 1967, 18.

23. This would embrace *Paint Your Wagon*, *On a Clear Day You Can See Forever* (1969), with Richard Harris originally assigned as the male lead, *The Little Prince* (1974) and *Coco* (never made).

24. Setlowe, Rick, "Baker, Ore, Paints Sinful Gold Rush Replica for Par's 16-Mil *Wagon*," *Variety*, September 25, 1969, 2.

25. "Evans Credo for Paramount," *Variety*, February 21, 1968, 77.

26. "News Vs. Handout," *Variety*, June 28, 1967, 4.

27. Archerd, Army, "Hollywood Cross Cuts," *Variety*, December 11, 1968, 28. Marvin turned down *The Wild Bunch* in favor of the musical.

28. "Clint Eastwood *Dollars* Pays Off in Italian Lire," *Variety*, June 12, 1968, 4. Eastwood had been paid $400,000 for *Hang 'Em High* plus 25 percent of the profits.

29. Siegel, Don, "The Anti Hero," *Films and Filming*, January, 1969, 22.

30. "*Wagon* Rolls Up $24 Million Budget," *International Motion Picture Exhibitor*, September 10, 1969, 3.

31. "When Big Pics Go Over Budget," *Variety*, February 19, 1969, 5.
32. Setlowe, "Baker, Ore, Paints."
33. *Ibid.*
34. "Josh Logan Exiting *Wagon*, He Shrugs," *Variety*, August 2, 19682.
35. "Big Budgets Bust Up," *Variety*, July 23, 1969, 3.
36. "*Paint* Roadshow Getting 'M' Rating; Is *Cowboy* 'X'?" *Variety*, April 30, 1969, 7.
The Loves of Isadora had also received an "M" but it only ran for one week in roadshow; Holston, *Movie Roadshows*, 239, Paramount fought the rating citing *Sweet Charity* but without success.
37. "Par Loses Rating Appeal on *Wagon* by 13–9 Vote," *Variety*, November 12, 1969, 4.
38. *Ibid.*
39. On stage, Rumson had a daughter. Elisa, Clint Eastwood's fantasy woman, was originally his dead wife. Pardner replaces the original Julio and is American to boot. In the stage version it was a character called Edgar who fell in love with Elizabeth. Legitimizing the love triangle by Elizabeth having two husbands is a movie device.
40. This is not to say the song was not appreciated. A single of the song went to number one in the British charts, although that success could be attributed to the novelty factor.
41. Review, *International Motion Picture Exhibitor*, October 22, 1969, 10.
42. This was a new song written for the movie with music by Andre Previn.
43. Review, *International Motion Picture Exhibitor*.
44. Pressbook Supplement, *Paint Your Wagon*. Lists of book sale representatives, record distributors and sheet music "jobbers" and stores nationwide participating in the Lurex promotion were supplied to help exhibitors get involved.

Chapter 13

1. There were four previous adaptations of the Gene Stratton-Porter novel—in 1917, 1928, 1935 and 1942.
2. Two previous versions of the John Fox, Jr., novel appeared in 1920 and 1928.
3. The fifth best film at that year's box office.
4. This picture had been on the stocks for more than a decade, first announced as a Hecht-Hill-Lancaster production to star Lancaster, Stewart and Gary Cooper. Earlier, John Wayne was connected to the movie project. Charlton Heston was also approached to star in the 1967 version.
5. Graham, Wheeler Winston, "Andrew V. McLaglen: Last of the Professionals," *Conversations on Film*, April 2009.
6. Montgomery Clift was not a star at the time of *Red River* (1948).
7. Dean Martin had been a massive star during the years of the Martin & Lewis comedy partnership and although still feeling his way into more serious roles with *The Young Lions* (1958) and *Some Came Running* (1958) was still considered a star in his own right toplining *Twelve Thousand Bedrooms* (1957) and *Career* (1959) as well as his impact as a singer and television performer. In his 1960s westerns, Martin, himself was often double-teamed with another top star, George Peppard in *Rough Night in Jericho* (1967), James Stewart in *Bandolero!* (1968) and Robert Mitchum in *5 Card Stud* (1968).
8. Published by Pantheon in 1963.
9. The movie had actually done reasonably well at the box office—19th in the annual rankings—but not well enough to cover its big budget.
10. As expected, the nudity was cut for American release, although some of it found its way into the European versions, which were more flexible when it came to such matters. The latest DVD restores this footage which took place at a wine festival.
11. Pressbook, *The Undefeated*, 3.
12. Solomon, Aubrey, *Twentieth Century Fox, a Corporate and Financial History* (Lanham, MD: Scarecrow, 2002) 230, 254–255. *Valley of the Dolls* cost $4.6 million and brought in $20 million in rentals, *Planet of the Apes* cost $5.8 million and rentals topped $15 million.
13. The background to the story is never properly explained, though it is highly likely American audiences would be familiar with the history. While America was engaged in a Civil War, French Emperor Napoleon III had tried to take advantage of the situation and get round the confines of the Monroe Doctrine by helping Maximilian and in so doing expand his own empire.
14. American audiences would be familiar with Juarez, already deified in Hollywood pictures, most notably in *Juarez* (1939) starring Paul Muni and Bette Davis which goes more thoroughly into the background of French involvement in Mexico.
15. Review, *Chicago Sun-Times*, December 2, 1969.
16. Review, *Variety*, October 1, 1969, 17.
17. Review, *The Showmen's Servisection,* November 19, 1969, 3.
18. Pressbook Supplement Tabloid Herald, *The Undefeated.*
19. Pressbook Advertisement Supplement, *The Undefeated.*
20. Advertisement, *International Motion Picture Exhibitor*, July 16, 1969, 5.

Chapter 14

1. Polonsky was a member of the Communist Party of the USA.
2. Bakley was a scandal-sheet dream, having been married nine times previously.
3. This was cut on appeal to $15million, but the appeals court upheld the decision of the civil court and Blake went bankrupt.
4. Later a television show.
5. He wrote *Golden Earrings* (1947) for Marlene Dietrich at Paramount but received no screen credit.
6. The movie won one Oscar, for Best Film Editing.
7. John O. Killens was the front. The way fronting worked was shown in Martin Ritt's *The Front* (1976) starring Woody Allen and *Trumbo* (2075) about blacklisted writer Dalton Trumbo.
8. "Five Universals in Title Switch," *Variety*, May 5, 1969, 15. Of the others, *Isadora* becomes *The Loves of Isadora*, *Patch* was changed to *Death of a Gunfighter*, *How Many Roads* altered to *The Lost Man*, and *Colossus* became *Colossus 1980*.
9. "Abe Polonsky Back," *Variety*, April 10, 1968, 8.
10. He appeared in 23 of these shorts. He also had bit parts in Laurel and Hardy film *The Big Noise* (1944), *The Treasure of the Sierra Madre* (1948) and *The Black Rose* (1950).
11. "Gutter Film-Talk," *Variety*, October 30, 1968, 78. Blake received some notoriety as the first actor to mutter the word "bullshit" in a movie.
12. "Col. Signs Robt. Blake," *Variety*, January 31, 1968,

14. Nothing came of this. He never made a picture for Columbia.

13. The sixth-best performing film of the year.

14. Ranked 15th in the annual box office charts.

15. "7 Going in States, U's Best for 11 Years," *Variety*, May 29, 1968, 4.

16. Ross met cinematographer Conrad Hall on this set and had a relationship with him.

17. Old Mike was murdered on September 16, 1909.

18. Advertisement, *International Motion Picture Exhibitor*, November 12, 1969, 16.

19. The film may well have opened in December in the hope of generating enough critical approval to push into contention for the Oscars. This proved to a misjudgment. The movie was not nominated in a single category.

20. Larkins, Robert, "Hollywood and the Indian," *Focus on Film*, March-April, 1970, 44–56.

21. *Ibid.*

22. *Ibid.*

23. *Ibid.*

24. *Ibid.*

25. *Ibid.*

26. *Ibid.*

27. The source material was *Willie Boy: A Desert Manhunt* by journalist Harry Lawton published in 1960. The book won the James D. Phelan prize for non-fiction and after Truman Capote's *In Cold Blood* it was retrospectively tabbed as a "non-fiction novel." Much of Lawton's findings have been hotly disputed and many Native Americans believe that Willie Boy was not, in fact, killed but escaped and died a natural death.

28. In 1970 the single most influential endeavor *Bury My Heart at Wounded Knee* by Dee Brown was published but came too late to influence the release of the movie.

29. Sizate, Julia, *Willie Boy, How a Manhunt Became a Myth*, KCET, Jun 27, 2018.Willie Boy had been trained to travel long distances as part of his spiritual beliefs. Sizate also pointed out that the reason Carlota's father objected to the marriage was that it was against tribal law since Willie Boy and Carlota were distant cousins. Also, the reason Willie Boy had to be shot at the end was because suicide was also against those laws.

30. Book jacket to the paperback movie tie-in.

31. Leonelli, Elisa, *Robert Redford and American West*, 24–25.

32. Sizate, *Willie Boy*, 24–25.

33. Review, *Variety*, October 22, 1969, 16.

34. "John Wayne Tactics," *Variety*, November 5, 1969, 27.

35. "New York Critics Dec 14–21," *Variety*, December 24, 1969, 7.

36. "Time for Year's 10 Best Lists," *Variety*, Dec 31, 1969, 7.

Chapter 15

1. Hannan Brian, *Coming Back to a Theater Near You, a History of the Hollywood Reissue, 1914–2014* (Jefferson, NC: McFarland, 2016), 1.

2. Hannan, *Coming Back*, 47–48.

3. Hannan, *Coming Back*, 52, 311. *A Rage in Heaven* earned rentals of $1.3 million in 1946–1947.

4. Hannan. *Coming Back*, 80–83, 311–312. The 1952 reissue of *King Kong* earned $2.7 million. It had previously been reissued in 1941–1942 in a double bill with *Gunga Din* for $390,000 in rentals and less successfully on its own in 1948 for $170,000. Its final revival was in 1956 in a double bill with *I Walked with a Zombie* (1943).

5. Hannan, *Coming Back*, 85–86, 311. *Duel in the Sun* brought in rentals of $2 million in 1954. Other reissue big hitters that year were *The Best Years of Our Lives* (1946) with rentals of $2.6 million, *Gone with the Wind* (1939) with $7 million, *Pinocchio* (1940) and *Reap the Wild Wind* (1942) both with $900,000.

6. Hannan, *Coming Back*, 65–67, 108–111, 127–128, 168–172 .*Gone with the Wind* earned $4 million in rentals in 1941, $1 million in 1942, $5 million in 1947, $7 million in 1954, $7 million 1961 and $35 million over 1967–1969 when it was initially reinvented as a 70mm roadshow before going out in 35mm general release.

7. Hannan, *Coming Back*, 128–129. MGM came up with the bright idea of playing oldies in a season lasting six-to-eight weeks, the movies shown one day a week, and season tickets sold to encourage loyalty. The first season comprised the "golden operettas" of *Rose Marie* (1936), *The Merry Widow* (1934), *The Great Waltz* (1938), *Sweethearts* (1938), *The Chocolate Soldier* (1941) and *Girl of the Golden West* (1938).

8. Hannan, *Coming Back*, 62–63, 101–103, 159–160, 174, 311. Each of Disney's animated features was reissued on a regular cycle about every 7–10 years. *Snow White and the Seven Dwarfs* (1939) earned $1.4 million in rentals in 1944, $2 million in rentals in 1952, and $4.75 million in 1967. *Bambi* (1942) earned $1.8 million in 1947, $2.5 million in 1957 and $4 million in 1966. *Swiss Family Robinson* earned $4.6 million in 1969. *Darby O'Gill and the Little People* made $2.3 million in 1968, compared to $2.6 million on original release.

9. Hannan, *Coming Back*, 127–128.

10. Hannan, *Coming Back*, 147–151.

11. Hannan, *Coming Back*, 177. *A Fistful of Dollars* earned $2 million in rentals in 1967 for 46th place on the annual chart and its stablemate $2.2 million the same year for 40th place according to the *Variety* annual chart.

12. Dates relate to the U.S. release rather than their original Italian release.

13. Stevens, Brad, *Monte Hellman: His Life and Films* (Jefferson, NC: McFarland, 2003) 200. It took until February 23, 1975, for *A Fistful of Dollars* to make its television debut on ABC, the eight-year window between U.S. release and small screen an astonishing long time given the fever with which studios threw movies at television. In an attempt to justify the violence, ABC inserted a prologue featuring Harry Dean Stanton and directed by Monte Hellman.

14. "Picture Grosses," *Variety*, April 16, 1969, 8–10, 11, 16.

15. Annual Rentals, *Variety*. It is not known how much the revival of the Eastwood films bit into the grosses of *Where Eagles Dare*, suffice to say that the MGM picture was generally considered to have underperformed.

16. "Picture Grosses," *Variety*, August 27, 1969, 9, 11, 13, 15, 20.

17. Annual Rentals, *Variety*.

18. Monaco, Paul, *The Sixties, the History of the American Cinema*, Vol. 8 (Berkeley: University of California Press, 2001), 15, 106. Spaghetti westerns and Sergio Leone were only mentioned in relation to the improvements in post-synchronization technology that allowed films made in foreign countries with an international cast to be dubbed into intelligible English and to the fact nobody "appeared to mind" that there were not shot on authentic U.S. locales.

19. *Sight & Sound*, September 2012, 60. The three films were ranked joint eighth.

20. Although primarily an actor, Anthony was also

an executive producer, though mostly uncredited, on virtually one picture a year from *Force of Impulse* (1961) starring Robert Alda which he co-wrote to 1967. The title in those days, as it pretty much does now, simply meant he had put money into the movie rather than undertaking actual producer duties. He put $4,000 into *A Stranger In Town*, for example. Except for George Sherman's Italian-American co-production bullfighting drama *Wound of Honor* (1963), he had not starred in any of the films—sometimes third billed, other times much further down the billing—that he made in Italy from 1963 to 1965.

21. One of Anthony's early filmmaking buddies was friends with Allen Klein, an MGM stockholder, who was persuaded to campaign within MGM to pick up the picture.

22. This had also been reissued in 1968 in a double bill with *The Carpetbaggers* (1964), thereby, effectively running as a double bill promoted around novelist Harold Robbins since Nevada Smith was a character in *The Carpetbaggers*.

23. "B.O. Charts 1969 Results," *Variety*, April 29, 1969, 26, 176, 180, 194, 196.

Chapter 16

1. "Five Universals in Title Switch," *Variety*, March 5, 1969, 15. *Isadora* changed to The Loves of Isadora, *Willie Boy* to *Tell Them Willie Boy Is Here*, *How Many Roads* starring Sidney Poitier to *The Lost Man* and Colossus to *Colossus 80*.

2. He worked primarily in television in the 1960s such as *Hawaiian Eye*, *The Virginian*, *Bonanza* and 25 episodes of *Gunsmoke* from 1966.

3. Review, *Variety*, April 30, 1969, 6.

4. Review, *The Showmen's Servisection*, November 19, 1969, 4.

5. Advertisement, *International Motion Picture Exhibitor*, April 16, 1969, 13.

6. B.O. Charts 1969 Results," *Variety*, April 29, 1970, 26. These figures are a rough estimate based on my own calculations. At the time *Variety* had started to run a computerized box office system for first run theaters across 20–24 cities and which covered more than 1,000 movies released in 1969. These figures were published as grosses so I used the rough standard that about only 50 percent of the grosses would end up in the pockets of the studios. Also *Variety*, due to the limitations of the survey, which did not cover every theater as it does today, conceded that these grosses represented only about 30 percent of the film's actual annual total. So my calculations have taken into account these factors.

7. Although born in San Francisco, Shenson primarily plied his trade in Britain where he made comedies *The Mouse That Roared* (1959) and *The Mouse of the Moon* (1963).

8. With Richard Lester, who had helmed the two previous Beatles offerings, directing.

9. Pre-Beatles, Quine had tried to get the picture off the ground in 1964 with Chuck Connors as star.

10. "Charro" means "horseman" in Spanish.

11. Although he sang the title song over the credits.

12. He was better known as a writer, having penned *Streets of Laredo* (1949), *Little Big Horn* (1951), *Springfield Rifle* (1952) and *Pony Express* (1953).

13. Victor French was the star of Robert Totten's debut *The Quick and the Dead*, incidentally also French's first picture. He also appeared in *Death of a Gunfighter*.

14. She had also appeared in *Seconds* (1966).

15. "Critics Wrap Up," *Variety*, September 10, 1969, 6.

16. Review, *International Motion Picture Exhibitor*, March 26, 1969, 9.

17. "Audie Murphy Re-Teams with Budd Boetticher; *Dying for Arizona*," *Variety*, April 23, 1969, 22.

18. Review, *Variety*, October 6, 1971, 16.

19. "New MPAA Ratings," *Variety*, September 3, 1969, 17.

20. "Producer Audie Murphy Places *Time for Dying*," *Variety*, April 29, 1970, 6.

21. "Netherlands Fest," *Variety*, December 10, 1969, 21.

22. From a script by Sam Peckinpah.

23. Review, *The Showmen's Servisection*, November 19, 1969, 4.

24. Review, *Variety*, June 11, 1969, 6.

25. Review, *The Showmen's Servisection*, November 19, 1969, 5.

26. Review, *International Motion Picture Exhibitor*, June 11, 1969, 7.

27. "B.O. Charts," *Variety*. It took $82,000 in rentals.

28. Review, *Variety*, July 16, 1969, 6.

29. Review, *The Showmen's Servisection*, November 19, 1969, 4.

30. Review, *International Motion Picture Exhibitor*, July 16, 1969, 9.

31. Review by Colin Heard, *Films and Filming*, June, 1969, 54.

32. "Picture Grosses," *Variety*.

33. "B.O. Charts," *Variety*.

34. Review, *International Motion Picture Exhibitor*, November 26, 1969, 9.

35. "Picture Grosses," *Variety*, December 10, 1969, 8, 9, 13, 16, 24.

36. "B.O. Charts," *Variety*.

37. "Picture Grosses," *Variety*, July 23, 1969, 8, 12, 13, 15, 17.

38. "B.O. Charts," *Variety*.

39. Pressbook, *The Great Bank Robbery*, 3—in a previous job as a literary agent, he claimed to have convinced Leon Uris to write *Exodus*.

40. "Mal Stuart's Sextet, He and Blatty Set for *O'rourke's Robbery*," *Variety*, April 26, 1967, 36. The Newman picture fell through and Stuart's name did not appear on the credits of *Scalawag* when it was released in 1973. Others in the original portfolio were *Face of the Enemy* and *Comedian*.

41. "Stuart H.Q. at Par," *Variety*, November 15, 1967, 7.

42. "Dassin's New Heist," *Variety*, October 25, 1967, 4.

43. "New York Sound Track," *Variety*, November 1, 1967, 6.

44. Winning three Tonys, achieving the rare feat of winning for drama (*Rhinoceros*), comedy (*A Funny Thing*) and musical (*Fiddler on the Roof*).

45. He had been working in television since 1951 and mainly known for directing comedy like *The Real McCoys* (1957–1960) and *Ensign O'Toole* (1962–1963) with Dean Jones.

46. Tamiroff had appeared in both *Monsieur LeCog* and *Great Catherine*.

47. Pressbook, *The Great Bank Robbery*, 3.

48. *Ibid.*, 4.

49. *Ibid.*, 7.

50. *Ibid.*, 8.

51. *Ibid.*, 9.

52. Hope, I.C., "WB-7 Fete Reaps World Word Harvest," *International Motion Picture Exhibitor*, June 25, 1969, 4. WB screened five other films—Francis Ford Coppola's *The Rain People* budgeted at $750,000, Luchino Visconti's *The Damned*, *The Learning Tree*, the $4.5 million *Madwoman of Chaillot* and *The Great Bank Robbery*.
53. "N.Y. News on Comedy," *Variety*, September 17, 1969, 17.
54. Review, *Variety*, June 25, 1969, 6.
55. Review, *Variety*, April 30, 1969, 6.
56. Review, *International Motion Picture Exhibitor*, April 30, 1969, 6.
57. "N.Y Critics," *Variety*, May 7, 1969, 24.
58. "Picture Grosses," *Variety*, May 7, 1969, 10, 11, 14, 18, 21.
59. Review, *Variety*, May 21, 1969, 6.
60. *Ibid.*, July 2, 1969, 8–10, 14, 18; *Ibid.*, September 17, 1969, 8–10, 12, 20.
61. *Ibid.*, February 26, 1969, 8–9, 12–13.
62. Review, *Variety*, October 29, 1969, 28.
63. *The Italian Job* topped the billing in New York and Seattle. In Portland and Toronto it was the other way round. In Dayton, Cincinnati, Minneapolis and Philadelphia *Ace High* it was the sole attraction.
64. Originally released in Italy in 1967.
65. "Guarantee Distribution Sums Key to RAf Industries Future," *Variety*, June 11, 1969, 30. This independent outfit bought the U.S. distribution rights for $40,000 for *Any Gun Can Play* and proceeded to gross $211,000 from 798 theaters. Even on a 50/50 rental split, and counting in marketing, that would produce a decent profit. Many of the movies went straight into theaters without being trade screened ("Distributed, Never Trade Screened," *Variety*, March 19, 1969, 23).
66. Originally released in Italy in 1967.
67. Review, *The Showmen's Sevisection*, November 19, 1969, 1. It was distributed by Columbia.
68. "B.O. Charts," *Variety*.
69. "Picture Grosses," *Variety*, September 3, 1969, 8–9, 12, 15.
70. "Picture Grosses," *Variety*, January 15, 1969, 8–10, 15; "Picture Grosses," *Variety*, February 5, 1969, 8, 11, 13. It played three weeks in New York and Boston and was remarkably consistent, pulling down $7,000 in the final week in the Big Apple and $6,000 in the third in Boston. It also ran for three weeks in Portland.
71. Lee Frost ended up directing 33 pictures including *Chrome and Hot Leather* (1971) and *Black Gestapo* (1975). He had several other pseudonyms—Carl Borch, Leoni Valentino, Robert Lee, F.C. Perl, Les Emerson and Elov Petersson. Virginia Gordon only made seven films.

Conclusion

1. In 1970 with *Chisum* and 1971 with *Big Jake* and 1972 with *The Cowboys* John Wayne starred in the top western of the year.

Bibliography

Agnes, Jeremy. *The Old West in Fact and Film: History vs. Hollywood.* Jefferson, NC: McFarland, 2012.

Allvine, Glendon. *The Greatest Fox of Them All.* New York: Lyle Stuart, 1969.

Armstrong, Stephen B. *Andrew V. McLaglen: The Life and Hollywood Career.* Jefferson, NC: McFarland, 2011.

Bacharach, Burt. *Anyone Who Had a Heart.* New York: Harper, 2013.

Balio, Tino. *Grand Design: Hollywood as a Modern Business Enterprise, 1930–1939.* New York: Charles Scribner's and Sons, 1993.

Balio, Tino. *United Artists: The Company That Changed the Film Industry.* Madison: University of Wisconsin Press, 1987.

Balio, Tino. *United Artists: The Company Built by the Stars.* Madison: University of Wisconsin Press, 1976.

Balio, Tino (ed.). *The American Film Industry,* 2nd revised edition. Madison: University of Wisconsin Press, 1985.

Basinger, Jeanine. *Anthony Mann.* Boston: Twayne, 1979.

Baxter, John. *The Cinema of John Ford.* London: A. Zwemmer, 1972.

Bergen, Ronald. *The United Artists Story.* London: Octopus, 1986.

Biskind, Peter. *Easy Riders, Raging Bulls.* New York: Simon & Schuster, 1998.

Bogdanovich, Peter, *John Ford.* Berkeley: University of California Press, 1967.

Brodwell, David, Janet Staiger and Kirstin Thompson. *The Classical Hollywood Cinema, Film Style and Mode of Production to 1960.* New York: Columbia University Press, 1985.

Brown, Gene. *Movie Time: A Chronology of Hollywood and the Movie Industry from Its Beginnings to the Present.* New York: Macmillan, 1995.

Buscombe, Edward. *The BFI Companion to the Western.* New York: Athenaum, 1988.

Buscombe, Edward. *The Searchers.* London: British Film Institute, 2002.

Buscombe, Edward. *Stagecoach.* London: British Film Institute, 1992.

Caewetti, John G. *The Six Gun Mystique.* Ohio: Bowling Green, 1971.

Calder, Jenni. *There Must Be a Lone Ranger.* London: Hamish Hamilton, 1974.

Callan, Michael Feeney. *Robert Redford: The Biography.* New York: Simon & Schuster, 2012.

Cameron, Ian, and Douglas Pye, eds. *The Movie Book of the Western.* London: Studio Vista, 1996.

Caspar, Drew. *Post-War Hollywood 1946–1962.* Hoboken, NJ: Wiley-Blackwell, 2007.

Clapham, Walter. *Western Movies: The Story of the West on Screen.* London: Octopus, 1974.

Corkin, Stanley. *Cowboys as Cold Warriors: The Western and U.S. History.* Philadelphia: Temple University Press, 2004.

Cumbow, Robert C. *Once Upon a Time: The Films of Sergio Leone.* Lanham, MD: Scarecrow, 1987.

Daniel, Douglass K. *Tough as Nails: The Life and Times of Richard Brooks.* Madison: University of Wisconsin Press, 2011.

Davis, Ronald L. *John Ford, Hollywood's Old Master.* Norman: University of Oklahoma Press, 1995.

Dick, Bernard F. *Engulfed: The Death of Paramount and the Birth of Corporate Hollywood.* Lexington: University Press of Kentucky, 2001.

Everson, William K. *The Hollywood Western.* New York: Citadel Press, 1992.

Eyles, Allen, *the Western: An Illustrated Guide.* London: A. Zwemmer, 1967.

Fenin, George N, and William K. Everson. *The Western: From Silents to Cinerama.* New York: Orion Press, 1962.

Fine, Marshall. *Bloody Sam: The Life and Films of Sam Peckinpah.* New York: Donald I. Fine, 1991.

Ford, Peter. *Glenn Ford a Life.* Madison: University of Wisconsin Press, 2011.

Frayling, Christopher. *Sergio Leone, Once Upon a Time in Italy.* London: Thames and Hudson, 2008.

Frayling, Christopher. *Sergio Leone, Something to Do with Death.* London: Faber & Faber, 2000.

Frayling, Christopher. *Spaghetti Westerns: Cowboys and Europeans from Karl May to Sergio Leone.* London: Routledge & Paul, 1981.

French, Philip. *Westerns, Aspects of a Genre.* Revised edition. Carcanet Films, 2001.

Garfield, Brian. *Western Films a Complete Guide.* New York: Da Capo Press, 1982.

Garner, Simmons. *Peckinpah: A Portrait in Montage.* Austin: University of Texas Press, 1982.

Goldman, William. *Butch Cassidy and the Sundance Kid.* New York: Bantam, 1969.

Grant, Barry Keith, ed. *American Cinema of the 1960s: Themes and Variations.* New Brunswick, NJ: Rutgers University Press, 2008.

Hannan, Brian. *Coming Back to a Theater Near You: A History of Hollywood Reissues 1914–2014.* Jefferson, NC: McFarland, 2016.

Hannan, Brian. *The Making of the Magnificent Seven: Behind the Scenes of the Pivotal Western.* Jefferson, NC: McFarland, 2015.

Hardy, Phil. *The Western.* New York: William Morrow, 1983.

Hoffman, Elizabeth DeLaney. *American Indians and Popular Culture.* Santa Barbara, CA: Praeger, 2012.

Hughes, Howard. *Aim for the Heart.* London: I.B. Tauris, 2009.

Hughes, Howard. *Once Upon a Time in the Italian West: The Filmgoers Guide to Spaghetti Westerns.* London: I.B. Tauris, 2004.

Hughes, Howard. *Stagecoach to Tombstone: The Filmgoers Guide to Great Westerns.* London: I.B. Tauris, 2008.

Izod, John. *Hollywood and the Box Office.* New York: Columbia University Press, 1992.

Kennedy, Burt. *Hollywood Trail Boss: Behind the Scenes of the Wild, Wild Westerns.* New York: Boulevard Books, 1997.

Kitses, Jim. *Horizons West.* Bloomington: Indiana University Press, 1969.

Kitses, Jim, and Greg Rickman eds. *The Western Reader.* New York: Limelight Editions, 1998.

Lenihan, John H. *Showdown: Confrontation in Modern America in the Western Film.* Urbana: University of Illinois Press, 1988.

Leonelli, Elisa. *Robert Redford and the American West.* Xlibris, 2007.

Lev, Peter. *The Fifties: Transforming the Screen 1950–1959.* New York: Charles Scribner's Sons, 2003.

Levy, Shawn. *Paul Newman: A Life.* New York: Harmony Books, 2009.

Lovell, Glenn. *Escape Artist, John Sturges.* Madison: University of Wisconsin Press, 2008.

Loy, R. Philip. *Westerns in a Changing America, 1955–2000.* Jefferson, NC: McFarland, 2004.

Lucas, George, Alex Ben Block and Lucy Autry Wilson, eds. *Blockbusting.* New York: IT Books, 2010.

Lusted, David. *The Western.* Harlow, Essex: Pearson Education, 2003.

Madsen, Axel. *The New Hollywood.* New York: Crowell, 1975.

Matthews, Leonard. *History of Western Movies.* New York: Crescent Books, 1984.

McBride, Joseph. *Searching for John Ford.* New York: St. Martin's Press, 2001.

McCarthy, Todd. *Howard Hawks: The Grey Fox of Hollywood.* New York: Grove Press, 2000.

McDonald, Archie P. *Shooting Stars, Heroes and Heroines of Western Film.* Bloomington: Indiana University Press, 1987.

McGee, P. *From Shane to Kill Bill, Rethinking the Western.* London: Wiley Blackwell, 2007.

McMahon, Jennifer L., and B. Steven Csaki, eds. *The Philosophy of the Western.* Lexington: University Press of Kentucky, 2010.

Meadows, Anne. *Digging Up Butch and Sundance.* New York: St. Martin's Press, 1994.

Mirisch, Walter. *I Thought We Were Making Movies, Not History.* Madison: University of Wisconsin Press, 2008.

Monaco, James. *American Film Now: The People, the Power, the Money, the Movies.* New York: Oxford University Press, 1979.

Monaco, Paul. *The Sixties: 1960–1969.* New York: Scribner's, 2001.

Munn, Michael. *Clint Eastwood: Hollywood's Loner.* London: Robson Books, 1992.

Nachbar Jack, *Focus on the Western.* Englewood Cliffs, NJ: Prentice-Hall, 1974.

O'Brien, Daniel. *Paul Newman.* London: Faber & Faber, 2004.

Parish, James Robert, *Fiasco—A History of Hollywood's Iconic Flops.* Hoboken, NJ: Wiley & Sons, 2006.

Pomainville, Harold N. *Henry Hathaway: The Lives of a Hollywood Director.* Lanham, MD: Rowman and Littlefield, 2016.

Prince, Stephen. *Savage Cinema: Sam Peckinpah and the Rise of Ultraviolent Movies.* Austin: University of Texas Press, 1998.

Roberts, Randy, and James S. Olson. *John Wayne American.* New York: The Free Press, 1995.

Sackett, Susan. *The Hollywood Reporter Book of Box Office Hits.* New York: Billboard Books, 1990.

Sandos, James A., and Burgess, Larry E. *The Hunt for Willie Boy: Indian-Hating & Popular Culture.* Norman: University of Oklahoma Press, 1994.

Sarf, Wayne Michael. *God Bless You, Buffalo Bill: A Layman's Guide to History and the Western Film.* East Brunswick, NJ: Associated University Press, 1993.

Sarris, Andrew. *American Cinema: Directors and Directions 1929–1968.* New York: E.P. Dutton, 1968.

Schatz, Thomas. *Boom or Bust: The American Cinema of the 1940s.* New York: Charles Scribner's Sons, 1997.

Siegel, Penina. *Steve McQueen: The Unauthorized Story of a Bad Boy in Hollywood.* Glasgow: William Collins, 1986.

Sinclair, Andrew. *John Ford: A Biography.* New York: Dial Press 1979.

Slotkin, Richard. *Gunfighter Nation: The Myth of the Frontier in Twentieth Century America.* New York: Maxwell MacMillan, 1992.

Solomon, Aubrey. *Twentieth Century Fox: A Corporate and Financial History.* Lanham, MD: Scarecrow, 1998.

Steinberg, Cobbett. *Reel Facts.* New York: Vintage, 1968.

Stowell, Peter. *John Ford.* Boston: Twayne, 1986.

Sydor, Paul. *Peckinpah: The Western Films: A Reconsideration.* Chicago: University of Illinois Press, 1997.

Tuska, Jon. *The American West in Film: Critical Approaches to the Western.* Westport, CT: Greenwood, 1985.

Wallach, Eli. *The Good, the Bad and Me.* New York: Harvest Harcourt 2006.

Wallis, Hal B. *Starmaker: The Autobiography of Hal Wallis.* London: Macmillan, 1980

Weddle, David. *If They Move ... Kill 'Em: The Life and Times of Sam Peckinpah.* New York: Grove Press, 1994.

Wood, Robin, *Howard Hawks.* London: Studio Vista, 1967.

Index

Numbers in ***bold italics*** indicate pages with illustrations